C++17 STL Cookb

Discover the latest enhancements to functional
programming and lambda expressions

Jacek Galowicz

BIRMINGHAM - MUMBAI

C++17 STL Cookbook

First published: June 2017

Production reference: 1230617

Published by Packt Publishing Ltd.

Livery Place
35 Livery Street
Birmingham
B3 2PB, UK.

ISBN 978-1-78712-049-5

www.packtpub.com

Credits

Author
Jacek Galowicz

Reviewer
Arne Mertz

Commissioning Editor
Aaron Lazar

Acquisition Editor
Nitin Dasan

Content Development Editor
Vikas Tiwari

Technical Editor
Hussain Kanchwala

Copy Editor
Muktikant Garimella

Project Coordinator
Ulhas Kambali

Proofreader
Safis Editing

Indexer
Francy Puthiry

Graphics
Abhinash Sahu

Production Coordinator
Shantanu Zagade

About the Author

Jacek Galowicz obtained his master of science in electrical engineering/computer engineering at RWTH Aachen University, Germany. While at university, he enjoyed working as a student assistant in teaching and research, and he participated in several scientific publications. During and after his studies, he worked as a freelancer and implemented applications as well as kernel drivers in C and C++, touching various areas, including 3D graphics programming, databases, network communication, and physics simulation. In recent years, he has been programming performance- and security-sensitive microkernel operating systems for Intel x86 virtualization at Intel and FireEye in Braunschweig, Germany. He has a strong passion for modern C++ implementations of low-level software, and he tries hard to combine high performance with an elegant coding style. Learning purely functional programming and Haskell in recent years triggered his drive to implement generic code with the aid of meta programming.

Writing a book and founding a company at the same time was a great and interesting experience in my life and a lot of fun. The fun aspects, however, were only possible because of the support and patience of my wonderful girlfriend Viktoria, my fellow co-founders, and all my friends. Special thanks go to Arne Mertz for his invaluable and meticulous review suggestions, as well as Torsten Robitzki and Oliver Bruns from the C++ user group Hannover for their great feedback.

About the Reviewer

Arne Mertz is a C++ expert with over a decade of experience. He studied physics at the university of Hamburg, and he switched careers to become a software developer. His main background is in financial enterprise applications written in C++. Arne works at Zühlke Engineering, Germany and is known for his blog, *Simplify C++!* (`https://arne-mertz.de`) on clean and maintainable C++.

www.PacktPub.com

For support files and downloads related to your book, please visit www.PacktPub.com.

Did you know that Packt offers eBook versions of every book published, with PDF and ePub files available? You can upgrade to the eBook version at www.PacktPub.com and as a print book customer, you are entitled to a discount on the eBook copy. Get in touch with us at service@packtpub.com for more details.

At www.PacktPub.com, you can also read a collection of free technical articles, sign up for a range of free newsletters and receive exclusive discounts and offers on Packt books and eBooks.

https://www.packtpub.com/mapt

Get the most in-demand software skills with Mapt. Mapt gives you full access to all Packt books and video courses, as well as industry-leading tools to help you plan your personal development and advance your career.

Why subscribe?

- Fully searchable across every book published by Packt
- Copy and paste, print, and bookmark content
- On demand and accessible via a web browser

Customer Feedback

Thanks for purchasing this Packt book. At Packt, quality is at the heart of our editorial process. To help us improve, please leave us an honest review on this book's Amazon page at `https://www.amazon.com/dp/178712049X`.

If you'd like to join our team of regular reviewers, you can e-mail us at customerreviews@packtpub.com. We award our regular reviewers with free eBooks and videos in exchange for their valuable feedback. Help us be relentless in improving our products!

Table of Contents

Chapter 5: STL Algorithm Basics   169

Preface

The *C++17 STL Cookbook* will teach you how to get the most out of C++17 by providing coding recipes that combine the C++ language and its standard library, the STL. Indeed, this book uses as much STL as possible, which is worth a bit of explanation.

C++ is such a great and powerful language. It allows us to hide complex solutions behind simple high-level interfaces but, at the same time, to write low-level code where high performance and low overhead really matter. The ISO C++ Standard Committee works hard on improving the C++ standard. C++11 brought a lot of great features to C++, and so did C++14 and C++17.

As of today, C++ is a language that provides language features and standard library facilities for sophisticated standard data structures and algorithms, automatic resource management pointers, lambda expressions, constant expressions, portable thread control for concurrent programming, regular expressions, random number generators, exceptions, variadic templates (the part of C++ for expressing template types is even Turing-complete!), user-defined literals, portable filesystem traversal, and so much more. This giant bunch of features makes it a general-purpose language ideal for implementing high-quality and high-performance software in all fields of the software industry.

However, many C++ programmers eagerly learn C++ as a language but put its standard library, the STL, in the second place. Using the C++ language without the help that the standard library provides often leads to programs that look like C with classes, but not what modern programs in the 21st century should look like. This is very sad because using C++ like that means dropping half its strength.

In the C++11 edition of his book, *The C++ Programming Language*, Bjarne Stroustrup writes, "Please remember that those libraries and language features exist to support programming techniques for developing quality software. They are meant to be used in combination--as bricks in a building set--rather than to be used individually in relative isolation to solve a specific problem."

This is exactly what this book and its recipes are about. All the recipes in this book are designed to be as near as possible to real-life problems, while at the same time, they do not rely on any external libraries other than the STL. This way, it is very simple to play around with each of them, without having to do confusing setup work. I really hope that you find inspiration in the recipes and, maybe, find some of them to be nice standard building blocks for solving higher-level problems with this great programming language.

What this book covers

Chapter 1, *The New C++17 Features*, specializes on the new and game-changing additions that the C++17 standard brought to C++ as a language, so we can concentrate on the additions to the STL in the following chapters.

Chapter 2, *STL Containers*, explains how the STL's rich variety of container data structures got some upgrades with C++17. After having a look at the entire collection of the different containers, we will have a closer look on the new additions they got.

Chapter 3, *Iterators*, explains iterators, which are an extremely important abstraction as they are the glue between the STL's algorithms and the container data structures, whenever they are combined. We are going to roll up the whole iterator concept from the ground to learn how to put them to the best use in all our programs.

Chapter 4, *Lambda Expressions*, explores lambda expressions, which allow for some very interesting programming patterns. Inspired by purely functional programming languages, lambda expressions, which were first introduced in C++11, got some new features with C++14 and C++17.

Chapter 5, *STL Algorithm Basics*, introduces the basics of the STL's standard algorithms that are easy to use, very performant, well-tested, and highly generic. We will learn how to use them, so we can be productive by concentrating on solutions, instead of wasting time reinventing the wheel.

Chapter 6, *Advanced Use of STL Algorithms*, demonstrates how to combine the STL's basic algorithms in order to compose more complex ones in clean ways without code duplication. In this chapter, we will be creative and stick tightly to the STL while implementing solutions to more complex problems, and we will learn how to combine existing algorithms to create new ones that really fit our needs.

Chapter 7, *Strings, Stream Classes, and Regular Expressions*, provides a detailed overview over the STL's powerful classes around strings, generic I/O streaming, and regular expressions. We will have an in-depth look into these parts of the STL in this chapter.

Chapter 8, *Utility Classes*, explains the STL ways of generating random numbers, taking and measuring the time, managing dynamic memory, elegantly signalizing error conditions, and more. We will have a look at the extremely useful and portable utility classes that the C++ STL provides for such tasks and introduce the brand new ones that came with C++17.

Chapter 9, *Parallelism and Concurrency*, showcases the existing C++ extensions for parallelism and concurrency which became very important topics at the time we entered the era of multi-core processors. First C++11, and then C++17, came with great additions that are of an enormous help whenever we need to implement programs that run on multiple cores and do things concurrently. So, we make sure we grasp these concepts in this chapter.

Chapter 10, *Filesystem*, shows that although the STL always provided support for reading and manipulating individual files, C++17 got a lot of new value with its whole new operating system-independent library for the handling of filesystem paths and the traversal of directories. In this chapter, we will learn how to use it.

What you need for this book

All recipes in this book are kept as simple and self-contained as possible. They are easy to compile and run, but depending on the reader's choice of operating system and compiler, there are differences. Let's have a look how to compile and run all the recipes, and what else to pay attention to.

Compiling and running the recipes

All the code in this book has been developed and tested on Linux and MacOS, using the GNU C++ compiler, **g++**, and the LLVM C++ compiler, **clang++**.

Building an example in the shell can be done with the following command using g++:

```
$ g++ -std=c++1z -o recipe_app recipe_code.cpp
```

Using clang++, the command is similar:

```
$ clang++ -std=c++1z -o recipe_app recipe_code.cpp
```

Both the command-line examples assume that the file `recipe_code.cpp` is the text file containing your C++ code. After compiling the program, the executable binary will have the filename `recipe_app` and can be executed as follows:

```
$ ./recipe_app
```

In a lot of examples, we read the content of entire files via standard input. In such cases, we use the standard UNIX pipes and the UNIX `cat` command to direct the file content into our app, as follows:

```
$ cat file.txt | ./recipe_app
```

This works on Linux and MacOS. In the Microsoft Windows shell, it works as follows:

```
> recipe_app.exe < file.txt
```

If you do not happen to run your programs from the command-line shell, but from the Microsoft Visual Studio IDE, then you need to open the dialogue, `"Configuration properties > Debugging"`, and add the `"< file.txt"` part to the command line of the app that Visual Studio uses for launching.

Requirements for early adopters

If you happen to read this book in the earliest days of C++17 and use bleeding- edge compilers to compile the code, you might experience that some recipes do not compile yet. This depends on how much of the C++17 STL has been implemented already in your STL distribution.
While writing this book, it was necessary to add the path prefix `experimental/` to the headers `<execution_policy>` and `<filesystem>`. There might also be additional includes such as algorithm, numeric, and so on, in the `experimental/` folder of your STL distribution, depending on how new and stable it is.

The same applies for the namespace of brand new features. The parts of the library that were included from the experimental part of the STL are usually exported not within the `std` namespace but the `std::experimental` namespace.

Who this book is for

This book is not for you if you have no prior knowledge of writing and compiling C++ programs. If you read about the basics of this language already, this book is the ideal second book about C++ to take your knowledge to an advanced level.

Apart from that, you are a good candidate for reading this book if you can identify yourself with one of the following bullet point descriptions:

- You have learned the basics of C++, but now, you don't have a clue where to go next, since the gap between your knowledge and the knowledge of an experienced C++ veteran is still large.
- You know C++ well, but your knowledge of the STL is limited.
- You know C++ from one of the older standards, such as C++98, C++11, or C++14. Depending on how far in the past you used C++ the last time, this book has a lot of nice new STL features and perks in store, ready for you to discover.

Sections

In this book, you will find several headings that appear frequently (Getting ready, How to do it, How it works, There's more, and See also).

To give clear instructions on how to complete a recipe, we use these sections as follows:

Getting ready

This section tells you what to expect in the recipe, and describes how to set up any software or any preliminary settings required for the recipe.

How to do it…

This section contains the steps required to follow the recipe.

How it works…

This section usually consists of a detailed explanation of what happened in the previous section.

There's more…

This section consists of additional information about the recipe in order to make the reader more knowledgeable about the recipe.

See also

This section provides helpful links to other useful information for the recipe.

Conventions

In this book, you will find a number of text styles that distinguish between different kinds of information. Here are some examples of these styles and an explanation of their meaning.

Code words in text, database table names, folder names, filenames, file extensions, pathnames, dummy URLs, user input, and Twitter handles are shown as follows: "The next step is to edit `build.properties` file."

A block of code is set as follows:

```
my_wrapper<T1, T2, T3> make_wrapper(T1 t1, T2 t2, T3 t3)
{
    return {t1, t2, t3};
}
```

New terms and **important words** are shown in bold. Words that you see on the screen, for example, in menus or dialog boxes, appear in the text like this: "Once done, click on **Activate**."

Warnings or important notes appear in a box like this.

Tips and tricks appear like this.

Reader feedback

Feedback from our readers is always welcome. Let us know what you think about this book-what you liked or disliked. Reader feedback is important for us as it helps us develop titles that you will really get the most out of. To send us general feedback, simply e-mail `feedback@packtpub.com`, and mention the book's title in the subject of your message. If there is a topic that you have expertise in and you are interested in either writing or contributing to a book, see our author guide at `www.packtpub.com/authors`.

Customer support

Now that you are the proud owner of a Packt book, we have a number of things to help you to get the most from your purchase.

Downloading the example code

You can download the example code files for this book from your account at `http://www.packtpub.com`. If you purchased this book elsewhere, you can visit `http://www.packtpub.com/support`and register to have the files e-mailed directly to you.

You can download the code files by following these steps:

1. Log in or register to our website using your e-mail address and password.
2. Hover the mouse pointer on the **SUPPORT** tab at the top.
3. Click on **Code Downloads & Errata**.
4. Enter the name of the book in the **Search** box.
5. Select the book for which you're looking to download the code files.
6. Choose from the drop-down menu where you purchased this book from.
7. Click on **Code Download**.

Once the file is downloaded, please make sure that you unzip or extract the folder using the latest version of:

- WinRAR / 7-Zip for Windows
- Zipeg / iZip / UnRarX for Mac
- 7-Zip / PeaZip for Linux

The code bundle for the book is also hosted on GitHub at `https://github.com/PacktPubl ishing/Cpp17-STL-Cookbook`. We also have other code bundles from our rich catalog of books and videos available at `https://github.com/PacktPublishing/`. Check them out!

Errata

Although we have taken every care to ensure the accuracy of our content, mistakes do happen. If you find a mistake in one of our books-maybe a mistake in the text or the code-we would be grateful if you could report this to us. By doing so, you can save other readers from frustration and help us improve subsequent versions of this book. If you find any errata, please report them by visiting `http://www.packtpub.com/submit-errata`, selecting your book, clicking on the **Errata Submission Form** link, and entering the details of your errata. Once your errata are verified, your submission will be accepted and the errata will be uploaded to our website or added to any list of existing errata under the Errata section of that title.

To view the previously submitted errata, go to `https://www.packtpub.com/books/conten t/support` and enter the name of the book in the search field. The required information will appear under the **Errata** section.

Piracy

Piracy of copyrighted material on the Internet is an ongoing problem across all media. At Packt, we take the protection of our copyright and licenses very seriously. If you come across any illegal copies of our works in any form on the Internet, please provide us with the location address or website name immediately so that we can pursue a remedy.

Please contact us at `copyright@packtpub.com` with a link to the suspected pirated material.

We appreciate your help in protecting our authors and our ability to bring you valuable content.

Questions

If you have a problem with any aspect of this book, you can contact us at `questions@packtpub.com`, and we will do our best to address the problem.

1
The New C++17 Features

In this chapter, we will cover the following recipes:

- Using structured bindings to unpack bundled return values
- Limiting variable scopes to `if` and `switch` statements
- Profiting from the new bracket initializer rules
- Letting the constructor automatically deduce the resulting template class type
- Simplifying compile-time decisions with constexpr-if
- Enabling header-only libraries with inline variables
- Implementing handy helper functions with fold expressions

Introduction

C++ got a lot of additions in C++11, C++14, and, most recently, C++17. By now, it is a completely different language compared to what it was just a decade ago. The C++ standard does not only standardize the language, as it needs to be understood by the compilers, but also the C++ standard template library (STL).

This book explains how to put the STL to the best use with a broad range of examples. But at first, this chapter will concentrate on the most important new language features. Mastering them will greatly help you write readable, maintainable, and expressive code a lot.

We will see how to access individual members of pairs, tuples, and structures comfortably with structured bindings and how to limit variable scopes with the new `if` and `switch` variable initialization capabilities. The syntactical ambiguities, which were introduced by C++11 with the new bracket initialization syntax, which looks the same for initializer lists, were fixed by *new bracket initializer rules*. The exact *type* of template class instances can now be *deduced* from the actual constructor arguments, and if different specializations of a template class will result in completely different code, this is now easily expressible with constexpr-if. The handling of variadic parameter packs in template functions became much easier in many cases with the new *fold expressions*. At last, it became more comfortable to define static globally accessible objects in header-only libraries with the new ability to declare inline variables, which was only possible for functions before.

Some of the examples in this chapter might be more interesting for implementers of libraries than for developers who implement applications. While we will have a look at such features for completeness reasons, it is not too critical to understand all the examples of this chapter immediately in order to understand the rest of this book.

Using structured bindings to unpack bundled return values

C++17 comes with a new feature, which combines syntactic sugar and automatic type deduction: **structured bindings**. These help to assign values from pairs, tuples, and structs into individual variables. In other programming languages, this is also called **unpacking**.

How to do it...

Applying a structured binding in order to assign multiple variables from one bundled structure is always one step. Let's first see how it was done before C++17. Then, we can have a look at multiple examples that show how we can do it in C++17:

- Accessing individual values of an `std::pair`: Imagine we have a mathematical function, `divide_remainder`, which accepts a *dividend* and a *divisor* parameter and returns the fraction of both as well as the remainder. It returns those values using an `std::pair` bundle:

```
std::pair<int, int> divide_remainder(int dividend, int divisor);
```

Consider the following way of accessing the individual values of the resulting pair:

```
const auto result (divide_remainder(16, 3));
std::cout << "16 / 3 is "
          << result.first << " with a remainder of "
          << result.second << '\n';
```

Instead of doing it as shown in the preceding code snippet, we can now assign the individual values to individual variables with expressive names, which is much better to read:

```
auto [fraction, remainder] = divide_remainder(16, 3);
std::cout << "16 / 3 is "
          << fraction << " with a remainder of "
          << remainder << '\n';
```

- Structured bindings also work with `std::tuple`: Let's take the following example function, which gets us online stock information:

```
std::tuple<std::string,
           std::chrono::system_clock::time_point, unsigned>
stock_info(const std::string &name);
```

  Assigning its result to individual variables looks just like in the example before:

```
const auto [name, valid_time, price] = stock_info("INTC");
```

- Structured bindings also work with custom structures: Let's assume a structure like the following:

```
struct employee {
    unsigned id;
    std::string name;
    std::string role;
    unsigned salary;
};
```

Now, we can access these members using structured bindings. We can even do that in a loop, assuming we have a whole vector of those:

```
int main()
{
    std::vector<employee> employees {
        /* Initialized from somewhere */};
    for (const auto &[id, name, role, salary] : employees) {
        std::cout << "Name: "   << name
```

```
                                << "Role: "   << role
                                << "Salary: " << salary << '\n';
                     }
            }
```

How it works...

Structured bindings are always applied with the same pattern:

```
auto [var1, var2, ...] = <pair, tuple, struct, or array expression>;
```

- The list of variables `var1`, `var2`, ... must exactly match the number of variables contained by the expression being assigned from.
- The `<pair, tuple, struct, or array expression>` must be one of the following:
  - An `std::pair`.
  - An `std::tuple`.
  - A `struct`. All members must be *non-static* and defined in the *same base class*. The first declared member is assigned to the first variable, the second member to the second variable, and so on.
  - An array of fixed size.
- The type can be `auto`, `const auto`, `const auto&`, and even `auto&&`.

 Not only for the sake of *performance,* always make sure to minimize needless copies by using references when appropriate.

If we write *too many* or *not enough* variables between the square brackets, the compiler will error out, telling us about our mistake:

```
std::tuple<int, float, long> tup {1, 2.0, 3};
auto [a, b] = tup; // Does not work
```

This example obviously tries to stuff a tuple variable with three members into only two variables. The compiler immediately chokes on this and tells us about our mistake:

```
error: type 'std::tuple<int, float, long>' decomposes into 3 elements, but
only 2 names were provided
auto [a, b] = tup;
```

There's more...

A lot of fundamental data structures from the STL are immediately accessible using structured bindings without us having to change anything. Consider, for example, a loop that prints all the items of an `std::map`:

```
std::map<std::string, size_t> animal_population {
    {"humans",    7000000000},
    {"chickens", 17863376000},
    {"camels",    24246291},
    {"sheep",     1086881528},
    /* … */
};

for (const auto &[species, count] : animal_population) {
    std::cout << "There are " << count << " " << species
              << " on this planet.\n";
}
```

This particular example works because when we iterate over an `std::map` container, we get the `std::pair<const key_type, value_type>` nodes on every iteration step. Exactly these nodes are unpacked using the structured bindings feature (`key_type` is the `species` string and `value_type` is the population count `size_t`) in order to access them individually in the loop body.

Before C++17, it was possible to achieve a similar effect using `std::tie`:

```
int remainder;
std::tie(std::ignore, remainder) = divide_remainder(16, 5);
std::cout << "16 % 5 is " << remainder << '\n';
```

This example shows how to unpack the resulting pair into two variables. The `std::tie` is less powerful than structured bindings in the sense that we have to define all the variables we want to bind to *before*. On the other hand, this example shows a strength of `std::tie` that structured bindings do *not* have: the value `std::ignore` acts as a dummy variable. The fraction part of the result is assigned to it, which leads to that value being dropped because we do not need it in that example.

When using structured bindings, we don't have `tie` dummy variables, so we have to bind all the values to named variables. Doing so and ignoring some of them is efficient, nevertheless, because the compiler can optimize the unused bindings out easily.

Back in the past, the `divide_remainder` function could have been implemented in the following way, using output parameters:

```
bool divide_remainder(int dividend, int divisor,
                      int &fraction, int &remainder);
```

Accessing it would have looked like the following:

```
int fraction, remainder;
const bool success {divide_remainder(16, 3, fraction, remainder)};
if (success) {
    std::cout << "16 / 3 is " << fraction << " with a remainder of "
              << remainder << '\n';
}
```

A lot of people will still prefer this over returning complex structures like pairs, tuples, and structs, arguing that this way the code would be *faster*, due to avoided intermediate copies of those values. This is *not true* any longer for modern compilers, which optimize intermediate copies away.

 Apart from the missing language features in C, returning complex structures via return value was considered slow for a long time because the object had to be initialized in the returning function and then copied into the variable that should contain the return value on the caller side. Modern compilers support **return value optimization** (RVO), which enables for omitting intermediate copies.

Limiting variable scopes to if and switch statements

It is good style to limit the scope of variables as much as possible. Sometimes, however, one first needs to obtain some value, and only if it fits a certain condition, it can be processed further.

For this purpose, C++17 comes with `if` and `switch` statements with initializers.

How to do it...

In this recipe, we use the initializer syntax in both the supported contexts in order to see how they tidy up our code:

- The `if` statements: Imagine we want to find a character in a character map using the `find` method of `std::map`:

```
if (auto itr (character_map.find(c)); itr != character_map.end()) {
    // *itr is valid. Do something with it.
} else {
    // itr is the end-iterator. Don't dereference.
}
// itr is not available here at all
```

- The `switch` statements: This is how it would look to get a character from the input and, at the same time, check the value in a `switch` statement in order to control a computer game:

```
switch (char c (getchar()); c) {
    case 'a': move_left();  break;
    case 's': move_back();  break;
    case 'w': move_fwd();   break;
    case 'd': move_right(); break;
    case 'q': quit_game();  break;

    case '0'...'9': select_tool('0' - c); break;

    default:
        std::cout << "invalid input: " << c << '\n';
}
```

How it works...

The `if` and `switch` statements with initializers are basically just syntax sugar. The following two samples are equivalent:

Before C++17:

```
{
    auto var (init_value);
    if (condition) {
        // branch A. var is accessible
    } else {
        // branch B. var is accessible
```

```
    }
    // var is still accessible
  }
```

Since C++17:

```
  if (auto var (init_value); condition) {
      // branch A. var is accessible
  } else {
      // branch B. var is accessible
  }
  // var is not accessible any longer
```

The same applies to `switch` statements:

Before C++17:

```
  {
      auto var (init_value);
      switch (var) {
      case 1: ...
      case 2: ...
      ...
      }
      // var is still accessible
  }
```

Since C++17:

```
  switch (auto var (init_value); var) {
  case 1: ...
  case 2: ...
      ...
  }
  // var is not accessible any longer
```

This feature is very useful to keep the scope of a variable as short as necessary. Before C++17, this was only possible using extra braces around the code, as the pre-C++17 examples show. The short lifetimes reduce the number of variables in the scope, which keeps our code tidy and makes it easier to refactor.

There's more...

Another interesting use case is the limited scope of critical sections. Consider the following example:

```
if (std::lock_guard<std::mutex> lg {my_mutex}; some_condition) {
    // Do something
}
```

At first, an `std::lock_guard` is created. This is a class that accepts a mutex argument as a constructor argument. It *locks* the mutex in its constructor, and when it runs out of scope, it *unlocks* it again in its destructor. This way, it is impossible to *forget* to unlock the mutex. Before C++17, a pair of extra braces was needed in order to determine the scope where it unlocks again.

Yet another interesting use case is the scope of weak pointers. Consider the following:

```
if (auto shared_pointer (weak_pointer.lock()); shared_pointer != nullptr) {
    // Yes, the shared object does still exist
} else {
    // shared_pointer var is accessible, but a null pointer
}
// shared_pointer is not accessible any longer
```

This is another example where we would have a useless `shared_pointer` variable leaking into the current scope, although it has a potentially useless state outside the `if` conditional block or noisy extra brackets!

The `if` statements with initializers are especially useful when using *legacy* APIs with output parameters:

```
if (DWORD exit_code; GetExitCodeProcess(process_handle, &exit_code)) {
    std::cout << "Exit code of process was: " << exit_code << '\n';
}
// No useless exit_code variable outside the if-conditional
```

`GetExitCodeProcess` is a Windows kernel API function. It returns the exit code for a given process handle but only if that handle is valid. After leaving this conditional block, the variable is useless, so we don't need it in any scope any longer.

Being able to initialize variables within `if` blocks is obviously very useful in a lot of situations and, especially, when dealing with legacy APIs that use output parameters.

Keep your scopes tight using `if` and `switch` statement initializers. This makes your code more compact, easier to read, and in code refactoring sessions, it will be easier to move around.

Profiting from the new bracket initializer rules

C++11 came with the new brace initializer syntax { }. Its purpose was to allow for *aggregate* initialization, but also for usual constructor calling. Unfortunately, it was too easy to express the wrong thing when combining this syntax with the `auto` variable type. C++17 comes with an enhanced set of initializer rules. In this recipe, we will clarify how to correctly initialize variables with which syntax in C++17.

How to do it...

Variables are initialized in one step. Using the initializer syntax, there are two different situations:

- Using the brace initializer syntax *without* `auto` type deduction:

```
// Three identical ways to initialize an int:
int x1 = 1;
int x2   {1};
int x3   (1);
std::vector<int> v1   {1, 2, 3}; // Vector with three ints: 1, 2, 3
std::vector<int> v2 = {1, 2, 3}; // same here
std::vector<int> v3   (10, 20);  // Vector with 10 ints,
                                 // each have value 20
```

- Using the brace initializer syntax *with* `auto` type deduction:

```
auto v   {1};        // v is int
auto w   {1, 2};     // error: only single elements in direct
                     // auto initialization allowed! (this is new)
auto x = {1};        // x is std::initializer_list<int>
auto y = {1, 2};     // y is std::initializer_list<int>
auto z = {1, 2, 3.0}; // error: Cannot deduce element type
```

How it works...

Without `auto` type deduction, there's not much to be surprised about in the brace `{}` operator, at least, when initializing regular types. When initializing containers such as `std::vector`, `std::list`, and so on, a brace initializer will match the `std::initializer_list` constructor of that container class. It does this in a *greedy* manner, which means that it is not possible to match non-aggregate constructors (non-aggregate constructors are usual constructors in contrast to the ones that accept an initializer list).

`std::vector`, for example, provides a specific non-aggregate constructor, which fills arbitrarily many items with the same value: `std::vector<int> v (N, value)`. When writing `std::vector<int> v {N, value}`, the `initializer_list` constructor is chosen, which will initialize the vector with two items: `N` and `value`. This is a special pitfall one should know about.

One nice detail about the `{}` operator compared to constructor calling using normal `()` parentheses is that they do no implicit type conversions: `int x (1.2);` and `int x = 1.2;` will initialize x to value 1 by silently rounding down the floating point value and converting it to int. `int x {1.2};`, in contrast, will not compile because it wants to *exactly* match the constructor type.

> One can controversially argue about which initialization style is the best one.
> Fans of the bracket initialization style say that using brackets makes it very explicit, that the variable is initialized with a constructor call, and that this code line is not reinitializing anything. Furthermore, using `{}` brackets will select the only matching constructor, while initializer lines using `()` parentheses try to match the closest constructor and even do type conversion in order to match.

The additional rule introduced in C++17 affects the initialization with `auto` type deduction-- while C++11 would correctly make the type of the variable `auto x {123};` an `std::initializer_list<int>` with only one element, this is seldom what we would want. C++17 would make the same variable an `int`.

Rule of thumb:

- `auto var_name {one_element};` deduces `var_name` to be of the same type as `one_element`
- `auto var_name {element1, element2, ...};` is invalid and does not compile
- `auto var_name = {element1, element2, ...};` deduces to an `std::initializer_list<T>` with `T` being of the same type as all the elements in the list

C++17 has made it harder to accidentally define an initializer list.

Trying this out with different compilers in C++11/C++14 mode will show that some compilers actually deduce `auto x {123};` to an `int`, while others deduce it to `std::initializer_list<int>`. Writing code like this can lead to problems regarding portability!

Letting the constructor automatically deduce the resulting template class type

A lot of classes in C++ are usually specialized on types, which could be easily deduced from the variable types the user puts in their constructor calls. Nevertheless, before C++17, this was not a standardized feature. C++17 lets the compiler *automatically* deduce template types from constructor calls.

How to do it...

A very handy use case for this is constructing `std::pair` and `std::tuple` instances. These can be specialized and instantiated and specialized in one step:

```
std::pair  my_pair  (123, "abc");        // std::pair<int, const char*>
std::tuple my_tuple (123, 12.3, "abc"); // std::tuple<int, double,
                                         //             const char*>
```

How it works...

Let's define an example class where automatic template type deduction would be of value:

```
template <typename T1, typename T2, typename T3>
class my_wrapper {
    T1 t1;
    T2 t2;
    T3 t3;

public:
    explicit my_wrapper(T1 t1_, T2 t2_, T3 t3_)
        : t1{t1_}, t2{t2_}, t3{t3_}
    {}

    /* ... */
};
```

Okay, this is just another template class. We previously had to write the following in order to instantiate it:

```
my_wrapper<int, double, const char *> wrapper {123, 1.23, "abc"};
```

We can now just omit the template specialization part:

```
my_wrapper wrapper {123, 1.23, "abc"};
```

Before C++17, this was only possible by implementing a *make function helper*:

```
my_wrapper<T1, T2, T3> make_wrapper(T1 t1, T2 t2, T3 t3)
{
    return {t1, t2, t3};
}
```

Using such helpers, it was possible to have a similar effect:

```
auto wrapper (make_wrapper(123, 1.23, "abc"));
```

 The STL already comes with a lot of helper functions such as that one: `std::make_shared`, `std::make_unique`, `std::make_tuple`, and so on. In C++17, these can now mostly be regarded as obsolete. Of course, they will be provided further for compatibility reasons.

There's more...

What we just learned about was *implicit template type deduction*. In some cases, we cannot rely on implicit type deduction. Consider the following example class:

```
template <typename T>
struct sum {
    T value;

    template <typename ... Ts>
    sum(Ts&& ... values) : value{(values + ...)} {}
};
```

This struct, sum, accepts an arbitrary number of parameters and adds them together using a fold expression (have a look at the fold expression recipe a little later in this chapter to get more details on fold expressions). The resulting sum is saved in the member variable value. Now the question is, what type is T? If we don't want to specify it explicitly, it surely needs to depend on the types of the values provided in the constructor. If we provide string instances, it needs to be std::string. If we provide integers, it needs to be int. If we provide integers, floats, and doubles, the compiler needs to figure out which type fits all the values without information loss. In order to achieve that, we provide an *explicit deduction guide*:

```
template <typename ... Ts>
sum(Ts&& ... ts) -> sum<std::common_type_t<Ts...>>;
```

This deduction guide tells the compiler to use the std::common_type_t trait, which is able to find out which common type fits all the values. Let's see how to use it:

```
sum s           {1u, 2.0, 3, 4.0f};
sum string_sum {std::string{"abc"}, "def"};

std::cout << s.value          << '\n'
          << string_sum.value << '\n';
```

In the first line we instantiate a sum object with constructor arguments of type unsigned, double, int, and float. The std::common_type_t returns double as the common type, so we get a sum<double> instance. In the second line, we provide an std::string instance and a C-style string. Following our deduction guide, the compiler constructs an instance of type sum<std::string>.

When running this code, it will print 10 as the numeric sum and abcdef as the string *sum*.

Simplifying compile time decisions with constexpr-if

In templated code, it is often necessary to do certain things differently, depending on the type the template is specialized for. C++17 comes with constexpr-if expressions, which simplify the code in such situations *a lot*.

How to do it...

In this recipe, we'll implement a little helper template class. It can deal with different template type specializations because it is able to select completely different code in some passages, depending on what type we specialize it for:

1. Write the part of the code that is generic. In our example, it is a simple class, which supports adding a type U value to the type T member value using an add function:

```
template <typename T>
class addable
{
    T val;
public:
    addable(T v) : val{v} {}
    template <typename U>
    T add(U x) const {
        return val + x;
    }
};
```

2. Imagine that type `T` is `std::vector<something>` and type `U` is just `int`. What shall it mean to add an integer to a whole vector? Let's say it means that we add the integer to every item in the vector. This will be done in a loop:

```
template <typename U>
T add(U x)
{
    auto copy (val); // Get a copy of the vector member
    for (auto &n : copy) {
        n += x;
    }
    return copy;
}
```

3. The next and last step is to *combine* both worlds. If `T` is a vector of `U` items, do the *loop* variant. If it is not, just implement the *normal* addition:

```
template <typename U>
T add(U x) const {
    if constexpr (std::is_same_v<T, std::vector<U>>) {
        auto copy (val);
        for (auto &n : copy) {
            n += x;
        }
        return copy;
    } else {
        return val + x;
    }
}
```

4. The class can now be put to use. Let's see how nicely it works with completely different types, such as `int`, `float`, `std::vector<int>`, and `std::vector<string>`:

```
addable<int>{1}.add(2);                    // is 3
addable<float>{1.0}.add(2);                // is 3.0
addable<std::string>{"aa"}.add("bb");      // is "aabb"

std::vector<int> v {1, 2, 3};
addable<std::vector<int>>{v}.add(10);
    // is std::vector<int>{11, 12, 13}

std::vector<std::string> sv {"a", "b", "c"};
addable<std::vector<std::string>>{sv}.add(std::string{"z"});
    // is {"az", "bz", "cz"}
```

How it works...

The new constexpr-if works exactly like usual if-else constructs. The difference is that the condition that it tests has to be evaluated at *compile time*. All runtime code that the compiler creates from our program will not contain any branch instructions from constexpr-if conditionals. One could also put it that it works in a similar manner to preprocessor `#if` and `#else` text substitution macros, but for those, the code would not even have to be syntactically well-formed. All the branches of a constexpr-if construct need to be *syntactically well-formed*, but the branches that are *not* taken do not need to be *semantically valid*.

In order to distinguish whether the code should add the value x to a vector or not, we use the type trait `std::is_same`. An expression `std::is_same<A, B>::value` evaluates to the Boolean value `true` if A and B are of the same type. The condition used in our recipe is `std::is_same<T, std::vector<U>>::value`, which evaluates to `true` if the user specialized the class on `T = std::vector<X>` and tries to call `add` with a parameter of type `U = X`.

There can, of course, be multiple conditions in one constexpr-if-else block (note that a and b have to depend on template parameters and not only on compile-time constants):

```
if constexpr (a) {
    // do something
} else if constexpr (b) {
    // do something else
} else {
    // do something completely different
}
```

With C++17, a lot of meta programming situations are much easier to express and to read.

There's more...

In order to relate how much constexpr-if constructs are an improvement to C++, we can have a look at how the same thing could have been implemented *before* C++17:

```
template <typename T>
class addable
{
    T val;

public:
    addable(T v) : val{v} {}
```

```
template <typename U>
std::enable_if_t<!std::is_same<T, std::vector<U>>::value, T>
add(U x) const { return val + x; }

template <typename U>
std::enable_if_t<std::is_same<T, std::vector<U>>::value,
                 std::vector<U>>
add(U x) const {
    auto copy (val);
    for (auto &n : copy) {
        n += x;
    }
    return copy;
}
};
```

Without using constexpr-if, this class works for all different types we wished for, but it looks super complicated. How does it work?

The implementations alone of the *two different* add functions look simple. It's their return type declaration, which makes them look complicated, and which contains a trick--an expression such as std::enable_if_t<condition, type> evaluates to type if condition is true. Otherwise, the std::enable_if_t expression does not evaluate to anything. That would normally considered an error, but we will see why it is not.

For the second add function, the same condition is used in an *inverted* manner. This way, it can only be true at the same time for one of the two implementations.

When the compiler sees different template functions with the same name and has to choose one of them, an important principle comes into play: **SFINAE**, which stands for **Substitution Failure is not an Error**. In this case, this means that the compiler does not error out if the return value of one of those functions cannot be deduced from an erroneous template expression (which std::enable_if is, in case its condition evaluates to false). It will simply look further and try the *other* function implementation. That is the trick; that is how this works.

What a hassle. It is nice to see that this became so much easier with C++17.

Enabling header-only libraries with inline variables

While it was always possible in C++ to declare individual functions *inline*, C++17 additionally allows us to declare *variables* inline. This makes it much easier to implement *header-only* libraries, which was previously only possible using workarounds.

How it's done...

In this recipe, we create an example class that could suit as a member of a typical header-only library. The target is to give it a static member and instantiate it in a globally available manner using the `inline` keyword, which would not be possible like this before C++17:

1. The `process_monitor` class should both contain a static member and be globally accessible itself, which would produce double-defined symbols when included from multiple translation units:

```
// foo_lib.hpp
class process_monitor {
public:
    static const std::string standard_string
        {"some static globally available string"};
};
process_monitor global_process_monitor;
```

2. If we now include this in multiple `.cpp` files in order to compile and link them, this would fail at the linker stage. In order to fix this, we add the `inline` keyword:

```
// foo_lib.hpp

class process_monitor {
public:
    static const inline std::string standard_string
        {"some static globally available string"};
};

inline process_monitor global_process_monitor;
```

Voila, that's it!

How it works...

C++ programs do often consist of multiple C++ source files (these do have .cpp or .cc suffices). These are individually compiled to modules/object files (which usually have **.o** suffices). Linking all the modules/object files together into a single executable or shared/static library is then the last step.

At the link stage, it is considered an error if the linker can find the definition of one specific symbol *multiple* times. Let's say, for example, we have a function with a signature such as int foo();. If two modules define the same function, which is the right one? The linker can't just roll the dice. Well, it could, but that's most likely not what any programmer would ever want to happen.

The traditional way to provide globally available functions is to *declare* them in the header files, which will be included by any C++ module that needs to call them. The definition of every of those functions will be then put *once* into separate module files. These are then linked together with the modules that desire to use these functions. This is also called the **One Definition Rule (ODR)**. Check out the following illustration for better understanding:

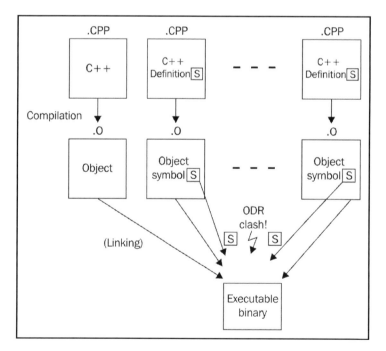

However, if this were the only way, then it would not have been possible to provide header-only libraries. Header-only libraries are very handy because they only need to be included using `#include` into any C++ program file and then are immediately available. In order to use libraries that are not header-only, the programmer must also adapt the build scripts in order to have the linker link the library modules together with his own module files. Especially for libraries with only very short functions, this is unnecessarily uncomfortable.

For such cases, the `inline` keyword can be used to make an exception in order to allow *multiple* definitions of the same symbol in different modules. If the linker finds multiple symbols with the same signature, but they are declared inline, it will just choose the first one and trust that the other symbols have the same definition. That all equal inline symbols are defined completely equal is basically a *promise* from the programmer.

Regarding our recipe example, the linker will find the `process_monitor::standard_string` symbol in every module that includes `foo_lib.hpp`. Without the `inline` keyword, it would not know which one to choose, so it would abort and report an error. The same applies to the `global_process_monitor` symbol. Which one is the right one?

After declaring both the symbols `inline`, it will just accept the first occurrence of each symbol and *drop* all the others.

Before C++17, the only clean way would be to provide this symbol via an additional C++ module file, which would force our library users to include this file in the linking step.

The `inline` keyword traditionally also has *another* function. It tells the compiler that it can *eliminate* the function call by taking its implementation and directly putting it where it was called. This way, the calling code contains one function call less, which can often be considered faster. If the function is very short, the resulting assembly will also be shorter (assuming that the number of instructions that do the function call, saving and restoring the stack, and so on, is higher than the actual payload code). If the inlined function is very long, the binary size will grow and this might sometimes not even lead to faster code in the end. Therefore, the compiler will only use the `inline` keyword as a hint and might eliminate function calls by inlining them. But it can also inline some functions *without* the programmer having it declared inline.

There's more...

One possible workaround before C++17 was providing a `static` function, which returns a reference to a `static` object:

```
class foo {
public:
    static std::string& standard_string() {
        static std::string s {"some standard string"};
        return s;
    }
};
```

This way, it is completely legal to include the header file in multiple modules but still getting access to exactly the same instance everywhere. However, the object is *not* constructed *immediately* at the start of program but only on the first call of this getter function. For some use cases, this is indeed a problem. Imagine that we want the constructor of the static, globally available object to do something important at *program start* (just as our reciple example library class), but due to the getter being called near the end of the program, it is too late.

Another workaround is to make the non-template class `foo` a template class, so it can profit from the same rules as templates.

Both strategies can be avoided in C++17.

Implementing handy helper functions with fold expressions

Since C++11, there are variadic template parameter packs, which enable implementing functions that accept arbitrarily many parameters. Sometimes, these parameters are all combined into one expression in order to derive the function result from that. This task became really easy with C++17, as it comes with fold expressions.

How to do it...

Let's implement a function that takes arbitrarily many parameters and returns their sum:

1. At first, we define its signature:

```
template <typename ... Ts>
auto sum(Ts ... ts);
```

2. So, we have a parameter pack `ts` now, and the function should expand all the parameters and sum them together using a fold expression. If we use any operator (+, in this example) together with ... in order to apply it to all the values of a parameter pack, we need to surround the expression with parentheses:

```
template <typename ... Ts>
auto sum(Ts ... ts)
{
    return (ts + ...);
}
```

3. We can now call it this way:

```
int the_sum {sum(1, 2, 3, 4, 5)}; // Value: 15
```

4. It does not only work with `int` types; we can call it with any type that just implements the + operator, such as `std::string`:

```
std::string a {"Hello "};
std::string b {"World"};
std::cout << sum(a, b) << '\n'; // Output: Hello World
```

How it works...

What we just did was a simple recursive application of a binary operator (+) to its parameters. This is generally called *folding*. C++17 comes with **fold expressions**, which help expressing the same idea with less code.

This kind of expression is called **unary fold**. C++17 supports folding parameter packs with the following binary operators: +, -, *, /, %, ^, &, |, =, <, >, <<, >>, +=, -=, *=, /=, %=, ^=, &=, |=, <<=, >>=, ==, !=, <=, >=, &&, ||, ,, .*, ->*.

By the way, in our example code, it does not matter if we write (ts + ...) or (... + ts); both work. However, there is a difference that may be relevant in other cases--if the ... dots are on the *right-hand* side of the operator, the fold is called a *right* fold. If they are on the *left-hand* side, it is a *left* fold.

In our sum example, a unary left fold expands to 1 + (2 + (3 + (4 + 5))), while a unary right fold will expand to (((1 + 2) + 3) + 4) + 5. Depending on the operator in use, this can make a difference. When adding numbers, it does not.

There's more...

In case someone calls sum() with *no* arguments, the variadic parameter pack contains no values that could be folded. For most operators, this is an error (for some, it is not; we will see this in a minute). We then need to decide if this should stay an error or if an empty sum should result in a specific value. The obvious idea is that the sum of nothing is 0.

This is how it's done:

```
template <typename ... Ts>
auto sum(Ts ... ts)
{
    return (ts + ... + 0);
}
```

This way, sum() evaluates to 0, and sum(1, 2, 3) evaluates to (1 + (2 + (3 + 0))). Such folds with an initial value are called **binary folds**.

Again, it works if we write (ts + ... + 0), or (0 + ... + ts), but this makes the binary fold a binary *right* fold or a binary *left* fold again. Check out the following diagram:

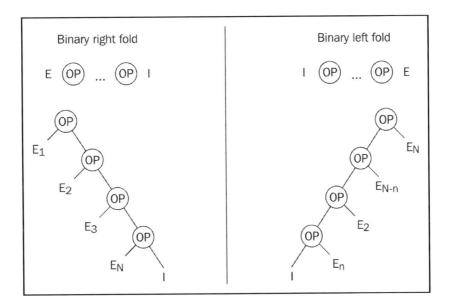

When using binary folds in order to implement the no-argument case, the notion of an *identity* element is often important--in this case, adding a 0 to any number changes nothing, which makes 0 an identity element. Because of this property, we can add a 0 to any fold expression with the operators + or −, which leads to the result 0 in case there are no parameters in the parameter pack. From a mathematical point of view, this is correct. From an implementation view, we need to define what is correct, depending on what we need.

The same principle applies to multiplication. Here, the identity element is 1:

```
template <typename ... Ts>
auto product(Ts ... ts)
{
    return (ts * ... * 1);
}
```

The result of `product(2, 3)` is 6, and the result of `product()` without parameters is 1.

The logical **and** (`&&`) and **or** (`||`) operators come with *built-in* identity elements. Folding an empty parameter pack with `&&` results in `true`, and folding an empty parameter pack with `||` results in `false`.

Another operator that defaults to a certain expression when applied on empty parameter packs is the comma operator (`,`), which then defaults to `void()`.

In order to ignite some inspiration, let's have a look at some more little helpers that we can implement using this feature.

Match ranges against individual items

How about a function that tells whether some range contains *at least one* of the values we provide as variadic parameters:

```
template <typename R, typename ... Ts>
auto matches(const R& range, Ts ... ts)
{
    return (std::count(std::begin(range), std::end(range), ts) + ...);
}
```

The helper function uses the `std::count` function from the STL. This function takes three parameters: the first two parameters are the *begin* and *end* iterators of some iterable range, and as the third parameter, it takes a *value* which will be compared to all the items of the range. The `std::count` method then returns the number of all the elements within the range that are equal to the third parameter.

In our fold expression, we always feed the *begin* and *end* iterators of the same parameter range into the `std::count` function. However, as the third parameter, each time we put one other parameter from the parameter pack into it. In the end, the function sums up all the results and returns it to the caller.

We can use it like this:

```
std::vector<int> v {1, 2, 3, 4, 5};

matches(v,         2, 5);         // returns 2
matches(v,         100, 200);     // returns 0
matches("abcdefg", 'x', 'y', 'z'); // returns 0
matches("abcdefg", 'a', 'd', 'f'); // returns 3
```

As we can see, the `matches` helper function is quite versatile--it can be called on vectors or even on strings directly. It would also work on initializer lists, on instances of `std::list`, `std::array`, `std::set`, and so on!

Check if multiple insertions into a set are successful

Let's write a helper that inserts an arbitrary number of variadic parameters into an
`std::set` and returns if all the insertions are *successful*:

```
template <typename T, typename ... Ts>
bool insert_all(T &set, Ts ... ts)
{
    return (set.insert(ts).second && ...);
}
```

So, how does this work? The `insert` function of `std::set` has the following signature:

```
std::pair<iterator, bool> insert(const value_type& value);
```

The documentation says that when we try to insert an item, the `insert` function will return
an `iterator` and a `bool` variable in a pair. The `bool` value is `true` if the insertion is
successful. If it is successful, the iterator points to the *new element* in the set. Otherwise, the
iterator points to the *existing* item, which would *collide* with the item to be inserted.

Our helper function accesses the `.second` field after insertion, which is just the `bool`
variable that reflects success or fail. If all the insertions lead to `true` in all the return pairs,
then all the insertions were successful. The fold expression combines all the insertion results
with the `&&` operator and returns the result.

We can use it like this:

```
std::set<int> my_set {1, 2, 3};

insert_all(my_set, 4, 5, 6); // Returns true
insert_all(my_set, 7, 8, 2); // Returns false, because the 2 collides
```

Note that if we try to insert, for example, three elements, but the second element can
already not be inserted, the `&& ...` fold will short-circuit and stop inserting all the other
elements:

```
std::set<int> my_set {1, 2, 3};

insert_all(my_set, 4, 2, 5); // Returns false
// set contains {1, 2, 3, 4} now, without the 5!
```

Check if all the parameters are within a certain range

If we can check if *one* variable is within some specific range, we can also do the same thing with *multiple* variables using fold expressions:

```
template <typename T, typename ... Ts>
bool within(T min, T max, Ts ...ts)
{
    return ((min <= ts && ts <= max) && ...);
}
```

The expression, `(min <= ts && ts <= max)`, does tell for every value of the parameter pack if it is between `min` and `max` (*including* `min` and `max`). We choose the `&&` operator to reduce all the Boolean results to a single one, which is only `true` if all the individual results are `true`.

This is how it looks in action:

```
within( 10,   20,   1, 15, 30);      // --> false
within( 10,   20,  11, 12, 13);      // --> true
within(5.0, 5.5,   5.1, 5.2, 5.3)    // --> true
```

Interestingly, this function is very versatile because the only requirement it imposes on the types we use is that they are *comparable* with the `<=` operator. And this requirement is also fulfilled by `std::string`, for example:

```
std::string aaa {"aaa"};
std::string bcd {"bcd"};
std::string def {"def"};
std::string zzz {"zzz"};

within(aaa, zzz,  bcd, def); // --> true
within(aaa, def,  bcd, zzz); // --> false
```

Pushing multiple items into a vector

It's also possible to write a helper that does not reduce any results but processes multiple actions of the same kind. Like inserting items into an `std::vector`, which does not return any results (`std::vector::insert()` signalizes error by throwing exceptions):

```
template <typename T, typename ... Ts>
void insert_all(std::vector<T> &vec, Ts ... ts)
{
    (vec.push_back(ts), ...);
}

int main()
{
    std::vector<int> v {1, 2, 3};
    insert_all(v, 4, 5, 6);
}
```

Note that we use the comma (,) operator in order to expand the parameter pack into individual `vec.push_back(...)` calls without folding the actual result. This function also works nicely with an *empty* parameter pack because the comma operator has an implicit identity element, `void()`, which translates to *do nothing*.

2
STL Containers

We will cover the following recipes in this chapter:

- Using the erase-remove idiom on `std::vector`
- Deleting items from an unsorted `std::vector` in *O(1)* time
- Accessing `std::vector` instances the fast or the safe way
- Keeping `std::vector` instances sorted
- Inserting items efficiently and conditionally into `std::map`
- Knowing the new insertion hint semantics of `std::map::insert`
- Efficiently modifying the keys of `std::map` items
- Using `std::unordered_map` with custom types
- Filtering duplicates from user input and printing them in alphabetical order with `std::set`
- Implementing a simple RPN calculator with `std::stack`
- Implementing a word frequency counter with `std::map`
- Implementing a writing style helper tool for finding very long sentences in texts with `std::set`
- Implementing a personal to-do list using `std::priority_queue`

Introduction

The C++ standard library comes with a wide range of standard containers. A container always contains a collection of data or objects. The cool thing is that containers can be used with practically any kind of object, so we just need to pick the right containers for our specific application. The STL gives us stacks, automatically growing vectors, maps, and so on. This way we can concentrate on our app and don't need to reinvent the wheel. Knowing all containers well is therefore crucial for every C++ programmer.

All containers the STL provides can be categorized as follows, which is explained in detail in the subsequent subsection:

- Contiguous storage
- List storage
- Search trees
- Hash tables
- Container adapters

Contiguous storage

The simplest way to store objects is to put them just next to each other in one large chunk of memory. Such memory can be accessed in a random access manner in *O(1)* time.

The easiest way to do that is using `std::array`, which is just a wrapper around normal C-style arrays. It should always be preferred over normal C-style arrays, because it comes with no runtime cost, but adds some comfort and safety. Just as C-style arrays, it has a *fixed* size once it is created.

The `std::vector` comes into play when array-like storage is needed, but with varying sizes. It uses memory from the heap to store objects. Whenever new objects are pushed into the vector exceeding its current size, it will automatically move all items to a larger chunk of newly allocated memory, and delete the old chunk. Furthermore, if a new item shall be inserted between old ones, it can even move the existing items back and forth. If an item somewhere in the middle shall be removed, the vector class will automatically close the gap by moving the other objects together.

If lots of objects are inserted/removed at the front and/back of an `std::vector` that leads to a lot of new memory allocations in order to gain space, with potentially costly object move, `std::deque` offers an interesting trade off here. The objects are stored in fixed-size chunks of contiguous memory, but these chunks are independent of each other. This makes it very simple and quick to arbitrarily grow the deque, because objects in existing chunks can stay where they are, whenever a new chunk is allocated and put at the front or the end of the container. Deque stands for *double-ended queue*.

List storage

The `std::list` is a classical doubly-linked list. Not less, and not more. If only uni-directional list traversal is needed, `std::forward_list` may be more performant in both space and maintenance complexity, because it maintains only list item pointers in one direction. Lists can only be traversed linearly with *O(n)* time. Inserting and removing items at specific positions can be done in *O(1)* time.

Search trees

Whenever objects have a natural order so that they can be sorted using some notion of the mathematical *smaller* < relation, they can be maintained in that order using *search trees*. As the name suggests, search trees can easily be searched for specific items using a search key, which allows *O(log(n))* search times.

The STL provides such trees in different flavors, where `std::set` is the simplest one of them, storing just *unique*, sortable objects in a tree structure.

`std::map` is different in that regard, that it stores data in *pairs*. A pair consists of a *key*, and a *value*. The search tree uses the key part for sorting the items, which enables for using `std::map` as an *associative container*. As in `std::set`, all key items must only exist once in the whole tree.

`std::multiset` and `std::multimap` are specializations, which drop the requirement for *uniqueness* of the key objects.

Hash tables

When talking about associative containers, search trees are not the only way to implement them. With *hash tables*, items can be found in *O(1)* time, but they ignore the natural order of the items, so they can't be easily traversed in a sorted manner. The *size* of the hash table can be manipulated by the user, and the *hash function* can also be chosen individually, which is important, because the performance versus space consumption characteristics depend on that.

`std::unordered_set` and `std::unordered_map` have so much interface in common with their `std::set` and `std::map` pendants, that they can be used almost interchangeably.

Just as for the search tree implementations, both containers have their multipendants: `std::unordered_multiset` and `std::unordered_multimap` both drop the constraint on the uniqueness of the objects/keys, so we can store multiple elements with the same key.

Container adapters

Arrays, lists, trees, and hash tables are not the only way to store and access data, as there are also stacks, queues, and so on. Similar, more sophisticated structures, however, can be implemented using the more primitive ones, and the STL does that with the following ones in the form of container *adapters*: `std::stack`, `std::queue`, and `std::priority_queue`.

The cool thing is that whenever we need such a data structure, we can just pick such an adapter. Then, when we realize that they do not work out well regarding their performance, we can just change a template parameter in order to let the adapter use a different container implementation, and that's it. In practice, this means, for example, that we can switch the implementation of an `std::stack` instance from `std::vector` to `std::deque`.

Using the erase-remove idiom on std::vector

A lot of novice C++ programmers learn about `std::vector`, that it basically works like an *automatically growing array*, and stop right there. Later, they only lookup its documentation in order to see how to do very specific things, for example, *removing* items. Using STL containers like this will only scratch the surface of how much they help writing *clean*, *maintainable*, and *fast* code.

This section is all about removing items from in-between a vector instance. When an item disappears from a vector, and sits somewhere in the middle *between* other items, then all items right from it must *move* one slot to the *left* (which gives this task a runtime cost within *O(n)*). Many novice programmers will do that using a *loop*, since it is also not really a hard thing to do. Unfortunately, they will potentially ignore a lot of optimization potential while doing that. And in the end, a hand crafted loop is neither *faster*, nor *prettier* to read than the STL way, which we will see next.

How to do it...

In this section, we are filling an `std::vector` instance with some example integers, and then prune some specific items away from it. The way we are doing it is considered the *correct* way of removing multiple items from a vector.

1. Of course we need to include some headers before we do anything.

   ```
   #include <iostream>
   #include <vector>
   #include <algorithm>
   ```

2. Then we declare that we are using namespace `std` to spare us some typing.

   ```
   using namespace std;
   ```

3. Now we create us a vector of integers and fill it with some example items.

   ```
   int main()
   {
       vector<int> v {1, 2, 3, 2, 5, 2, 6, 2, 4, 8};
   ```

4. The next step is to remove the items. What do we remove? There are multiple 2 values. Let's remove them.

   ```
   const auto new_end (remove(begin(v), end(v), 2));
   ```

5. Interestingly, that was only one of the two steps. The vector still has the same size. The next line makes it actually shorter.

   ```
   v.erase(new_end, end(v));
   ```

6. Let's stop by here in order to print the vector's content to the terminal, and then continue.

```
for (auto i : v) {
    cout << i << ", ";
}
cout << '\n';
```

7. Now, let's remove a whole *class* of items, instead of specific *values*. In order to do that, we define a predicate function first, which accepts a number as parameter, and returns true, if it is an *odd* number.

```
const auto odd ([](int i) { return i % 2 != 0; });
```

8. Now we use the remove_if function and feed it with the predicate function. Instead of removing in two steps as we did before, we do it in one.

```
v.erase(remove_if(begin(v), end(v), odd), end(v));
```

9. All odd items are gone now, but the vector's *capacity* is still at the old 10 elements. In a last step, we reduce that also to the actual *current* size of the vector. Note that this might lead the vector code to allocate a new chunk of memory that fits and moves all items from the old chunk to the new one.

```
v.shrink_to_fit();
```

10. Now, let's print the content after the second run of removing items and that's it.

```
for (auto i : v) {
    cout << i << ", ";
}
cout << '\n';
}
```

11. Compiling and running the program yields the following two output lines from the two item removing approaches.

```
$ ./main
1, 3, 5, 6, 4, 8,
6, 4, 8,
```

How it works...

What became obvious in the recipe is that when removing items from the middle of a vector, they first need to be *removed* and then *erased*. At least the functions we used have names like this. This is admittedly confusing, but let's have a closer look at it to make sense of these steps.

The code which removes all values of 2 from the vector, looked like this:

```
const auto new_end (remove(begin(v), end(v), 2));
v.erase(new_end, end(v));
```

The `std::begin` and `std::end` functions both accept a vector instance as parameter, and return us iterators, which point to the *first* item, and *past the last* item, just as sketched in the upcoming diagram.

After feeding these and the value 2 to the `std::remove` function, it will move the non-2 values forward, just like we could do that with a manually programmed loop. The algorithm will strictly preserve the order of all non-2 values while doing that. A quick look at the illustration might be a bit confusing. In step 2, there still is a value of 2, and the vector should have become shorter, as there were four values of 2, which all ought to be removed. Instead, the 4 and the 8 which were in the initial array, are duplicated. What's that?

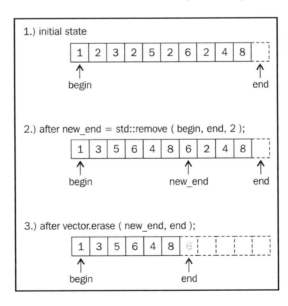

Let's only take a look at all the items, which are within the range and which spans from the `begin` iterator on the illustration, to the `new_end` iterator. The item, to which the `new_end` iterator points, is the *first item past* the range, so it's not included. Just concentrating on that region (these are only the items from 1 to including 8), we realize that *this* is the *correct* range from which all values of 2 are removed.

This is where the `erase` call comes into play: We must tell the vector that it shall not consider all items from `new_end` to `end` to be items of the vector any longer. This order is easy to follow for the vector, as it can just point its `end` iterator to the position of `new_end` and it's done. Note that `new_end` was the return value of the `std::remove` call, so we can just use that.

 Note that the vector did more magic than just moving an internal pointer. If that vector was a vector of more complicated objects, it would have called all the destructors of the to-be-removed items.

Afterward, the vector looks like in step 3 of the diagram: it's considered *smaller* now. The old items which are now out of the range, are *still in memory*.

In order to make the vector occupy only as much memory as it needs, we make the `shrink_to_fit` call in the end. During that call, it allocates exactly as much memory as needed, moves over all the items and deletes the larger chunk we don't need any longer.

In step 8, we define a *predicate* function and use it with `std::remove_if` in only one step. This works, because whatever iterator the remove function returns, it is safe to be used in the vector's erase function. Even if *no odd item* was found, the `std::remove_if` function will do just *nothing*, and return the `end` iterator. Then, a call like `v.erase(end, end);` also does nothing, hence it is harmless.

There's more...

The `std::remove` function also works on other containers. When used with `std::array`, note that it does not support the second step of calling `erase`, because they do not have automatic size handling. Just because `std::remove` effectively only moves items around and does not perform their actual deletion, it can also be used on data structures such as arrays that do not support resizing. In the array case, one could overwrite the values past the new end iterator with sentinel values such as `'\0'` for strings, for example.

Deleting items from an unsorted std::vector in O(1) time

Deleting items from somewhere in the middle of an `std::vector` takes *O(n)* time. This is because the resulting gap from removing an item must be filled by moving all the items which come after the gap one slot to the left.

While moving items around like this, which might be expensive if they are complex and/or very large and include many items, we preserve their order. If preserving the order is not important, we can optimize this, as this section shows.

How to do it...

In this section, we will fill an `std::vector` instance with some example numbers, and implement a quick remove function, which removes any item from a vector in *O(1)* time.

1. First, we need to include the required header files.

```
#include <iostream>
#include <vector>
#include <algorithm>
```

2. Then, we define a main function where we instantiate a vector with example numbers.

```
int main()
{
    std::vector<int> v {123, 456, 789, 100, 200};
```

3. The next step is to delete the value at index 2 (counting from zero of course, so it's the third number 789). The function we will use for that task is not implemented yet. We do that some steps later. Afterward, we print the vector's content.

```
quick_remove_at(v, 2);
for (int i : v) {
    std::cout << i << ", ";
}
std::cout << '\n';
```

4. Now, we will delete another item. It will be the value `123`, and let's say we don't know its index. Therefore, we will use the `std::find` function, which accepts a range (the vector), and a value, and then searches for the value's position. Afterward, it returns us an *iterator* pointing to the `123` value. We will use the same `quick_remove_at` function, but this is an *overloaded* version of the *previous* one which accepts *iterators*. It is also not implemented, yet.

```
    quick_remove_at(v, std::find(std::begin(v), std::end(v), 123));
    for (int i : v) {
        std::cout << i << ", ";
    }
    std::cout << '\n';
}
```

5. Apart from the two `quick_remove_at` functions, we are done. So let's implement these. (Note that they should be at least declared before the main function. So let's just define them there.)
   Both the functions accept a reference to a vector of *something* (in our case, its `int` values), so we leave that open what kind of vector the user will come up with. For us, it's a vector of `T` values. The first `quick_remove_at` function we used accepts *index* values, which are *numbers*, so the interface looks like the following:

```
template <typename T>
void quick_remove_at(std::vector<T> &v, std::size_t idx)
{
```

6. Now comes the meat of the recipe--how do we remove the item quickly without moving too many others? First, we simply take the value of the last item in the vector and use it to overwrite the item which shall be deleted. Second, we cut off the last item of the vector. These are the two steps. We surround this code with a little sanity check. If the index value is obviously out of the vector range, we do nothing. Otherwise, the code would, for example, crash on an empty vector.

```
    if (idx < v.size()) {
        v[idx] = std::move(v.back());
        v.pop_back();
    }
}
```

7. The other implementation of `quick_remove_at` works similar. Instead of accepting a numeric index, it accepts an iterator for `std::vector<T>`. Obtaining its type in a generic manner is not complicated because STL containers already define such types.

```
template <typename T>
void quick_remove_at(std::vector<T> &v,
                     typename std::vector<T>::iterator it)
{
```

8. Now, we will access the value, at which the iterator is pointing. Just as in the other function, we will overwrite it by the last element in the vector. Because we are handling not a numeric index, but an iterator this time, we need to check a bit differently if the iterator position is sane. If it points to the artificial end position, we are not allowed to dereference it.

```
    if (it != std::end(v)) {
```

9. Within that if block, we do the same thing as before--we overwrite the item to be removed with the value of the item from the last position--then we cut off the last element from the vector:

```
        *it = std::move(v.back());
        v.pop_back();
    }
}
```

10. That's it. Compiling and running the program leads to the following output:

```
$ ./main
123, 456, 200, 100,
100, 456, 200,
```

How it works...

The `quick_remove_at` function removes items pretty quickly without touching too many other items. It does this in a relatively creative way: It kind of *swaps* the *actual item,* which shall be removed with the *last* item in the vector. Although the last item has *no connection* to the actually selected item, it is in a *special position*: Removing the last item is *cheap*! The vector's size just needs to be shrunk down by one slot, and that's it. No items are moved during that step. Have a look at the following diagram which helps imaging how this happens:

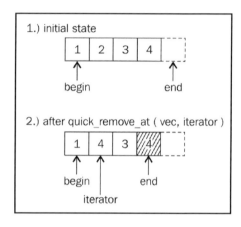

Both the steps in the recipe code look like this:

```
v.at(idx) = std::move(v.back());
v.pop_back();
```

This is the iterator version, which looks nearly identical:

```
*it = std::move(v.back());
v.pop_back();
```

Logically, we *swap* the selected item and the last one. But the code does not swap items, it *moves* the last one over the first one. Why? If we swapped the items, then we would have to store the selected item in a *temporary* variable, move the last item to the selected item, and then store the temporary value in the last slot again. This seems *useless*, as we are just about to *delete* the last item anyway.

Ok, fine, so the swap is useless, and a one-way overwrite is a better thing to do. Having seen that, we can argue that this step could also be performed with a simple `*it = v.back();`, right? Yes, this would be completely *correct*, but imagine we stored some very large strings in every slot, or even another vector or map--in that situation, that little assignment would lead to a very expensive copy. The `std::move` call in between is just an *optimization:* In the example case of *strings*, the string item internally points to a large string in the *heap*. We do not need to copy that. Instead, when *moving* a string, the destination of the move gets to *point at the string data of the other*. The move source item is left intact, but in a useless state, which is fine because we are removing it anyway.

Accessing std::vector instances the fast or the safe way

The `std::vector` is probably the most widely used container in the STL, because it holds data just like an array, and adds a lot of comfort around that representation. However, wrong access to a vector can still be dangerous. If a vector contains 100 elements, and by accident our code tries to access an element at index 123, this is obviously bad. Such a program could just crash, which might be the best case, because that behavior would make it very obvious that there is a bug! If it does not crash, we might observe that the program just behaves *strangely* from time to time, which could lead to even more headaches than a crashing program. The experienced programmer might add some checks before any directly indexed vector access. Such checks do not increase the readability of the code, and many people do not know that `std::vector` already has built-in bound checks!

How to do it...

In this section, we will use the two different ways to access an `std::vector`, and then see how we can utilize them to write safer programs without decreasing readability.

1. Let's include all the needed header files, and fill an example vector with `1000` times the value `123`, so we have something we can access:

   ```
   #include <iostream>
   #include <vector>

   using namespace std;
   ```

```
int main()
{
    const size_t container_size {1000};
    vector<int> v (container_size, 123);
```

2. Now, we access the vector out of bounds using the `[]` operator:

```
cout << "Out of range element value: "
     << v[container_size + 10] << '\n';
```

3. Next, we access it out of bounds using the `at` function:

```
cout << "Out of range element value: "
     << v.at(container_size + 10) << '\n';
}
```

4. Let's run the program and see what happens. The error message is GCC specific. Other compilers would emit different but similar error messages. The first read succeeds in a strange way. It doesn't lead the program to crash, but it's a completely different *value* than `123`. We can't see the output line of the other access because it purposefully crashed the whole program. If that out of bounds access was an accident, we would catch it much earlier!

```
Out of range element value: -726629391
terminate called after throwing an instance of 'std::out_of_range'
  what():  array::at: __n (which is 1010) >= _Nm (which is 1000)
Aborted (core dumped)
```

How it works...

The `std::vector` provides the `[]` operator and the `at` function, and they basically do exactly the same job. The `at` function, however, performs additional bounds checks and throws an *exception* if the vector bounds are exceeded. This is super useful in situations like ours, but also makes the program a little bit *slower*.

Especially when doing numeric computations with indexed members which need to be really fast, it is advantageous to stick to `[]` indexed access. In any other situation, the `at` function helps uncovering bugs with usually negligible performance loss.

 It is good practice to use the `at` function by default. If the resulting code is too slow but has proven to be bug-free, the `[]` operator can be used in performance-sensitive sections instead.

There's more...

Of course, we can *handle* out of bounds accesses, instead of letting the whole app *crash*. In order to handle it, we *catch* the exception, in case it was thrown by the `at` function. Catching such an exception is simple. We just surround the `at` call with a `try` block and define the error handling in a `catch` block.

```
try {
    std::cout << "Out of range element value: "
              << v.at(container_size + 10) << '\n';
} catch (const std::out_of_range &e) {
    std::cout << "Ooops, out of range access detected: "
              << e.what() << '\n';
}
```

By the way, `std::array` also provides an `at` function.

Keeping std::vector instances sorted

Arrays and vectors do not sort their payload objects themselves. But if we need that, this does not mean that we always have to switch to data structures, which were designed to do that automatically. If an `std::vector` is perfect for our use case, it is still very simple and practical to add items to it in a *sorting manner*.

How to do it...

In this section, we will fill an `std::vector` with random words, sort it, and then insert more words while keeping the vector's sorted word order intact.

1. Let's first include all headers we're going to need.

```
#include <iostream>
#include <vector>
#include <string>
#include <algorithm>
#include <iterator>
#include <cassert>
```

2. We also declare that we are using namespace `std` in order to spare us some `std::` prefixes:

```
using namespace std;
```

3. Then we write a little main function, which fills a vector with some random strings.

```
int main()
{
    vector<string> v {"some", "random", "words",
                      "without", "order", "aaa",
                      "yyy"};
```

4. The next thing we do is *sorting* that vector. Let's do that with some assertions and the `is_sorted` function from the STL before, which shows that the vector really was *not* sorted before, but *is* sorted afterward.

```
assert(false == is_sorted(begin(v), end(v)));
sort(begin(v), end(v));
assert(true == is_sorted(begin(v), end(v)));
```

5. Now, we finally add some random words into the sorted vector using a new `insert_sorted` function, which we still need to implement afterward. These words shall be put at the right spot so that the vector is still sorted afterward:

```
insert_sorted(v, "foobar");
insert_sorted(v, "zzz");
```

6. So, let's now implement `insert_sorted` a little earlier in the source file.

```
void insert_sorted(vector<string> &v, const string &word)
{
    const auto insert_pos (lower_bound(begin(v), end(v), word));
    v.insert(insert_pos, word);
}
```

7. Now, back in the main function where we stopped, we can now continue printing the vector and see that the insert procedure works:

```
for (const auto &w : v) {
    cout << w << " ";
}
cout << '\n';
}
```

8. Compiling and running the program yields the following nicely sorted output:

```
aaa foobar order random some without words yyy zzz
```

How it works...

The whole program is constructed around the `insert_sorted` function, which does what this section is about: For any new string, it locates the position in the sorted vector, at which it must be inserted, in order to *preserve* the order of the strings in the vector. However, we assume that the vector was sorted before. Otherwise, this would not work.

The locating step is done by the STL function `lower_bound`, which accepts three arguments. The first two denote *beginning* and *end* of the underlying range. The range is our vector of words in this case. The third argument is the word, which shall be inserted. The function then finds the first item in the range, which is *greater than or equal* to that third parameter and returns an iterator pointing to it.

Having the right position at hand, we gave it to the `std::vector` member method `insert`, which accepts just two arguments. The first argument is an iterator, which points to the position in the vector, at which the second parameter shall be inserted. It appears very handy that we can use the same iterator, which just dropped out of the `lower_bound` function. The second argument is, of course, the item to be inserted.

There's more...

The `insert_sorted` function is pretty generic. If we generalize the types of its parameters, it will also work on other container payload types, and even on other containers such as `std::set`, `std::deque`, `std::list`, and so on! (Note that set has its own `lower_bound` member function that does the same as `std::lower_bound`, but is more efficient because it is specialized for sets.)

```
template <typename C, typename T>
void insert_sorted(C &v, const T &item)
{
    const auto insert_pos (lower_bound(begin(v), end(v), item));
    v.insert(insert_pos, item);
}
```

When trying to switch the type of the vector in the recipe from `std::vector` to something else, note that not all containers support `std::sort`. That algorithm requires random access containers, which `std::list`, for example, does not fulfill.

Inserting items efficiently and conditionally into std::map

Sometimes we want to fill a map with key-value pairs and while filling the map up, we might run into two different cases:

1. The key does not exist yet. Create a *fresh* key-value pair.
2. The key does exist already. Take the *existing* item and *modify* it.

We could just naively use the `insert` or `emplace` methods of map and see if they succeed. If it doesn't, we have case 2 and modify the existing item. In both cases, insert and emplace create the item which we try to insert, and in case 2 the freshly created item is dropped. We get a useless constructor call in both cases.

Since C++17, there is the `try_emplace` function, which enables us to create items only conditionally upon insertion. Let's implement a program that takes a list of billionaires and constructs a map that tells us the number of billionaires per country. In addition to that, it stores the wealthiest person in every country. Our example will not contain expensive to create items, but whenever we find ourselves in such a situation in real-life projects, we know how to master it with `try_emplace`.

How to do it...

In this section, we will implement an application that creates a map from a list of billionaires. The map maps from each country to a reference to the wealthiest person in that country and a counter that tells how many billionaires that country has.

1. As always, we need to include some headers first and we declare that we use namespace `std` by default.

```
#include <iostream>
#include <functional>
#include <list>
#include <map>

using namespace std;
```

2. Let's define a structure that represents billionaire items for our list.

```
struct billionaire {
    string name;
    double dollars;
    string country;
};
```

3. In the main function, we first define the list of billionaires. There are *many* billionaires in the world, so let's construct a limited list with just some of the richest persons in some countries. This list is already ordered. The rankings are actually taken from the Forbes 2017 list *The World's Billionaires* at `https://www.fo rbes.com/billionaires/list/`:

```
int main()
{
    list<billionaire> billionaires {
        {"Bill Gates", 86.0, "USA"},
        {"Warren Buffet", 75.6, "USA"},
        {"Jeff Bezos", 72.8, "USA"},
        {"Amancio Ortega", 71.3, "Spain"},
        {"Mark Zuckerberg", 56.0, "USA"},
        {"Carlos Slim", 54.5, "Mexico"},
        // ...
        {"Bernard Arnault", 41.5, "France"},
        // ...
        {"Liliane Bettencourt", 39.5, "France"},
        // ...
        {"Wang Jianlin", 31.3, "China"},
        {"Li Ka-shing", 31.2, "Hong Kong"}
```

```
        // ...
    };
```

4. Now, let's define the map. It maps from the country string to a pair. The pair contains a (const) copy of the first billionaire of every country from our list. That is automatically the richest billionaire per country. The other variable in the pair is a counter, which we will increment for every following billionaire in that country.

```
    map<string, pair<const billionaire, size_t>> m;
```

5. Now, let's go through the list and try to emplace a new payload pair for every country. The pair contains a reference to the billionaire we are currently looking at and a counter value of 1.

```
    for (const auto &b : billionaires) {
        auto [iterator, success] = m.try_emplace(b.country, b, 1);
```

6. If that step was successful, then we don't need to do anything else. The pair for which we provided the constructor arguments b, 1 has been constructed and inserted into the map. If the insertion was *not* successful because the country key exists already, then the pair was not constructed. If our billionaire structure was very large, this would have saved us the runtime cost of copying it.
   However, in the nonsuccessful case, we still need to increment the counter for this country.

```
        if (!success) {
            iterator->second.second += 1;
        }
    }
```

7. Ok, that's it. We can now print how many billionaires there are per country, and who is the wealthiest one in each country.

```
    for (const auto & [key, value] : m) {
        const auto &[b, count] = value;
        cout << b.country << " : " << count
            << " billionaires. Richest is "
            << b.name << " with " << b.dollars
            << " B$\n";
    }
}
```

8. Compiling and running the program yields the following output. (Of course, the output is limited, because we limited our input map.)

```
$ ./efficient_insert_or_modify
China : 1 billionaires. Richest is Wang Jianlin with 31.3 B$
France : 2 billionaires. Richest is Bernard Arnault with 41.5 B$
Hong Kong : 1 billionaires. Richest is Li Ka-shing with 31.2 B$
Mexico : 1 billionaires. Richest is Carlos Slim with 54.5 B$
Spain : 1 billionaires. Richest is Amancio Ortega with 71.3 B$
USA : 4 billionaires. Richest is Bill Gates with 86 B$
```

How it works...

The whole recipe revolves around the `try_emplace` function of `std::map`, which is a new C++17 addition. It has the following signature:

```
std::pair<iterator, bool> try_emplace(const key_type& k, Args&&... args);
```

Thus, the key being inserted is parameter `k` and the associated value is constructed from the parameter pack `args`. If we succeed in inserting the item, then the function returns an *iterator*, which points to the new node in the map, *paired* with a Boolean value being set to `true`. If the insertion was *not* successful, the Boolean value in the return pair is set to `false`, and the iterator points to the item with which the new item would clash.

This characteristic is very useful in our case--when we see a billionaire from a specific country for the first time, then this country is not a key in the map yet. In that case, we must *insert* it, accompanied with a new counter being set to 1. If we *did* see a billionaire from a specific country already, we have to get a reference to its existing counter, in order to increment it. This is exactly what happened in step 6:

```
if (!success) {
    iterator->second.second += 1;
}
```

 Note that both the `insert` and `emplace` functions of `std::map` work exactly the same way. A crucial difference is that `try_emplace` will *not* construct the object associated with the key if the key already exists. This boosts the performance in case objects of that type are expensive to create.

There's more...

The whole program still works if we switch the type of the map from `std::map` to `std::unordered_map`. This way, we can simply switch from one implementation to another, which has different performance characteristics. In this recipe, the only observable difference is that the billionaire map is not printed in alphabetical order any longer, because hash maps do not order their objects the same way as search trees do.

Knowing the new insertion hint semantics of std::map::insert

Looking up items in an `std::map` takes $O(log(n))$ time. This is the same for inserting new items, because the position where to insert them must be looked up. Naive insertion of *M* new items would thus take $O(M * log(n))$ time.

In order to make this more efficient, `std::map` insertion functions accept an optional *insertion hint* parameter. The insertion hint is basically an iterator, which points near the future position of the item that is to be inserted. If the hint is correct, then we get *amortized O(1)* insertion time.

How to do it...

In this section, we will insert multiple items into an `std::map`, and use insertion hints for that, in order to reduce the number of lookups.

1. We are mapping strings to numbers, so we need the header files included for `std::map` and `std::string`.

   ```
   #include <iostream>
   #include <map>
   #include <string>
   ```

2. The next step is to instantiate a map, which already contains some example characters.

   ```
   int main()
   {
       std::map<std::string, size_t> m {{"b", 1}, {"c", 2}, {"d", 3}};
   ```

3. We will insert multiple items now, and for each item we will use an insertion hint. Since we have no hint in the beginning to start with, we will just do the first insertion pointing to the `end` iterator of the map.

```
auto insert_it (std::end(m));
```

4. We will now insert items from the alphabet backward while always using the iterator hint we have, and then reinitialize it to the return value of the `insert` function. The next item will be inserted just *before* the hint.

```
for (const auto &s : {"z", "y", "x", "w"}) {
    insert_it = m.insert(insert_it, {s, 1});
}
```

5. And just for the sake of showing how it is *not* done, we insert a string which will be put at the leftmost position in the map, but give it a completely *wrong* hint, which points to the rightmost position in the map--the `end`.

```
m.insert(std::end(m), {"a", 1});
```

6. Finally, we just print what we have.

```
for (const auto & [key, value] : m) {
    std::cout << "\"" << key << "\": " << value << ", ";
}
std::cout << '\n';
```

7. And this is the output we get when we compile and run the program. Obviously, the wrong insertion hint did not hurt too much, as the map ordering is still correct.

```
"a": 1, "b": 1, "c": 2, "d": 3, "w": 1, "x": 1, "y": 1, "z": 1,
```

How it works...

The only difference to normal map insertions in this recipe was the additional hint iterator. And we spoke about *correct* and *wrong* hints.

A *correct* hint will point to an existing element, which is *greater* than the element to be inserted so that the newly inserted key will be just *before* the hint. If this does not apply for the hint the user provided during an insertion, the insert function will fall back to a nonoptimized insertion, yielding *O(log(n))* performance again.

For the first insertion, we got the `end` iterator of the map, because we had no better hint to start with. After installing a "z" in the tree, we knew that installing "y" will insert a new item just in front of the "z", which qualified it to be a correct hint. This applies to "x" as well, if put into the tree after inserting the "y", and so on. This is why it is possible to use the iterator, which was returned by the *last* insertion for the *next* insertion.

> It is important to know, that before C++11, insertion hints were considered correct when they pointed *before* the position of the newly inserted item.

There's more...

Interestingly, a wrong hint does not even destroy or disturb the order of the items in the map, so how does that even work, and what did that mean, that the insertion time is amortized *O(1)*?

The `std::map` is usually implemented using a binary search tree. When inserting a new key into a search tree, it is compared against the keys of the other nodes, beginning from the top. If the key is smaller or larger than the key of one node, then the search algorithm branches left or right to go down to the next deeper node. While doing that, the search algorithm will stop at the point where it reached the maximum depth of the current tree, where it will put the new node with its key. It is possible that this step destroyed the tree's balance, so it will also correct that using a re-balancing algorithm afterward as a housekeeping task.

When we insert items into a tree with key values which are direct neighbors of each other (just as the integer 1 is a neighbor of the integer 2, because no other integer fits between them), they can *often* also be inserted just next to each other in the tree, too. It can easily be checked if this is true for a certain key and an accompanying hint. And if this situation applies, the search algorithm step can be omitted, which spares some crucial runtime. Afterward, the re-balancing algorithm might nevertheless have to be run. When such an optimization can *often* be done, but not *always*, this can still lead to an *average* performance gain. It is possible to show a *resulting* runtime complexity which settles down after *multiple* insertions, and then it's called **amortized complexity**.

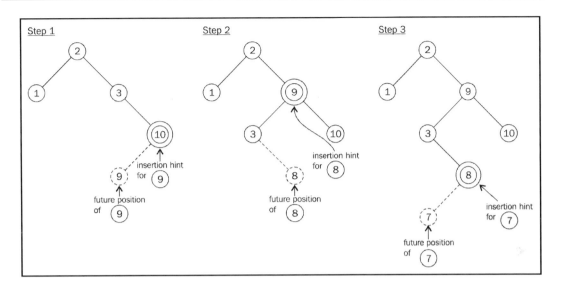

If the insertion hint is wrong, the insertion function will simply *waive* the hint and start over using the search algorithm. This works correctly but is obviously *slower*.

Efficiently modifying the keys of std::map items

Since the `std::map` data structure maps from keys to values in a way that the keys are always unique and sorted, it is of crucial value that users cannot modify the keys of map nodes that are already inserted. In order to prevent the user from modifying the key items of perfectly sorted map nodes, the `const` qualifier is added to the key type.

This kind of restriction is perfectly sane because it makes it harder for the user to use `std::map` the wrong way. But what shall we do if we really need to change the keys of some map items?

Prior to C++17, we had to remove the items of which we need to change the key value from the tree, in order to reinsert them. The downside of this approach is that this always needlessly reallocates some memory, which sounds bad in terms of performance.

Since C++17, we can remove and reinsert map nodes *without* any reallocation of memory. We will see how that works in this recipe.

How to do it...

We implement a little application that orders the placement of drivers in a fictional race in an `std::map` structure. While drivers pass each other during the race, we need to change their placement keys, which we do the new C++17 way.

1. Let's first include the necessary headers and declare that we use namespace `std`.

```
#include <iostream>
#include <map>

using namespace std;
```

2. We will print the race placements before and after manipulating the map structure, so let's implement a little helper function for that.

```
template <typename M>
void print(const M &m)
{
    cout << "Race placement:\n";
    for (const auto &[placement, driver] : m) {
        cout << placement << ": " << driver << '\n';
    }
}
```

3. In the main function, we instantiate and initialize a map that maps from integer values that denote the driver's place to strings that contain the driver's name. We also print the map because we will modify it in the next steps.

```
int main()
{
    map<int, string> race_placement {
        {1, "Mario"}, {2, "Luigi"}, {3, "Bowser"},
        {4, "Peach"}, {5, "Yoshi"}, {6, "Koopa"},
        {7, "Toad"}, {8, "Donkey Kong Jr."}
    };
    print(race_placement);
```

4. Let's say that during one race lap, Bowser had a little accident and dropped to the last place and Donkey Kong Jr. took the chance to jump from the last place to the third place. In that case, we first need to extract their map nodes from the map because this is the only way to manipulate their keys. The extract function is a new C++17 feature. It removes items from a map without any allocation-related side effects. Let's also open a new scope for this task.

```
{
    auto a (race_placement.extract(3));
    auto b (race_placement.extract(8));
```

5. Now we can swap Bowser's and Donkey Kong Jr.'s keys. While the keys of map nodes are usually not mutable because they are declared const, we can modify the keys of items which we extracted using the extract method.

```
    swap(a.key(), b.key());
```

6. std::map's insert method got a new overload in C++17 that accepts the handles of extracted nodes, in order to insert them without touching the allocator.

```
    race_placement.insert(move(a));
    race_placement.insert(move(b));
}
```

7. After leaving the scope, we're done. We print the new race placement and let the application terminate.

```
    print(race_placement);
}
```

8. Compiling and running the program yields the following output. We see the race placement in the fresh map instance first, and then we see it again after swapping Bowser's and Donkey Kong Jr.'s positions.

```
$ ./mapnode_key_modification
Race placement:
1: Mario
2: Luigi
3: Bowser
4: Peach
5: Yoshi
6: Koopa
7: Toad
8: Donkey Kong Jr.
Race placement:
1: Mario
```

```
2: Luigi
3: Donkey Kong Jr.
4: Peach
5: Yoshi
6: Koopa
7: Toad
8: Bowser
```

How it works...

In C++17, `std::map` got a new member function extract. It comes in two flavors:

```
node_type extract(const_iterator position);
node_type extract(const key_type& x);
```

In this recipe, we used the second one, which accepts a key and then finds and extracts the map node that matches the key parameter. The first one accepts an iterator, which implies that it is *faster* because it doesn't need to search for the item.

If we try to extract an item that doesn't exist with the second method (the one that searches using a key), it returns an *empty* `node_type` instance. The `empty()` member method returns us a Boolean value that tells whether a `node_type` instance is empty or not. Accessing any other method on an empty instance leads to undefined behavior.

After extracting nodes, we were able to modify their keys using the `key()` method, which gives us nonconst access to the key, although keys are usually const.

Note that in order to reinsert the nodes into the map again, we had to *move* them into the `insert` function. This makes sense because `extract` is all about avoiding unnecessary copies and allocations. Note that while we move a `node_type` instance, this does not result in actual moves of any of the container values.

There's more...

Map nodes that have been extracted using the extract method are actually very versatile. We can extract nodes from a `map` instance and insert it into any other `map` or even `multimap` instance. It does also work between `unordered_map` and `unordered_multimap` instances, as well as with `set`/`multiset` and respective `unordered_set`/`unordered_multiset`.

In order to move items between different map/set structures, the types of key, value, and allocator need to be identical. Note that even if that is the case, we cannot move nodes from a `map` to an `unordered_map`, or from a `set` to an `unordered_set`.

Using std::unordered_map with custom types

If we use `std::unordered_map` instead of `std::map`, we have a different degree of freedom for the choice of the key type which shall be used. `std::map` demands that there is a natural order between all key items. This way, items can be sorted. But what if we want, for example, mathematical vectors as a key type? There is no *meaning* in a *smaller* < relation for such types, as a vector `(0, 1)` is not *smaller* or *larger* than `(1, 0)`. They just point in different directions. This is completely fine for `std::unordered_map` because it will not distinguish items via their smaller/greater ordering relationship but via *hash values*. The only thing we need to do is to implement a *hash function* for our own type, and an *equal to* == operator implementation, which tells whether two objects are identical. This section will demonstrate this in an example.

How to do it...

In this section, we will define a simple `coord` struct, which has no *default* hash function, so we need to define it ourselves. Then we put it to use by mapping `coord` values to numbers.

1. We first include what's needed in order to print and use `std::unordered_map`.

```
#include <iostream>
#include <unordered_map>
```

2. Then we define our own custom struct, which is not trivially hashable by *existing* hash functions:

```
struct coord {
    int x;
    int y;
};
```

3. We do not only need a hash function in order to use the structure as a key for a hash map, it also needs a comparison operator implementation:

```
bool operator==(const coord &l, const coord &r)
{
    return l.x == r.x && l.y == r.y;
}
```

4. In order to extend the STL's own hashing capabilities, we will open the std namespace and create our own std::hash template struct specialization. It contains the same using type alias clauses as other hash specializations.

```
namespace std
{
template <>
struct hash<coord>
{
    using argument_type = coord;
    using result_type   = size_t;
```

5. The meat of this struct is the operator() definition. We are just adding the numeric member values of struct coord, which is a poor hashing technique, but for the sake of showing how to implement it, it's good enough. A good hash function tries to distribute values as evenly over the whole value range as possible, in order to reduce the amount of *hash collisions*.

```
    result_type operator()(const argument_type &c) const
    {
        return static_cast<result_type>(c.x)
            + static_cast<result_type>(c.y);
    }
};
}
```

6. We can now instantiate a new `std::unordered_map` instance, which accepts `struct coord` instances as a key, and maps it to arbitrary values. As this recipe is about enabling our own types for `std::unordered_map`, this is pretty much it already. Let's instantiate a hash-based map with our own type, fill it with some items, and print its :

```
int main()
{

    std::unordered_map<coord, int> m {{{0, 0}, 1}, {{0, 1}, 2},
                                      {{2, 1}, 3}};
    for (const auto & [key, value] : m) {
        std::cout << "{(" << key.x << ", " << key.y
                  << "): " << value << "} ";
    }
    std::cout << '\n';
}
```

7. Compiling and running the program yields the following output:

```
$ ./custom_type_unordered_map
{(2, 1): 3} {(0, 1): 2} {(0, 0): 1}
```

How it works...

Usually, when we instantiate a hash-based map implementation like `std::unordered_map`, we write:

```
std::unordered_map<key_type, value_type> my_unordered_map;
```

It is not too obvious that there happens a lot of magic in the background when the compiler creates our `std::unordered_map` specialization. So, let's have a look at the complete template-type definition of it:

```
template<
    class Key,
    class T,
    class Hash      = std::hash<Key>,
    class KeyEqual  = std::equal_to<Key>,
    class Allocator = std::allocator< std::pair<const Key, T> >
> class unordered_map;
```

The first two template types are those we filled with `coord` and `int`, which is the simple and obvious part. The other three template types are optional, as they are automatically filled with existing standard template classes, which themselves take template types. Those are fed with our choice for the first two parameters as default values.

Regarding this recipe, the `class Hash` template parameter is the interesting one: when we do not explicitly define anything else, it is going to be specialized on `std::hash<key_type>`. The STL already contains `std::hash` specializations for a lot of types such as `std::hash<std::string>`, `std::hash<int>`, `std::hash<unique_ptr>`, and many more. These classes know how to deal with such specific types in order to calculate optimal hash values from them.

However, the STL does not know how to calculate a hash value from our `struct coord`, yet. So what we did was to just define *another* specialization, which knows how to deal with it. The compiler can now go through the list of all `std::hash` specializations it knows, and will find our implementation to match it with the type we provided as key type.

If we did not add a new `std::hash<coord>` specialization, and named it `my_hash_type` instead, we could still use it with the following instantiation line:

```
std::unordered_map<coord, value_type, my_hash_type> my_unordered_map;
```

That is obviously more to type, and not as nice to read as when the compiler finds the right hashing implementation itself.

Filtering duplicates from user input and printing them in alphabetical order with std::set

`std::set` is a strange container: It kind of works like `std::map`, but it contains only keys as values, no key-value pairs. So it can hardly be used as a way to map values of one type to the other. Seemingly, just because there are less obvious use cases for it, a lot of developers do not even know about its existence. Then they start to implement things themselves, although `std::set` would be of great help in some of these situations.

This section shows how to put `std::set` to use in an example where we collect potentially many different items, in order to *filter* them and output a selection of the *unique* ones.

How to do it...

In this section, we will read a stream of words from the standard input. All *unique* words are put into an `std::set` instance. This way we can then enumerate all unique words from the stream.

1. We will use several different STL types, for which we need to include multiple headers.

```
#include <iostream>
#include <set>
#include <string>
#include <iterator>
```

2. In order to spare us some typing, we will declare that we are using namespace std:

```
using namespace std;
```

3. Now we're already writing the actual program, which begins with the `main` function instantiating an `std::set` which stores strings.

```
int main()
{
    set<string> s;
```

4. The next thing to do is to get the user input. We're just reading from standard input, and do that using the handy `istream_iterator`.

```
    istream_iterator<string> it {cin};
    istream_iterator<string> end;
```

5. Having a pair of `begin` and `end` iterators, which represent the user input, we can just fill the set from it using an `std::inserter`.

```
    copy(it, end, inserter(s, s.end()));
```

6. That's already it. In order to see what *unique* words we got from standard input, we just print the content of our set.

```
    for (const auto word : s) {
        cout << word << ", ";
    }
    cout << '\n';
}
```

7. Let's compile and run our program with the following input. We get the following output for the preceding input, where all duplicates are stripped out, and the words which were unique, are sorted alphabetically.

```
$ echo "a a a b c foo bar foobar foo bar bar" | ./program
a, b, bar, c, foo, foobar,
```

How it works...

This program consists of two interesting parts. The first part is using `std::istream_iterator` to access the user input, and the second part is to combine this with our `std::set` instance using the `std::copy` algorithm, after we wrapped it into an `std::inserter` instance! It might look surprising that there is only one line of code which does all the work of *tokenizing* the input, *putting* it into the alphabetically *sorted* set, and *dropping* all duplicates.

std::istream_iterator

This class is really interesting in cases where we want to process masses of data of the *same* type from a stream, which is exactly the case in this recipe: we parse the whole input word by word and put it into the set in the form of `std::string` instances.

The `std::istream_iterator` takes one template parameter. That is the type of the input we want to have. We chose `std::string` because we assume text words, but it could also have been `float` numbers, for example. It can basically be every type for which it is possible to write `cin >> var;`. The constructor accepts an `istream` instance. The standard input is represented by the global input stream object `std::cin`, which is an acceptable `istream` parameter in this case.

```
istream_iterator<string> it {cin};
```

The input stream iterator `it` which we have instantiated, is able to do two things: when it is dereferenced (`*it`), it yields the current input symbol. As we have typed the iterator to `std::string` via its template parameter, that symbol will be a string containing one word. When it is incremented (`++it`), it will jump to the next word, which we can access by dereferencing again.

But wait, we need to be careful after every increment before we dereference it again. If the standard input ran *empty*, the iterator must *not* be dereferenced again. Instead, we should terminate the loop in which we dereference the iterator to get at every word. The abort condition, which lets us know that the iterator became invalid, is a comparison with the `end` iterator. If `it == end` holds, we are past the end of the input.

We create the end iterator by creating an `std::istream_iterator` instance with its parameterless standard constructor. It has the purpose of being the counterpart of the comparison which shall act as the abort condition in every iteration:

```
istream_iterator<string> end;
```

As soon as `std::cin` runs empty, our `it` iterator instance will *notice* that and make a comparison with `end` returning `true`.

std::inserter

We used the `it` and `end` pair as *input* iterators in the `std::copy` call. The third parameter must be an *output* iterator. For that, we cannot just take `s.begin()` or `s.end()`. In an empty set, both are the same, so we are not even allowed to *dereference* it, regardless if that is for reading from it or assigning to it.

This is where `std::inserter` comes into play. It is a function which returns an `std::insert_iterator` that behaves like an iterator but does something else than what usual iterators do. When we increment it, it does nothing. When we dereference it and assign something to it, it will take the container it is attached to, and *insert* that value as a *new* item into it!

When instantiating an `std::insert_iterator` via `std::inserter`, two parameters are needed:

```
auto insert_it = inserter(s, s.end());
```

The `s` is our set, and `s.end()` is an iterator that points to where the new item shall be inserted. For an empty set which we start with, this makes as much sense as `s.begin()`. When used for other data structures as vectors or lists, that second parameter is crucial for defining where the insert iterator shall insert new items.

Putting it together

In the end, *all* the action happens during the `std::copy` call:

```
copy(input_iterator_begin, input_iterator_end, insert_iterator);
```

This call pulls the next word token out of `std::cin` via the input iterator and pushes it into our `std::set`. Afterward, it increments both iterators, and checks whether the input iterator is equal to the input end iterator counterpart. If it is not, then there are still words left in the standard input, so it will *repeat*.

Duplicate words are automatically dropped. If the set already contains a specific word, adding it again has *no effect*. This would be different in an `std::multiset` as, in contrast, it would accept duplicates.

Implementing a simple RPN calculator with std::stack

The `std::stack` is an adapter class which lets the user push objects *onto* it like on a real stack of objects, and pop objects *down from* it again. In this section, we construct a reverse polish notation (RPN) calculator around that data structure, in order to show how to use it.

The RPN is a notation that can be used to express mathematical expressions in a way that is really simple to parse. In RPN, `1 + 2` is `1 2 +`. Operands first, then the operation. Another example: `(1 + 2) * 3` would be `1 2 + 3 *` in RPN and that already shows why it is easier to parse, as we do not need *parentheses* to define subexpressions.

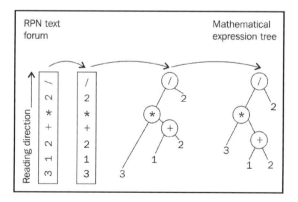

How to do it...

In this section, we will read a mathematical expression in RPN from the standard input, and then feed it into a function that evaluates it. In the end, we print the numeric result back to the user.

1. We will use a lot of helpers from the STL, so there are a few includes:

```
#include <iostream>
#include <stack>
#include <iterator>
#include <map>
#include <sstream>
#include <cassert>
#include <vector>
#include <stdexcept>
#include <cmath>
```

2. And we do also declare that we are using namespace `std` in order to spare us some typing.

```
using namespace std;
```

3. Then, we immediately start implementing our RPN parser. It will accept an iterator pair, which denotes the beginning and end of a mathematical expression in string form, which will be consumed token by token.

```
template <typename IT>
double evaluate_rpn(IT it, IT end)
{
```

4. While we iterate through the tokens, we need to memorize all *operands* on the way until we see an *operation*. This is where we need a stack. All the numbers will be parsed and saved in double precision floating point, so it's going to be a stack of `double` values.

```
stack<double> val_stack;
```

5. In order to comfortably access elements on the stack, we implement a helper. It modifies the stack by pulling the highest item from it and then returns that item. This way we can perform this task in one single step later.

```
auto pop_stack ([&](){
    auto r (val_stack.top());
    val_stack.pop();
    return r;
});
```

6. Another preparation is to define all the supported mathematical operations. We save them in a map, which associates every operation token with the actual operation. The operations are represented by callable lambdas, which take two operands, add or multiply them, for example, and then return the result.

```
map<string, double (*)(double, double)> ops {
    {"+", [](double a, double b) { return a + b; }},
    {"-", [](double a, double b) { return a - b; }},
    {"*", [](double a, double b) { return a * b; }},
    {"/", [](double a, double b) { return a / b; }},
    {"^", [](double a, double b) { return pow(a, b); }},
    {"%", [](double a, double b) { return fmod(a, b); }},
};
```

7. Now we can finally iterate through the input. Assuming that the input iterators give us strings, we feed a new `std::stringstream` per token, because it can parse numbers.

```
for (; it != end; ++it) {
    stringstream ss {*it};
```

8. Now with every token, we try to get a `double` value out of it. If that succeeds, we have an *operand*, which we push on the stack.

```
if (double val; ss >> val) {
    val_stack.push(val);
}
```

9. If it does *not* succeed, it must be something other than an operator; in that case, it can only be an *operand*. Knowing that all the operations we support are *binary*, we need to pop the last *two* operands from the stack.

```
else {
    const auto r {pop_stack()};
    const auto l {pop_stack()};
```

10. Now we get the operand from dereferencing the iterator `it`, which already emits strings. By querying the `ops` map, we get a lambda object which accepts the two operands `l` and `r` as parameters.

```
try {
    const auto & op        (ops.at(*it));
    const double result {op(l, r)};
    val_stack.push(result);
}
```

11. We surrounded the application of the math part with a `try` clause, so we can catch possibly occurring exceptions. The `at` call of the map will throw an `out_of_range` exception in case the user provides a mathematical operation we don't know of. In that case, we will rethrow a different exception, which says `invalid argument` and carries the operation string which was unknown to us.

```
catch (const out_of_range &) {
    throw invalid_argument(*it);
}
```

12. That's already it. As soon as the loop terminates, we have the final result on the stack. So we return just that. (At this point, we could assert if the stack size is 1. If it wasn't, then there would be missing operations.)

```
        }
    }
    return val_stack.top();
}
```

13. Now we can use our little RPN parser. In order to do this, we wrap the standard input into an `std::istream_iterator` pair, and feed that into the RPN parser function. Finally, we print the result:

```
int main()
{
    try {
        cout << evaluate_rpn(istream_iterator<string>{cin}, {})
             << '\n';
    }
```

14. We do again have that line wrapped into a `try` clause because there's still the possibility that the user input contains operations we did not implement. In that case, we must catch the exception which we throw in such cases, and print an error message:

```
    catch (const invalid_argument &e) {
        cout << "Invalid operator: " << e.what() << '\n';
    }
}
```

15. After compiling the program, we can play around with it. The input `"3 1 2 + *  2 /"` represents the expression (3 * (1 + 2)) / 2 and yields the correct result:

```
$ echo "3 1 2 + * 2 /" | ./rpn_calculator
4.5
```

How it works...

The whole recipe revolves around pushing operands onto the stack until we see an operation in the input. In that situation, we pop the last two operands from the stack again, apply the operation to them, and push the result onto the stack again. In order to understand all of the code in this recipe, it is important to understand how we distinguish *operands* and *operations* from the input, how we handle our stack, and how we select and apply the right mathematical operation.

Stack handling

We push items onto the stack, simply using the `push` function of `std::stack`:

```
val_stack.push(val);
```

Popping values from it looks a bit more complicated because we implemented a lambda for that, which captures a reference to the `val_stack` object. Let's look at the same code, enhanced with some more comments:

```
auto pop_stack ([&](){
    auto r (val_stack.top());  // Get top value copy
    val_stack.pop();           // Throw away top value
    return r;                  // Return copy
});
```

This lambda is necessary to get the top value of the stack and *remove* it from there in *one* step. The interface of `std::stack` is not designed in a way which would allow doing that in a *single* call. However, defining a lambda is quick and easy, so we can now get values like this:

```
double top_value {pop_stack()};
```

Distinguishing operands from operations from user input

In the main loop of `evaluate_rpn`, we take the current string token from the iterator and then see whether it is an operand or not. If the string can be parsed into a `double` variable, then it is a number, and hence also an operand. We consider everything which is not easily parseable as a number (such as "+", for example) to be an *operation*.

The naked code skeleton for exactly this task is as follows:

```
stringstream ss {*it};
if (double val; ss >> val) {
    // It's a number!
} else {
    // It's something else than a number - an operation!
}
```

The stream operator >> tells us if it is a number. First, we wrapped the string into an `std::stringstream`. Then we use the `stringstream` object's capability to stream from an `std::string` into a `double` variable, which involves parsing. If the parsing *fails*, we know that it does so, because we asked it to parse something into a number, which is *no number*.

Selecting and applying the right mathematical operation

After we realize that the current user input token is not a number, we just assume that it is an operation, such as + or *. Then we query our map, which we called `ops`, to look that operation up and return us a function, which accepts two operands, and returns the sum, or the product, or whatever is appropriate.

The type of the map itself looks relatively complicated:

```
map<string, double (*)(double, double)> ops { ... };
```

It maps from `string` to `double (*)(double, double)`. What does the latter mean? This type description shall read *"pointer to a function which takes two doubles, and returns a double"*. Imagine that the `(*)` part is the name of the function, such as in `double sum(double, double)`, which is immediately easier to read. The trick here is that our lambda `[](double, double) { return /* some double */ }` is convertible to a function pointer that actually matches that pointer description. Lambdas that *don't capture* anything are generally convertible to function pointers.

This way, we can conveniently ask the map for the correct operation:

```
const auto & op      (ops.at(*it));
const double result {op(l, r)};
```

The map implicitly does another job for us: If we say `ops.at("foo")`, then `"foo"` is a valid key value, but we did not store any operation named like this. In such a case, the map will throw an exception, which we catch in the recipe. We rethrow a different exception whenever we catch it, in order to provide a descriptive meaning of this error case. The user will know better what an `invalid argument` exception means, compared to an `out of range` exception. Note that the user of the `evaluate_rpn` function might not have read its implementation, hence it might be unknown that we are using a map inside at all.

There's more...

As the `evaluate_rpn` function accepts iterators, it is very easy to feed it with different inputs than the standard input stream. This makes it very easy to test, or to adapt to different sources of user input.

Feeding it with iterators from a string stream or from a string vector, for example, looks like the following code, for which `evaluate_rpn` does not have to be changed at all:

```
int main()
{
    stringstream s {"3 2 1 + * 2 /"};
    cout << evaluate_rpn(istream_iterator<string>{s}, {}) << '\n';

    vector<string> v {"3", "2", "1", "+", "*", "2", "/"};
    cout << evaluate_rpn(begin(v), end(v)) << '\n';
}
```

Use iterators wherever it makes sense. This makes your code very composable and reusable.

Implementing a word frequency counter with std::map

The `std::map` is very useful when categorizing something in order to collect statistics about that data. By attaching modifiable payload objects to every key which represents an object category, it is pretty simple to implement a histogram of word frequencies for example. This is what we will do in this section.

How to do it...

In this section, we will read all user input from standard input, which might, for example, be a text file containing an essay. We tokenize the input to words, in order to count which word occurs how often.

1. As always, we need to include all the headers from the data structures we are going to use.

    ```
    #include <iostream>
    #include <map>
    #include <vector>
    #include <algorithm>
    #include <iomanip>
    ```

2. To spare us some typing, we declare that we use namespace `std`.

```
using namespace std;
```

3. We will use one helper function in order to crop possibly appended commas, dots, or colons from words.

```
string filter_punctuation(const string &s)
{
    const char *forbidden {".,:; "};
    const auto  idx_start (s.find_first_not_of(forbidden));
    const auto  idx_end   (s.find_last_not_of(forbidden));
    return s.substr(idx_start, idx_end - idx_start + 1);
}
```

4. Now we start with the actual program. We will collect a map that associates every word we see with a counter of that word's frequency. Additionally, we maintain a variable which records the size of the longest word we've seen so far, so we can indent the word frequency table nicely when we print it at the end of the program.

```
int main()
{
    map<string, size_t> words;
    int max_word_len {0};
```

5. When we stream from `std::cin` into an `std::string` variable, the input stream will cut out white space on the way. This way we get the input word by word.

```
string s;
while (cin >> s) {
```

6. The word which we have now, could contain a comma, dots, or a colon, because it might be at the end of a sentence or similar. We filter that out with the helper function we defined before.

```
auto filtered (filter_punctuation(s));
```

7. In case this word is the longest word so far, we need to update the `max_word_len` variable.

```
max_word_len = max<int>(max_word_len, filtered.length());
```

8. Now we will increment the counter value of the word in our `words` map. If it occurs for the first time, it is implicitly created before we increment it.

```
    ++words[filtered];
}
```

9. After the loop terminated, we know that we saved all unique words from the input stream in the `words` map, paired with a counter denoting every word's frequency. The map uses words as keys and is sorted by their *alphabetical* order. What we want is to print all words sorted by their *frequency*, so the words with the highest frequency shall come first. In order to get that, we will first instantiate a vector where all these word-frequency pairs fit in and move them from the map to the vector.

```
    vector<pair<string, size_t>> word_counts;
    word_counts.reserve(words.size());
    move(begin(words), end(words), back_inserter(word_counts));
```

10. The vector does now still contain all word-frequency pairs in the same order as the `words` map maintained them. Now we sort it again, in order to have the most frequent words at the beginning, and the least frequent ones at the end.

```
    sort(begin(word_counts), end(word_counts),
        [](const auto &a, const auto &b) {
            return a.second > b.second;
        });
```

11. All data is in order now, so we push it out to the user terminal. Using the `std::setw` stream manipulator, we format the data in a nicely indented format, so it looks kind of like a table.

```
    cout << "# " << setw(max_word_len) << "<WORD>" << " #<COUNT>\n";
    for (const auto & [word, count] : word_counts) {
        cout << setw(max_word_len + 2) << word << " #"
            << count << '\n';
    }
}
```

12. After compiling the program, we can pipe any text file into it in order to get a frequency table.

```
$ cat lorem_ipsum.txt | ./word_frequency_counter
#        <WORD> #<COUNT>
            et #574
         dolor #302
           sed #273
          diam #273
           sit #259
         ipsum #259
...
```

How it works...

This recipe concentrates on collecting all words in an `std::map` and then shoves all items out of the map and into an `std::vector`, which is then sorted differently, in order to print the data. Why?

Let's look at an example. When we count the word frequency in the string "a a b c b b b d c c", we would get the following map content:

```
a -> 2
b -> 4
c -> 3
d -> 1
```

However, that is not the order which we want to present to the user. The program should print b first because it has the highest frequency. Then c, then a, then d. Unfortunately, we cannot request the map to give us the "*key with the highest associated value*", then the "*key with the second highest associated value*", and so on.

Here, the vector comes into play. We typed the vector to contain pairs of strings and counter values. This way it can hold items exactly in the form as they drop out of the map.

```
vector<pair<string, size_t>> word_counts;
```

Then we fill the vector using the word-frequency pairs using the `std::move` algorithm. This has the advantage that the part of the strings which is maintained on the heap will not be duplicated, but will be moved over from the map to the vector. This way we can avoid a lot of copies.

```
move(begin(words), end(words), back_inserter(word_counts));
```

 Some STL implementations use short string optimization--if the string is not too long, it will *not* be allocated on the heap and stored in the string object directly instead. In that case, a move is not faster. But moves are also never slower!

The next interesting step is the sort operation, which uses a lambda as a custom comparison operator:

```
sort(begin(word_counts), end(word_counts),
        [](const auto &a, const auto &b) { return a.second > b.second; });
```

The sort algorithm will take items pairwise, and compare them, which is what sort algorithms do. By providing that lambda function, the comparison does not just compare if `a` is smaller than `b` (which is the default implementation), but also compares if `a.second` is larger than `b.second`. Note that all objects are *pairs* of strings and their counter values, and by writing `a.second` we access the word's counter value. This way we move all high-frequency words toward the beginning of the vector, and the low-frequency ones to the back.

Implement a writing style helper tool for finding very long sentences in text with std::multimap

Whenever a lot of items shall be stored in a sorted manner, and the key by which they are sorted can occur multiple times, `std::multimap` is a good choice.

Let's find an example use case: When writing text in German, it is okay to use very long sentences. When writing texts in English, it is *not*. We will implement a tool that helps German authors to analyze their English text files, focusing on the length of all sentences. In order to help the author in improving the text style, it will group the sentences by their length. This way the author can pick the longest ones and break them down.

How to do it...

In this section, we will read all user input from standard input, which we will tokenize by whole sentences, and not words. Then we will collect all sentences in an `std::multimap` paired with a variable carrying their length. Afterward, we output all sentences, sorted by their length, back to the user.

1. As usual, we need to include all needed headers. `std::multimap` comes from the same header as `std::map`.

```
#include <iostream>
#include <iterator>
#include <map>
#include <algorithm>
```

2. We use a lot of functions from namespace `std`, so we declare its use automatically.

```
using namespace std;
```

3. When we tokenize strings by extracting what's between dot characters in the text, we will get text sentences surrounded by white space such as spaces, new line symbols, and so on. These would increase their size in a wrong way, so we filter them out using a helper function, which we now define.

```
string filter_ws(const string &s)
{
    const char *ws {" \r\n\t"};
    const auto a (s.find_first_not_of(ws));
    const auto b (s.find_last_not_of(ws));
    if (a == string::npos) {
        return {};
    }
    return s.substr(a, b);
}
```

4. The actual sentence length counting function shall take a giant string containing all the text, and then return an `std::multimap`, which maps sorted sentence lengths to the sentences.

```
multimap<size_t, string> get_sentence_stats(const string &content)
{
```

5. We begin by declaring the `multimap` structure, which is intended to be the return value, and some iterators. As we will have a loop, we need an `end` iterator. Then we use two iterators in order to point to consecutive dots within the text. Everything between is a text sentence.

```
multimap<size_t, string> ret;
const auto end_it (end(content));
auto it1 (begin(content));
auto it2 (find(it1, end_it, '.'));
```

6. The `it2` will be always one dot further than `it1`. As long as `it1` did not reach the end of the text, we are fine. The second condition checks whether `it2` is really at least some characters further. If that was not the case, there would be no characters left to read between them.

```
while (it1 != end_it && distance(it1, it2) > 0) {
```

7. We create a string from all characters between the iterators, and filter all white space from its beginning and end, in order to count the length of the pure sentence.

```
string s {filter_ws({it1, it2})};
```

8. It's possible that the sentence does not contain anything other than white space. In that case, we simply drop it. Otherwise, we count its length by determining how many words there are. This is easy, as there are single spaces between all words. Then we save the word count together with the sentence in the `multimap`.

```
if (s.length() > 0) {
    const auto words (count(begin(s), end(s), ' ') + 1);
    ret.emplace(make_pair(words, move(s)));
}
```

9. For the next loop iteration, we put the leading iterator `it1` on the next sentence's dot character. The following iterator `it2` is put one character after the *old* position of the leading iterator.

```
it1 = next(it2, 1);
it2 = find(it1, end_it, '.');
}
```

10. After the loop is terminated, the `multimap` contains all sentences paired with their word count and can be returned.

```
        return ret;
    }
```

11. Now we put the function to use. First, we tell `std::cin` to not skip white space, as we want sentences with spaces in one piece. In order to read the whole file, we initialize an `std::string` from input stream iterators which encapsulate `std::cin`.

```
int main()
{
    cin.unsetf(ios::skipws);
    string content {istream_iterator<char>{cin}, {}};
```

12. As we only need the `multimap` result for printing, we put the `get_sentence_stats` call directly in the loop and feed it with our string. In the loop body, we print the items line by line.

```
    for (const auto & [word_count, sentence]
            : get_sentence_stats(content)) {
        cout << word_count << " words: " << sentence << ".\n";
    }
}
```

13. After compiling the code, we can feed the app with text from any text file. An example Lorem Ipsum text yields the following output. As the output is very long for long text with many sentences, it prints the shortest sentences first and the longest last. This way we see the longest sentences first as terminals usually scroll to the end of the output automatically.

```
$ cat lorem_ipsum.txt | ./sentence_length
...
10 words: Nam quam nunc, blandit vel, luctus pulvinar,
hendrerit id, lorem.
10 words: Sed consequat, leo eget bibendum sodales,
augue velit cursus nunc,.
12 words: Cum sociis natoque penatibus et magnis dis
parturient montes, nascetur ridiculus mus.
17 words: Maecenas tempus, tellus eget condimentum rhoncus,
sem quam semper libero, sit amet adipiscing sem neque sed ipsum.
```

How it works...

The whole recipe concentrates on breaking down a large string into sentences of text, which are assessed for their length, and then ordered in a `multimap`. Because `std::multimap` itself is so easy to use, the complex part of the program is the loop, which iterates over the sentences:

```
const auto end_it (end(content));
auto it1 (begin(content));        // (1) Beginning of string
auto it2 (find(it1, end_it, '.')); // (1) First '.' dot

while (it1 != end_it && std::distance(it1, it2) > 0) {
    string sentence {it1, it2};

    // Do something with the sentence string...

    it1 = std::next(it2, 1);      // One character past current '.' dot
    it2 = find(it1, end_it, '.'); // Next dot, or end of string
}
```

Let's look at the code with the following diagram in mind, which consists of three sentences:

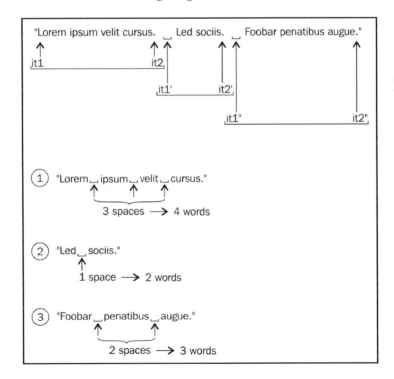

The `it1` and `it2` are always moved forward through the string together. This way they always point to the beginning and end of *one* sentence. The `std::find` algorithm helps us a lot in that regard because it works like "*start at the current position and then return an iterator to the next dot character. If there is none, return the end iterator.*"

After we extract a sentence string, we determine how many words it contains, so we can insert it into the `multimap`. We are using the *number of words* as the *key* for the map nodes, and the string itself as the payload object associated with it. There can easily be multiple sentences which have the same length. This would render us unable to insert them all into one `std::map`. But since we use `std::multimap`, this is no problem, because it can easily handle multiple keys of the same value. It will keep them all *ordered* in line, which is what we need to enumerate all sentences by their length and output them to the user.

There's more...

After having read the whole file into one large string, we iterate through the string and create copies of every sentence again. This is not necessary, as we also could have used `std::string_view`, which will be covered later in this book.

Another way to iteratively get the strings between two consecutive dots is `std::regex_iterator`, which will also be covered in a later chapter of this book.

Implementing a personal to-do list using std::priority_queue

The `std::priority_queue` is another container adapter class, such as `std::stack`. It is a wrapper around another data structure (`std::vector` by default) and provides a queue-like interface for it. This means that items can stepwise be pushed into it, and stepwise be popped out of it again. What is pushed into it *first*, will be popped out of it *first*. This is usually also abbreviated as a **first in, first out** (**FIFO**) queue. This is the opposite of a stack, where the *last* item pushed onto it is popped out of it *first*.

While we just described the behavior of `std::queue`, this section shows how `std::priority_queue` works. That adapter is special, as it does not only take FIFO characteristics into account but also mixes it with priorities. This means that the FIFO principle is kind of broken down into sub-FIFO queues, which are ordered by the priorities their items have.

How to do it...

In this section, we will set up a cheap *to-do list organizing* structure. We do not parse user input in order to keep this program short and concentrate on `std::priority_queue`. So we're just filling an unordered list of to-do items with priorities and descriptions into a priority queue, and then read them out like from a FIFO queue data structure, but grouped by the priorities of the individual items.

1. We need to include some headers first. `std::priority_queue` is in the header file `<queue>`.

   ```
   #include <iostream>
   #include <queue>
   #include <tuple>
   #include <string>
   ```

2. How do we store to-do items in the priority queue? The thing is, we cannot add items and additionally attach a priority to them. The priority queue will try to use the *natural order* of all items in the queue. We could now implement our own `struct todo_item`, and give it a priority number, and a string to-do description, and then implement the comparison operator < in order to make them orderable. Alternatively, we can just take `std::pair`, which enables us to aggregate two things in one type and implements comparison for us automatically.

   ```
   int main()
   {
       using item_type = std::pair<int, std::string>;
   ```

3. We now have a new type `item_type`, which consists of an integer priority and a string description. So, let's instantiate a priority queue, which maintains such items.

   ```
   std::priority_queue<item_type> q;
   ```

4. We will now fill the priority queue with different items which have different priorities. The goal is to provide an *unstructured* list, and then the priority queue tells us *what* to do in *which order*. If there are comics to read, and homework to do, of course, the homework must be done first. Unfortunately, `std::priority_queue` has no constructor, which accepts the initializer lists, which we can use to fill the queue from the beginning on. (With a vector or a normal list, it would have worked that way.) So we first define the list and insert it in the next step.

```
std::initializer_list<item_type> il {
    {1, "dishes"},
    {0, "watch tv"},
    {2, "do homework"},
    {0, "read comics"},
};
```

5. We can now comfortably iterate through the unordered list of to-do items and insert them step by step using the `push` function.

```
for (const auto &p : il) {
    q.push(p);
}
```

6. All items are implicitly sorted, and therefore we have a queue which gives us out items with the highest priority.

```
while(!q.empty()) {
    std::cout << q.top().first << ": " << q.top().second << '\n';
    q.pop();
}
std::cout << '\n';
}
```

7. Let's compile and run our program. Indeed, it tells us, to do our homework first, and after washing the dishes, we can finally watch TV and read comics.

```
$ ./main
2: do homework
1: dishes
0: watch tv
0: read comics
```

How it works...

The `std::priority` list is very easy to use. We have only used three functions:

1. The `q.push(item)` pushes an item into the queue.
2. The `q.top()` returns a reference to the item which is coming out of the queue first.
3. The `q.pop()` removes the frontmost item in the queue.

But how did the item ordering work? We grouped a priority integer and a to-do item description string into an `std::pair` and got automatic ordering. If we have an `std::pair<int, std::string>` instance p, we can write `p.first` to access the *integer* part, and `p.second` to access the *string* part. We did that in the loop which prints out all to-do items.

But how did the priority queue infer that `{2, "do homework"}` is *more important* than `{0, "watch tv"}`, without us telling it to compare the numeric part?

The comparison operator < handles different cases. Let's assume we compare `left < right` and `left` and `right` are pairs.

1. The `left.first != right.first`, then it returns `left.first < right.first`.
2. The `left.first == right.first`, then it returns `left.second < right.second`.

This way, we can order the items as we need. The only important thing is that the priority is the *first* member of the pair, and the description is the *second* member of the pair. Otherwise, `std::priority_queue` would order the items in a way where it looks like the alphabetic order of the items is more important than their priorities. (In that case, *watch TV* would be suggested as the *first* thing to do, and *do homework* some time *later*. That would at least be great for those of us who are lazy!)

3
Iterators

We cover the following recipes in this chapter:

- Building your own iterable range
- Making your own iterators compatible with STL iterator categories
- Using iterator wrappers to fill generic data structures
- Implementing algorithms in terms of iterators
- Iterating the other way around using reverse iterator adapters
- Terminating iterations over ranges with iterator sentinels
- Automatically checking iterator code with checked iterators
- Building your own zip iterator adapter

Introduction

Iterators are an *extremely important concept* in C++. The STL aims to be as flexible and generic as possible, and iterators are a great help in that regard. Unfortunately, they are sometimes a bit tedious to use, which is why many novices *avoid* them and fall back to *C-Style C++*. A programmer who avoids iterators basically waives *half* the potential of the STL. This chapter deals with iterators and quickly casts some light on how they work. That very quick introduction is probably not enough, but the *recipes* are really here to give a good feeling for iterator internals.

Most container classes, but also old-school C-style arrays, in one or the other way, contain a *range* of data items. A lot of day-to-day tasks that process a lot of data items do not care how to get at that data. However, if we regard, for example, an array of integers and a *linked list* of integers and want to calculate the *sum* of all the items of both the structures, we would end up with two different algorithms, which could look like the following:

- One algorithm, which deals with the array by checking its size and summing it up as follows:

```
int sum {0};
for (size_t i {0}; i < array_size; ++i) { sum += array[i]; }
```

- Another algorithm, which deals with the linked list by iterating until it reaches its end:

```
int sum {0};
while (list_node != nullptr) {
    sum += list_node->value; list_node = list_node->next;
}
```

Both of them are about *summing up integers*, but how large is the percentage of characters that we typed, which is directly related to the *actual* summing up task? And does one of them work with a third kind of data structure, let's say `std::map`, or do we have to implement another version of it? Without iterators, this would lead us into ridiculous directions.

Only with the help of iterators is it possible to implement this in a generic form:

```
int sum {0};
for (int i : array_or_vector_or_map_or_list) { sum += i; }
```

This pretty and short, so-called, range-based `for` loop has been in existence since C++11. It is just a syntax sugar, which expands to something similar to the following code:

```
{
    auto && __range = array_or_vector_or_map_or_list ;
    auto __begin = std::begin(__range);
    auto __end   = std::end(__range);
    for ( ; __begin != __end; ++__begin) {
        int i = *__begin;
        sum += i;
    }
}
```

This is an old hat for everyone who has worked with iterators already and looks completely magic for everyone who didn't. Imagine our vector of integers looks like the following:

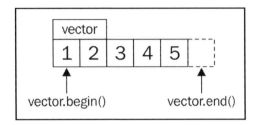

The `std::begin(vector)` command is the same as `vector.begin()` and returns us an iterator that points to the first item (the **1**). `std::end(vector)` is the same as `vector.end()` and returns an iterator that points at one item *past the last* item (past the **5**).

In every iteration, the loop checks if the begin iterator is non-equal to the end iterator. If so, it will *dereference* the begin iterator and thus access the integer value it points to. Then, it *increments* the iterator, repeats the comparison against the end iterator, and so on. In that moment, it helps to read the loop code again while imagining that the iterators are plain C-style pointers. In fact, plain C-style pointers are also a valid kind of iterators.

Iterator categories

There are multiple categories of iterators, and they have different limitations. They are not too hard to memorize, just remember that the capabilities one category requires are inherited from the next powerful category. The whole point of iterator categories is that if an algorithm knows what kind of iterator it is dealing with, it can be implemented in an optimized way. This way, the programmer can lean back and express his intent, while the compiler can choose the *optimal implementation* for the given task.

Let's go through them in the right order:

Iterator category					Multi pass support	Defined operations
Input Iterator					multiple passes <u>not</u> supported	*it (read-access) ++it or it++
Forward Iterator						++it or it++
Bidirectional Iterator					multiple passes supported	--it or it--
Random Access Iterator						it+=n or it-=n
Contiguous Iterator						contiguous storage (like an array)

Input iterator

Input iterators can be dereferenced only for *reading* the values they point to. Once they are incremented, the last value they pointed to has been *invalidated* during the incrementation. This means that it is not possible to iterate over such a range multiple times.
The `std::istream_iterator` is an example for this category.

Forward iterator

Forward iterators are the same as input iterators, but they differ in that regard that the ranges they represent can be iterated over multiple times.
The `std::forward_list` iterators are an example of that. Such a list can only be iterated over *forward*, not backward, but it can be iterated over as often as we like to.

Bidirectional iterator

The bidirectional iterator, as the name suggests, can be incremented and decremented, in order to iterate forward or backward. The iterators of `std::list`, `std::set`, and `std::map`, for example, support that.

Random access iterator

Random access iterators allow jumping over multiple values at once, instead of single-stepping. This is the case for iterators of `std::vector` and `std::deque`.

Contiguous iterator

This category specifies all of the aforementioned requirements, plus the requirement that the data that is being iterated through lies in contiguous memory, like it does in an array, or `std::vector`.

Output iterator

Output iterators are detached from the other categories. This is because an iterator can be a pure output iterator, which can only be incremented and used to *write* to the data it points to. If they are being read from, the value will be undefined.

Mutable iterator

If an iterator is an output iterator and one of the other categories at the same time, it is a mutable iterator. It can be read from and written to. If we obtain an iterator from a non-const container instance, it will usually be of this kind.

Building your own iterable range

We already realized that iterators are, kind of, the *standard interface* for iterations over containers of all kinds. We just need to implement the prefix increment operator, ++, the dereference operator, *, and the object comparison operator, ==, and then we already have a primitive iterator that fits into the fancy C++11 range-based `for` loop.

In order to get used to this a bit more, this recipe shows how to implement an iterator that just emits a range of numbers when iterating through it. It is not backed by any container structure or anything similar. The numbers are generated ad hoc while iterating.

How to do it...

In this recipe, we will implement our own iterator class, and then, we will iterate through it:

1. First, we include the header, which enables us to print to the terminal:

   ```
   #include <iostream>
   ```

2. Our iterator class will be called `num_iterator`:

   ```
   class num_iterator {
   ```

3. Its only data member is an integer. That integer is used for counting. The constructor is for initializing it. It is generally a good form to make constructors *explicit*, which create a type from another type to avoid *accidental* implicit conversion. Note that we also provide a default value for `position`. This makes the instances of the `num_iterator` class default-constructible. Although we will not use the default constructor in the whole recipe, this is really important because some STL algorithms depend on iterators being default-constructible:

   ```
       int i;
   public:

       explicit num_iterator(int position = 0) : i{position} {}
   ```

4. When dereferencing our iterator (`*it`), it will emit an integer:

   ```
       int operator*() const { return i; }
   ```

5. Incrementing the iterator (`++it`) will just increment its internal counter, `i`:

   ```
       num_iterator& operator++() {
           ++i;
           return *this;
       }
   ```

6. A `for` loop will compare the iterator against the end iterator. If they are *unequal*, it will continue iterating:

   ```
       bool operator!=(const num_iterator &other) const {
           return i != other.i;
       }
   };
   ```

7. That was the iterator class. We still need an intermediate object for writing `for (int i : intermediate(a, b)) {...}`, which then contains the begin and end iterator, which is preprogrammed to iterate from a to b. We call it `num_range`:

```
class num_range {
```

8. It contains two integer members, which denote at which number the iteration shall start, and which number is the first number past the last number. This means if we want to iterate from 0 to 9, a is set to 0 and b to 10:

```
    int a;
    int b;

public:
    num_range(int from, int to)
        : a{from}, b{to}
    {}
```

9. There are only two member functions that we need to implement: the `begin` and `end` functions. Both return iterators that point to the beginning and the end of the numeric range:

```
    num_iterator begin() const { return num_iterator{a}; }
    num_iterator end()   const { return num_iterator{b}; }
};
```

10. That's it. We can use it. Let's write a main function which just iterates over a range that goes from 100 to 109 and prints all its values:

```
int main()
{
    for (int i : num_range{100, 110}) {
        std::cout << i << ", ";
    }
    std::cout << '\n';
}
```

11. Compiling and running the program yields the following terminal output:

```
100, 101, 102, 103, 104, 105, 106, 107, 108, 109,
```

How it works...

Consider that we write the following code:

```
for (auto x : range) { code_block; }
```

The compiler will evaluate it to the following:

```
{
    auto __begin = std::begin(range);
    auto __end   = std::end(range);
    for ( ; __begin != __end; ++__begin) {
        auto x = *__begin;
        code_block
    }
}
```

While looking at this code, it becomes obvious that the only requirements for the iterators are the following three operators:

- `operator!=`: unequal comparison
- `operator++`: prefix increment
- `operator*`: dereference

The requirements of the range are that it has a `begin` and an `end` method, which return two iterators that denote the beginning and the end of a range.

In this book, we're mostly using `std::begin(x)` instead of `x.begin()`. This is generally a good style because `std::begin(x)` automatically calls `x.begin()` if that member method is available. If `x` is an array that does not have a `begin()` method, `std::begin(x)` will automatically find out how to deal with it. The same applies to `std::end(x)`. User defined types that do not provide `begin()`/`end()` members do not work with `std::begin`/`std::end`.

What we did in this recipe is just fit a simple number counting algorithm into the forward iterator interface. Implementing an iterator and a range always involves this minimum amount of boilerplate code, which can be a little bit annoying on the one hand. A look at the loop that uses `num_range` is, on the other hand, very rewarding because it looks so *perfectly simple*!

Scroll back and have a thorough look on which of the methods of the iterator and the range class are `const`. Forgetting to make those functions `const` can make the compiler *reject* your code in a lot of situations because it is a common thing to iterate over `const` objects.

Making your own iterators compatible with STL iterator categories

Whatever own container data structure we come up with, in order to effectively *mix* it with all the STL goodness, we need to make them provide iterator interfaces. In the last section, we learned how to do that, but we do soon realize that *some* STL algorithms *do not compile* well with our custom iterators. Why?

The problem is that a lot of STL algorithms try to find out more about the iterators they are asked by us to deal with. Different iterator *categories* have different capabilities, and hence, there might be different possibilities to implement the *same* algorithm. For example, if we copy *plain numbers* from one `std::vector` to another, this may be implemented with a fast `memcpy` call. If we copy data from or to `std::list`, this is *not* possible any longer and the items have to be copied individually one by one. The implementers of the STL algorithms put a lot of thought into this kind of automatic optimization. In order to help them, we can equip our iterators with some *information* about them. This section shows how to achieve the same.

How to do it...

In this section, we will implement a primitive iterator that counts numbers and use it together with an STL algorithm, which initially does not compile with it. Then we do what's necessary to make it STL-compatible.

1. First, we need to include some headers, as always:

```
#include <iostream>
#include <algorithm>
```

2. Then we implement a primitive number counting iterator, as in the previous section. When iterating over it, it will emit plain increasing integers. The num_range acts as a handy *begin* and *end* iterator donor:

```
class num_iterator
{
    int i;
public:
    explicit num_iterator(int position = 0) : i{position} {}
    int operator*() const { return i; }
    num_iterator& operator++() {
        ++i;
        return *this;
    }
    bool operator!=(const num_iterator &other) const {
        return i != other.i;
    }
    bool operator==(const num_iterator &other) const {
        return !(*this != other);
    }
};
class num_range {
    int a;
    int b;
public:
    num_range(int from, int to)
        : a{from}, b{to}
    {}
    num_iterator begin() const { return num_iterator{a}; }
    num_iterator end()   const { return num_iterator{b}; }
};
```

3. In order to keep the std:: namespace prefix out and keep the code readable, we declare that we use namespace std:

```
using namespace std;
```

4. Let's now just instantiate a range that goes from `100` to `109`. Note that the value `110` is the position of the end iterator. This means that `110` is the *first* number that is *outside* the range (which is why it goes from `100` to `109`):

```
int main()
{
    num_range r {100, 110};
```

5. And now, we use it with `std::minmax_element`. This algorithm returns us `std::pair` with two members: an iterator pointing to the lowest value and another iterator pointing to the highest value in the range. These are, of course, `100` and `109` because that's how we constructed the range:

```
    auto [min_it, max_it] (minmax_element(begin(r), end(r)));
    cout << *min_it << " - " << *max_it << '\n';
}
```

6. Compiling the code leads to the following error message. It's some error related to `std::iterator_traits`. More on that later. It *might* happen that there are *other* errors on other compilers and/or STL library implementations or *no* errors at all. This error message occurs with clang version 5.0.0 (trunk 299766):

```
error: no type named 'value_type' in 'std::__1::iterator_traits<num_iterator>'
                __less<typename iterator_traits<_ForwardIterator>::value_type>());

main.cpp:56:24:       in instantiation of function template specialization 'std::
__1::minmax_element<num_iterator>' requested here
    auto min_max (std::minmax_element(std::begin(r), std::end(r)));
                  ^

1 error generated.
```

7. In order to fix this, we need to activate iterator trait functionality for our iterator class. Just after the definition of `num_iterator`, we write the following template structure specialization of the `std::iterator_traits` type. It tells the STL that our `num_iterator` is of the category forward iterator, and it iterates over `int` values:

```
namespace std {
template <>
struct iterator_traits<num_iterator> {
    using iterator_category = std::forward_iterator_tag;
    using value_type        = int;
};
}
```

8. Let's compile it again; we can see that it works! The output of the min/max function is the following, which is just what we expect:

```
100 - 109
```

How it works...

Some STL algorithms need to know the characteristics of the iterator type they are used with. Some others need to know the type of items the iterators iterate over. This has different implementation reasons.

However, all STL algorithms will access this type information via `std::iterator_traits<my_iterator>`, assuming that the iterator type is `my_iterator`. This traits class contains up to five different type member definitions:

- `difference_type`: What type results from writing `it1 - it2`?
- `value_type`: Of what type is the item which we access with `*it` (note that this is `void` for pure output iterators)?
- `pointer`: Of what type must a pointer be in order to point to an item?
- `reference`: Of what type must a reference be in order to reference an item?
- `iterator_category`: Which category does the iterator belong to?

The `pointer`, `reference`, and `difference_type` type definitions do not make sense for our `num_iterator`, as it doesn't iterate over real *memory* values (we just *return* `int` values but they are not persistently available like in an array). Therefore it's better to not define them because if an algorithm depends on those items being referenceable in memory, it might be *buggy* when combined with our iterator.

There's more...

Until C++17, it was encouraged to let iterator types just inherit from `std::iterator<...>`, which automatically populates our class with all the type definitions. This still works, but it is discouraged since C++17.

Using iterator adapters to fill generic data structures

In a lot of situations, we want to fill any container with masses of data, but the data source and the container have *no common interface*. In such a situation, we would need to write our own hand-crafted algorithms that just deal with the question of how to shove data from the source to the sink. Usually, this distracts us from our actual work of *solving* a specific *problem*.

Tasks where we simply transport data between conceptually different data structures can be implemented with a one-liner code, thanks to another abstraction provided by the STL: **iterator adapters**. This section demonstrates the use of some of them in order to give a feeling how useful they are.

How to do it...

In this section, we use some iterator wrappers just for the sake of showing that they exist and how they can help us in everyday programming tasks.

1. We need to include some headers first:

```
#include <iostream>
#include <string>
#include <iterator>
#include <sstream>
#include <deque>
```

2. Declaring that we use namespace `std` spares us some typing later:

```
using namespace std;
```

3. We start with `std::istream_iterator`. We specialize it on `int`. This way, it will try to parse the standard input to integers. For example, if we iterate over it, it will look as if it was `std::vector<int>`. The end iterator is instantiated of the same type but without any constructor arguments:

```
int main()
{
    istream_iterator<int> it_cin {cin};
    istream_iterator<int> end_cin;
```

4. Next, we instantiate `std::deque<int>` and just copy over all the integers from the standard input into the deque. The deque itself is not an iterator, so we wrap it into `std::back_insert_iterator` using the `std::back_inserter` helper function. This special iterator wrapper will execute `v.push_back(item)` with each of the items we get from the standard input. This way the deque is grown automatically!

```
deque<int> v;

copy(it_cin, end_cin, back_inserter(v));
```

5. In the next exercise, we use `std::istringstream` to copy items into the *middle* of the deque. So, let's first define some example numbers in the form of a string and instantiate the stream object from it:

```
istringstream sstr {"123 456 789"};
```

6. Then, we need a hint of where to insert into the deque. It will be the middle, so we use the begin pointer of the deque and feed it to the `std::next` function. The second argument of this function says that it will return an iterator advanced by `v.size() / 2` steps, that is, *half* the deque. (We cast `v.size()` to `int` because the second parameter of `std::next` is `difference_type` of the iterator used as the first parameter. In this case, this is a signed integer type. Depending on the compiler flags, the compiler might *warn* at this point if we didn't cast explicitly.)

```
auto deque_middle (next(begin(v),
                   static_cast<int>(v.size()) / 2));
```

7. Now, we can copy parsed integers step by step from the input string stream into the deque. Again, the end iterator of a stream iterator wrapper is just an empty `std::istream_iterator<int>` without constructor arguments (that is, the empty `{}` braces in the code line). The deque is wrapped into an inserter wrapper, which is an `std::insert_iterator`, which is pointed to the deque's middle using the `deque_middle` iterator:

```
copy(istream_iterator<int>{sstr}, {}, inserter(v, deque_middle));
```

8. Now, let's use `std::front_insert_iterator` to insert some items at the front of the deque:

```
initializer_list<int> il2 {-1, -2, -3};
copy(begin(il2), end(il2), front_inserter(v));
```

9. In the last step, we print the whole content of the deque out to the user shell. The `std::ostream_iterator` works like an output iterator which, in our case, just forwards all the integers it gets copied from to `std::cout` and then appends ", " after each item:

```
    copy(begin(v), end(v), ostream_iterator<int>{cout, ", "});
    cout << '\n';
}
```

10. Compiling and running the program yields the following output. Can you identify which number was inserted by which code line?

```
$ echo "1 2 3 4 5" | ./main
-3, -2, -1, 1, 2, 123, 456, 789, 3, 4, 5,
```

How it works...

We used a lot of different iterator adapters in this section. They all have one thing in common, which is they wrap an object into an iterator that is not an iterator itself.

std::back_insert_iterator

The `back_insert_iterator` can be wrapped around `std::vector`, `std::deque`, `std::list`, and so on. It will call the container's `push_back` method, which inserts the new item *past* the existing items. If the container instance is not large enough, it will be grown automatically.

std::front_insert_iterator

The `front_insert_iterator` does exactly the same thing as `back_insert_iterator`, but it calls the container's `push_front` method, which inserts the new item *before* all the existing items. Note that for a container like `std::vector`, this means that all the existing items need to be moved one slot further in order to leave space for the new item at the front.

std::insert_iterator

This iterator adapter is similar to the other inserters, but is able to insert new items *between* existing ones. The `std::inserter` helper function which constructs such a wrapper takes two arguments. The first argument is the container and the second argument is an iterator that points to the position where new items shall be inserted.

std::istream_iterator

The `istream_iterator` is another very handy adapter. It can be used with any `std::istream` object (which can be the standard input or files for example) and will try to parse the input from that stream object according to the template parameter it was instantiated with. In this section, we used `std::istream_iterator<int>(std::cin)`, which pulls integers out of the standard input for us.

The special thing about streams is that we often cannot know in advance how long the stream is. That leaves the question, where will the *end* iterator point to if we do not know where the stream's end is? The way this works is that the iterator *knows* when it reaches the end of the stream. When it is compared to the end iterator, it will effectively *not really* compare itself with the end iterator but return if the stream has any tokens *left*. That's why the end iterator constructor does not take any arguments.

std::ostream_iterator

The `ostream_iterator` is the same thing as the `istream_iterator`, but it works the other way around: It doesn't take tokens *from* an *input* stream--it pushes tokens *into* an *output* stream. Another difference to `istream_iterator` is that its constructor takes a second argument, which is a string that shall be pushed into the output stream after each item. That is useful because this way we can print a separating ", " or a new line after each item.

Implementing algorithms in terms of iterators

Iterators usually iterate by *moving* their *position* from one item of a container to another. But they do not necessarily need to iterate over data structures at all. Iterators can also be used to implement algorithms, in which case, they would calculate the next value when they are incremented (`++it`) and return that value when they are dereferenced (`*it`).

In this section, we demonstrate this by implementing the Fibonacci function in form of an iterator. The Fibonacci function is recursively defined like this: F(n) = F(n - 1) + F(n - 2). It starts with the beginning values of F(0) = 0 and F(1) = 1. This leads to the following number sequence:

- F(0) = 0
- F(1) = 1
- F(2) = F(1) + F(0) = 1
- F(3) = F(2) + F(1) = 2
- F(4) = F(3) + F(2) = 3
- F(5) = F(4) + F(3) = 5
- F(6) = F(5) + F(4) = 8
- ... and so on

If we implement this in the form of a callable function that returns the Fibonacci value for any number, *n*, we will end up with a recursive self-calling function, or a loop implementation. This is fine, but what if we write some program where have to consume Fibonacci numbers in some pattern, one after the other? We would have two possibilities-- either we recalculate all the recursive calls for every new Fibonacci number, which is a waste of computing time, or we save the last two Fibonacci numbers as temporary variables and use them to calculate the next. In the latter case, we reimplemented the Fibonacci algorithm loop implementation. It seems that we would end up *mixing* Fibonacci code with our actual code, which solves a different problem:

```
size_t a {0};
size_t b {1};

for (size_t i {0}; i < N; ++i) {
    const size_t old_b {b};
    b += a;
    a  = old_b;
    // do something with b, which is the current fibonacci number
}
```

Iterators are an interesting way out of this. How about wrapping the steps that we do in the loop-based iterative Fibonacci implementation in the prefix increment ++ operator implementation of a Fibonacci value *iterator*? This is pretty easy, as this section demonstrates.

How to do it...

In this section, we concentrate on implementing an iterator that generates numbers from the Fibonacci number sequence while iterating over it.

1. In order to be able to print the Fibonacci numbers to the terminal, we need to include a header first:

```
#include <iostream>
```

2. We call the Fibonacci iterator, `fibit`. It will carry a member `i`, which saves the index position in the Fibonacci sequence, and `a` and `b` will be the variables that hold the last two Fibonacci values. If instantiated with the default constructor, a Fibonacci iterator will be initialized to the value `F(0)`:

```
class fibit
{
    size_t i {0};
    size_t a {0};
    size_t b {1};
```

3. Next, we define the standard constructor and another constructor, which allows us to initialize the iterator at any Fibonacci number step:

```
public:
    fibit() = default;
    explicit fibit(size_t i_)
        : i{i_}
    {}
```

4. When dereferencing our iterator (`*it`), it will just emit the Fibonacci number of the current step:

```
size_t operator*() const { return b; }
```

5. When incrementing the iterator (++it), it will move its state to the next Fibonacci number. This function contains the same code as the loop-based Fibonacci implementation:

```
fibit& operator++() {
    const size_t old_b {b};
    b += a;
    a = old_b;
    ++i;
    return *this;
}
```

6. When used in a loop, the incremented iterator is compared against an end iterator, for which we need to define the != operator. We are only comparing the *step* at which the Fibonacci iterators currently reside, which makes it easier to define the end iterator for step 1000000, for example, as we do not need to expensively calculate such a high Fibonacci number *in advance*:

```
    bool operator!=(const fibit &o) const { return i != o.i; }
};
```

7. In order to be able to use the Fibonacci iterator in the range-based for loop, we have to implement a range class beforehand. We call it fib_range, and its constructor will accept one parameter that tells how far in the Fibonacci range we want to iterate:

```
class fib_range
{
    size_t end_n;
public:
    fib_range(size_t end_n_)
        : end_n{end_n_}
    {}
```

8. Its begin and end functions return iterators which point to the positions, F(0) and F(end_n):

```
    fibit begin() const { return fibit{}; }
    fibit end()   const { return fibit{end_n}; }
};
```

9. Okay, now let's forget about all the iterator-related boilerplate code. We do not need to touch it again as we have a helper class now which nicely hides all the implementation details from us! Let's print the first 10 Fibonacci numbers:

```
int main()
{
    for (size_t i : fib_range(10)) {
        std::cout << i << ", ";
    }
    std::cout << '\n';
}
```

10. Compiling and running the program yields the following shell output:

```
1, 1, 2, 3, 5, 8, 13, 21, 34, 55,
```

There's more...

In order to use this iterator with the STL, it must support the `std::iterator_traits` class. To see how to do that, have a look at the *other* recipe, which deals with exactly that matter: *Making your own iterators compatible with STL iterator categories*.

> Try to think in terms of iterators. This leads to very elegant code in many situations. Don't worry about performance: compilers find it *trivial* to optimize away the iterator-related boilerplate code!

In order to keep the example simple, we did not do anything about this, but if we do publish the Fibonacci iterator as a library, it would become apparent that it has a usability flaw--a `fibit` instance that was created with a constructor parameter will only be used as an end iterator because it does not contain valid Fibonacci values. Our tiny library does not enforce such usage. There are different possibilities to fix it:

- Make the `fibit(size_t i_)` constructor private and declare the `fib_range` class as a friend of the `fibit` class. This way, users can only use it the right way.
- Use iterator sentinels in order to prevent users to dereference the end iterator. Have a look at the recipe in which we introduce those: *Terminating iterations over ranges with iterator sentinels*

Iterating the other way around using reverse iterator adapters

Sometimes, it is valuable to iterate over a range the other way around, not forward but *backward*. The range-based `for` loop, as well as all STL algorithms usually iterate over the given ranges by *incrementing* iterators, although iterating backward requires *decrementing* them. Of course, it is possible to *wrap* iterators into a layer that transforms an *increment* call effectively into a *decrement* call. This sounds like a lot of boilerplate code for every type on which we would like to support that.

The STL provides a helpful *reverse-iterator adapter*, which helps us set up such iterators.

How to do it...

In this section, we will use reverse iterators in different ways, just to show how they are used:

1. We need to include some headers first, as always:

   ```
   #include <iostream>
   #include <list>
   #include <iterator>
   ```

2. Next, we declare that we use namespace `std` in order to spare us some typing:

   ```
   using namespace std;
   ```

3. For the sake of having something to iterate over, let's instantiate a list of integers:

   ```
   int main()
   {
       list<int> l {1, 2, 3, 4, 5};
   ```

4. Now let's print these integers in the reverse form. In order to do that, we iterate over the list by using the `rbegin` and `rend` functions of `std::list` and shove those values out via the standard output using the handy `ostream_iterator` adapter:

   ```
   copy(l.rbegin(), l.rend(), ostream_iterator<int>{cout, ", "});
   cout << '\n';
   ```

5. If a container does not provide handy `rbegin` and `rend` functions but at least provides bidirectional iterators, the `std::make_reverse_iterator` function helps out. It accepts *normal* iterators and converts them to *reverse* iterators:

```
copy(make_reverse_iterator(end(l)),
    make_reverse_iterator(begin(l)),
    ostream_iterator<int>{cout, ", "});
cout << '\n';
}
```

6. Compiling and running our program yields the following output:

```
5, 4, 3, 2, 1,
5, 4, 3, 2, 1,
```

How it works...

In order to be able to transform a normal iterator into a reverse iterator, it must at least have support for bidirectional iteration. This requirement is fulfilled by any iterator of the *bidirectional* category or higher.

A reverse iterator kind of *contains* a normal iterator and *mimics* its interface completely, but it *rewires* the increment operation to a decrement operation.

The next detail is about the begin and end iterator positions. Let's have a look at the following diagram, which shows a standard numeric sequence kept in an iterable range. If the sequence goes from 1 to 5, then the begin iterator has to point to the element 1, and the end iterator must point one element past 5:

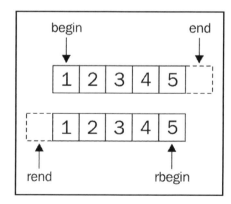

When defining reverse iterators, the `rbegin` iterator must point to 5, and the `rend` iterator must point to the element *before* 1. Turn the book upside down, and see that it completely makes sense.

If we want our own custom container classes to support reverse iteration, we do not need to implement all these details ourselves; we can just wrap the normal iterators into reverse iterators by using the `std::make_reverse_iterator` helper function, and it does all the operator rewiring and offset corrections for us.

Terminating iterations over ranges with iterator sentinels

Both STL algorithms and the range-based `for` loop assume that the begin and end positions of the iteration are known *in advance*. In some situations, however, it is hardly possible to know the end position *before reaching* it by iteration.

A very simple example for this is iterating over plain C-Style strings, the length of which is not known before *runtime*. The code which iterates over such strings usually looks like this:

```
for (const char *c_ponter = some_c_string; *c_pointer != '\0'; ++c_pointer)
{
    const char c = *c_pointer;
    // do something with c
}
```

The only way to put this into a range-based `for` loop seems to be wrapping it into an `std::string`, which has `begin()` and `end()` functions:

```
for (char c : std::string(some_c_string)) { /* do something with c */ }
```

However, the constructor of `std::string` will iterate over the whole string before our `for` loop can iterate over it. Since C++17, we also have `std::string_view`, but its constructor will also iterate through the string once. This is not worth the real hassle for *short* strings, but this is also only an example for a problem *class*, which can be worth the hassle in *other situations*. The `std::istream_iterator` also has to deal with this when it captures input from `std::cin`, as its end iterator cannot realistically point to the end of the user input while the user is *still typing* keys.

C++17 comes with the great news that it does not constrain begin and end iterators to be of the same type. This section demonstrates how to put this *little rule change* to *great use*.

How to do it...

In this section, we will build an iterator together with a range class, which enables us to iterate over a string with unknown length, without finding the *end* position *in advance*.

1. First, as always, we need to include headers:

```
#include <iostream>
```

2. The iterator sentinel is a very central element of this section. Surprisingly, its class definition can stay completely empty:

```
class cstring_iterator_sentinel {};
```

3. Now we implement the iterator. It will contain a string pointer, which is the *container* we iterate over:

```
class cstring_iterator {
    const char *s {nullptr};
```

4. The constructor just initializes the internal string pointer to whatever string the user provides. Let's make the constructor explicit in order to prevent accidental implicit conversions from strings to string iterators:

```
public:
    explicit cstring_iterator(const char *str)
        : s{str}
    {}
```

5. When dereferencing the iterator at some point, it will just return the character value at this position:

```
char operator*() const { return *s; }
```

6. Incrementing the iterator just increments the position in the string:

```
cstring_iterator& operator++() {
    ++s;
    return *this;
}
```

7. This is the interesting part. We implement the `!=` operator for comparison, as it is used by STL algorithms and the range-based `for` loop. However, this time, we do not implement it for the comparison of iterators with other *iterators*, but for comparing iterators with *sentinels*. When we compare an iterator with another iterator we can only check if their internal string pointers both point to the same address, which is somewhat limiting. By comparing against an empty sentinel object, we can perform a completely different semantic–we check if the character our iterator points to is a terminating `'\0'` character because this represents the *end* of the string!

```
        bool operator!=(const cstring_iterator_sentinel) const {
            return s != nullptr && *s != '\0';
        }
    };
```

8. In order to use this in a range-based `for` loop, we need a range class around it, which emits the begin and end iterators:

```
class cstring_range {
    const char *s {nullptr};
```

9. The only thing the user needs to provide during instantiation is the string that will be iterated over:

```
public:
    cstring_range(const char *str)
        : s{str}
    {}
```

10. We return a normal `cstring_iterator` from the `begin()` function, which points to the beginning of the string. From the `end()` function, we just return the *sentinel type*. Note that without the sentinel type, we would also return an iterator, but from where should we know the end of the string if we didn't search for it in advance?

```
        cstring_iterator begin() const {
            return cstring_iterator{s};
        }
        cstring_iterator_sentinel end() const {
            return {};
        }
    };
```

11. That's it. We can immediately use it. Strings that come from the user are one example of an input we cannot know the length of in advance. In order to force the user to give some input, we will abort the program if the user did not provide at least one parameter when launching the program in the shell:

```
int main(int argc, char *argv[])
{
    if (argc < 2) {
        std::cout << "Please provide one parameter.\n";
        return 1;
    }
```

12. If the program is still being executed up to this point, then we know that `argv[1]` contains some user string:

```
    for (char c : cstring_range(argv[1])) {
        std::cout << c;
    }
    std::cout << '\n';
}
```

13. Compiling and running the program yields the following output:

```
$ ./main "abcdef"
abcdef
```

That the loop prints what we just entered is not a surprise, as this is just quite a micro-example for the implementation of a sentinel-based iterator range. This iteration termination method will help you in implementing your own iterators wherever you run into a situation where the *comparison with an end position* approach is not helpful.

Automatically checking iterator code with checked iterators

No matter how useful iterators are, and what generic interface they represent, iterators can easily be *misused*, just as pointers. When dealing with pointers, code must be written in a way that it *never* dereferences them when they point to invalid memory locations. Same applies to iterators, but there are *a lot of rules* that state when an iterator is valid and when it is invalidated. Those can easily be learned by studying the STL documentation a bit, but it will still *always* be possible to write buggy code.

In the best case, such buggy code blows up in front of the *developer* while it is being *tested*, and *not* on the client's machine. However, in many cases, the code just silently seems to work, although it dereferences dangling pointers, iterators, and so on. In such cases, we want to be *eagerly alarmed* if we produce code showing undefined behavior.

Fortunately, there's help! The GNU STL implementation has a *debug mode*, and the GNU C++ compiler as well as the LLVM clang C++ compiler both support *additional libraries* that can be used to produce *extra-sensitive* and *verbose* binaries for us, which immediately blow up on a large variety of bugs. This is *easy to use* and *super useful*, as we will demonstrate in this section. The Microsoft Visual C++ standard library also provides a possibility to activate additional checks.

How to do it...

In this section, we'll write a program that deliberately accesses an invalidated iterator:

1. First, we include headers.

   ```
   #include <iostream>
   #include <vector>
   ```

2. Now, let's instantiate a vector of integers and get an iterator to the first item, the value 1. We apply `shrink_to_fit()` on the vector in order to ensure that its capacity is *really* 3, as its implementation *might* allocate more memory than necessary as a little reserve to make future item insertions faster:

   ```
   int main()
   {
       std::vector<int> v {1, 2, 3};
       v.shrink_to_fit();
       const auto it (std::begin(v));
   ```

3. Then we print the dereferenced iterator, which is completely fine:

   ```
   std::cout << *it << '\n';
   ```

4. Next, let's append a new number to the vector. As the vector is not large enough to take another number, it will automatically increase its size. It does this by allocating a new and larger chunk of memory, moving all the existing items to that new chunk and then deleting the *old* memory chunk:

   ```
   v.push_back(123);
   ```

5. Now, let's print 1 from the vector through this iterator again. This is bad. Why? Well, when the vector moved all its values to the new chunk of memory and threw away the old chunk, it did not tell the iterator about this change. This means that the iterator is still pointing to the old location, and we cannot know what really happened to it since then:

```
        std::cout << *it << '\n'; // bad bad bad!
}
```

6. Compiling and running this program leads to a flawless execution. The app doesn't crash, but what it prints when dereferencing the invalidated pointer is pretty much random. Leaving it like this is pretty dangerous, but at this point, no one tells us about that bug if we don't see it ourselves:

```
$ g++ -std=c++17 main.cpp -o main
$ ./main
1
0
```

7. Debug flags come to the rescue! The *GNU* STL implementation supports a preprocessor macro called _GLIBCXX_DEBUG, which activates a lot of sanity checking code in the STL. This makes the program slower, but it *finds bugs*. We can activate it by adding a -D_GLIBCXX_DEBUG flag to our compiler command line, or define it in the head of the code file before the include lines. As you can see, it kills the app in the mactivate different sanitizers. Let's compile the code with clan useful (the activation flag for checked iterators with the Microsoft Visual C++ compiler is /D_ITERATOR_DEBUG_LEVEL=1):

```
$ g++ -std=c++17 main.cpp -D_GLIBCXX_DEBUG -o main
$ ./main
1
/opt/gcc_latest/include/c++/7.0.0/debug/safe_iterator.h:270:
Error: attempt to dereference a singular iterator.

Objects involved in the operation:
    iterator "this" @ 0x0x7ffc06323730 {
      type = __gnu_debug::_Safe_iterator<__gnu_cxx::__normal_iterator<int*, std::__cxx1998::vecto
r<int, std::allocator<int> > >, std::__debug::vector<int, std::allocator<int> > > (mutable iterat
or);
      state = singular;
      references sequence with type 'std::__debug::vector<int, std::allocator<int> >' @ 0x0x7ffc0
6323760
    }
Aborted (core dumped)
```

8. The LLVM/clang implementation of the STL also has debug flags, but they serve the purpose of debugging *the STL* itself, not user code. For user code, you can activate different sanitizers. Let's compile the code with clang using the `-fsanitize=address -fsanitize=undefined` flags and see what happens:

```
$ clang++ -std=c++1z -fsanitize=address -fsanitize=undefined main.cpp -o main
$ ./main
1

==========================================================================
==20639==ERROR: AddressSanitizer: heap-use-after-free on address 0x60200000eff0 at pc 0x0000004eb
519 bp 0x7ffc0fe5d730 sp 0x7ffc0fe5d728
READ of size 4 at 0x60200000eff0 thread T0
    #0 0x4eb518  (/home/tfc/src/stl_cookbook/03/checked_iterator/main+0x4eb518)
    #1 0x7f1c89f893f0  (/lib/x86_64-linux-gnu/libc.so.6+0x203f0)
    #2 0x4187f9  (/home/tfc/src/stl_cookbook/03/checked_iterator/main+0x4187f9)

0x60200000eff0 is located 0 bytes inside of 12-byte region [0x60200000eff0,0x60200000effc)
freed by thread T0 here:
    #0 0x4e83c0  (/home/tfc/src/stl_cookbook/03/checked_iterator/main+0x4e83c0)
    #1 0x4ee64b  (/home/tfc/src/stl_cookbook/03/checked_iterator/main+0x4ee64b)
    #2 0x4ee619  (/home/tfc/src/stl_cookbook/03/checked_iterator/main+0x4ee619)
    #3 0x4ee4ae  (/home/tfc/src/stl_cookbook/03/checked_iterator/main+0x4ee4ae)
    #4 0x4f09c7  (/home/tfc/src/stl_cookbook/03/checked_iterator/main+0x4f09c7)
    #5 0x4ef2a7  (/home/tfc/src/stl_cookbook/03/checked_iterator/main+0x4ef2a7)
    #6 0x4ec1af  (/home/tfc/src/stl_cookbook/03/checked_iterator/main+0x4ec1af)
    #7 0x4eb364  (/home/tfc/src/stl_cookbook/03/checked_iterator/main+0x4eb364)
    #8 0x7f1c89f893f0  (/lib/x86_64-linux-gnu/libc.so.6+0x203f0)

previously allocated by thread T0 here:
    #0 0x4e7dc0  (/home/tfc/src/stl_cookbook/03/checked_iterator/main+0x4e7dc0)
```

Wow, this is a very precise description of what went wrong. The screenshot would have spanned *multiple pages* of this book if it had not been truncated. Note that this is not a clang-only feature, as it also works with GCC.

 If you get runtime errors because some library is missing, then your compiler did not automatically ship with **libasan** and **libubsan**. Try to install them via your package manager or something similar.

How it works...

As we have seen, we did not need to *change* anything in the code in order to get this kind of *tripwire* feature for buggy code. It basically came for *free*, just by appending some compiler flags to the command line when compiling the program.

This feature is implemented by *sanitizers*. A sanitizer usually consists of an additional compiler module and a runtime library. When sanitizers are activated, the compiler will add *additional information* and *code* to the binary, which results from our program. At runtime, the sanitizer libraries that are then linked into the program binary can, for example, replace the `malloc` and `free` functions in order to *analyze* how the program deals with the memory it acquires.

Sanitizers can detect different kinds of bugs. Just to list a few valuable examples:

- **Out-of-bounds**: This triggers whenever we access an array, vector, or anything similar outside its legitimate memory range.
- **Use-after-free**: This triggers if we reference heap memory after it was already freed (which we did in this section).
- **Integer overflow**: This triggers if an integer variable overflows by calculating with values that do not fit into the variable. For signed integers, the arithmetic wraparound is undefined behavior.
- **Pointer alignment**: Some architectures cannot access memory if it has a weird alignment in memory.

There are many more such bugs that sanitizers can detect.

It is *not feasible* to *always* activate all available sanitizers because they make the program *slower*. However, it is good style to always activate sanitizers in your *unit tests* and *integration tests*.

There's more...

There are a lot of different sanitizers for different bug categories, and they are all still under development. We can and should inform ourselves on the internet about how we can improve our test binaries. The GCC and LLVM project homepages list their sanitizing capabilities in their online documentation pages:

- `https://gcc.gnu.org/onlinedocs/gcc/Instrumentation-Options.html`
- `http://clang.llvm.org/docs/index.html` (look for *sanitizers* in the table of contents)

Thorough testing with sanitizers is something that *every* programmer should be aware of and should *always* be doing. Unfortunately, this is not the case in alarmingly many companies, although buggy code is the most important entry point for all the *malware* and *computer viruses* out there.

When you get a new job as a software developer, check if your team really uses all the sanitizing possibilities there are. If not, you have the unique chance to fix important and sneaky bugs on your first day at work!

Building your own zip iterator adapter

Different programming languages lead to different programming styles. This is, because there are different ways to express things, and they are differing in their elegance for each use case. That is no surprise because every language was designed with specific objectives.

A very special kind of programming style is *purely functional programming*. It is magically different from the *imperative* programming which C or C++ programmers are used to. While this style is very different, it enables extremely elegant code in many situations.

One example of this elegance is the implementation of formulas, such as the mathematical dot product. Given two mathematical vectors, applying the dot product to them means pairwise multiplying of the numbers at the same positions in the vector and then summing up all of those multiplied values. The dot product of two vectors $(a, b, c) * (d, e, f)$ is $(a * e + b * e + c * f)$. Of course, we can do that with C and C++, too. It could look like the following:

```
std::vector<double> a {1.0, 2.0, 3.0};
std::vector<double> b {4.0, 5.0, 6.0};

double sum {0};
for (size_t i {0}; i < a.size(); ++i) {
    sum += a[i] * b[i];
}
// sum = 32.0
```

How does it look like in those languages that can be considered *more elegant*?

Haskell is a purely functional language, and this is how you can calculate the dot product of two vectors with a magical one-liner:

```
Prelude> a = [1.0, 2.0, 3.0]
Prelude> b = [4.0, 5.0, 6.0]
Prelude> sum $ zipWith (*) a b
32.0
```

Python is not a purely functional language, but it supports similar patterns to some extent, as seen in the next example:

```
>>> a = [1.0, 2.0, 3.0]
>>> b = [4.0, 5.0, 6.0]
>>> sum([ p[0] * p[1] for p in zip(a, b) ])
32.0
```

The STL provides a specific algorithm called `std::inner_product`, which solves this specific problem in one line, too. But the point is that in many other languages, such code can be written *on the fly* in only one line *without* specific library functions that support that exact purpose.

Without delving into the explanations of such foreign syntax, an important commonality in both examples is the magical `zip` function. What does it do? It takes the two vectors a and b and transforms them to a *mixed* vector. Example: `[a1, a2, a3]` and `[b1, b2, b3]` result in `[ (a1, b1), (a2, b2), (a3, b3) ]` when they are zipped together. Have a close look at it; it's really similar to how zip fasteners work!

The relevant point is that it is now possible to iterate over *one* combined range where pairwise multiplications can be done and then summed up to an accumulator variable. Exactly the same happens in the Haskell and Python examples, without adding any loop or index variable noise.

It will not be possible to make the C++ code exactly as elegant and generic as in Haskell or Python, but this section explains how to implement similar magic using iterators, by implementing a *zip iterator*. The example problem of calculating the dot product of two vectors is solved more elegantly by specific libraries, which are beyond the scope of this book. However, this section tries to show how much iterator-based libraries can help in writing expressive code by providing extremely generic building blocks.

How to do it...

In this section, we will recreate the *zip* function as known from Haskell or Python. It will be hardcoded to vectors of `double` variables in order to not distract from iterator mechanics:

1. First, we need to include some headers:

```
#include <iostream>
#include <vector>
#include <numeric>
```

2. Next, we define the `zip_iterator` class. While iterating over a `zip_iterator` range, we will get a pair of values from the two containers at every iteration step. This means that we iterate over two containers at the same time:

```
class zip_iterator {
```

3. The zip iterator needs to save two iterators, one for each container:

```
using it_type = std::vector<double>::iterator;

it_type it1;
it_type it2;
```

4. The constructor simply saves the iterators from the two containers that we would like to iterate over:

```
public:
    zip_iterator(it_type iterator1, it_type iterator2)
        : it1{iterator1}, it2{iterator2}
    {}
```

5. Incrementing the zip iterator means incrementing both the member iterators:

```
zip_iterator& operator++() {
    ++it1;
    ++it2;
    return *this;
}
```

6. Two zip iterators are unequal if both the member iterators are unequal to their counterparts in the other zip iterator. Usually, one would use logical or (| |) instead of and (&&), but imagine that the ranges are not of equal length. In such a case, it would not be possible to match *both* the end iterators at the same time. This way, we can abort the loop when we reach the *first* end iterator of *either* range:

```
bool operator!=(const zip_iterator& o) const {
    return it1 != o.it1 && it2 != o.it2;
}
```

7. The equality comparison operator is just implemented using the other operator, but negating the result:

```
bool operator==(const zip_iterator& o) const {
    return !operator!=(o);
}
```

8. Dereferencing the zip iterator gives access to the elements of both the containers at the same position:

```
std::pair<double, double> operator*() const {
    return {*it1, *it2};
}
};
```

9. This was the iterator code. We need to make the iterator compatible with STL algorithms, so we define the needed type trait boilerplate code for that. It basically says that this iterator is just a forward iterator, and it returns pairs of double values when dereferenced. Although we do not use difference_type in this recipe, different implementations of the STL might need it in order to compile:

```
namespace std {
template <>
struct iterator_traits<zip_iterator> {
    using iterator_category = std::forward_iterator_tag;
    using value_type = std::pair<double, double>;
    using difference_type = long int;
};
}
```

10. The next step is to define a range class that returns us zip iterators from its `begin` and `end` functions:

```
class zipper {
    using vec_type = std::vector<double>;
    vec_type &vec1;
    vec_type &vec2;
```

11. It needs to reference two existing containers in order to form zip iterators from them:

```
public:
    zipper(vec_type &va, vec_type &vb)
        : vec1{va}, vec2{vb}
    {}
```

12. The `begin` and `end` functions just feed pairs of begin and end pointers in order to construct zip iterator instances from that:

```
    zip_iterator begin() const {
        return {std::begin(vec1), std::begin(vec2)};
    }
    zip_iterator end() const {
        return {std::end(vec1), std::end(vec2)};
    }
};
```

13. Just as in the Haskell and Python examples, we define two vectors of `double` values. We also define that we use namespace `std` within the main function by default:

```
int main()
{
    using namespace std;
    vector<double> a {1.0, 2.0, 3.0};
    vector<double> b {4.0, 5.0, 6.0};
```

14. The zipper object combines them to one vector-like range where we see pairs of `a` and `b` values:

```
    zipper zipped {a, b};
```

15. We will use `std::accumulate` in order to sum all the items of the range together. We can't do it directly because that would mean that we sum up the instances of `std::pair<double, double>` for which the concept of sum is not defined. Therefore, we will define a helper lambda that takes a pair, multiplies its members, and adds it to an accumulator. The `std::accumulate` works well with lambdas with such a signature:

```
const auto add_product ([](double sum, const auto &p) {
    return sum + p.first * p.second;
});
```

16. Now, we feed it to `std::accumulate`, together with the begin and end iterator pair of the zipped ranges and a start value of `0.0` for the accumulator variable, which, in the end, contains the sum of the products:

```
const auto dot_product (accumulate(
        begin(zipped), end(zipped), 0.0, add_product));
```

17. Let's print the dot product result:

```
cout << dot_product << '\n';
}
```

18. Compiling and running the program yields the correct result:

```
32
```

There's more...

OK, that was a *lot* of work for a little bit of syntax sugar, and it's still not as elegant as Haskell code can be without any effort. A big flaw is the hardcoded nature of our little zip iterator--it only works on the `std::vector` ranges of double variables. With a bit of template code and some type traits, the zipper can be made more generic. This way, it could combine lists and vectors, or deques and maps, even if these are specialized on completely different container item types.

The amount of work and thought needed in order to really and correctly make such classes generic is not to be underestimated. Luckily, such libraries do already exist. One popular non-STL library is the *Boost* `zip_iterator`. It is very generic and easy to use.

By the way, if you came here to see the most elegant way to do a *dot product* in C++, and don't really care about the concept of zip-iterators, you should have a look at `std::valarray`. See for yourself:

```cpp
#include <iostream>
#include <valarray>

int main()
{
    std::valarray<double> a {1.0, 2.0, 3.0};
    std::valarray<double> b {4.0, 5.0, 6.0};

    std::cout << (a * b).sum() << '\n';
}
```

Ranges library

There is a very, very interesting C++ library, which supports zippers and all other kinds of magic iterator adapters, filters, and so on: the *ranges* library. It is inspired by the Boost ranges library, and for some time, it looked like it would find its way into C++17, but unfortunately, we will have to wait for the *next* standard. The reason why this is so unfortunate is that it will *vigorously* improve the possibilities of writing *expressive* and *fast* code in C++ by composing *complex* functionality from *generic* and *simple* blocks of code.

There are some very simple examples in its documentation:

1. Calculating the sum of the squares of all numbers from 1 to 10:

```cpp
const int sum = accumulate(view::ints(1)
                    | view::transform([](int i){return i*i;})
                    | view::take(10), 0);
```

2. Filtering out all uneven numbers from a numeric vector, and transforming the rest to strings:

```cpp
std::vector<int> v {1,2,3,4,5,6,7,8,9,10};
auto rng = v | view::remove_if([](int i){return i % 2 == 1;})
            | view::transform([](int i){return std::to_string(i);});
// rng == {"2"s,"4"s,"6"s,"8"s,"10"s};
```

If you are interested and can't wait for the next C++ standard, have a look at the ranges documentation at `https://ericniebler.github.io/range-v3/`.

4
Lambda Expressions

We will cover the following recipes in this chapter:

- Defining functions on the run using lambda expressions
- Adding polymorphy by wrapping lambdas into `std::function`
- Composing functions by concatenation
- Creating complex predicates with logical conjunction
- Calling multiple functions with the same input
- Implementing `transform_if` using `std::accumulate` and lambdas
- Generating cartesian product pairs of any input at compile time

Introduction

One important new feature of C++11 was **lambda expressions**. In C++14 and C++17, the lambda expressions got some new additions, which have made them even more powerful. But first, what *is* a lambda expression?

Lambda expressions or lambda functions construct closures. A closure is a very generic term for *unnamed objects* that can be *called* like functions. In order to provide such a capability in C++, such an object must implement the `()` function calling operator, with or without parameters. Constructing such an object without lambda expressions before C++11 could still look like the following:

```
#include <iostream>
#include <string>

int main() {
    struct name_greeter {
        std::string name;
```

```
            void operator()() {
                std::cout << "Hello, " << name << '\n';
            }
        };

        name_greeter greet_john_doe {"John Doe"};
        greet_john_doe();
    }
```

Instances of the `name_greeter` struct obviously carry a string with them. Note that both this structure type and instance are not unnamed but lambda expressions can be, as we will see. In terms of closures, we would say they *capture* a string. When the example instance is called like a function without parameters, it prints `"Hello, John Doe"` because we constructed it with this name.

Since C++11, it has become easier to create such closures:

```
    #include <iostream>

    int main() {
        auto greet_john_doe ([] {
            std::cout << "Hello, John Doe\n";
        });

        greet_john_doe();
    }
```

That's it. The whole struct, `name_greeter`, is replaced by a little `[] { /* do something */ }` construct, which might look a bit like magic at first, but the first section of this chapter will explain it thoroughly in all the possible variants.

Lambda expressions are of a great help to make code *generic* and *tidy*. They can be used as parameters for very generic algorithms in order to specialize what those do when processing specific user-defined types. They can also be used to wrap work packages together with data in order to be run in threads or just to save work and postpone the actual execution. Since C++11 came out, more and more libraries work with lambda expressions because they became a very natural thing in C++. Another use case is metaprogramming, because lambda expressions can also be evaluated at compile time. However, we are not going much into *that* direction, as this would quickly blast the scope of this book.

This chapter does heavily rely on some *functional programming* patterns, which might look weird to novices or programmers who are already experienced but not with such patterns. If you see lambda expressions in the coming recipes that return lambda expressions, which again return lambda expressions, please don't feel frustrated or confused too quickly. We are pushing the boundaries a bit in order to prepare ourselves for modern C++, where functional programming patterns occur with increasing regularity. If some code in the following recipes looks a bit too complex, take your time to understand it. Once you got through this, complex lambda expressions in real projects in the wild will not confuse you any longer.

Defining functions on the run using lambda expressions

With lambda expressions, we can encapsulate code in order to call it later, and that also might be somewhere else because we can copy them around. We can also just encapsulate code to call it multiple times with slightly different parameters without having to implement a whole new function class for that task.

The syntax of lambda expressions was really new in C++11, and it has slightly evolved with the next two standard versions until C++17. In this section, we will see what lambda expressions can look like and what they mean.

How to do it...

We are going to write a little program in which we play with lambda expressions in order to get a feeling for them:

1. Lambda expressions do not need any library support, but we are going to write messages to the terminal and use strings, so we need the headers for this:

```
#include <iostream>
#include <string>
```

2. Everything happens in the main function this time. We define two function objects that take no parameters and return integer constants with the values, 1 and 2. Note that the return statement is surrounded by curly brackets { }, like it is in normal functions, and the () parentheses, which denote a parameterless function, are *optional*, we don't provide them in the second lambda expression. But the [] brackets have to be there:

```
int main()
{
    auto just_one ( [](){ return 1; } );
    auto just_two ( []   { return 2; } );
```

3. Now, we can call both the function objects just by writing the names of the variables they are saved to and appending the parentheses. In this single line, they are indistinguishable from *normal functions* for the reader:

```
std::cout << just_one() << ", " << just_two() << '\n';
```

4. Now let's forget about those and define another function object, which is called plus because it takes two parameters and returns their sum:

```
auto plus ( [](auto l, auto r) { return l + r; } );
```

5. This is also easy to use, just like any other binary function. As we defined its parameters to be of the auto type, it will work with anything that defines the plus operator +, just as strings do:

```
std::cout << plus(1, 2) << '\n';
std::cout << plus(std::string{"a"}, "b") << '\n';
```

6. We do not need to store a lambda expression in a variable in order to use it. We can also define it *in place* and then write the parameters in parentheses just behind it (1, 2):

```
std::cout
    << [](auto l, auto r){ return l + r; }(1, 2)
    << '\n';
```

7. Next, we will define a closure that carries an integer counter value around with it. Whenever we call it, it increments its counter value and returns the new value. In order to tell it that it has an internal counter variable, we write count = 0 within the brackets to tell it that there is a variable count initialized to the integer value 0. In order to allow it to modify its own captured variables, we use the mutable keyword, as the compiler would not allow it otherwise:

```
auto counter (
    [count = 0] () mutable { return ++count; }
);
```

8. Now, let's call the function object five times and print the values it returns, so we can see the increasing number values later:

```
for (size_t i {0}; i < 5; ++i) {
    std::cout << counter() << ", ";
}
std::cout << '\n';
```

9. We can also take existing variables and capture them by *reference* instead of giving a closure its own value copy. This way, the captured variable can be incremented by the closure, but it is still accessible outside. In order to do so, we write &a between the brackets, where the & means that we store only a *reference* to the variable, not a *copy*:

```
int a {0};
auto incrementer ( [&a] { ++a; } );
```

10. If this works, then we should be able to call this function object multiple times, and then observe that it has really changed the value of variable a:

```
incrementer();
incrementer();
incrementer();

std::cout
  << "Value of 'a' after 3 incrementer() calls: "
  << a << '\n';
```

11. The last example is *currying*. Currying means that we take a function that can accept some parameters and store it in another function object, which accepts *fewer* parameters. In this case, we store the `plus` function and only accept *one* parameter, which we forward to the `plus` function. The other parameter is the value `10`, which we save in the function object. This way, we get a function, which we call `plus_ten` because it can add that value to the single parameter it accepts:

```
    auto plus_ten ( [=] (int x) { return plus(10, x); } );
    std::cout << plus_ten(5) << '\n';
}
```

12. Before compiling and running the program, go through the code again and try to foresee what it will print to the terminal. Then run it and check against the real output:

```
1, 2
3
ab
3
1, 2, 3, 4, 5,
Value of a after 3 incrementer() calls: 3
15
```

How it works...

What we just did was not overly complicated--we added numbers, and incremented and printed them. We even concatenated strings with a function object, which was implemented to add up numbers. But for anyone who didn't know lambda expression syntax yet, it might have looked confusing.

So, let's first have a look at all the lambda expression peculiarities:

```
[capture list] (parameters)
        mutable          (optional)
        constexpr        (optional)
        exception attr   (optional)
        -> return type   (optional)
    {
        body
    }
```

We can usually omit most of this, which spares us some typing, in the average case. The shortest lambda expression possible is `[]{}`. It accepts no parameters, captures nothing, and essentially *does* nothing.

So what does the rest mean?

Capture list

Specifies if and what we capture. There are several forms to do so. There are two lazy variants:

- If we write `[=]` `()` `{...}`, we capture every variable the closure references from outside by value, which means that the values are *copied*
- Writing `[&]` `()` `{...}` means that everything the closure references outside is only captured by *reference*, which does *not* lead to a copy.

Of course, we can set the capturing settings for every variable individually. Writing `[a, &b]` `()` `{...}` means, that we capture the variable a by *value*, and b by *reference*. This is more typing work, but it's generally safer to be that verbose because we cannot accidentally capture something we don't want to capture from outside.

In the recipe, we defined a lambda expression as such: `[count=0]` `()` `{...}`. In this special case, we did not capture any variable from outside, but we defined a new one called `count`. Its type is deduced from the value we initialized it with, namely 0, so it's an `int`.

It is also possible to capture some variables by value and some, by reference, as in:

- `[a, &b]` `()` `{...}`: This captures a by copy and b by reference.
- `[&, a]` `()` `{...}`: This captures a by copy and any other used variable by reference.
- `[=, &b, i{22}, this]` `()` `{...}`: This captures b by reference, `this` by copy, initializes a new variable i with value 22, and captures any other used variable by copy.

> If you try to capture a member variable of an object, you cannot do this directly using `[member_a]` `()` `{...}`. Instead, you have to capture either `this` or `*this`.

mutable (optional)

If the function object should be able to *modify* the variables it captures by *copy* (`[=]`), it must be defined `mutable`. This includes calling non-const methods of captured objects.

constexpr (optional)

If we mark the lambda expression explicitly as `constexpr`, the compiler will *error* out if it does not satisfy the criteria of `constexpr` functions. The advantage of `constexpr` functions and lambda expressions is that the compiler can evaluate their result at compile time if they are called with compile-time constant parameters. This leads to less code in the binary later.

If we do not explicitly declare the lambda expression to be `constexpr` but it fits the requirements for that, it will be implicitly `constexpr` *anyway*. If we *want* a lambda expression to be `constexpr`, it helps to be explicit because the compiler will then help us by erroring out if we did it *wrong*.

exception attr (optional)

This is the place to specify if the function object can throw exceptions when it's called and runs into an error case.

return type (optional)

If we want to have ultimate control over the return type, we may not want the compiler to deduce it for us automatically. In such a case, we can just write `[] () -> Foo {}`, which tells the compiler that we will really always return the `Foo` type.

Adding polymorphy by wrapping lambdas into std::function

Let's say we want to write an observer function for some kind of value, which might change sometimes, which then notifies other objects; like a gas pressure indicator, or a stock price, or something similar. Whenever the value changes, a list of observer objects should be called, which then react their way.

In order to implement this, we could store a range of observer function objects in a vector, which all accept an `int` variable as the parameter, which represents the observed value. We do not know what these function objects do in particular when they are called with the new value, but we also don't care.

Of what type will that vector of function objects be? The `std::vector<void (*)(int)>` type would be correct if we were capturing pointers to *functions* with signatures such as `void f(int);`. This would indeed also work with any lambda expression that does *not* capture any variables, such as `[](int x) {...}`. But a lambda expression that captures something is actually a *completely different type* compared with a normal function because it's not just a function pointer. It is an *object* that couples a certain amount of data with a function! Think of pre-C++11 times, when there were no lambdas. Classes and structs are the natural way of coupling data with functions, and if you change the data member types of a class, you get a completely different class type. It's just *natural* that a vector can't store completely different types using the same type name.

Telling the user that it's only possible to save observer function objects that do not capture anything is bad because it limits the number of use cases very much. How can we allow the user to store any kind of function object, only constraining to the call interface, which takes a specific set of parameters that represent the value that shall be observed?

This section shows how to solve this problem using `std::function`, which can act as a polymorphic wrapper around any lambda expression, no matter if and what it captures.

How to do it...

In this section, we are going to create several lambda expressions that are completely different in regard to the variable types they capture but have the same function call signature in common. These will be saved in one vector using `std::function`:

1. Let's first do some necessary includes:

```
#include <iostream>
#include <deque>
#include <list>
#include <vector>
#include <functional>
```

2. We implement a little function that returns a lambda expression. It accepts a container and returns a function object that captures that container by reference. The function object itself accepts an integer parameter. Whenever that function object is fed with an integer, it will *append* that integer to the container it captures:

```
static auto consumer (auto &container){
    return [&] (auto value) {
        container.push_back(value);
    };
}
```

3. Another little helper function will print whatever container instance we provide as a parameter:

```
static void print (const auto &c)
{
    for (auto i : c) {
        std::cout << i << ", ";
    }
    std::cout << '\n';
}
```

4. In the main function, we first instantiate a deque, a list, and a vector, which all store integers:

```
int main()
{
    std::deque<int>  d;
    std::list<int>   l;
    std::vector<int> v;
```

5. Now we use the consumer function with our container instances, d, l, and v: we produce consumer function objects for those and store them all in a vector instance. Then we have a vector that stores three function objects. These function objects each capture a reference to one of the container objects. These container objects are of completely different types and so are the function objects. Nevertheless, the vector holds instances of std::function<void(int)>. All the function objects are implicitly wrapped into such std::function objects, which are then stored in the vector:

```
const std::vector<std::function<void(int)>> consumers
    {consumer(d), consumer(l), consumer(v)};
```

6. Now, we feed 10 integer values to all the data structures by looping over the values and then looping over the consumer function objects, which we call with those values:

```
for (size_t i {0}; i < 10; ++i) {
    for (auto &&consume : consumers) {
        consume(i);
    }
}
```

7. All the three containers should now contain the same 10 number values. Let's print their content:

```
    print(d);
    print(l);
    print(v);
}
```

8. Compiling and running the program yields the following output, which is just what we expect:

```
$ ./std_function
0, 1, 2, 3, 4, 5, 6, 7, 8, 9,
0, 1, 2, 3, 4, 5, 6, 7, 8, 9,
0, 1, 2, 3, 4, 5, 6, 7, 8, 9,
```

How it works...

The complicated part of this recipe is the following line:

```
const std::vector<std::function<void(int)>> consumers
        {consumer(d), consumer(l), consumer(v) };
```

The objects d, l, and v are each wrapped into a consumer(...) call. This call returns function objects, which then each capture references to one of d, l, and v. Although these function objects all accept int values as parameters, the fact that they capture completely *different* variables also makes them completely different *types*. This is like trying to stuff variables of type A, B, and C into a vector, although these types have *nothing* in common.

In order to fix this, we need to find a *common* type, which can store very *different* function objects, that is, `std::function`. An `std::function<void(int)>` object can store any function object or traditional function, which accepts an integer parameter and returns nothing. It decouples its type from the underlying function object type, using polymorphy. Consider we write something like this:

```
std::function<void(int)> f (
    [&vector](int x) { vector.push_back(x); });
```

Here, the function object which is constructed from the lambda expression is wrapped into an `std::function` object, and whenever we call `f(123)`, this leads to a *virtual function call*, which is *redirected* to the actual function object inside it.

While storing function objects, `std::function` instances apply some intelligence. If we capture more and more variables in a lambda expression, it must grow larger. If its size is not too large, `std::function` can store it within itself. If the size of the stored function object is too large, `std::function` will allocate a chunk of memory on the heap and then store the large function object there. This does not affect the functionality of our code, but we should know about this because this can impact the *performance* of our code.

 A lot of novice programmers think or hope that `std::function<...>` actually expresses the *type* of a lambda expression. No, it doesn't. It is a polymorphic library helper, which is useful for wrapping lambda expressions and erasing their type differences.

Composing functions by concatenation

A lot of tasks are not really worthy of being implemented in completely custom code. Let's, for example, have a look on how a programmer might solve the task of finding out how many unique words a text contains with the programming language Haskell. The first line defines a function `unique_words` and the second one demonstrates its use with an example string:

```
Prelude> unique_words = length . group . sort . words . (map toLower)
Prelude> unique_words "A B c d a b c d e"
5
```

Wow, that is short! Without explaining Haskell syntax too much, let's see what the code does. It defines the function called `unique_words`, which applies a series of functions to its input. It first maps all the characters from the input to lowercase with `map toLower`. This way, words like `FOO` and `foo` can be regarded as the *same* word. Then, the `words` function splits a sentence into individual words, as from `"foo bar baz"` to `["foo", "bar", "baz"]`. Next step is sorting the new list of words. This way, a word sequence such as `["a", "b", "a"]` becomes `["a", "a", "b"]`. Now, the `group` function takes over. It groups consecutive equal words into grouped lists, so `["a", "a", "b"]` becomes `[ ["a", "a"], ["b"] ]`. The job is now nearly done, as we now only need to count *how many* groups of equal words we got, which is exactly what the `length` function does.

This is a *wonderful* style of programming, as we can read *what* happens from right to left because we are just, kind of, describing a transformation pipeline. We don't need to care *how* the individual pieces are implemented (unless it turns out that they are slow or buggy).

However, we are not here to praise Haskell but to improve our C++ skills. It is possible to work like this in C++ too. We will not completely reach the elegance of the Haskell example but we still have the fastest programming language there is. This example explains how to imitate *function concatenation* in C++ with lambda expressions.

How to do it...

In this section, we define some simple toy function objects and *concatenate* them, so we get a single function that applies the simple toy functions after each other to the input we give it. In order to do so, we write our own concatenation helper function:

1. First, we need some includes:

   ```
   #include <iostream>
   #include <functional>
   ```

2. Then, we implement the helper function, `concat`, which arbitrarily takes many parameters. These parameters will be functions, such as f, g, and h, and the result will be another function object that applies `f(g(h(...)))` on any input:

   ```
   template <typename T, typename ...Ts>
   auto concat(T t, Ts ...ts)
   {
   ```

3. Now, it gets a little complicated. When the user provides functions f, g, and h, we will evaluate this to f (concat(g, h)), which again expands to f (g (concat(h))), where the recursion aborts, so we get f (g (h(...))). This chain of function calls representing the concatenation of these user functions is captured by a lambda expression, which can later take some parameters, p, and then forward them to f(g(h(p))). This lambda expression is what we return. The if constexpr construct checks whether we are in a recursion step with more than one function to concatenate left:

```
if constexpr (sizeof...(ts) > 0) {
    return [=](auto ...parameters) {
        return t(concat(ts...)(parameters...));
    };
}
```

4. The other branch of the if constexpr construct is selected by the compiler if we are at the *end* of the recursion. In such a case, we just return the function, t, because it is the only parameter left:

```
else {
    return t;
}
}
```

5. Now, let's use our cool new function concatenation helper with some functions we want to see concatenated. Let's begin with the main function, where we define two cheap simple function objects:

```
int main()
{
    auto twice  ([] (int i) { return i * 2; });
    auto thrice ([] (int i) { return i * 3; });
```

6. Now let's concatenate. We concatenate our two multiplier function objects with the STL function, std::plus<int>, which takes two parameters and simply returns their sum. This way, we get a function that does twice(thrice(plus(a, b))).

```
auto combined (
    concat(twice, thrice, std::plus<int>{})
);
```

7. Now let's use it. The `combined` function looks like a single normal function now, and the compiler is also able to concatenate those functions without any unnecessary overhead:

```
    std::cout << combined(2, 3) << '\n';
}
```

8. Compiling and running our program yields the following output, which we also expected, because 2 * 3 * (2 + 3) is 30:

```
$ ./concatenation
30
```

How it works...

The complicated thing in this section is the `concat` function. It looks horribly complicated because it unpacks the parameter pack `ts` into another lambda expression, which recursively calls `concat` again, with less parameters:

```
template <typename T, typename ...Ts>
auto concat(T t, Ts ...ts)
{
    if constexpr (sizeof...(ts) > 0) {
        return [=](auto ...parameters) {
            return t(concat(ts...)(parameters...));
        };
    } else {
        return [=](auto ...parameters) {
            return t(parameters...);
        };
    }
}
```

Let's write a simpler version, which concatenates exactly *three* functions:

```
template <typename F, typename G, typename H>
auto concat(F f, G g, H h)
{
    return [=](auto ... params) {
        return f( g( h( params... ) ) );
    };
}
```

This already looks similar, but less complicated. We return a lambda expression, which captures f, g, and h. This lambda expression arbitrarily accepts many parameters and just forwards them to a call chain of f, g, and h. When we write `auto combined (concat(f, g, h))`, and later call that function object with two parameters, such as `combined(2, 3)`, then the `2, 3` are represented by the `params` pack from the preceding `concat` function.

Looking at the much more complex, generic `concat` function again; the only thing we do really differently is the `f ( g( h( params... ) ) )` concatenation. Instead, we write `f( concat(g, h) )(params...)`, which evaluates to `f( g( concat(h) ) )(params...)` in the next recursive call, which then finally results in `f( g( h( params... ) ) )`.

Creating complex predicates with logical conjunction

When filtering data with generic code, we end up defining **predicates**, which tell what data we want, and what data we do not want. Sometimes predicates are the *combinations* of different predicates.

When filtering strings, for example, we could implement a predicate that returns `true` if its input string *begins* with `"foo"`. Another predicate could return true if its input string *ends* with `"bar"`.

Instead of writing custom predicates all the time, we can *reuse* predicates by combining them. If we want to filter strings that begin with `"foo"` and end with `"bar"`, we can just pick our *existing* predicates and *combine* them with a logical *and*. In this section, we play with lambda expressions in order to find a comfortable way to do this.

How to do it...

We will implement very simple string filter predicates, and then we will combine them with a little helper function that does the combination for us in a generic way.

1. As always, we'll include some headers first:

```
#include <iostream>
#include <functional>
#include <string>
#include <iterator>
#include <algorithm>
```

2. Because we are going to need them later, we implement two simple predicate functions. The first one tells if a string begins with the character 'a' and the second one tells if a string ends with the character 'b':

```
static bool begins_with_a (const std::string &s)
{
    return s.find("a") == 0;
}

static bool ends_with_b (const std::string &s)
{
    return s.rfind("b") == s.length() - 1;
}
```

3. Now, let's implement a helper function, which we call combine. It takes a binary function as its first parameter, which could be the logical AND function or the logical OR function, for example. Then, it takes two other parameters, which shall be two predicate functions that are then combined:

```
template <typename A, typename B, typename F>
auto combine(F binary_func, A a, B b)
{
```

4. We simply return a lambda expression that captures the new predicate *combination*. It forwards a parameter to both predicates and, then, puts the results of both into the binary function and returns its result:

```
    return [=](auto param) {
        return binary_func(a(param), b(param));
    };
}
```

5. Let's state that we use the std namespace to spare us some typing in the main function:

```
using namespace std;
```

6. Now, let's combine our two predicate functions in another predicate function, which tells if a given string begins with a *and* ends with b, as "ab" does or "axxxb". As the binary function, we choose `std::logical_and`. It is a template class that needs to be instantiated, so we use it with curly braces in order to instantiate it. Note that we don't provide a template parameter because for this class, it defaults to `void`. This specialization of the class deduces all parameter types automatically:

```cpp
int main()
{
    auto a_xxx_b (combine(
        logical_and<>{},
        begins_with_a, ends_with_b));
```

7. We iterate over the standard input and print all words back to the terminal, which satisfies our predicate:

```cpp
copy_if(istream_iterator<string>{cin}, {},
        ostream_iterator<string>{cout, ", "},
        a_xxx_b);
cout << '\n';
}
```

8. Compiling and running the program yields the following output. We feed the program with four words, but only two satisfy the predicate criteria:

```
$ echo "ac cb ab axxxb" | ./combine
ab, axxxb,
```

There's more...

The STL already provides a useful bunch of functional objects such as `std::logical_and`, `std::logical_or`, as well as many others, so we do not need to reimplement them in every project. It's a good idea to have a look at the C++ reference and explore what's there already:
http://en.cppreference.com/w/cpp/utility/functional

Calling multiple functions with the same input

There are a lot of tasks, which lead to repetitive code. A lot of repetitive code can be eliminated easily using lambda expressions and a lambda expression helper that wraps such repetitive tasks is created very quickly.

In this section, we will play with lambda expressions in order to forward a single call with all its parameters to multiple receivers. This is going to happen without any data structures in between, so the compiler has a simple job to generate a binary without overhead.

How to do it...

We are going to write a lambda expression helper, which forwards a single call to multiple objects, and another lambda expression helper, which forwards a single call to multiple calls of other functions. In our example, we are going to use this to print a single message with different printer functions:

1. Let's include the STL header we need for printing first:

   ```
   #include <iostream>
   ```

2. At first, we implement the `multicall` function, which is central to this recipe. It accepts an arbitrary number of functions as parameters and returns a lambda expression that accepts one parameter. It forwards this parameter to all the functions that were provided before. This way, we can define `auto call_all (multicall(f, g, h))`, and then, `call_all(123)` leads to a sequence of calls, `f(123); g(123); h(123);`. This function looks really complicated because we need a syntax trick in order to expand the parameter pack, `functions`, into a series of calls by using an `std::initializer_list` constructor:

   ```
   static auto multicall (auto ...functions)
   {
       return [=](auto x) {
           (void)std::initializer_list<int>{
               ((void)functions(x), 0)...
           };
       };
   }
   ```

3. The next helper accepts a function, f, and a pack of parameters, xs. What it does is it calls f with each of those parameters. This way, a for_each(f, 1, 2, 3) call leads to a series of calls: f(1); f(2); f(3);. This function essentially uses the same syntax trick to expand the parameter pack, xs, to a series of function calls, as the other function before:

```
static auto for_each (auto f, auto ...xs) {
    (void)std::initializer_list<int>{
        ((void)f(xs), 0)...
    };
}
```

4. The brace_print function accepts two characters and returns a new function object, which accepts one parameter, x. It will *print* it, surrounded by the two characters we just captured before:

```
static auto brace_print (char a, char b) {
    return [=] (auto x) {
        std::cout << a << x << b << ", ";
    };
}
```

5. Now, we can finally put everything to use in the main function. At first, we define functions f, g, and h. They represent print functions that accept values and print them surrounded by different braces/parentheses each. The nl function takes any parameter and just prints a line break character:

```
int main()
{
    auto f  (brace_print('(', ')'));
    auto g  (brace_print('[', ']'));
    auto h  (brace_print('{', '}'));
    auto nl ([] (auto) { std::cout << '\n'; });
```

6. Let's combine all of them using our multicall helper:

```
    auto call_fgh (multicall(f, g, h, nl));
```

7. For each of the numbers we provide, we want to see them individually printed three times surrounded by different pairs of braces/parentheses. This way, we can do a single function call and end up with five calls to our multifunction, which does another four calls to f, g, h, and nl.

```
        for_each(call_fgh, 1, 2, 3, 4, 5);
    }
```

8. Before compiling and running, think about what output to expect:

```
$ ./multicaller
(1), [1], {1},
(2), [2], {2},
(3), [3], {3},
(4), [4], {4},
(5), [5], {5},
```

How it works...

The helpers we just implemented look horribly complicated. This is because we expand parameter packs with std::initializer_list. Why did we even use that data structure? Let's have a look at for_each again:

```
auto for_each ([](auto f, auto ...xs) {
    (void)std::initializer_list<int>{
        ((void)f(xs), 0)...
    };
});
```

The heart of this function is the f(xs) expression. xs is a parameter pack, and we need to *unpack* it in order to get the individual values out of it and feed them to individual f calls. Unfortunately, we cannot just write f(xs) ... using the . . . notation, which we already know.

What we can do is constructing a list of values using `std::initializer_list`, which has a variadic constructor. An expression such as `return std::initializer_list<int>{f(xs)...};` does the job, but it has *downsides*. Let's have a look at an implementation of `for_each` which does just this, so it looks simpler than what we have:

```
auto for_each ([](auto f, auto ...xs) {
    return std::initializer_list<int>{f(xs)...};
});
```

This is easier to grasp, but its downsides are the following:

1. It constructs an actual initializer list of return values from all the `f` calls. At this point, we do not care about the return values.
2. It *returns* that initializer list, although we want a *"fire and forget"* function, which returns *nothing*.
3. It's possible that `f` is a function, which does not even return anything, in which case, this would not even compile.

The much more complicated `for_each` function fixes all these problems. It does the following things to achieve that:

1. It does not *return* the initializer list, but it *casts* the whole expression to void using `(void)std::initializer_list<int>{...}`.
2. Within the initializer expression, it wraps `f(xs)...` into an `(f(xs), 0)...` expression. This leads to the return value being *thrown away*, while `0` is put into the initializer list.
3. The `f(xs)` in the `(f(xs), 0)...` expression is again cast to void, so the return value is really not processed anywhere *if* it has any.

Putting all this together unluckily leads to an *ugly* construct, but it does it's work right and compiles with a whole variety of function objects, regardless of whether they return anything or what they return.

A nice detail of this technique is that the order in which the function calls are applied is guaranteed to be in a *strict sequence*.

 Casting anything using the old C-style notation `(void)expression` is advised against because C++ has its own cast operators. We should have used `reinterpret_cast<void>(expression)` instead, but this would have decreased the *readability* of the code further.

Implementing transform_if using std::accumulate and lambdas

Most developers who have used `std::copy_if` and `std::transform` may have asked themselves already, why there is no `std::transform_if`. The `std::copy_if` function copies items from a source range to a destination range, but *skips* the items that are not selected by a user-defined *predicate* function. The `std::transform` unconditionally copies all items from a source range to a destination range but transforms them in between. The transformation is provided by a user-defined function, which might do simple things, such as multiplying numbers or transforming items to completely different types.

Such functions have been there for a long time now, but there is *still* no `std::transform_if` function. In this section, we are going to implement this function. It would be easy to do this by just implementing a function that iterates over the ranges while copying all the items that are selected by a predicate function and transforming them in between. However, we'll use this occasion to delve deeper into lambda expressions.

How to do it...

We are going to build our own `transform_if` function which works by supplying `std::accumulate` with the right function objects:

1. We need to include some headers, as always:

   ```
   #include <iostream>
   #include <iterator>
   #include <numeric>
   ```

2. First, we will implement a function called `map`. It accepts an input-transforming function as parameter and returns a function object, which works well together with `std::accumulate`:

   ```
   template <typename T>
   auto map(T fn)
   {
   ```

3. What we return is a function object that accepts a *reduce* function. When this object is called with such a reduce function, it returns another function object, which accepts an *accumulator* and an input parameter. It calls the reduce function on this accumulator and the `fn` transformed input variable. Don't worry if this looks complicated, we'll put it together later and see how it really works:

```
return [=] (auto reduce_fn) {
    return [=] (auto accum, auto input) {
        return reduce_fn(accum, fn(input));
    };
};
}
```

4. Now we implement a function called `filter`. It works exactly the same way as the `map` function, but it leaves the input *untouched*, while the `map` function *transforms* it using a transform function. Instead, we accept a predicate function and *skip* input variables without reducing them in case they are not accepted by the predicate function:

```
template <typename T>
auto filter(T predicate)
{
```

5. The two lambda expressions have exactly the same function signature as the expressions in the `map` function. The only difference is that the `input` parameter is left untouched. The predicate function is used to distinguish if we call the `reduce_fn` function on the input or if we just reach the accumulator forward without any change:

```
return [=] (auto reduce_fn) {
    return [=] (auto accum, auto input) {
        if (predicate(input)) {
            return reduce_fn(accum, input);
        } else {
            return accum;
        }
    };
};
}
```

6. Now let's finally use those helpers. We instantiate iterators that let us read integer values from the standard input:

```
int main()
{
    std::istream_iterator<int> it {std::cin};
    std::istream_iterator<int> end_it;
```

7. Then we define a predicate function, even, which just returns true if we have an *even number*. The transformation function twice multiplies its integer parameter with the factor 2:

```
auto even  ([](int i) { return i % 2 == 0; });
auto twice ([](int i) { return i * 2; });
```

8. The std::accumulate function takes a range of values and *accumulates* them. Accumulating means *summing* the values up with the + operator in the default case. We want to provide our own accumulation function. This way, we do not maintain a *sum* of the values. What we do is we assign each value of the range to the dereferenced iterator, it, and then return this iterator after *advancing* it further:

```
auto copy_and_advance ([](auto it, auto input) {
    *it = input;
    return ++it;
});
```

9. Now we finally put together the pieces. We iterate over the standard input and provide an output, ostream_iterator, which prints to the terminal. The copy_and_advance function object works on that output iterator by assigning the user input integers to it. Assigning to the output iterator effectively *prints* the assigned items. But we only want the *even* numbers from the user input, and we want to *multiply* them. To achieve this, we wrap the copy_and_advance function into an even *filter* and then into a twice *mapper*:

```
std::accumulate(it, end_it,
    std::ostream_iterator<int>{std::cout, ", "},
    filter(even) (
        map(twice) (
            copy_and_advance
        )
    ));
std::cout << '\n';
}
```

10. Compiling and running the program leads to the following output. The values 1, 3, and 5 are dropped because they are not even, and the values 2, 4, and 6 are printed after they have been doubled:

```
$ echo "1 2 3 4 5 6" | ./transform_if
4, 8, 12,
```

How it works...

This recipe looks really complicated because we are nesting lambda expressions a lot. In order to understand how this works, let's first have a look at the inner workings of std::accumulate. This is how it will look like in a typical STL implementation:

```
template <typename T, typename F>
T accumulate(InputIterator first, InputIterator last, T init, F f)
{
    for (; first != last; ++first) {
        init = f(init, *first);
    }
    return init;
}
```

The function parameter, f, does the main work here, while the loop collects its results in the user provided init variable. In a usual example case, the iterator range may represent a vector of numbers, such as 0, 1, 2, 3, 4, and the init value is 0. The f function is then just a binary function that might calculate the *sum* of two items using the + operator.

In this example case, the loop just sums up all the items into the init variable, such as in init = (((0 + 1) + 2) + 3) + 4. Writing it down like this makes obvious that std::accumulate is just a general *folding* function. Folding a range means applying a binary operation to an accumulator variable and stepwise every item contained in the range (the result of each operation is then the accumulator value for the next one). As this function is so general, we can do all kinds of things with it, just like implementing std::transform_if! The f function is then also called the *reduce* function.

A very direct implementation of `transform_if` will look as follows:

```
template <typename InputIterator, typename OutputIterator,
          typename P, typename Transform>
OutputIterator transform_if(InputIterator first, InputIterator last,
                            OutputIterator out,
                            P predicate, Transform trans)
{
    for (; first != last; ++first) {
        if (predicate(*first)) {
            *out = trans(*first);
            ++out;
        }
    }
    return out;
}
```

This looks quite *similar* to `std::accumulate`, if we regard the parameter `out` as the `init` variable, and *somehow* get function `f` to substitute the if-construct and its body!

We actually did that. We constructed that if-construct and its body with the binary function object we provided as a parameter to `std::accumulate`:

```
auto copy_and_advance ([](auto it, auto input) {
    *it = input;
    return ++it;
});
```

The `std::accumulate` function puts the `init` variable into the binary function's `it` parameter. The second parameter is the current value from the source range per loop iteration step. *We* provided an *output iterator* as the `init` parameter of `std::accumulate`.. This way, `std::accumulate` does not calculate a sum, but forwards the items it iterates over to another range. This means that we just reimplemented `std::copy` without any predicate and transformation, yet.

The filtering using a predicate was added by us by wrapping the `copy_and_advance` function object into *another* function object, which employs a predicate function:

```
template <typename T>
auto filter(T predicate)
{
    return [=] (auto reduce_fn) {
        return [=] (auto accum, auto input) {
            if (predicate(input)) {
                return reduce_fn(accum, input);
            } else {
```

```
                        return accum;
                }
        };
    };
}
```

This construction does not look too simple at first but have a look at the `if` construct. If the `predicate` function returns `true`, it forwards the parameters to the `reduce_fn` function, which is `copy_and_advance` in our case. If the predicate returns `false`, the `accum` variable, which is the `init` variable of `std::accumulate`, is just returned without change. This implements the *skipping* part of a filter operation. The `if` construct is located within the inner lambda expression, which has the same binary function signature as the `copy_and_advance` function, which makes it a fitting substitute.

Now we are able to *filter* but are still not *transforming*. This is done with the `map` function helper:

```
template <typename T>
auto map(T fn)
{
    return [=] (auto reduce_fn) {
        return [=] (auto accum, auto input) {
            return reduce_fn(accum, fn(input));
        };
    };
}
```

This code looks much easier. It again contains an inner lambda expression, which has the same signature as `copy_and_advance` has, so it can substitute it. The implementation just forwards the input values but *transforms* the *right* parameter of the binary function call with the `fn` function.

Later, when we used those helpers, we wrote the following expression:

```
filter(even)(
    map(twice)(
        copy_and_advance
    )
)
```

The `filter(even)` call captures the `even` predicate and gives us a function, which takes a binary function in order to wrap it into *another* binary function, which does additional *filtering*. The `map(twice)` function does the same with the `twice` transformation function but wraps the binary function, `copy_and_advance`, into another binary function, which always *transforms* the right parameter.

Without any optimization, we would get a horribly complicated nested construction of functions that call functions and do only a very little amount of work in between. However, it is a very simple task for the compiler to optimize all the code. The resulting binary is as simple as if it resulted from a more direct implementation of `transform_if`. We pay nothing in terms of performance this way. But what we get is a very nice composability of functions because we were able to stick the `even` predicate together with the `twice` transformation function, nearly as simply as if they were *lego* bricks.

Generating cartesian product pairs of any input at compile time

Lambda expressions in combination with parameter packs can be used for complex tasks. In this section, we will implement a function object that accepts an arbitrary number of input parameters and generates the **cartesian product** of this set with *itself*.

The cartesian product is a mathematical operation. It is noted as A x B, meaning the cartesian product of set A and set B. The result is another *single set*, which contains pairs of *all* item combinations of the sets A and B. The operation basically means, *combine every item from A with every item from B.* The following diagram illustrates the operation:

		B		
		1	2	3
	x	(x, 1)	(x, 2)	(x, 3)
A	y	(y, 1)	(y, 2)	(y, 3)
	z	(z, 1)	(z, 2)	(z, 3)

In the preceding diagram, if A = (x, y, z), and B = (1, 2, 3), then the cartesian product is (x, 1), (x, 2), (x, 3), (y, 1), (y, 2), and so on.

If we decide that A and B are the *same* set, say (1, 2), then the cartesian product of that is (1, 1), (1, 2), (2, 1), and (2, 2). In some cases, this might be declared *redundant*, because the combination of items with *themselves* (like in (1, 1)) or redundant combinations of (1, 2) and (2, 1) may not be needed. In such a case, the cartesian product can be filtered with a simple rule.

In this section, we will implement the cartesian product without any loops but with lambda expressions and parameter pack unpacking.

How to do it...

We implement a function object that accepts a function, f, and a set of parameters. The function object will *create* the cartesian product of the parameter set, *filter* out the redundant parts, and *call* the f function with each of them:

1. We only need to include the STL header that is needed for printing:

   ```
   #include <iostream>
   ```

2. Then, we define a simple helper function that prints a pair of values, and we begin implementing the main function:

   ```
   static void print(int x, int y)
   {
       std::cout << "(" << x << ", " << y << ")\n";
   }

   int main()
   {
   ```

3. The hard part starts now. We first implement a helper for the cartesian function that we are going to implement in the next step. This function accepts a parameter, f, which will be the print function when we use it later. The other parameters are x and the parameter pack rest. These contain the actual items of which we want to have the cartesian product. Look at the f(x, rest) expression: for x=1 and rest=2, 3, 4, this will result in calls such as f(1, 2); f(1, 3); f(1, 4);. The (x < rest) test is for removing redundancy in the generated pairs. We will look at this in more detail later:

   ```
   constexpr auto call_cart (
       [=](auto f, auto x, auto ...rest) constexpr {
           (void)std::initializer_list<int>{
               (((x < rest)
                   ? (void)f(x, rest)
                   : (void)0)
               ,0)...
           };
       });
   ```

4. The `cartesian` function is the most complex piece of code in this whole recipe. It accepts the parameter pack `xs` and returns a function object that captures it. The returned function object accepts a function object, `f`.

For a parameter pack, `xs=1, 2, 3`, the inner lambda expression will generate the following calls: `call_cart(f, `**`1`**`, 1, 2, 3)`; `call_cart(f, `**`2`**`, 1, 2, 3)`; `call_cart(f, `**`3`**`, 1, 2, 3)`;. From that range of calls, we can generate all the cartesian product pairs we need.

Note that we use the . . . notation for expanding the `xs` parameter pack *twice*, which looks weird at first. The first occurrence of . . . expands the entire `xs` parameter pack into the `call_cart` call. The second occurrence leads to multiple `call_cart` calls with a differing *second* parameter:

```
constexpr auto cartesian ([=](auto ...xs) constexpr {
    return [=] (auto f) constexpr {
        (void) std::initializer_list<int>{
            ((void) call_cart(f, xs, xs...), 0)...
        };
    };
});
```

5. Now, let's generate the cartesian product of the numeric set `1, 2, 3` and print the pairs. Without the redundant pairs, this should result in the number pairs, `(1, 2)`, `(2, 3)`, and `(1, 3)`. More combinations are not possible if we ignore the order and do not want the same number in one pair. This means that we do *not* want `(1, 1)`, and consider `(1, 2)` and `(2, 1)` the *same* pair.

First, we let `cartesian` generate a function object that already contains all possible pairs and accepts our print function. Then, we use it to let our `print` function being called with all these pairs.

We declare the `print_cart` variable, `constexpr`, so we can guarantee that the function object it holds (and all the pairs it generates) is created at compile time:

```
constexpr auto print_cart (cartesian(1, 2, 3));

print_cart(print);
}
```

6. Compiling and running yields the following output, just as expected. Play around with the code by removing the `(x < xs)` conditional in the `call_cart` function and see that we get the full cartesian product with redundant pairs and the same number pairs:

```
$ ./cartesian_product
(1, 2)
(1, 3)
(2, 3)
```

How it works...

That was another really complicated-looking lambda expression construct. But as soon as we understand this thoroughly, we will not be confused by any lambda expression anytime soon!

So, let's have a detailed look at it. We should get a mental picture of what needs to happen:

$$1, 2, 3 \longrightarrow \begin{array}{l} 1, [1, 2, 3] \longrightarrow (1, 1), (1, 2), (1, 3) \\ 2, [1, 2, 3] \longrightarrow (2, 1), (2, 2), (2, 3) \\ 3, [1, 2, 3] \longrightarrow (3, 1), (3, 2), (3, 3) \end{array}$$

These are three steps:

1. We take our set 1, 2, 3 and compose *three new* sets from it. The first part of each of these sets is consecutively a single item from the set, and the second part is the whole set itself.
2. We combine the first item with every item from the set and get as many *pairs* out of it.
3. From these resulting pairs, we only pick the ones that are *not redundant* (as for example (1, 2) and (2, 1) are redundant) and not same-numbered (as for example (1, 1)).

Now, back to the implementation:

```
constexpr auto cartesian ([=](auto ...xs) constexpr {
    return [=](auto f) constexpr {
        (void)std::initializer_list<int>{
            ((void)call_cart(f, xs, xs...), 0)...
        };
    };
});
```

The inner expression, `call_cart(xs, xs...)`, exactly represents the separation of (1, 2, 3) into those new sets, such as `1, [1, 2, 3]`. The full expression, `((void)call_cart(f, xs, xs...), 0)...` with the other `...` outside, does this separation for every value of the set, so we also get `2, [1, 2, 3]` and `3, [1, 2, 3]`.

Step 2 and step 3 are done by `call_cart`:

```
auto call_cart ([](auto f, auto x, auto ...rest) constexpr {
    (void)std::initializer_list<int>{
        (((x < rest)
            ? (void)f(x, rest)
            : (void)0)
        ,0)...
    };
});
```

Parameter `x` always contains the single value picked from the set, and `rest` contains the whole set again. Let's ignore the `(x < rest)` conditional at first. Here, the expression `f(x, rest)`, together with the `...` parameter pack expansion generates the function calls `f(1, 1)`, `f(1, 2)`, and so on, which results in the pairs being printed. This was step 2.

Step 3 is achieved by filtering out only the pairs where `(x < rest)` applies.

We made all lambda expressions and the variables holding them `constexpr`. By doing so, we can now guarantee that the compiler will evaluate their code at compile time and compile a binary that already contains all the number pairs instead of calculating them at runtime. Note that this *only* happens if all the function arguments we provide to a constexpr function are *known at compile time* already.

5
STL Algorithm Basics

We will cover the following recipes in this chapter:

- Copying items from containers to other containers
- Sorting containers
- Removing specific items from containers
- Transforming the contents of containers
- Finding items in ordered and unordered vectors
- Limiting the values of a vector to a specific numeric range with `std::clamp`
- Locating patterns in strings with `std::search` and choosing the optimal implementation
- Sampling large vectors
- Generating permutations of input sequences
- Implementing a dictionary merging tool

Introduction

The STL does not only contain data structures but also *algorithms*, of course. While data structures help *store* and *maintain* data in different ways with different motivations and targets, algorithms apply specific *transformations* to the data in such data structures.

Let's have a look at a standard task, such as summing up items from a vector. This can be done easily by looping over the vector and summing up all the items into an accumulator variable called `sum`:

```
vector<int> v {100, 400, 200 /*, ... */ };

int sum {0};
for (int i : v) { sum += i; }

cout << sum << '\n';
```

But because this is quite a standard task, there is also an STL algorithm for this:

```
cout << accumulate(begin(v), end(v), 0) << '\n';
```

In this case, the handcrafted loop variant is not much longer, and it is also not significantly harder to read than a one-liner which says what it does: `accumulate`. In a lot of cases, however, it is awkward to read a 10-line code loop just to realize, "Did I just have to study the whole loop in order to understand that it does a standard task, X?", rather than seeing one line of code, which uses a standard algorithm whose name clearly states what it does, such as `accumulate`, `copy`, `move`, `transform`, or `shuffle`.

The basic idea is to provide a rich variety of algorithms that can be used by programmers on a daily basis in order to reduce the need to repeatedly reimplement them. This way, programmers can just use off the shelf algorithm implementations and concentrate on the *new* problems, instead of wasting time on problems that *already have been solved* by the STL. Another perspective is correctness--if a programmer implements the same thing again and again for a hundred times, there is some probability that this may introduce a slight *error* in one or the other attempt. This would be completely unnecessary and also very *embarrassing* if, for example, it is pointed out by a colleague during code review, whereas at the same time, a standard algorithm could have been used.

Another important point of STL algorithms is *efficiency*. Many STL algorithms provide multiple *specialized* implementations of the same algorithm, which do things differently, depending on the *iterator type* they are being used with. For example, if all the elements in a vector of integers should be zeroed, this can be done with the STL algorithm `std::fill`. Because the iterator of a vector can already tell the compiler that it iterates over *contiguous* memory, it can select the implementation of `std::fill` which uses the C procedure `memset`. If the programmer changes the container type from `vector` to `list`, then the STL algorithm cannot use `memset` any longer and has to iterate over the list in order to zero the items individually. In case the programmer uses `memset` himself, the implementation would be unnecessarily hardcoded to using vectors or arrays because most other data structures do not save their data in contiguous memory chunks. In most cases, it makes little sense to try to be smart, as the implementers of the STL may already have implemented the same ideas, which can be used for free.

Let's summarize the preceding points. Using STL algorithms is good for:

- **Maintainability**: The names of the algorithms already state in a straightforward manner what they do. Explicit loops are rarely both better to read and as data-structure agnostic as standard algorithms.
- **Correctness**: The STL has been written and reviewed by experts, and used and tested by so many people that you are pretty unlikely to reach the same degree of correctness when reimplementing the complex parts of it.
- **Efficiency**: STL algorithms are, by default, at least as efficient as most handcrafted loops.

Most algorithms work on *iterators*. The concept of how iterators work is already explained in `Chapter 3`, *Iterators*. In this chapter, we'll concentrate on using STL algorithms for different problems in order to get a feeling of how they can be profitably put to use. Showing *all* STL algorithms would blow up this book to a very boring C++ reference, although there is already a C++ reference publicly available.

The best way to become an STL ninja is having the C++ reference always at hand or, at least, saved in a browser bookmark. When solving a task, every programmer should have a look at it with the question back in his mind, "Is there an STL algorithm for my problem?", before writing code himself.

A very good and complete C++ reference is available for online viewing at:

`http://cppreference.com`

It can also be downloaded for offline viewing.

 In job interviews, good fluency with the STL algorithms is often regarded as an indicator of a strong knowledge of C++.

Copying items from containers to other containers

The most important STL data structures have iterator support. This means that it is at least possible to get iterators via `begin()` and `end()` functions, which point to the data structure's underlying payload data and allow to iterate over that data. The iteration always looks the same, no matter what kind of data structure is iterated over.

We can get iterators from vectors, lists, deques, maps, and so on. Using iterator adaptors, we can even get iterators as an interface to files, standard input, and standard output. Moreover, as we saw in the previous chapter, we can even wrap iterator interfaces around algorithms. Now, where we can access everything with iterators, we can combine them with STL algorithms, which accept iterators as parameters.

A really nice way to show how iterators help abstract the nature of different data structures away is the `std::copy` algorithm, which just copies items from one set of iterators to an output iterator. Where such algorithms are used, the nature of the underlying data structure is not really relevant any longer. In order to demonstrate this, we will play a bit with `std::copy`.

How to do it...

In this section, we will use different variants of `std::copy`:

1. Let's first include all headers we need for the data structures we use. Additionally, we declare that we use the `std` namespace:

```
#include <iostream>
#include <vector>
#include <map>
#include <string>
#include <tuple>
#include <iterator>
#include <algorithm>

using namespace std;
```

2. We will use pairs of integer and string values in the following. In order to nicely print them, we should first overload the `<<` stream operator for them:

```
namespace std {
ostream& operator<<(ostream &os, const pair<int, string> &p)
{
    return os << "(" << p.first << ", " << p.second << ")";
}
}
```

3. In the `main` function, we fill a `vector` of integer-string pairs with some default values. And we declare a `map` variable, which associates integer values with string values:

```
int main()
{
    vector<pair<int, string>> v {
        {1, "one"}, {2, "two"}, {3, "three"},
        {4, "four"}, {5, "five"}};
    map<int, string> m;
```

4. Now, we use `std::copy_n` to copy exactly three integer-string pairs from the front of the vector to the map. Because vectors and maps are completely different data structures, we need to transform the items from the vector using the `insert_iterator` adapter. The `std::inserter` function produces such an adapter for us. Please be always aware that using algorithms like `std::copy_n` combined with insert iterators is the most *generic* way to copy/insert items to other data structures, but not the *fastest*. Using the data structure-specific member functions for inserting items is usually the most efficient way:

```
copy_n(begin(v), 3, inserter(m, begin(m)));
```

5. Let's print what's in the map afterward. Throughout the book, we have often been printing a container's content using the `std::copy` function. The `std::ostream_iterator` helps a lot in that regard because it allows us to treat the user shell's standard output as *another container* we can copy data into:

```
auto shell_it (ostream_iterator<pair<int, string>>{cout,
                                                    ", "});
copy(begin(m), end(m), shell_it);
cout << '\n';
```

6. Let's clear the map again for the next experiment. This time, we *move* items from the vector to the map, and this time, it's *all* the items:

```
m.clear();
move(begin(v), end(v), inserter(m, begin(m)));
```

7. We print the new content of the map again. Moreover, as `std::move` is an algorithm that also alters the data *source*, we will print the source vector too. This way, we can see what happened to it when it acted as a move source:

```
copy(begin(m), end(m), shell_it);
cout << '\n';
copy(begin(v), end(v), shell_it);
cout << '\n';
}
```

8. Let's compile and run the program and see what it says. The first two lines are simple. They reflect what the map contained after applying the `copy_n` and move algorithms. The third line is interesting because it shows that the strings in the vector that we used as move source are now empty. This is because the content of the strings has not been copied but efficiently *moved* (which means that the map uses the string data in heap memory that was previously referenced by the string objects in the vector). We should usually not access items that were a move source before we reassigned them, but let's ignore that for the sake of this experiment:

```
$ ./copying_items
(1, one), (2, two), (3, three),
(1, one), (2, two), (3, three), (4, four), (5, five),
(1, ), (2, ), (3, ), (4, ), (5, ),
```

How it works...

As `std::copy` is one of the simplest STL algorithms, its implementation is very short. Let's have a look at how it could be implemented:

```
template <typename InputIterator, typename OutputIterator>
OutputIterator copy(InputIterator it, InputIterator end_it,
                    OutputIterator out_it)
{
    for (; it != end_it; ++it, ++out_it) {
        *out_it = *it;
    }
    return out_it;
}
```

This looks exactly as one would implement the copying of items from one iterable range to the other by hand, naively. At this point, one could also ask, "So why not implementing it by hand, the loop is simple enough and I don't even need the return value?", which is, of course, a good question.

While `std::copy` is not the best example for making code significantly shorter, a lot of other algorithms with more complex implementations are. What is not obvious is the hidden automatic optimization of such STL algorithms. If we happen to use `std::copy` with data structures that store their items in contiguous memory (as `std::vector` and `std::array` do), *and* the items themselves are *trivially copy assignable,* then the compiler will select a completely different implementation (which assumes the iterator types to be pointers):

```
template <typename InputIterator, typename OutputIterator>
OutputIterator copy(InputIterator it, InputIterator end_it,
                    OutputIterator out_it)
{
    const size_t num_items (distance(it, end_it));
    memmove(out_it, it, num_items * sizeof(*it));
    return it + num_items;
}
```

This is a simplified version of how the `memmove` variant of the `std::copy` algorithm can look in a typical STL implementation. It is *faster* than the standard loop version, and *this time,* it is also not as nice to read. But nevertheless, `std::copy` users automatically profit from it if their argument types comply with the requirements of this optimization. The compiler selects the fastest implementation possible for the chosen algorithm, while the user code nicely expresses *what* the algorithm does without tainting the code with too many details of the *how.*

STL algorithms often simply provide the best trade-off between *readability* and *optimal implementation.*

 Types are usually trivially copy assignable if they only consist of one or multiple (wrapped by a class/struct) scalar types or classes, which can safely be moved using `memcopy`/`memmove` without the need to invoke a user-defined copy assignment operator.

We also used `std::move`. It works exactly like `std::copy`, but it applies `std::move(*it)` to the source iterator in the loop in order to cast *lvalues* to *rvalues.* This makes the compiler select the move assignment operator of the target object instead of the copy assignment operator. For a lot of complex objects, this *performs* better but *destroys* the source object.

Sorting containers

Sorting values is quite a standard task, and it can be done in various ways. Every computer science student who was tortured with having to learn a majority of existing sorting algorithms (together with their performance and stability trade-offs for exams) knows that.

Because this is a solved problem, programmers should not waste their time in solving it *again*, except if it is for learning purposes.

How to do it...

In this section, we are going to play with `std::sort` and `std::partial_sort`:

1. First, we include all that's necessary and declare that we use the `std` namespace:

```
#include <iostream>
#include <algorithm>
#include <vector>
#include <iterator>
#include <random>

using namespace std;
```

2. We will print the state of a vector of integers multiple times, so let's abbreviate this task by writing a small procedure:

```
static void print(const vector<int> &v)
{
    copy(begin(v), end(v), ostream_iterator<int>{cout, ", "});
    cout << '\n';
}
```

3. We begin with a vector that contains some example numbers:

```
int main()
{
    vector<int> v {1, 2, 3, 4, 5, 6, 7, 8, 9, 10};
```

4. Because we will shuffle the vector multiple times in order to play with different sort functions, we need a random number generator:

```
random_device rd;
mt19937 g {rd()};
```

5. The `std::is_sorted` function tells us if the content of a container is sorted. This line should print 1:

```
cout << is_sorted(begin(v), end(v)) << '\n';
```

6. With `std::shuffle`, we shake around the content of the vector in order to sort it again later. The first two arguments denote the range that will be shuffled and the third argument is the random number generator:

```
shuffle(begin(v), end(v), g);
```

7. The `is_sorted` function should now return `false` so that 0 is printed, and the values in the vector should be the same but in a different order. We will see after we have printed both again to the shell:

```
cout << is_sorted(begin(v), end(v)) << '\n';
print(v);
```

8. Now, we reestablish the original item ordering by using `std::sort`. The same prints to the terminal should now again give us the sorted ordering from the beginning:

```
sort(begin(v), end(v));
cout << is_sorted(begin(v), end(v)) << '\n';
print(v);
```

9. Another interesting function is `std::partition`. Maybe, we do not want to fully sort the list because it is sufficient to just have the items that are smaller than some value at the front. So, let's *partition* the vector in order to move all the items that are smaller than 5 to the front and print it:

```
shuffle(begin(v), end(v), g);
partition(begin(v), end(v), [] (int i) { return i < 5; });
print(v);
```

10. The next sort-related function is `std::partial_sort`. We can use it to sort the content of a container, but only to some extent. It will put the N smallest of all vector elements in the first half of the vector in a sorted order. The rest will reside in the second half, which will not be sorted:

```
shuffle(begin(v), end(v), g);
auto middle (next(begin(v), int(v.size()) / 2));
partial_sort(begin(v), middle, end(v));
print(v);
```

11. What if we want to sort a data structure that has *no* comparison operator? Let's define one and make a vector of such items:

```
struct mystruct {
    int a;
    int b;
};
vector<mystruct> mv {{5, 100}, {1, 50}, {-123, 1000},
                     {3, 70}, {-10, 20}};
```

12. The `std::sort` function optionally accepts a comparison function as its third argument. Let's use that and provide it with such a function. Just to show that this is possible, we compare them by their *second* field, b. This way, they will appear in the order of `mystruct::b` and not `mystruct::a`:

```
sort(begin(mv), end(mv),
    [] (const mystruct &lhs, const mystruct &rhs) {
        return lhs.b < rhs.b;
    });
```

13. The last step is printing the sorted vector of `mystruct` items:

```
for (const auto &[a, b] : mv) {
    cout << "{" << a << ", " << b << "} ";
}
cout << '\n';
}
```

14. Let's compile and run our program.

The first 1 results from the `std::is_sorted` call after initializing the sorted vector. Then, we shuffled the vector and got a 0 from the second `is_sorted` call. The third line shows all the vector items after the shuffling. The next 1 is the result of the `is_sorted` call after sorting it again with `std::sort`.

Then, we shuffled the whole vector again and *partitioned* it using `std::partition`. We can see that all the items that are less than 5 are also to the left of 5 in the vector. All items that are greater than 5 are to its right. Apart from that, they seem shuffled.

The second last line shows the result of `std::partial_sort`. All items up to the middle appear strictly sorted but the rest do not.

In the last line, we can see our vector of `mystruct` instances. They are strictly sorted by their *second* member values:

```
$ ./sorting_containers
1
0
7, 1, 4, 6, 8, 9, 5, 2, 3, 10,
1
1, 2, 3, 4, 5, 6, 7, 8, 9, 10,
1, 2, 4, 3, 5, 7, 8, 10, 9, 6,
1, 2, 3, 4, 5, 9, 8, 10, 7, 6,
{-10, 20} {1, 50} {3, 70} {5, 100} {-123, 1000}
```

How it works...

We have used different algorithms, which have to do with sorting:

Algorithm	Purpose
std::sort	Accepts a range as arguments and simply sorts it.
std::is_sorted	Accepts a range as argument and tells *if* that range is sorted.
std::shuffle	This is, kind of, the *reverse* operation to sorting; it accepts a range as arguments and *shuffles* its items around.
std::partial_sort	Accepts a range as arguments and another iterator, which tells until where the input range should be sorted. Behind that iterator, the rest of the items appear unsorted.
std::partition	Accepts a range and a *predicate function*. All items for which the predicate function returns true are moved to the front of the range. The rest is moved to the back.

For objects that do not have a comparison operator < implementation, it is possible to provide custom comparison functions. These should always have a signature such as bool function_name(const T &lhs, const T &rhs) and should not have any side effects during execution.

There are also other algorithms such as std::stable_sort, which also sort but preserve the order of items with the same sort key and std::stable_partition.

std::sort has different implementations for sorting. Depending on the nature of the iterator arguments, it is implemented as selection sort, insertion sort, merge sort, or completely optimized for a smaller number of items. On the user side, we usually do not even need to care.

Removing specific items from containers

Copying, transforming, and filtering are perhaps the most common operations on ranges of data. In this section, we concentrate on filtering items.

Filtering items out of data structures, or simply removing specific ones, works completely differently for different data structures. In linked lists (such as `std::list`), for example, a node can be removed by making its predecessor point to its successor. After a node is removed from the link chain in this way, it can be given back to the allocator. In contiguously storing data structures (`std::vector`, `std::array`, and, to some extent, `std::deque`), items can only be removed by overwriting them with other items. If an item slot is marked to be removed, all the items that are behind it must be moved one slot further to the front in order to fill the gap. This sounds like a lot of hassle, but if we want to simply remove whitespace from a string, for example, this should be achievable without much code.

When having either data structure at hand, we do not really want to care *how* to remove an item. It should just happen. This is what `std::remove` and `std::remove_if` can do for us.

How to do it...

We will transform a vector's content by removing items in different ways:

1. Let's import all the needed headers and declare that we use the `std` namespace:

```
#include <iostream>
#include <vector>
#include <algorithm>
#include <iterator>

using namespace std;
```

2. A short print helper function will print our vector:

```
void print(const vector<int> &v)
{
    copy(begin(v), end(v), ostream_iterator<int>{cout, ", "});
    cout << '\n';
}
```

3. We'll begin with an example vector containing some simple integer values. We'll also print it, so we can see how it changes with the function we apply to it later:

```
int main()
{
    vector<int> v {1, 2, 3, 4, 5, 6};
    print(v);
```

4. Now let's remove all the items with the value 2 from the vector. std::remove moves the other items in a way that the one value 2 we actually have in the vector vanishes. Because the vector's actual content is shorter after removing items, std::remove returns us an iterator pointing to the *new end*. The items between the new end iterator and the old end iterator are to be considered garbage, so we tell the vector to *erase* them. We surround the two removal lines with a new scope because the new_end iterator is invalidated afterward anyway, so it can go out of scope immediately:

```
    {
        const auto new_end (remove(begin(v), end(v), 2));
        v.erase(new_end, end(v));
    }
    print(v);
```

5. Now let's remove all the *odd* numbers. In order to do so, we implement a predicate, which tells us if a number is odd and feed it into the std::remove_if function, which accepts such predicates:

```
    {
        auto odd_number ([](int i) { return i % 2 != 0; });
        const auto new_end (
            remove_if(begin(v), end(v), odd_number));
        v.erase(new_end, end(v));
    }
    print(v);
```

6. The next algorithm we try out is `std::replace`. We use it to overwrite all values of 4 with the value 123. The `std::replace` function also exists as `std::replace_if`, which also accepts predicate functions:

```
replace(begin(v), end(v), 4, 123);
print(v);
```

7. Let's pump completely new values into the vector and create two new empty vectors in order to do another experiment with those:

```
v = {1, 2, 3, 4, 5, 6, 7, 8, 9, 10};
vector<int> v2;
vector<int> v3;
```

8. Then, we implement a predicate for odd numbers again and another predicate function, which tells the opposite if a number is even:

```
auto odd_number  ([](int i) { return i % 2 != 0; });
auto even_number ([](int i) { return i % 2 == 0; });
```

9. The next two lines do exactly the same thing. They copy *even* values to the vectors, v2 and v3. The first line does this with the `std::remove_copy_if` algorithm, which copies everything from a source container to another container which does *not* fulfill the predicate constraint. The other line uses `std::copy_if`, which copies everything that *does* fulfill the predicate constraint:

```
remove_copy_if(begin(v), end(v),
               back_inserter(v2), odd_number);
copy_if(begin(v), end(v),
        back_inserter(v3), even_number);
```

10. Printing both the vectors should now result in the same output:

```
print(v2);
print(v3);
}
```

11. Let's compile and run the program. The first output line shows the vector after its initialization. The second line shows it after removing all the values of 2. The next line shows the result of removing all the odd numbers. Before the fourth line, we replaced all the values of 4 with 123.

The last two lines show vectors v2 and v3:

```
$ ./removing_items_from_containers
1, 2, 3, 4, 5, 6,
1, 3, 4, 5, 6,
4, 6,
123, 6,
2, 4, 6, 8, 10,
2, 4, 6, 8, 10,
```

How it works...

We have used different algorithms, which have to do with filtering:

Algorithm	Purpose
std::remove	Accepts a range and a value as arguments and removes any occurrence of the value. Returns a new end iterator of the modified range.
std::replace	Accepts a range and two values as arguments and replaces all the occurrences of the first value with the second value.
std::remove_copy	Accepts a range, an output iterator, and a value as arguments and copies all the values that are *not* equal to the given value from the range to the output iterator.
std::replace_copy	Works similar to std::replace but analogous to std::remove_copy. The source range is not altered.
std::copy_if	Works like std::copy but additionally accepts a predicate function as an argument in order to copy only the values that the predicate accepts, which makes it a *filter* function.

 For every one of the listed algorithms, there also exists an *_if version, which accepts a predicate function instead of a value, which then decides which values are to be removed or replaced.

Transforming the contents of containers

If `std::copy` is the simplest STL algorithm for application on ranges, `std::transform` is the second simplest STL algorithm. Just as `copy`, it copies items from one range to another but additionally accepts a transformation function. This transformation function can alter the value of the input type before it is assigned to an item in the destination range. Furthermore, it can even construct a completely different type, which is useful if the source range and destination range differ in their payload item types. It is simple to use but still very useful, which makes it an ordinary standard component used in portable day-to-day programs.

How to do it...

In this section, we are going to use `std::transform` in order to modify the items of a vector while copying them:

1. As always, we first need to include all the necessary headers and to spare us some typing, we declare that we use the `std` namespace:

```
#include <iostream>
#include <vector>
#include <string>
#include <sstream>
#include <algorithm>
#include <iterator>

using namespace std;
```

2. A vector with some simple integers will do the job as an example source data structure:

```
int main()
{
    vector<int> v {1, 2, 3, 4, 5};
```

3. Now, we copy all the items to an `ostream_iterator` adapter in order to print them. The `transform` function accepts a function object, which accepts items of the container payload type and transforms them during each copy operation. In this case, we calculate the *square* of each number item, so the code will print the squares of the items in the vector without us having to store them anywhere:

```
transform(begin(v), end(v),
    ostream_iterator<int>{cout, ", "},
    [] (int i) { return i * i; });
cout << '\n';
```

4. Let's do another transformation. From the number 3, for example, we could generate a nicely readable string such as 3^2 = 9. The following `int_to_string` function object does just that using the `std::stringstream` object:

```
auto int_to_string ([](int i) {
    stringstream ss;
    ss << i << "^2 = " << i * i;
    return ss.str();
});
```

5. The function we just implemented returns us string values from integer values. We could also say it *maps* from integers to strings. Using the `transform` function, we can copy all such mappings from the integer vector into a string vector:

```
vector<string> vs;
transform(begin(v), end(v), back_inserter(vs),
          int_to_string);
```

6. After printing those, we're done:

```
copy(begin(vs), end(vs),
    ostream_iterator<string>{cout, "\n"});
}
```

7. Let's compile and run the program:

```
$ ./transforming_items_in_containers
1, 4, 9, 16, 25,
1^2 = 1
2^2 = 4
3^2 = 9
4^2 = 16
5^2 = 25
```

How it works...

The `std::transform` function works exactly like `std::copy` but while copy-assigning the values from the source iterator to the destination iterator, it applies the user-provided transformation function to the value before assigning the result to the destination iterator.

Finding items in ordered and unordered vectors

Often, we need to tell *if* some kind of item exists within some range. And if it does, we often also need to modify it or to access other data associated with it.

There are different strategies for finding items. If the items are present in a sorted order, then we can do a binary search, which is faster than linearly going through the items one by one. If it is not sorted, we are stuck with linear traversal again.

The typical STL search algorithms can do both for us, so it's good to know them and their characteristics. This section is about the simple linear search algorithm `std::find`, the binary search version `std::equal_range`, and their variants.

How to do it...

In this section, we are going to use linear and binary search algorithms on a small example data set:

1. We first include all the necessary headers and declare that we use the `std` namespace:

```
#include <iostream>
#include <vector>
#include <list>
#include <algorithm>
#include <string>

using namespace std;
```

2. Our data set will consist of `city` structs, which just save a city's name, and its population count:

```
struct city {
    string name;
    unsigned population;
};
```

3. Search algorithms need to be able to compare one item to the other, so we overload the `==` operator for the `city` struct instances:

```
bool operator==(const city &a, const city &b) {
    return a.name == b.name && a.population == b.population;
}
```

4. We also want to print the `city` instances, so we overload the stream operator, `<<`:

```
ostream& operator<<(ostream &os, const city &city) {
    return os << "{" << city.name << ", "
             << city.population << "}";
}
```

5. Search functions typically return iterators. These iterators point to the item if they found it or, otherwise, to the end iterator of the underlying container. In the last case, we are not allowed to access such an iterator. Because we are going to print our search results, we implement a function that returns us another function object, which encapsulates the end iterator of a data structure. When used for printing, it will compare its iterator argument against the end iterator and then print the item or, otherwise, just <end>:

```
template <typename C>
static auto opt_print (const C &container)
{
    return [end_it (end(container))] (const auto &item) {
        if (item != end_it) {
            cout << *item << '\n';
        } else {
            cout << "<end>\n";
        }
    };
}
```

6. We start with an example vector of some German cities:

```
int main()
{
    const vector<city> c {
        {"Aachen",        246000},
        {"Berlin",        3502000},
        {"Braunschweig",  251000},
        {"Cologne",       1060000}
    };
```

7. Using this helper, we build a city printer function, which captures the end iterator of our city vector c:

```
auto print_city (opt_print(c));
```

8. We use `std::find` to find the item in the vector, which saves the city item of Cologne. At first, this search looks pointless because we get exactly the item we searched for. But we did not know its position in the vector before, and the `find` function returns us just that. However, we could, for example, make the operator `==` of the `city` struct that we overloaded only compare the city name, then we could search just using the city name, without even knowing its population. But that would not be a good design. In the next step, we will do it differently:

```
{
    auto found_cologne (find(begin(c), end(c),
        city{"Cologne", 1060000})));
    print_city(found_cologne);
}
```

9. Without knowing the population count of a city, and also without tampering with its `==` operator, we can search only by comparing its name with the vector's content. The `std::find_if` function accepts a predicate function object instead of a specific value. This way, we can search for the Cologne city item when we only know its name:

```
{
    auto found_cologne (find_if(begin(c), end(c),
        [] (const auto &item) {
            return item.name == "Cologne";
        }));
    print_city(found_cologne);
}
```

10. In order to make searching a bit prettier and expressive, we can implement predicate builders. The `population_higher_than` function object accepts a population size and returns us a function that tells if a `city` instance has a larger population than the captured value. Let's use it to search for a German city with more than two million inhabitants in our small example set. Within the given vector, that city is only Berlin:

```
{
    auto population_more_than ([](unsigned i) {
        return [=] (const city &item) {
            return item.population > i;
        };
    });
    auto found_large (find_if(begin(c), end(c),
        population_more_than(2000000)));
    print_city(found_large);
}
```

11. The search functions we just used, traverse our containers linearly. Thus they have a runtime complexity of *O(n)*. The STL also has binary search functions, which work within *O(log(n))*. Let's generate a new example data set, which just consists of some integer values, and build another `print` function for that:

    ```
    const vector<int> v {1, 2, 3, 4, 5, 6, 7, 8, 9, 10};

    auto print_int (opt_print(v));
    ```

12. The `std::binary_search` function returns boolean values and just tells us *if* it found an item, but it does *not* return the item itself. It is important that the container we are searching in is *sorted* because otherwise, binary search doesn't work correctly:

    ```
    bool contains_7 {binary_search(begin(v), end(v), 7)};
    cout << contains_7 << '\n';
    ```

13. In order to get the items we are searching for, we need other STL functions. One of them is `std::equal_range`. It does not return an iterator for the item we found, but a *pair* of iterators. The first iterator points to the first item that is *not smaller* than the value we've been looking for. The second iterator points to the first item that is *larger* than it. In our range, which goes from 1 to 10, the first iterator points to the actual 7, because it is the first item, that is not smaller than 7. The second iterator points to the 8 because it's the first item that is larger than 7. If we had multiple values of 7, both the iterators would, in fact, represent a *subrange* of items:

    ```
    auto [lower_it, upper_it] (
        equal_range(begin(v), end(v), 7));
    print_int(lower_it);
    print_int(upper_it);
    ```

14. If we just need one iterator; we can use `std::lower_bound` or `std::upper_bound`. The `lower_bound` function only returns an iterator to the first item that is not smaller than what we searched. The `upper_bound` function returns an iterator to the first item that is larger than what we searched for:

```
print_int(lower_bound(begin(v), end(v), 7));
print_int(upper_bound(begin(v), end(v), 7));
}
```

15. Let's compile and run the program to see if the output matches our assumptions:

```
$ ./finding_items
{Cologne, 1060000}
{Cologne, 1060000}
{Berlin, 3502000}
1
7
8
7
8
```

How it works...

These are the search algorithms we have used in this recipe:

Algorithm	Purpose
`std::find`	Accepts a search range and a comparison value as arguments. Returns an iterator that points to the first item equal to the comparison value. Searches linearly.
`std::find_if`	Works like `std::find` but uses a predicate function instead of a comparison value.
`std::binary_search`	Accepts a search range and a comparison value as arguments. Performs a binary search and returns `true` if the range contains that value.
`std::lower_bound`	Accepts a search range and a comparison value, and then performs a binary search for the first item that is *not smaller* than the comparison value. Returns an iterator pointing to that item.
`std::upper_bound`	Works like `std::lower_bound` but returns an iterator to the first item that is *larger* than the comparison value.

`std::equal_range`	Accepts a search range and a comparison value and, then, returns a pair of iterators. The first iterator is the result of `std::lower_bound` and the second iterator is the result of `std::upper_bound`.

All these functions accept custom comparison functions as an optional additional argument. This way, the search can be customized, as we did in the recipe.

Let's have a closer look at how `std::equal_range` works. Imagine that we have a vector, v = {0, 1, 2, 3, 4, 5, 6, 7, 7, 7, 8}, and call `equal_range(begin(v), end(v), 7)`; in order to perform a binary search for the value 7. As `equal_range` returns us a pair of lower bound and upper bound iterators, these should afterward denote the range {7, 7, 7}, as there are so many values of 7 in the sorted vector. Check out the following diagram for more clarity:

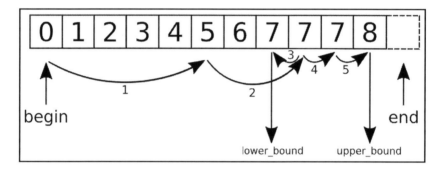

At first, `equal_range` uses the typical binary search approach until it trips into the range of values *not smaller* than the search value. Then, it splits up to a `lower_bound` call and an `upper_bound` call in order to bundle their return values in a pair as the return value.

In order to get a binary search function, which just returns the first item that fits the requirements, we could implement the following:

```
template <typename Iterator, typename T>
Iterator standard_binary_search(Iterator it, Iterator end_it, T value)
{
    const auto potential_match (lower_bound(it, end_it, value));
    if (potential_match != end_it && value == *potential_match) {
        return potential_match;
    }
    return end_it;
}
```

This function uses `std::lower_bound` in order to find the first item not smaller than `value`. The resulting `potential_match` can then have three different cases it points to:

- No item is not smaller than `value`. In this case, it is identical to `end_it`.
- The first item that is not smaller than `value` is also *larger* than `value`. Therefore we must signal that we did *not* find it by returning `end_it`.
- The item that `potential_match` points to is equal to `value`. So, it is not only a *potential* match, but it is an *actual* match. Therefore we can return it.

If our type `T` does not support the `==` operator, it must at least support the `<` operator for the binary search. Then, we can rewrite the comparison to `!(value < *potential_match) && !(*potential_match < value)`. If it is neither smaller, nor larger, then it must be equal.

One potential reason why the STL does not provide such a function out of the box is the missing knowledge about the possibility that there are multiple hits, as in the diagram where we have multiple values of `7`.

 Note that data structures such as `std::map`, `std::set`, and so on have their *own* `find` functions. These are, of course, faster than the more general algorithms because they are tightly coupled with the data structure's implementation and data representation.

Limiting the values of a vector to a specific numeric range with std::clamp

In a lot of applications, we get numeric data from somewhere. Before we can plot or otherwise process it, it may need to be normalized because the values differ randomly far from each other.

Usually, this would mean a little `std::transform` call over the data structure that holds all these values, combined with a simple *scaling* function. But if we *do not know* how large or small the values are, we need to go through the data first in order to find the right *dimensions* for the scaling function.

The STL contains useful functions for this purpose: `std::minmax_element` and `std::clamp`. Using these and combining them with some lambda expression glue, we can perform such a task easily.

How to do it...

In this section, we will normalize the values of a vector from an example numeric range to a normalized one in two different ways, one of them using `std::minmax_element` and one using `std::clamp`:

1. As always, we first need to include the following headers and declare that we use the `std` namespace:

```
#include <iostream>
#include <vector>
#include <algorithm>
#include <iterator>

using namespace std;
```

2. We implement a function for later use, which accepts the minimum and maximum values of a range, and a new maximum so that it can project values from the old range to a smaller range that we want to have. The function object takes such values and returns another function object, which does exactly that transformation. For the sake of simplicity, the new minimum is 0, so no matter what offset the old data had, its normalized values will always be relative to 0. For the sake of readability, we ignore the possibility that max and min could be of the same value, which would lead to a division by zero:

```
static auto norm (int min, int max, int new_max)
{
    const double diff (max - min);
    return [=] (int val) {
        return int((val - min) / diff * new_max);
    };
}
```

3. Another function object builder called `clampval` returns a function object that captures the min and max values and calls `std::clamp` on values with those values, in order to limit their values to this range:

```
static auto clampval (int min, int max)
{
    return [=] (int val) -> int {
        return clamp(val, min, max);
    };
}
```

4. The data we are going to normalize is a vector of varying values. This could be, for example, some kind of heat data, landscape height, or stock prices over time:

```
int main()
{
    vector<int> v {0, 1000, 5, 250, 300, 800, 900, 321};
```

5. In order to be able to normalize the data, we need the *highest* and *lowest* values. The `std::minmax_element` function is of a great help here. It returns us a pair of iterators to exactly those two values:

```
const auto [min_it, max_it] (
    minmax_element(begin(v), end(v)));
```

6. We will copy all the values from the first vector to a second one. Let's instantiate the second vector and prepare it to accept as many new items as we have in the first vector:

```
vector<int> v_norm;
v_norm.reserve(v.size());
```

7. Using `std::transform`, we copy the values from the first vector to the second. While copying the items, they will be transformed with our normalization helper. The minimum and maximum values of the old vector are 0 and 1000. The minimum and maximum values after normalization are 0 and 255:

```
transform(begin(v), end(v), back_inserter(v_norm),
          norm(*min_it, *max_it, 255));
```

8. Before we implement the other normalization strategy, we print what we have by now:

```
copy(begin(v_norm), end(v_norm),
     ostream_iterator<int>{cout, ", "});
cout << '\n';
```

9. We reuse the same normalized vector with the other helper `clampval`, which *clamps* the old range to the range with the minimum of 0 and the maximum of 255:

```
transform(begin(v), end(v), begin(v_norm),
          clampval(0, 255));
```

10. After printing these values too, we're done:

```
copy(begin(v_norm), end(v_norm),
    ostream_iterator<int>{cout, ", "});
cout << '\n';
}
```

11. Let's compile and run the program. Having the values reduced to values from 0 to 255, we could use them as brightness values for RGB color codes, for example:

```
$ ./reducing_range_in_vector
0, 255, 1, 63, 76, 204, 229, 81,
0, 255, 5, 250, 255, 255, 255, 255,
```

12. When we plot the data, we get the following graphs. As we can see, the approach where we *divide* the values by the difference between the min and max values is a linear transformation of the original data. The *clamped* graph loses some information. Both variations can be useful in different situations:

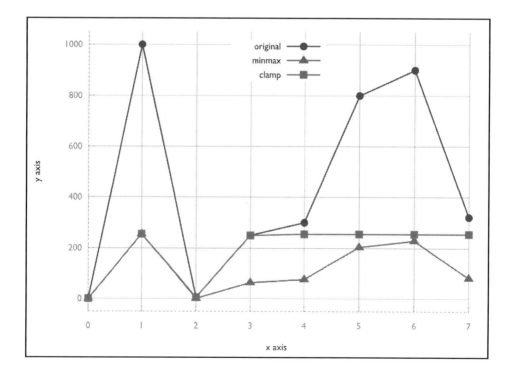

How it works...

Apart from `std::transform` we used two algorithms:

`std::minmax_element` simply accepts the begin and end iterators of an input range. It loops through the range and records the largest and the smallest element on the way to its end. These values are returned in a pair, which we then used for our scaling function.

The `std::clamp` function, in contrast, does not operate on an iterable range. It accepts three values: an input value, a min value, and a max value. The output of this function is the input value cut-off in a way that it lies between the allowed minimum and maximum. We could also write `max(min_val, min(max_val, x))` instead of `std::clamp(x, min_val, max_val)`.

Locating patterns in strings with std::search and choosing the optimal implementation

Searching for a string in a string is a slightly different problem than finding *one* object in a range. On the one hand, a string is, of course, an iterable range (of characters) too. On the other hand, finding a string in a string means finding a range in *another* range. And this comes along with multiple comparisons per potential match position, so we need some other algorithm for that.

`std::string` already contains a `find` function, which can do exactly what we are talking about; nevertheless we'll concentrate on `std::search` in this section. Although `std::search` might be used on strings mostly, it works on all kinds of containers. The more interesting feature of `std::search` is that since C++17, it has a slightly different additional interface and allows for simply exchanging the search algorithm itself. These algorithms are optimized and can be freely chosen by the user, depending on what is better in which use case. Additionally, we could implement our own search algorithms and plug them into `std::search` if we ever come up with anything better than what is already provided.

How to do it...

We will use the new `std::search` function with strings and try its different variations with searcher objects:

1. First, we will include all the necessary headers and declare that we use the `std` namespace:

```
#include <iostream>
#include <string>
#include <algorithm>
#include <iterator>
#include <functional>

using namespace std;
```

2. We will print substrings from the positions the search algorithm returns to us, so let's implement a little helper for that:

```
template <typename Itr>
static void print(Itr it, size_t chars)
{
    copy_n(it, chars, ostream_iterator<char>{cout});
    cout << '\n';
}
```

3. A *lorem-ipsum style* string will work as our example string, within which we will search a substring. In this case, this is `"elitr"`:

```
int main()
{
    const string long_string {
        "Lorem ipsum dolor sit amet, consetetur"
        " sadipscing elitr, sed diam nonumy eirmod"};
    const string needle {"elitr"};
```

4. The old `std::search` interface accepts the begin/end iterators of the string within which we are searching a specific substring and the begin/end iterators of the substring. It then returns an iterator pointing to the substring it was able to find. If it didn't find the string, the returned iterator will be the end iterator:

```
{
    auto match (search(begin(long_string), end(long_string),
                       begin(needle), end(needle)));
    print(match, 5);
}
```

5. The C++17 version of `std::search` does not accept two pairs of iterators but one pair of begin/end iterators and a *searcher* object. The `std::default_searcher` takes the begin/end pair of iterators of the substring that we are searching for in the larger string:

```
{
    auto match (search(begin(long_string), end(long_string),
        default_searcher(begin(needle), end(needle))));
    print(match, 5);
}
```

6. The point of this change is that it is easy to switch the search algorithm this way. The `std::boyer_moore_searcher` uses the *Boyer-Moore search algorithm* for a faster search:

```
{
    auto match (search(begin(long_string), end(long_string),
        boyer_moore_searcher(begin(needle),
                             end(needle))));
    print(match, 5);
}
```

7. The C++17 STL comes with three different searcher object implementations. The third one is the *Boyer-Moore-Horspool search algorithm* implementation:

```
    {
        auto match (search(begin(long_string), end(long_string),
            boyer_moore_horspool_searcher(begin(needle),
                                          end(needle)))));
        print(match, 5);
    }
}
```

8. Let's compile and run our program. We should see the same string everywhere if it runs correctly:

```
$ ./pattern_search_string
elitr
elitr
elitr
elitr
```

How it works...

We utilized four different ways to use `std::search` in order to get exactly the same result. Which one should we prefer in what situation?

Let's assume our large string within which we search the pattern is called s, and the pattern is called p. Then, `std::search(begin(s), end(s), begin(p), end(p));` and `std::search(begin(s), end(s), default_searcher(begin(p), end(p)));` do exactly the same thing.

The other searcher function objects are implemented with more sophisticated search algorithms:

- `std::default_searcher`: This redirects to legacy `std::search` implementation
- `std::boyer_moore_searcher`: This uses the *Boyer-Moore* search algorithm
- `std::boyer_moore_horspool_searcher`: This analogously uses the *Boyer-Moore-Horspool* algorithm

What makes the other algorithms so special? The Boyer-Moore algorithm was developed with a specific idea--the search pattern is compared with the string, beginning at the pattern's *end*, from right to left. If the character in the search string *differs* from the character in the pattern at the overlay position and does *not even occur* in the pattern, then it is clear that the pattern can be shifted over the search string by its *full length*. Have a look at the following diagram, where this happens in step 1. If the character being currently compared differs from the pattern's character at this position but is *contained* by the pattern, then the algorithm knows by how many characters the pattern needs to be shifted to the right in order to correctly align to at least that character, and then, it starts over with the right-to-left comparison. In the diagram, this happens in step 2. This way, the Boyer-Moore algorithm can omit a whole lot of *unnecessary* comparisons, compared with a naive search implementation:

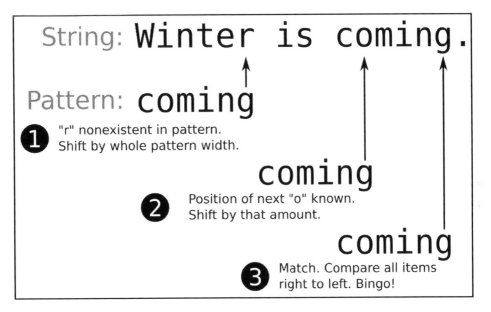

Of course, this would have become the new default search algorithm if it hadn't brought its own *trade-offs*. It is faster than the default algorithm, but it needs fast lookup data structures in order to determine which characters are contained in the search pattern and at which offset they are located. The compiler will select differently complex implementations of those, depending on the underlying types of which the pattern consists (varying between hash maps for complex types and primitive lookup tables for types such as char). In the end, this means that the default search implementation will be faster if the search string is not too large. If the search itself takes some significant time, then the Boyer-Moore algorithm can lead to performance gains in the dimension of a *constant factor*.

The **Boyer-Moore-Horspool** algorithm is a simplification of the Boyer-Moore algorithm. It drops the *bad character* rule, which leads to shifts of the whole pattern width if a search string character that does not occur in the pattern string is found. The trade-off of this decision is that it is *slightly slower* than the unmodified version of Boyer-Moore, but it also needs *fewer data structures* for its operation.

Do not try to *reason* about which algorithm *should* be faster in a specific case. Always *measure* the performance of your code with data samples that are typical for your users and base your decision on the *results*.

Sampling large vectors

When there are *very* large amounts of numeric data that need to be processed in some situations, it may not be possible to process it all in feasible time. In such situations, the data could be *sampled* in order to reduce the total amount of data for further processing, which then *speeds up* the whole program. In other situations, this might be done not to reduce the amount of work for processing but for *saving* or *transferring* the data.

A naive idea of sampling could be to only pick every N^{th} data point. This might be fine in a lot of cases, but in signal processing, for example, it *could* lead to a mathematical phenomenon called **aliasing**. If the distance between every sample is varied by a small random offset, aliasing can be reduced. Have a look at the following diagram, which shows an *extreme case* just to illustrate the point--while the original signal consists of a sine wave, the triangle points on the graph are sampling points that are sampled at exactly every *100th* data point. Unfortunately, the signal has the *same y-value* at these points! The graph which results from connecting the dots looks like a perfectly straight *horizontal line*. The square points, however, show what we get when we sample every `100 + random(-15, +15)` points. Here, the signal still looks very different from the original signal, but it is at least not completely *gone* as in the fixed step size sampling case.

The `std::sample` function does not add random alterations to sample points with fixed offset but chooses completely random points; therefore, it works a bit differently from this example:

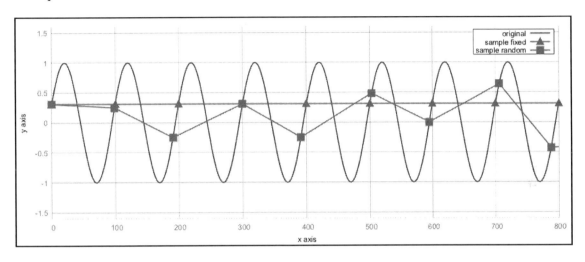

How to do it...

We will sample a very large vector of random data. This random data shows a normal distribution. After sampling it, the resulting points should still show a normal distribution, which we will check:

1. First, we need to include everything we use and declare that we use the `std` namespace in order to spare us some typing:

```
#include <iostream>
#include <vector>
#include <random>
#include <algorithm>
#include <iterator>
#include <map>
#include <iomanip>

using namespace std;
```

2. It is easier to play around with the code if we configure specific characteristics of our algorithm in their own constant variables. These are the size of the large random vector and the number of samples that we are going to take from it:

```
int main()
{
    const size_t data_points    {100000};
    const size_t sample_points {100};
```

3. The large, randomly filled vector should get numbers from a random number generator, which gives out numbers from a normal distribution. Any normal distribution can be characterized by the mean value and the standard deviation from the mean value:

```
    const int     mean {10};
    const size_t dev   {3};
```

4. Now, we set up the random generator. First, we instantiate a random device and call it once to get a seed for the constructor of a random generator. Then, we instantiate a distribution object that applies normal distribution to the random output:

```
    random_device rd;
    mt19937 gen {rd()};
    normal_distribution<> d {mean, dev};
```

5. Now, we instantiate a vector of integers and fill it with a lot of random numbers. This is achieved using the `std::generate_n` algorithm, which will call a generator function object to feed its return value into our vector using a `back_inserter` iterator. The generator function object just wraps around the `d(gen)` expression, which gets a random number from the random device and feeds it into the distribution object:

```
    vector<int> v;
    v.reserve(data_points);
    generate_n(back_inserter(v), data_points,
        [&] { return d(gen); });
```

6. Now, we instantiate another vector that will contain the much smaller set of samples:

```
vector<int> samples;
v.reserve(sample_points);
```

7. The `std::sample` algorithm works similar to `std::copy`, but it takes two additional parameters: the *number of samples*, which it shall take from the input range, and a *random number generator* object, which it will consult to get random sampling positions:

```
sample(begin(v), end(v), back_inserter(samples),
       sample_points, mt19937{random_device{}()});
```

8. We're already done with the sampling. The rest of the code is for displaying purposes. The input data has a normal distribution, and if the sampling algorithm works well, then the sampled vector should show a normal distribution too. To see how much of a normal distribution is left, we will print a *histogram* of the values:

```
map<int, size_t> hist;

for (int i : samples) { ++hist[i]; }
```

9. Finally, we loop over all the items in order to print our histogram:

```
for (const auto &[value, count] : hist) {
    cout << setw(2) << value << " "
         << string(count, '*') << '\n';
}
}
```

10. After compiling and running the program, we see that the sampled vector still roughly shows the characteristics of a normal distribution:

```
$ ./sampling_vectors
 1 *
 3 *
 4 **
 5 *****
 6 *****
 7 ******
 8 *************
 9 *************
10 *****************
11 *********
12 ********
13 *******
14 ***
15 ***
16 ***
```

How it works...

The `std::sample` algorithm is a new algorithm, which came with C++17. Its signature looks like this:

```
template<class InIterator, class OutIterator,
        class Distance, class UniformRandomBitGenerator>
OutIterator sample(InIterator first, InIterator last,
                SampleIterator out, Distance n,
                UniformRandomBitGenerator&& g);
```

The input range is denoted by the `first` and `last` iterators, while `out` is the output operator. These iterators have exactly the same function as in `std::copy`; items are copied from one range to the other. The `std::sample` algorithm is special in the regard that it will copy only a part of the input range because it samples only n items. It uses uniform distribution internally, so every data point in the source range gets chosen with the same probability.

Generating permutations of input sequences

When testing code that must deal with sequences of inputs where the order of the arguments is not important, it is beneficial to test whether it results in the same output for *all* possible permutations of that input. Such a test could, for example, check whether a self-implemented *sort* algorithm sorts correctly.

No matter for what reason we need all permutations of some value range, `std::next_permutation` can conveniently do it for us. We can invoke it on a modifiable range, and it changes the *order* of its items to the next *lexicographical permutation*.

How to do it...

In this section, we will write a program that reads multiple word strings from a standard input, and then we will use `std::next_permutation` to generate and print all the permutations of those strings:

1. First things first again; we include all the necessary headers and declare that we use the `std` namespace:

```
#include <iostream>
#include <vector>
#include <string>
#include <iterator>
#include <algorithm>

using namespace std;
```

2. We begin with a vector of strings, which we feed with the whole standard input. The next step is *sorting* the vector:

```
int main()
{
    vector<string> v {istream_iterator<string>{cin}, {}};
    sort(begin(v), end(v));
```

3. Now, we print the vector's content on the user terminal. Afterward, we call `std::next_permutation`. It systematically shuffles the vector to generate a permutation of its items, which we then print again. The `next_permutation` will return `false` as soon as the *last* permutation was reached:

```
do {
    copy(begin(v), end(v),
        ostream_iterator<string>{cout, ", "});
    cout << '\n';
} while (next_permutation(begin(v), end(v)));
}
```

4. Let's compile and run the function with some example input:

```
$ echo "a b c" | ./input_permutations
a, b, c,
a, c, b,
b, a, c,
b, c, a,
c, a, b,
c, b, a,
```

How it works...

The `std::next_permutation` algorithm is a bit weird to use. This is because it accepts only a begin/end pair of iterators and then returns `true` if it is able to find the next permutation. Otherwise, it returns `false`. But what does the *next permutation* even mean?

The algorithm with which `std::next_permutation` finds the next lexicographical order of the items, works as follows:

1. Find the largest index `i` such that `v[i - 1] < v[i]`. If there is none, then return `false`.
2. Now, find the largest index `j` such that `j >= i` and `v[j] > v[i - 1]`.
3. *Swap* the items at position `j` and position `i - 1`.
4. Reverse the order of the items from position `i` to the end of the range.
5. Return `true`.

The individually permuted orders we get out of this will always appear in the same sequence. In order to see all the possible permutations, we sorted the array first, because if we entered "c b a", for example, the algorithm would terminate *immediately*, as this already *is* the last lexicographic order of the elements.

Implementing a dictionary merging tool

Imagine that we have a sorted list of things, and someone else comes up with *another* sorted list of things, and we want to share the lists with each other. The best idea is to combine both the lists. The combination of both the lists should be sorted too, as this way, it is easy to look it up for specific items.

Such an operation is also called a **merge**. In order to merge two sorted ranges of items, we would intuitively create a new range and feed it with items from both the lists. For every item transfer, we would have to compare the frontmost items of our input ranges in order to always select the *smallest* one from what is left from the input. Otherwise, the output range would not be sorted any longer. The following diagram illustrates it better:

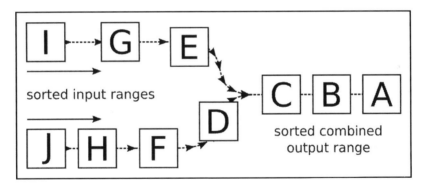

The std::merge algorithm can do exactly that for us, so we do not need to fiddle around too much. In this section, we will see how to use the algorithm.

How to do it...

We are going to build up a cheap dictionary of one-to-one mappings from English words to their German translations, and store them in `std::deque` structures. The program will read such a dictionary from a file and one from standard input, and print one large merged dictionary on the standard output again.

1. There are a lot of headers to include this time, and we declare that we use the `std` namespace:

   ```
   #include <iostream>
   #include <algorithm>
   #include <iterator>
   #include <deque>
   #include <tuple>
   #include <string>
   #include <fstream>

   using namespace std;
   ```

2. A dictionary entry should consist of a symmetric mapping from a string in one language to a string in another language:

   ```
   using dict_entry = pair<string, string>;
   ```

3. We are going to both print such pairs to the terminal and read them from user input, so we need to overload the << and >> operators:

   ```
   namespace std {
   ostream& operator<<(ostream &os, const dict_entry p)
   {
       return os << p.first << " " << p.second;
   }
   istream& operator>>(istream &is, dict_entry &p)
   {
       return is >> p.first >> p.second;
   }
   }
   ```

4. A helper function that accepts any input stream object will help us in building a dictionary from it. It constructs `std::deque` of dictionary entry pairs, and they are all read from the input stream until it is empty. Before returning it, we sort it:

```
template <typename IS>
deque<dict_entry> from_instream(IS &&is)
{
    deque<dict_entry> d {istream_iterator<dict_entry>{is}, {}};
    sort(begin(d), end(d));
    return d;
}
```

5. We create two individual dictionary data structures from different input streams. One input stream is opened from the `dict.txt` file, which we assume to exist. It contains word pairs, line by line. The other stream is the standard input:

```
int main()
{
    const auto dict1 (from_instream(ifstream{"dict.txt"}));
    const auto dict2 (from_instream(cin));
```

6. As the helper function, `from_instream`, has already sorted both the dictionaries for us, we can feed them directly into the `std::merge` algorithm. It accepts two input ranges via its begin/end iterator pairs, and one output. The output will be the user shell:

```
    merge(begin(dict1), end(dict1),
          begin(dict2), end(dict2),
          ostream_iterator<dict_entry>{cout, "\n"});
}
```

7. We can compile the program now, but before running it, we should create the `dict.txt` file with some example content. Let's fill it with some English words and their translations to German:

```
car        auto
cellphone  handy
house      haus
```

8. Now, we can launch the program while piping some English-German translations into its standard input. The output is a merged and still sorted dictionary, which contains the translations of both the inputs. We could create a new dictionary file from that:

```
$ echo "table tisch fish fisch dog hund" | ./dictionary_merge
car auto
cellphone handy
dog hund
fish fisch
house haus
table tisch
```

How it works...

The `std::merge` algorithm accepts two pairs of begin/end iterators, which denote the input ranges. These ranges must be *sorted*. The fifth parameter is an output iterator that accepts the incoming items during the merge.

There is also a variant called `std::inplace_merge`. This algorithm does the same as the other, but it does not need an output iterator because it works *in place*, as the name already suggests. It takes three parameters: a *begin* iterator, a *middle* iterator, and an *end* iterator. These iterators must all reference data in the same data structure. The middle iterator is at the same time the end iterator of the first range, and the begin iterator of the second range. This means that this algorithm handles a single range, which actually consists of two consecutive ranges, such as, for example, {A, C, B, D}. The first subrange is {A, C} and the second subrange is {B, D}. The `std::inplace_merge` algorithm can then merge both within the same data structure, which results in {A, B, C, D}.

6
Advanced Use of STL Algorithms

We will cover the following recipes in this chapter:

- Implementing a trie class using STL algorithms
- Implementing a search input suggestion generator with tries
- Implementing the Fourier transform formula with STL numeric algorithms
- Calculating the error sum of two vectors
- Implementing an ASCII Mandelbrot renderer
- Building our own algorithm - split
- Composing useful algorithms from standard algorithms - gather
- Removing consecutive whitespace between words
- Compressing and decompressing strings

Introduction

In the last chapter, we visited basic STL algorithms and performed simple tasks with them in order to get a feeling of the typical STL interface: most STL algorithms accept one or more ranges in the form of iterator pairs as input/output parameters. They often also accept predicate functions, custom comparison functions, or transformation functions. In the end, they mostly return iterators again because these can often be fed into some other algorithm afterward.

While STL algorithms aim to be minimal, their interfaces also try to be as general as possible. This enables maximum code reuse potential but does not always look too pretty. An experienced C++ coder who knows all algorithms has a better time reading other people's code if it tries to express as many ideas using STL algorithms as possible. This leads to a maximized common ground of comprehension between coder and reader. A programmer's brain can simply parse the name of a well-known algorithm more quickly than it can understand a complex loop, which does a mainly similar, but in some detail a slightly different, job.

At this point, we are using STL data structures so intuitively that we can nicely avoid pointers, raw arrays, and other crude legacy structures. The next step is lifting our comprehension of STL algorithms up to the levels where we can avoid the use of handcrafted loop-control-structure complexes by expressing them in terms of well-known STL algorithms. Often, this is a real improvement because code becomes simply shorter and more readable while at the same time being more general and data-structure agnostic. It is practically always possible to avoid writing handcrafted loops and taking an algorithm out of the `std` namespace instead, but sometimes, it admittedly leads to *awkward code*. We are not going to differentiate between what is awkward and what is not; we'll only explore the possibilities.

In this chapter, we will use STL algorithms in creative ways in order to look for new horizons and to see how things can be implemented with modern C++. On the way, we will implement our own STL-like algorithms, which can easily be combined with existing data structures and other algorithms designed in the same way. We will also *combine* existing STL algorithms to get *new* algorithms, which were not there before. Such combined algorithms allow for more complex algorithms on top of the existing ones, while they are themselves extremely short and readable this way. While on this little trip, we will also see where exactly STL algorithms suffer from reusability or prettiness. Only when we know *all* the ways well can we best decide which way is the right one.

Implementing a trie class using STL algorithms

The so-called **trie** data structure poses an interesting way to store data in an easily searchable manner. When segmenting sentences of text into lists of words, it is often possible to combine the first few words that some sentences have in common.

Let's have a look at the following diagram, where the sentences "hi how are you" and "hi how do you do" are saved in a tree-like data structure. The first words they have in common are "hi how", and then they differ and split up like a tree:

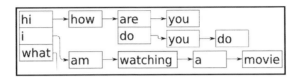

Because the trie data structure combines common prefixes, it is also called *prefix tree*. It is very easy to implement such a data structure with what the STL gives us already. This section concentrates on implementing our own trie class.

How to do it...

In this section, we will implement our own prefix tree only made from STL data structures and algorithms.

1. We will include all the headers from the STL parts we use and declare that we use the std namespace by default:

```
#include <iostream>
#include <optional>
#include <algorithm>
#include <functional>
#include <iterator>
#include <map>
#include <vector>
#include <string>

using namespace std;
```

2. The entire program revolves around a trie for which we have to implement a class first. In our implementation, a trie is basically a recursive map of maps. Every trie node contains a map, which maps from an instance of the payload type T to the next trie node:

```
template <typename T>
class trie
{
    map<T, trie> tries;
```

3. The code for inserting new item sequences is simple. The user provides a begin/end iterator pair and we loop through it recursively. If the user input sequence is {1, 2, 3}, then we look up 1 in the subtrie and then look up 2 in the next subtrie, in order to get the subtrie for 3. If any of those subtries did not exist before, they are implicitly added by the [] operator of std::map:

```
public:
    template <typename It>
    void insert(It it, It end_it) {
        if (it == end_it) { return; }
        tries[*it].insert(next(it), end_it);
    }
```

4. We also define convenience functions, which enable the user to just provide a container of items, which are then automatically queried for iterators:

```
    template <typename C>
    void insert(const C &container) {
        insert(begin(container), end(container));
    }
```

5. In order to allow the user to write my_trie.insert({"a", "b", "c"});, we must help the compiler a bit to correctly deduce all the types from that line, so we add a function, which overloads the insert interface with an initializer_list parameter:

```
    void insert(const initializer_list<T> &il) {
        insert(begin(il), end(il));
    }
```

6. We will also want to see what's in a trie, so we need a print function. In order to print, we can do a depth-first-search through the trie. On the way from the root node down to the first leaf, we record all payload items we have seen already. This way, we have a complete sequence together once we reach the leaf, which is trivially printable. We see that we reached a leaf when tries.empty() is true. After the recursive print call, we pop off the last added payload item again:

```
    void print(vector<T> &v) const {
        if (tries.empty()) {
            copy(begin(v), end(v),
                ostream_iterator<T>{cout, " "});
            cout << '\n';
        }
        for (const auto &p : tries) {
            v.push_back(p.first);
```

```
            p.second.print(v);
            v.pop_back();
        }
    }
```

7. The recursive `print` function passes around a reference to a printable list of payload items, but the user should call it without any parameters. Therefore, we define a parameterless `print` function, which constructs the helper list object:

```
void print() const {
    vector<T> v;
    print(v);
}
```

8. Now that we can construct and print tries, we may want to search for subtries. The idea is that if the trie contains sequences such as {a, b, c} and {a, b, d, e}, and we give it a sequence, {a, b}, for search, it would return us the subtrie that contains the {c} and {d, e} parts. If we find the subtrie, we return a `const` reference to it. The possibility exists that there is no such subtrie in case the trie does not contain the sequence we are searching for. In such cases, we still need to return *something*. The `std::optional` is a nice helper because we can return an *empty* optional object if there is no match:

```
template <typename It>
optional<reference_wrapper<const trie>>
subtrie(It it, It end_it) const {
    if (it == end_it) { return ref(*this); }
    auto found (tries.find(*it));
    if (found == end(tries)) { return {}; }
    return found->second.subtrie(next(it), end_it);
}
```

9. Similar to the `insert` method, we provide a one-parameter version of the `subtrie` method, which automatically takes iterators from the input container:

```
template <typename C>
auto subtrie(const C &c) {
    return subtrie(begin(c), end(c));
}
};
```

10. That's already it. Let's put the new trie class to use in our main function by instantiating a trie specialized on `std::string` objects and fill it with some example content:

```
int main()
{
    trie<string> t;
    t.insert({"hi", "how", "are", "you"});
    t.insert({"hi", "i", "am", "great", "thanks"});
    t.insert({"what", "are", "you", "doing"});
    t.insert({"i", "am", "watching", "a", "movie"});
```

11. Let's first print the whole trie:

```
    cout << "recorded sentences:\n";
    t.print();
```

12. Then we obtain the subtrie for all the input sentences that start with `"hi"`, and print it:

```
    cout << "\npossible suggestions after \"hi\":\n";
    if (auto st (t.subtrie(initializer_list<string>{"hi"}));
        st) {
        st->get().print();
    }
}
```

13. Compiling and running the program shows that it does indeed return us only the two sentences that start with `"hi"`, when we query the trie for exactly that subtrie:

```
$ ./trie
recorded sentences:
hi how are you
hi i am great thanks
i am watching a movie
what are you doing
possible suggestions after "hi":
how are you
i am great thanks
```

How it works...

Interestingly, the code for word sequence *insertion* is shorter and simpler than the code for *looking up* a given word sequence in a subtrie. So, let's first have a look at the insertion code:

```
template <typename It>
void trie::insert(It it, It end_it) {
    if (it == end_it) { return; }
    tries[*it].insert(next(it), end_it);
}
```

The pair of iterators, `it` and `end_it`, represent the word sequence to be inserted. The `tries[*it]` element looks up the first word in the sequence in the subtrie, and then, `.insert(next(it), end_it)` restarts the same function on that lower subtrie, with the iterator one word *further* advanced. The `if (it == end_it) { return; }` line just aborts the recursion. The empty `return` statement does *nothing*, which is a bit weird at first. All the insertion happens in the `tries[*it]` statement. The bracket operator `[]` of `std::map` either returns an existing item for the given key or it *creates* one with that key. The associated value (the mapped type is a trie in this recipe) is constructed from its default constructor. This way, we are *implicitly creating* a new trie branch whenever we are looking up unknown words.

Looking up in a subtrie looks more complicated because we were not able to *hide* so much in implicit code:

```
template <typename It>
optional<reference_wrapper<const trie>>
subtrie(It it, It end_it) const {
    if (it == end_it) { return ref(*this); }
    auto found (tries.find(*it));
    if (found == end(tries)) { return {}; }

    return found->second.subtrie(next(it), end_it);
}
```

This code basically revolves around the `auto found (tries.find(*it));` statement. Instead of looking up the next deeper trie node using the bracket operator (`[]`), we use `find`. If we use the `[]` operator for lookups, the trie will *create* missing items for us, which is *not* what we want when just looking up whether an item exists! (By the way, try doing that. The class method is `const`, so this will not even be possible. This can be quite a life saver, which helps us in preventing bugs.)

Another scary looking detail is the return type, `optional<reference_wrapper<const trie>>`. We chose `std::optional` as the wrapper because it is possible that there is no such subtrie for the input sequence we are looking for. If we only inserted `"hello my friend"`, there will be no `"goodbye my friend"` sequence to look up. In such cases, we just return `{}`, which gives the caller an empty optional object. This still does not explain why we use `reference_wrapper` instead of just writing `optional<const trie &>`. The point here is that an optional instance with a member variable of the `trie&` type is not reassignable and hence would not compile. Implementing a reference using `reference_wrapper` leads to reassignable objects.

Implementing a search input suggestion generator with tries

When entering something into a search engine on the Internet, the interface often tries to guess how the full search query will look. This guessing is usually based on popular search queries from the past. Sometimes, such search engine guesses are quite funny because it appears that people type weird queries into search engines.

In this section, we are going to use the trie class that we implemented in the previous recipe and build a little search query suggestion engine.

How to do it...

In this section, we will implement a terminal app, which accepts some input and then tries to guess what the user might want to look for, based on a cheap text file database:

1. As always, includes come first, and we define that we use the std namespace:

```
#include <iostream>
#include <optional>
#include <algorithm>
#include <functional>
#include <iterator>
#include <map>
#include <list>
#include <string>
#include <sstream>
#include <fstream>

using namespace std;
```

2. We use the trie implementation from the trie recipe:

```
template <typename T>
class trie
{
    map<T, trie> tries;
public:
    template <typename It>
    void insert(It it, It end_it) {
        if (it == end_it) { return; }
        tries[*it].insert(next(it), end_it);
    }

    template <typename C>
    void insert(const C &container) {
        insert(begin(container), end(container));
    }
    void insert(const initializer_list<T> &il) {
        insert(begin(il), end(il));
    }
    void print(list<T> &l) const {
        if (tries.empty()) {
            copy(begin(l), end(l),
                ostream_iterator<T>{cout, " "});
            cout << '\n';
        }
        for (const auto &p : tries) {
```

```
                l.push_back(p.first);
                p.second.print(l);
                l.pop_back();
            }
        }
        void print() const {
            list<T> l;
            print(l);
        }
        template <typename It>
        optional<reference_wrapper<const trie>>
        subtrie(It it, It end_it) const {
            if (it == end_it) { return ref(*this); }
            auto found (tries.find(*it));
            if (found == end(tries)) { return {}; }
          return found->second.subtrie(next(it), end_it);
        }
        template <typename C>
        auto subtrie(const C &c) const {
            return subtrie(begin(c), end(c));
        }
    };
```

3. Let's add a little helper function that prints a line that prompts the user to enter some text:

```
static void prompt()
{
    cout << "Next input please:\n > ";
}
```

4. In the main function, we open a text file, which acts as our sentence database. We read that text file line by line and feed those lines into a trie:

```
int main()
{
    trie<string> t;
    fstream infile {"db.txt"};
    for (string line; getline(infile, line);) {
        istringstream iss {line};
        t.insert(istream_iterator<string>{iss}, {});
    }
```

5. Now that we have constructed the trie from the content in the text file, we need to implement an interface for the user to query it. We prompt the user to enter some text and wait for a whole line of input:

```
    prompt();
    for (string line; getline(cin, line);) {
        istringstream iss {line};
```

6. With that text input, we query the trie in order to get a subtrie from it. If we have such an input sequence in the text file already, then we can print how the input can be continued, just as in the search engine suggestion feature. If we do not find a matching subtrie, we just tell the user:

```
        if (auto st (t.subtrie(istream_iterator<string>{iss}, {}));
            st) {
            cout << "Suggestions:\n";
            st->get().print();
        } else {
            cout << "No suggestions found.\n";
        }
```

7. Afterward, we print the prompt text again and wait for the next line of user input. That's it.

```
        cout << "---------------\n";
        prompt();
    }
}
```

8. Before thinking about launching the program, we need to fill some content into
   `db.txt`. The input can be really anything, and it does not even need to be sorted.
   Each line of text will be one trie sequence:

```
do ghosts exist
do goldfish sleep
do guinea pigs bite
how wrong can you be
how could trump become president
how could this happen to me
how did bruce lee die
how did you learn c++
what would aliens look like
what would macgiver do
what would bjarne stroustrup do
...
```

9. We need to create `db.txt` before we can run the program. Its content could look
   like this:

```
hi how are you
hi i am great thanks
do ghosts exist
do goldfish sleep
do guinea pigs bite
how wrong can you be
how could trump become president
how could this happen to me
how did bruce lee die
how did you learn c++
what would aliens look like
what would macgiver do
what would bjarne stroustrup do
what would chuck norris do
why do cats like boxes
why does it rain
why is the sky blue
why do cats hate water
why do cats hate dogs
why is c++ so hard
```

10. Compiling and running the program and entering some input looks like the following:

```
$ ./word_suggestion
Next input please:
 > what would
Suggestions:
aliens look like
bjarne stroustrup do
chuck norris do
macgiver do
----------------
Next input please:
 > why do
Suggestions:
cats hate dogs
cats hate water
cats like boxes
----------------
Next input please:
 >
```

How it works...

How a trie works was explained in the last recipe, but how we fill it and how we query it looks a bit strange here. Let's have a closer look at the code snippet that fills the empty trie with the content of the text database file:

```
fstream infile {"db.txt"};
for (string line; getline(infile, line);) {
    istringstream iss {line};
    t.insert(istream_iterator<string>{iss}, {});
}
```

The loop fills the string `line` with the content of the text file, line by line. Then, we copy the string into an `istringstream` object. From such an input stream object, we can create an `istream_iterator`, which is useful because our trie does not only accept a container instance for looking up subtries but also primarily iterators. This way, we do not need to construct a vector or a list of words and can directly consume the string. The last piece of unnecessary memory allocations could be avoided by *moving* the content of `line` into `iss`. Unfortunately, `std::istringstream` does not provide a constructor that accepts `std::string` values to be *moved*. It will *copy* its input string, nevertheless.

When reading the user's input to look it up in the trie, we use exactly the same strategy but we do not use an input *file* stream. We use `std::cin`, instead. This works completely identically for our use case because `trie::subtrie` works with iterators just as `trie::insert` does.

There's more...

It is possible to add *counter variables* to each node of the trie. This way, it is possible to count *how often* a prefix occurs in some input. From that, we could *sort* our suggestions by their occurrence frequency, which is actually what search engines do. Word suggestions for smartphone touchscreen text input could also be implemented this way.

This modification is left as an exercise for the reader.

Implementing the Fourier transform formula with STL numeric algorithms

The **Fourier transformation** is a very important and famous formula in signal processing. It was invented nearly 200 years ago, but with computers, the number of use cases for it really skyrocketed. It is used in audio/image/video compression, audio filters, medical imaging devices, cell phone apps that identify music tracks while listening to them on the fly, and so on.

Because of the vastness of general numeric application scenarios (not only because of the Fourier transformation of course), the STL also tries to be useful in the context of numeric computation. The Fourier transformation is only one example among them but a tricky one too. The formula itself looks like the following:

$$\hat{s}_k = \sum_{j=0}^{N-1} s_j \cdot e^{-i2\pi\frac{kj}{N}}$$

The transformation it describes is basically a *sum*. Each element of the sum is the multiplication of a data point of the input signal vector, and the expression *exp(-2 * i * ...)*. The maths behind this is a bit scary for everyone who does not know about complex numbers (or who just does not like maths), but it is also not really necessary to completely understand the maths in order to *implement* it. When having a close look at the formula, it says that the sum symbol loops over every data point of the signal (which is N elements long) using the loop variable j. The variable k is another loop variable because the Fourier transformation is not for calculating a single value, but a vector of values. In this vector, every data point represents the intensity and phase of a certain repetitive wave frequency, which is or is not a part of the original signal. When implementing this with manual loops, we will end up with code similar to the following:

```
csignal fourier_transform(const csignal &s) {
    csignal t(s.size());
    const double pol {-2.0 * M_PI / s.size()};

    for (size_t k {0}; k < s.size(); ++k) {
        for (size_t j {0}; j < s.size(); ++j) {
            t[k] += s[j] * polar(1.0, pol * k * j);
        }
    }
    return t;
}
```

The csignal type may be an std::vector vector of complex numbers. For complex numbers, there is an std::complex STL class, which helps represent those. The std::polar function basically does the *exp(-i * 2 * ...)* part.

This works well already, but we are going to implement it using STL tools.

How to do it...

In this section, we are going to implement the Fourier transformation and its backward transformation and then play around with it to transform some signals:

1. First, we include all the headers and declare that we use the std namespace:

```
#include <iostream>
#include <complex>
#include <vector>
#include <algorithm>
#include <iterator>
#include <numeric>
```

```
#include <valarray>
#include <cmath>

using namespace std;
```

2. A data point of a signal is a complex number and shall be represented by
   `std::complex`, specialized on the `double` type. This way, the type alias `cmplx`
   stands for two coupled `double` values, which represent the *real* and the *imaginary*
   parts of a complex number. A whole signal is a vector of such items, which we
   alias to the `csignal` type:

```
using cmplx   = complex<double>;
using csignal = vector<cmplx>;
```

3. In order to iterate over an up-counting numeric sequence, we take the *numeric
   iterator* from the numeric iterator recipe. The variables k and j in the formula
   shall iterate over such sequences:

```
class num_iterator {
    size_t i;
public:
    explicit num_iterator(size_t position) : i{position} {}
    size_t operator*() const { return i; }
    num_iterator& operator++() {
        ++i;
        return *this;
    }
    bool operator!=(const num_iterator &other) const {
        return i != other.i;
    }
};
```

4. The Fourier transformation function shall just take a signal and return a new signal. The returned signal represents the Fourier transformation of the input signal. As the back transformation from a Fourier transformed signal back to the original signal is very similar, we provide an optional `bool` parameter, which chooses the transformation direction. Note that `bool` parameters are generally bad practice, especially if we use multiple `bool` parameters in a function signature. Here we just have one for brevity.
   The first thing we do is allocate a new signal vector with the size of the initial signal:

```
csignal fourier_transform(const csignal &s, bool back = false)
{
    csignal t (s.size());
```

5. There are two factors in the formula, which always look the same. Let's pack them in their own variables:

```
        const double pol {2.0 * M_PI * (back ? -1.0 : 1.0)};
        const double div {back ? 1.0 : double(s.size())};
```

6. The `std::accumulate` algorithm is a fitting choice for executing formulas that sum up items. We are going to use `accumulate` on a range of up-counting numeric values. From these values, we can form the individual summands of each step. The `std::accumulate` algorithm calls a binary function on every step. The first parameter of this function is the current value of the part of sum that was already calculated in the previous steps, and its second parameter is the next value from the range. We look up the value of signal s at the current position and multiply it with the complex factor, `pol`. Then, we return the new partly sum. The binary function is wrapped into *another* lambda expression because we are going to use different values of j for every `accumulate` call. Because this is a two-dimensional loop algorithm, the inner lambda is for the inner loop and the outer lambda is for the outer loop:

```
        auto sum_up ([=, &s] (size_t j) {
            return [=, &s] (cmplx c, size_t k) {
                return c + s[k] *
                    polar(1.0, pol * k * j / double(s.size()));
            };
        });
```

7. The inner loop part of the Fourier transform is now executed by `std::accumulate`. For every `j` position of the algorithm, we calculate the sum of all the summands for positions $i = 0...N$. This idea is wrapped into a lambda expression, which we will execute for every data point in the resulting Fourier transformation vector:

```
auto to_ft ([=, &s](size_t j){
    return accumulate(num_iterator{0},
                      num_iterator{s.size()},
                      cmplx{},
                      sum_up(j))
        / div;
});
```

8. None of the Fourier code has been executed until this point. We only prepared a lot of functional code, which we'll put to action now. An `std::transform` call will generate values $j = 0...N$, which is our outer loop. The transformed values all go to the vector `t`, which we then return to the caller:

```
transform(num_iterator{0}, num_iterator{s.size()},
          begin(t), to_ft);
return t;
}
```

9. We are going to implement some functions that help us set up function objects for signal generation. The first one is a cosine signal generator. It returns a lambda expression that can generate a cosine signal with the period length that was provided as a parameter. The signal itself can be of arbitrary length, but it has a fixed period length. A period length of N means that the signal will repeat itself after N steps. The lambda expression does not accept any parameters. We can call it repeatedly, and for every call, it returns us the signal data point of the next point in time:

```
static auto gen_cosine (size_t period_len){
    return [period_len, n{0}] () mutable {
        return cos(double(n++) * 2.0 * M_PI / period_len);
    };
}
```

10. Another signal we are going to generate is the square wave. It oscillates between the values −1 and +1 and has no other values than those. The formula looks complicated, but it simply transforms the linearly up-counting value n to +1 and −1, with an oscillating period length of `period_len`.

    Note that we initialize n to a different value from 0 this time. This way, our square wave starts at the phase where its output values begin at +1:

```
static auto gen_square_wave (size_t period_len)
{
    return [period_len, n{period_len*7/4}] () mutable {
        return ((n++ * 2 / period_len) % 2) * 2 - 1.0;
    };
}
```

11. Generating an actual signal from such generators can be achieved by allocating a new vector and filling it with the values generated from repeating signal generator function calls. The `std::generate` does this job. It accepts a begin/end iterator pair and a generator function. For every valid iterator position, it does `*it = gen()`. By wrapping this code into a function, we can easily generate signal vectors:

```
template <typename F>
static csignal signal_from_generator(size_t len, F gen)
{
    csignal r (len);
    generate(begin(r), end(r), gen);
    return r;
}
```

12. In the end, we need to print the resulting signals. We can simply print a signal by copying its values into an output stream iterator, but we need to transform the data first because the data points of our signals are complex value pairs. At this point, we are only interested in the real value part of every data point; hence, we throw it through an `std::transform` call, which extracts only this part:

```
static void print_signal (const csignal &s)
{
    auto real_val ([](cmplx c) { return c.real(); });
    transform(begin(s), end(s),
              ostream_iterator<double>{cout, " "}, real_val);
    cout << '\n';
}
```

13. The Fourier formula is now implemented, but we have no signals to transform yet. That is what we do in the main function. Let's first define a standard signal length to which all the signals comply.

```
int main()
{
    const size_t sig_len {100};
```

14. Let's now generate signals, transform them, and print them, which happens in the next three steps. The first step is to generate a cosine signal and a square wave signal. Both have the same total signal length and period length:

```
auto cosine      (signal_from_generator(sig_len,
        gen_cosine(     sig_len / 2)));
auto square_wave (signal_from_generator(sig_len,
        gen_square_wave(sig_len / 2)));
```

15. We have a cosine function and a square wave signal now. In order to generate a third one in the middle between them, we take the square wave signal and calculate its Fourier transform (saved in the `trans_sqw` vector). The Fourier transform of a square wave has a specific form, and we are going to manipulate it a bit. All items from index 10 till (`signal_length` − 10) are set to 0.0. The rest remains *untouched*. Transforming this altered Fourier transformation back to the signal time representation will give us a different signal. We will see how that looks in the end:

```
auto trans_sqw (fourier_transform(square_wave));
fill (next(begin(trans_sqw), 10), prev(end(trans_sqw), 10), 0);
auto mid (fourier_transform(trans_sqw, true));
```

16. Now we have three signals: `cosine`, `mid`, and `square_wave`. For every signal, we print the signal itself and its Fourier transformation. The output of the whole program will consist of six very long lines of printed double value lists:

```
print_signal(cosine);
print_signal(fourier_transform(cosine));
print_signal(mid);
print_signal(trans_sqw);
print_signal(square_wave);
print_signal(fourier_transform(square_wave));
}
```

17. Compiling and running the program leads to the terminal getting filled with lots of numeric values. If we plot the output, we get the following image:

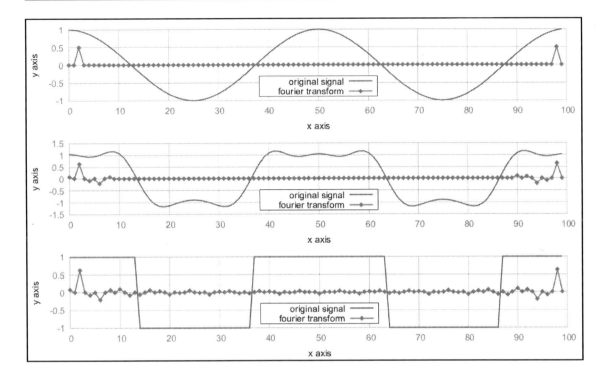

How it works...

This program contains two complicated sections. One is the Fourier transformation itself, and the other is the generation of signals with mutable lambda expressions.

Let's concentrate on the Fourier transformation first. The core of the raw loop implementation (which we did not use for our implementation but had a look at in the introduction) looks like the following:

```
for (size_t k {0}; k < s.size(); ++k) {
    for (size_t j {0}; j < s.size(); ++j) {
        t[k] += s[j] * polar(1.0, pol * k * j / double(s.size()));
    }
}
```

With the STL algorithms, `std::transform` and `std::accumulate`, we wrote code, which can be summarized to the following pseudo code:

```
transform(num_iterator{0}, num_iterator{s.size()}, ...
    accumulate((num_iterator0}, num_iterator{s.size()}, ...
        c + s[k] * polar(1.0, pol * k * j / double(s.size())));
```

The result is exactly the same compared with the loop variant. This is arguably an example situation where the strict use of STL algorithms does *not* lead to better code. Nevertheless, this algorithm implementation is agnostic over the data structure choice. It would also work on lists (although that would not make too much sense in our situation). Another upside is that the C++17 STL algorithms are easy to *parallelize* (which we examine in another chapter of this book), whereas raw loops have to be restructured to support multiprocessing (unless we use external libraries like *OpenMP* for example, but these do actually restructure the loops for us).

The other complicated part was the signal generation. Let's have another look at `gen_cosine`:

```
static auto gen_cosine (size_t period_len)
{
    return [period_len, n{0}] () mutable {
        return cos(double(n++) * 2.0 * M_PI / period_len);
    };
}
```

Each instance of the lambda expression represents a function object that modifies its own state on every call. Its state consists of the variables, `period_len` and n. The n variable is the one which is modified on every call. The signal has a different value at every time point, and `n++` represents the increasing time points. In order to get an actual signal vector out of it, we created the helper `signal_from_generator`:

```
template <typename F>
static auto signal_from_generator(size_t len, F gen)
{
    csignal r (len);
    generate(begin(r), end(r), gen);
    return r;
}
```

This helper allocates a signal vector with a length of choice and calls `std::generate` to fill it with data points. For every item of the vector `r`, it calls the function object `gen` once, which is just the kind of self-modifying function object we can create with `gen_cosine`.

 Unfortunately, the STL way does *not* make this code more elegant. As soon as the ranges library joins the STL club (which is hopefully the case with C++20), this will most probably change.

Calculating the error sum of two vectors

There are different possibilities to calculate the numerical *error* between a target value and an actual value. Measuring the difference between signals consisting of many data points usually involves loops and subtraction of corresponding data points, and so on.

One simple formula to calculate this error between a signal `a` and a signal `b` is the following:

$$e = \sum_{i=0}^{N-1} \left(a_i - b_i \right)^2$$

For every *i*, it calculates *a[i] - b[i]*, squares that difference (this way, negative and positive differences become comparable), and, finally, sums those values up. This is again a situation where one could use a loop, but for fun reasons, we will do it with an STL algorithm. The good thing is that we get data-structure independence for free this way. Our algorithm will work on vectors and on list-like data structures, where no direct indexing is possible.

How to do it...

In this section, we are going to create two signals and calculate their error sum:

1. As always, the include statements come first. Then, we declare that we use the `std` namespace:

    ```
    #include <iostream>
    #include <cmath>
    #include <algorithm>
    #include <numeric>
    ```

```
#include <vector>
#include <iterator>

using namespace std;
```

2. We are going to calculate the error sum of two signals. The two signals will be a sine wave and a copy of it, but with a different value type--the original sine wave is saved in a vector of `double` variables and its copy is saved in a vector of `int` variables. Because copying a value from a `double` variable to an `int` variable cuts its decimal part after the point, we have some *loss*. Let's name the vector of `double` values as, which stands for *analog signal* and the vector of `int` values ds, which stands for *digital signal*. The error sum will then later tell us how large the loss actually is:

```
int main()
{
    const size_t sig_len {100};
    vector<double> as (sig_len); // a for analog
    vector<int>    ds (sig_len); // d for digital
```

3. In order to generate a sine wave signal, we implement a little lambda expression with a *mutable* counter value n. We can call it as often as we want, and for every call, it will return us the value for the next point in time of a sine wave. The `std::generate` call fills the signal vector with the generated signal, and the `std::copy` call copies all the values from the vector of `double` variables to the vector of `int` variables afterward:

```
auto sin_gen ([n{0}] () mutable {
    return 5.0 * sin(n++ * 2.0 * M_PI / 100);
});
generate(begin(as), end(as), sin_gen);
copy(begin(as), end(as), begin(ds));
```

4. Let's first print the signals, as this way, they can be plotted later:

```
copy(begin(as), end(as),
    ostream_iterator<double>{cout, " "});
cout << '\n';
copy(begin(ds), end(ds),
    ostream_iterator<double>{cout, " "});
cout << '\n';
```

5. Now to the actual error sum, we use `std::inner_product` because it can easily be adapted to calculate the difference between every two corresponding elements of our signal vectors. It will iterate through both the ranges, pick items at the same corresponding positions in the ranges, calculate the difference between them, square it, and accumulate the results:

```
cout << inner_product(begin(as), end(as), begin(ds),
                      0.0, std::plus<double>{},
                      [](double a, double b) {
                          return pow(a - b, 2);
                      })
     << '\n';
}
```

6. Compiling and running the program gives us two long lines of signal output and a third line, which contains a single output value, which is the error between both the signals. The error is `40.889`. If we calculate the error in a continuous manner, first for the first pair of items, then for the first two pairs of items, then for the first three pairs of items, and so on, then we get the accumulated error curve, which is visible on the plotted graph as shown:

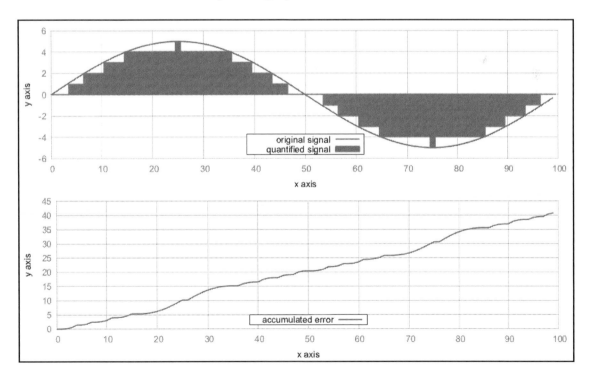

How it works...

In this recipe, we stuffed the task of looping through two vectors, getting the difference between their corresponding values, squaring them, and finally summing them up into one `std::inner_product` call. On the way, the only code we crafted ourselves was the lambda expression `[](double a, double b) { return pow(a - b, 2); }`, which takes the difference of its arguments and squares it.

A glance at a possible implementation of `std::inner_product` shows us why and how this works:

```
template<class InIt1, class InIt2, class T, class F, class G>
T inner_product(InIt1 it1, InIt1 end1, InIt2 it2, T val,
                F bin_op1, G bin_op2)
{
    while (it1 != end1) {
        val = bin_op1(val, bin_op2(*it1, *it2));
        ++it1;
        ++it2;
    }
    return value;
}
```

The algorithm accepts a pair of begin/end iterators of the first range, and another begin iterator of the second range. In our case, they are the vectors from which we want to calculate the error sum. The next character is the initial value `val`. We have initialized it to `0.0`. Then, the algorithm accepts two binary functions, namely `bin_op1` and `bin_op2`.

At this point, we might realize that this algorithm is really similar to `std::accumulate`. The only difference is that `std::accumulate` works on only *one* range. If we exchange the `bin_op2(*it1, *it2)` statement with `*it`, then we have basically restored the `accumulate` algorithm. We can, therefore, regard `std::inner_product` as a version of `std::accumulate` that *zips* a pair of input ranges.

In our case, the *zipper* function is `pow(a - b, 2)`, and that's it. For the other function, `bin_op1`, we chose `std::plus<double>` because we want all the squares to be summed together.

Implementing an ASCII Mandelbrot renderer

In 1975, the mathematician Benoît Mandelbrot coined the term **fractal**. A fractal is a mathematical figure or set, which has certain interesting mathematical properties, but in the end, it just looks like a piece of art. Fractals also look *infinitely repetitive* when being zoomed in. One of the most popular fractals is the *Mandelbrot set*, which can be seen on the following poster:

A picture of the Mandelbrot set can be generated by iterating a specific formula:

$$z_0 = 0$$
$$z_{n+1} = z_n^2 + c$$

The variables *z* and *c* are *complex* numbers. The Mandelbrot set consists of all such values of *c* for which the formula *converges* if it is applied often enough. This is the colored part of the poster. Some values converge earlier, some converge later, so they can be visualized with different colors. Some do not converge at all--these are painted black.

The STL comes with the useful `std::complex` class, and we will try to implement the formula without explicit loops, just for the sake of getting to know the STL better.

How to do it...

In this section, we are going to print the same image from the wall poster as a little piece of ASCII art in the terminal:

1. First, we include all the headers and declare that we use the `std` namespace:

```
#include <iostream>
#include <algorithm>
#include <iterator>
#include <complex>
#include <numeric>
#include <vector>

using namespace std;
```

2. The Mandelbrot set and formula operate on complex numbers. So, we define a type alias, `cmplx` to be of class `std::complex`, specializing on double values.

```
using cmplx = complex<double>;
```

3. It is possible to hack together all the code for an ASCII Mandelbrot image in something around 20 lines of code, but we will implement each logical step in a separate form, and then assemble all the steps in the end. The first step is implementing a function that scales from integer coordinates to floating point coordinates. What we have in the beginning is columns and rows of character positions on the terminal. What we want are complex-typed coordinates in the coordinate system of the Mandelbrot set. For this, we implement a function that accepts parameters that describe the geometry of the user terminal coordinate system, and the system we want to transform to. Those values are used to build a lambda expression, which is returned. The lambda expression accepts an `int` coordinate and returns a `double` coordinate:

```
static auto scaler(int min_from, int max_from,
                   double min_to, double max_to)
```

```
{
    const int    w_from   {max_from - min_from};
    const double w_to      {max_to - min_to};
    const int    mid_from  {(max_from - min_from) / 2 + min_from};
    const double mid_to    {(max_to - min_to) / 2.0 + min_to};
    return [=] (int from) {
        return double(from - mid_from) / w_from * w_to + mid_to;
    };
}
```

4. Now we can transform points on one dimension, but the Mandelbrot set exists in a two-dimensional coordinate system. In order to translate from one (x, y) coordinate system to another, we combine an x-scaler and a y-scaler and construct a `cmplx` instance from their output:

```
template <typename A, typename B>
static auto scaled_cmplx(A scaler_x, B scaler_y)
{
    return [=](int x, int y) {
        return cmplx{scaler_x(x), scaler_y(y)};
    };
}
```

5. After being able to transform coordinates to the right dimensions, we can now implement the Mandelbrot formula. The function that we're implementing now knows absolutely nothing about the concept of terminal windows or linear plane transformations, so we can concentrate on the Mandelbrot math. We square z and add c to it in a loop until its `abs` value is smaller than 2. For some coordinates, this never happens, so we also break out of the loop if the number of iterations exceeds `max_iterations`. In the end, we return the number of iterations we had to do until the `abs` value converged:

```
static auto mandelbrot_iterations(cmplx c)
{
    cmplx z {};
    size_t iterations {0};
    const size_t max_iterations {1000};
    while (abs(z) < 2 && iterations < max_iterations) {
        ++iterations;
        z = pow(z, 2) + c;
    }
    return iterations;
}
```

6. We can now begin with the main function, where we define the terminal dimensions and instantiate a function object, `scale`, which scales our coordinate values for both axes:

```
int main()
{
    const size_t w {100};
    const size_t h {40};
    auto scale (scaled_cmplx(
        scaler(0, w, -2.0, 1.0),
        scaler(0, h, -1.0, 1.0)
    ));
```

7. In order to have a one-dimensional iteration over the whole image, we write another transformation function that accepts a one-dimensional `i` coordinate. It calculates `(x, y)` coordinates from that, based on our assumed line of characters width. After breaking `i` down to the row and column numbers, it transforms them with our `scale` function and returns the complex coordinate.

```
auto i_to_xy ([=](int i) { return scale(i % w, i / w); });
```

8. What we can do now is transform from one-dimensional coordinates (the `int` type), via two-dimensional coordinates (the `(int, int)` type), to Mandelbrot set coordinates (the `cmplx` type), and then calculate the number of iterations from there (the `int` type again). Let's combine all that in one function, which sets up this call chain for us:

```
auto to_iteration_count ([=](int i) {
    return mandelbrot_iterations(i_to_xy(i));
});
```

9. Now we can set up all the data. We assume that our resulting ASCII image is w characters wide and h characters high. This can be saved in a one-dimensional vector that has w * h elements. We fill this vector using `std::iota` with the value range, *0 ... (w*h - 1)*. These numbers can be used as an input source for our constructed transformation function range, which we just encapsulated in `to_iteration_count`:

```
vector<int> v (w * h);
iota(begin(v), end(v), 0);
transform(begin(v), end(v), begin(v), to_iteration_count);
```

10. That's basically it. We now have the v vector, which we initialized with one-dimensional coordinates, but which then got overwritten by Mandelbrot iteration counters. From this, we can now print a pretty image. We could just make the terminal window w characters wide, then we would not need to print line break symbols in between. But we can also kind of *creatively misuse* `std::accumulate` to do the line breaks for us. The `std::accumulate` uses a binary function to reduce a range. We provide it a binary function, which accepts an output iterator (and which we will link to the terminal in the next step), and a single value from the range. We print this value as a * character if the number of iterations is higher than 50. Otherwise, we just print a space character. If we are on a *row end* (because the counter variable n is evenly divisible by w), we print a line break symbol:

```
auto binfunc ([w, n{0}] (auto output_it, int x) mutable {
    *++output_it = (x > 50 ? '*' : ' ');
    if (++n % w == 0) { ++output_it = '\n'; }
    return output_it;
});
```

11. By calling `std:accumulate` on the input range, combined with our binary print function and an `ostream_iterator`, we can flush the calculated Mandelbrot set out to the terminal window:

```
accumulate(begin(v), end(v), ostream_iterator<char>{cout},
           binfunc);
}
```

12. Compiling and running the program leads to the following output, which looks like the initial detailed Mandelbrot image, but in a simplified form:

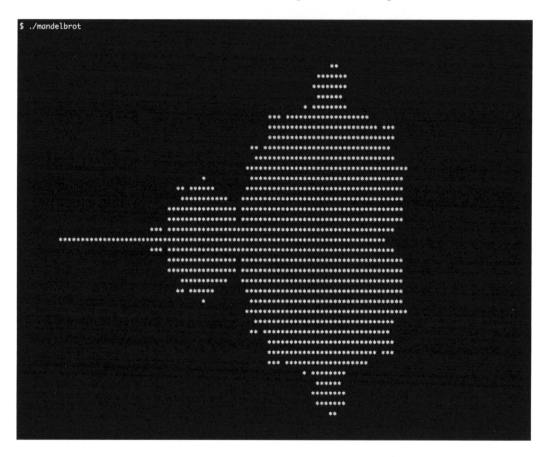

How it works...

The whole calculation took part during an `std::transform` call over a one-dimensional array:

```
vector<int> v (w * h);
iota(begin(v), end(v), 0);
transform(begin(v), end(v), begin(v), to_iteration_count);
```

So, what exactly happened, and why does it work this way? The `to_iteration_count` function is basically a call chain from `i_to_xy`, over `scale` to `mandelbrot_iterations`. The following diagram illustrates the transformation steps:

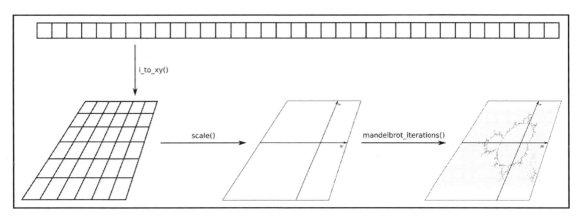

This way, we can use the index of a one-dimensional array as input, and get the number of Mandelbrot formula iterations at the point of the two-dimensional plane, which this array point represents. The good thing is that these three transformations are completely agnostic about each other. Code with such a separation of concerns can be tested very nicely because each component can be tested individually without the others. This way, it is easy to find and fix bugs, or just reason about its correctness.

Building our own algorithm - split

In some situations, the existing STL algorithms are not enough. But nothing hinders us from implementing our own. Before solving a specific problem, we should think about it firmly in order to realize that many problems can be solved in generic ways. If we regularly pile up some new library code while solving our own problems, then we are also helping our fellow programmers when they have similar problems to solve. Key is to know when it is generic enough and when not to go for more genericity than needed--else we end up with a new general purpose language.

In this recipe, we are implementing an algorithm, which we will call `split`. It can split any range of items at each occurrence of a specific value, and it copies the chunks that result from that into an output range.

How to do it...

In this section, we are going to implement our own STL-like algorithm called `split`, and then we check it out by splitting an example string:

1. First things first, we include some STL library parts and declare that we use the `std` namespace:

```
#include <iostream>
#include <string>
#include <algorithm>
#include <iterator>
#include <list>

using namespace std;
```

2. The whole algorithm this section revolves around is `split`. It accepts a begin/end pair of input iterators, and an output iterator, which makes it similar to `std::copy` or `std::transform` at first. The other parameters are `split_val` and `bin_func`. The `split_val` parameter is the value we are searching for in the input range, which represents a splitting point at which we cut the input interval. The `bin_func` parameter is a function that transforms a pair of iterators that mark the beginning and the end of such a split chunk subrange. We iterate through the input range using `std::find`, so we jump from occurrence to occurrence of `split_val` values. When splitting a long string into its individual words, we would jump from space character to space character. On every split value, we stop by to form a chunk and feed it into the output range:

```
template <typename InIt, typename OutIt, typename T, typename F>
InIt split(InIt it, InIt end_it, OutIt out_it, T split_val,
           F bin_func)
{
    while (it != end_it) {
        auto slice_end (find(it, end_it, split_val));
        *out_it++ = bin_func(it, slice_end);
        if (slice_end == end_it) { return end_it; }
        it = next(slice_end);
    }
    return it;
}
```

3. Let's use the new algorithm. We construct a string that we want to split. The item that marks the end of the last chunk, and the beginning of the next chunk, shall be the dash character `'-'`:

```
int main()
{
    const string s {"a-b-c-d-e-f-g"};
```

4. Whenever the algorithm calls its `bin_func` on a pair of iterators, we want to construct a new string from it:

```
auto binfunc ([](auto it_a, auto it_b) {
    return string(it_a, it_b);
});
```

5. The output range will be an `std::list` of strings. We can now call the `split` algorithm, which has a similar design compared to all the other STL algorithms:

```
list<string> l;
split(begin(s), end(s), back_inserter(l), '-', binfunc);
```

6. In order to see what we got, let's print the new chunked list of strings:

```
copy(begin(l), end(l), ostream_iterator<string>{cout, "\n"});
}
```

7. Compiling and running the program yields the following output. It contains no dashes anymore and shows that it has isolated the individual words (which are, of course, only single characters in our example string):

```
$ ./split
a
b
c
d
e
f
g
```

How it works...

The split algorithm works in a similar manner to std::transform because it accepts a pair of begin/end iterators of an input range and an output iterator. It does something with the input range, which, in the end, results in assignments to the output iterator. Apart from that, it accepts an item value called split_val and a binary function. Let's revisit the whole implementation to fully understand it:

```
template <typename InIt, typename OutIt, typename T, typename F>
InIt split(InIt it, InIt end_it, OutIt out_it, T split_val, F bin_func)
{
    while (it != end_it) {
        auto slice_end (find(it, end_it, split_val));
        *out_it++ = bin_func(it, slice_end);

        if (slice_end == end_it) { return end_it; }
        it = next(slice_end);
    }
    return it;
}
```

The loop demands to iterate until the end of the input range. During each iteration, an std::find call is used to find the next element in the input range, which equals to split_val. In our case, that element is the dash character ('-') because we want to split our input string at all the dash positions. The next dash position is now saved in slice_end. After the loop iteration, the it iterator is put on the next item past that split position. This way, the loop jumps directly from dash to dash, instead of over every individual item.

In this constellation, the iterator it points to the beginning of the last slice, while slice_end points to the end of the last slice. Both these iterators, in combination, mark the beginning and end of the subrange that represents exactly one slice between two dash symbols. In a string, "foo-bar-baz", this would mean that we have three loop iterations and we get a pair of iterators every time, which surround one word. But we do not actually want iterators but substrings. The binary function, bin_func, does just that for us. When we called split, we gave it the following binary function:

```
[] (auto it_a, auto it_b) {
    return string(it_a, it_b);
}
```

The `split` function throws every pair of iterators through `bin_func`, before feeding it into the output iterator. And we actually get string instances out of `bin_func`, which results in `"foo"`, `"bar"`, and `"baz"`:

There's more...

An interesting alternative to implementing our own algorithm for splitting strings would be implementing an *iterator* that does the same. We are not going to implement such an iterator at this point, but let's have a brief look at such a scenario.

The iterator would need to jump between delimiters on every increment. Whenever it is dereferenced, it needs to create a string object from the iterator positions it currently points to, which it could do using a binary function such as `binfunc`, which we used before.

If we had an iterator class called `split_iterator`, instead of an algorithm `split`, the user code would look as follows:

```
string s {"a-b-c-d-e-f-g"};
list<string> l;

auto binfunc ([](auto it_a, auto it_b) {
    return string(it_a, it_b);
});

copy(split_iterator{begin(s), end(s), '-', binfunc},{}, back_inserter(l));
```

The downside of this approach is that implementing an iterator is usually more *complicated* than a single function. Also, there are many subtle edges in iterator code that can lead to bugs, so an iterator solution needs more tedious testing. On the other hand, it is very simple to combine such an iterator with the other STL algorithms.

Composing useful algorithms from standard algorithms - gather

A very nice example for the composability of STL algorithms is `gather`. Sean Parent, principal scientist at Adobe Systems at the time, popularized this algorithm because it is both useful and short. The way it is implemented, it is the ideal poster child for the idea of STL algorithm composition.

The gather algorithm operates on ranges of arbitrary item types. It modifies the order of the items in such a way that specific items are gathered around a specific position, chosen by the caller.

How to do it...

In this section, we will implement the gather algorithm and a bonus variation of it. Afterward, we see how it can be put to use:

1. First, we add all the STL include statements. Then, we declare that we use the std namespace:

```
#include <iostream>
#include <algorithm>
#include <string>
#include <functional>

using namespace std;
```

2. The gather algorithm is a nice example of standard algorithm composition. gather accepts a begin/end iterator pair, and another iterator gather_pos, which points somewhere in between. The last parameter is a predicate function. Using this predicate function, the algorithm will push all that items that *do* satisfy the predicate near the gather_pos iterator. The implementation of the item movement is done by std::stable_partition. The return value of the gather algorithm is a pair of iterators. These iterators are returned from the stable_partition calls, and this way, they mark the beginning and the end of the now gathered range:

```
template <typename It, typename F>
pair<It, It> gather(It first, It last, It gather_pos, F predicate)
{
    return {stable_partition(first, gather_pos, not_fn(predicate)),
            stable_partition(gather_pos, last, predicate)};
}
```

3. Another variant of gather is `gather_sort`. It basically works the same way as `gather`, but it does not accept a unary predicate function; it accepts a binary comparison function instead. This way, it is possible to gather the values near `gather_pos`, which appear *smallest* or *largest*:

```
template <typename It, typename F>
void gather_sort(It first, It last, It gather_pos, F comp_func)
{
    auto inv_comp_func ([&](const auto &...ps) {
        return !comp_func(ps...);
    });
    stable_sort(first,      gather_pos, inv_comp_func);
    stable_sort(gather_pos, last,       comp_func);
}
```

4. Let's put those algorithms to use. We start with a predicate, which tells if a given character argument is the `'a'` character. We construct a string, which consists of wildly interleaved `'a'` and `'_'` characters:

```
int main()
{
    auto is_a ([](char c) { return c == 'a'; });
    string a {"a_a_a_a_a_a_a_a_a_a"};
```

5. We construct an iterator, which points to the middle of our new string. Let's call `gather` on it and see what happens. The `'a'` characters should be gathered around the middle afterward:

```
    auto middle (begin(a) + a.size() / 2);

    gather(begin(a), end(a), middle, is_a);
    cout << a << '\n';
```

6. Let's call `gather` again, but this time, the `gather_pos` iterator is not in the middle but the beginning:

```
    gather(begin(a), end(a), begin(a), is_a);
    cout << a << '\n';
```

7. In a third call, we gather items around the end iterator:

```
    gather(begin(a), end(a), end(a), is_a);
    cout << a << '\n';
```

8. With a last call of `gather`, we try to gather all the `'a'` characters around the middle again. This will not work as expected, and we will later see why:

```
// This will NOT work as naively expected
gather(begin(a), end(a), middle, is_a);
cout << a << '\n';
```

9. We construct another string with underscore characters and some number values. On that input sequence, we apply `gather_sort`. The `gather_pos` iterator is the middle of the string, and the binary comparison function is `std::less<char>`:

```
string b {"_9_2_4_7_3_8_1_6_5_0_"};
gather_sort(begin(b), end(b), begin(b) + b.size() / 2,
            less<char>{});
cout << b << '\n';
}
```

10. Compiling and running the program yields the following interesting output. The first three lines look like expected, but the fourth line looks like `gather` did *nothing* to the string.
    In the last line, we can see the result of the `gather_short` function. The numbers appear sorted towards either direction:

```
$ ./gather
_____aaaaaaaaaaa_____
aaaaaaaaaaa_____
_____aaaaaaaaaaa
_____aaaaaaaaaaa
_____9743201568_____
```

How it works...

Initially, the `gather` algorithm is hard to grasp because it is very short but has a seemingly complex task. Therefore, let's step through it:

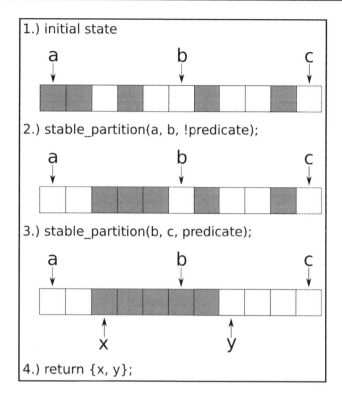

1. The initial state is a range of items, for which we present a predicate function. In the diagram, all items for which our predicate function returns `true`, are painted in *gray*. The iterators `a` and `c` mark the whole range, and iterator `b` points to a *pivot* element. The pivot element is the element around which we want to *gather* all the gray items.

2. The `gather` algorithm calls `std::stable_partition` on the range `[a, b)` and while doing that, it uses a *negated* version of the predicate. It negates the predicate because `std::stable_partition` moves all items for which the predicate returns `true` to the *front*. We want exactly the *opposite* to happen.

3. Another `std::stable_partition` call is done but, this time, on the range, `[b, c)`, and *without* negating the predicate. The gray items are moved to the front of the input range, which means they are all moved towards the pivot element pointed at by `b`.

4. The items are now gathered around `b` and the algorithm returns iterators to the beginning and the end of the now consecutive range of gray items.

We called `gather` multiple times on the same range. At first, we gathered all the items around the middle of the range. Then we gathered the items around `begin()` and then around `end()` of the range. These cases are interesting because they always lead *one* of the `std::stable_partition` calls to operate on an *empty* range, which results in *no action*.

We did the last call to gather again with the parameters (`begin, end, middle`) of the range, and that did not work. Why? At first, this looks like a bug, but actually, it is not.

Imagine the character range, `"aabb"`, together with a predicate function, `is_character_a`, which is only true for the `'a'` items--if we call it with a third iterator pointing to the middle of the character range, we would observe the same *bug*. The reason is that the first `stable_partition` call would operate on the subrange, `"aa"`, and the other `stable_partition` call operates on the range, `"bb"`. This series of calls cannot result in `"baab"`, which we initially naively hoped.

In order to get what we want in the last case, we could use
`std::rotate(begin, begin + 1, end);`

The `gather_sort` modification is basically the same as `gather`. The only difference is that it does not accept a unary *predicate* function but a binary *comparison* function, just like `std::sort`. And instead of calling `std::stable_partition` twice, it calls `std::stable_sort` twice.

The negation of the comparison function cannot be done with `not_fn`, just like we did in the `gather` algorithm because `not_fn` does not work on binary functions.

Removing consecutive whitespace between words

Because strings are often read from user input, they may contain wild formatting and often need to be sanitized. One example of this is strings containing too many whitespace.

In this section, we will implement a slick whitespace filtering algorithm, which removes excess whitespace from strings but leaves single whitespace characters untouched. We call that algorithm `remove_multi_whitespace`, and its interface will look very STL-like.

How to do it...

In this section, we will implement the `remove_multi_whitespace` algorithm and check out how it works:

1. As always, we do some includes first and then declare that we use the `std` namespace by default:

```
#include <iostream>
#include <string>
#include <algorithm>

using namespace std;
```

2. We implement a new STL-style algorithm called `remove_multi_whitespace`. This algorithm removes clustered occurrences of whitespace, but no single spaces. This means that a string line `"a b"` stays unchanged, but a string like `"a     b"` is shrunk to `"a b"`. In order to accomplish this, we use `std::unique` with a custom binary predicate function. The `std::unqiue` walks through an iterable range and always looks at consecutive pairs of payload items. Then it asks the predicate functions whether two items are equal. If they are, then `std::unique` removes one of them. Afterward, the range does not contain subranges with equal items sitting next to each other. Predicate functions that are usually applied in this context tell whether two items are equal. What we do, is give `std::unique` a predicate, which tells if there are two consecutive *spaces* in order to get those removed. Just like `std::unique`, we accept a pair of begin/end iterators, and then return an iterator pointing to the new end of the range:

```
template <typename It>
It remove_multi_whitespace(It it, It end_it)
{
    return unique(it, end_it, [](const auto &a, const auto &b) {
        return isspace(a) && isspace(b);
    });
}
```

3. That is already it. Let's construct a string that contains some unnecessary whitespace:

```
int main()
{
    string s {"fooo      bar    \t    baz"};
    cout << s << '\n';
```

4. Now, we use the *erase-remove idiom* on the string in order to get rid of the excess whitespace characters:

```
    s.erase(remove_multi_whitespace(begin(s), end(s)), end(s));

    cout << s << '\n';
}
```

5. Compiling and running the program yields the following output:

```
$ ./remove_consecutive_whitespace
fooo      bar          baz
fooo bar baz
```

How it works...

We solved the whole complexity of the problem without any loop or manual comparison of items. We only provided a predicate function, which tells if two given characters are *whitespace* characters. Then we fed that predicate into `std::unique` and *poof*, all the excess whitespace vanished. While this chapter also contains some recipes where we had to fight a bit more to express our programs with STL algorithms, this algorithm is a *really* nice and short example.

How does this interesting combination work in detail? Let's have a look at a possible implementation of `std::unique` first:

```
template<typename It, typename P>
It unique(It it, It end, P p)
{
    if (it == end) { return end; }

    It result {it};
    while (++it != end) {
        if (!p(*result, *it) && ++result != it) {
            *result = std::move(*it);
        }
    }
}
```

```
        return ++result;
    }
```

The loop steps over the range items, while they do not satisfy the predicate condition. At the point where an item satisfies the predicate, it moves such an item one item past the old position, where the predicate fired the last time. The version of `std::unique` that does not accept an additional predicate function checks whether two neighbor items are equal. This way, it wipes out *repeated* characters as it can , for example, transform `"abbbbbbc"` to `"abc"`.

What we want is not wiping out *all* characters which are repetitive, but repetitive *whitespace*. Therefore, our predicate does not say *"both argument characters are equal"*, but *"both argument characters are whitespace characters"*.

One last thing to note is that neither `std::unique` nor `remove_multi_whitespace` really removes character items from the underlying string. They only move characters within the string according to their semantics and tell where its new end is. The removal of all now-obsolete characters from the new end till the old end must still be done. This is why we wrote the following:

```
s.erase(remove_multi_whitespace(begin(s), end(s)), end(s));
```

This adheres to the *erase-remove* idiom, which we already know from vectors and lists.

Compressing and decompressing strings

This section deals with a relatively popular task in coding interviews. The basic idea is a function, which takes a string like `"aaaaabbbbbbbccc"` and transforms it to a shorter string `"a5b7c3"`. It is `"a5"` because there are five `'a'` characters. And then it is `"b7"` because there are seven `'b'` characters. This is a very simple *compression* algorithm. For normal text, it is of reduced utility because normal language is usually not so repetitive that its text representation would become shorter with this compression scheme. However, it is relatively easy to implement even if we have to do it on a whiteboard without a computer. The tricky part is that it is easy to write a buggy code if the program is not structured very well from the beginning. Dealing with strings is generally not a hard thing, but the chances of implementing buffer overflow bugs lurk around *a lot* here if legacy C-style formatting functions are used.

Let's try an STL approach to implementing string compression and decompression using this simple scheme.

How to do it...

In this section, we will implement simple `compress` and `decompress` functions for strings:

1. We include some STL libraries first, then we declare that we use the `std` namespace:

```
#include <iostream>
#include <string>
#include <algorithm>
#include <sstream>
#include <tuple>

using namespace std;
```

2. For our cheap compression algorithm, we try to find chunks of text containing ranges of the same characters, and we compress those individually. Whenever we start at one string position, we want to find the first position where it contains a different character. We use `std::find` to find the first character in the range, which is different than the character at the current position. Afterward, we return a tuple containing an iterator to that first different item, the character variable c, which fills the range at hand, and the number of occurrences that this subrange contains:

```
template <typename It>
tuple<It, char, size_t> occurrences(It it, It end_it)
{
    if (it == end_it) { return {it, '?', 0}; }
    const char c {*it};
    const auto diff (find_if(it, end_it,
                     [c](char x) { return c != x; }));
    return {diff, c, distance(it, diff)};
}
```

3. The `compress` algorithm continuously calls the `occurrences` function. This way, we jump from one same character group to another. The `r << c << n` line pushes the character into the output stream and then the number of occurrences it has in this part of the input string. The output is a string stream that automatically grows with our output. In the end, we return a string object from it, which contains the compressed string:

```
string compress(const string &s)
{
    const auto end_it (end(s));
    stringstream r;

    for (auto it (begin(s)); it != end_it;) {
        const auto [next_diff, c, n] (occurrences(it, end_it));
        r << c << n;
        it = next_diff;
    }
    return r.str();
}
```

4. The `decompress` method works similarly, but it is much simpler. It continuously tries to get a character value out of the input stream and, then, the following number. From those two values, it can construct a string containing the character as often as the number says. In the end, we again return a string from the output stream. By the way, this `decompress` function is *not safe*. It can be exploited easily. Can you guess, how? We will have a look at this problem later:

```
string decompress(const string &s)
{
    stringstream ss{s};
    stringstream r;
    char c;
    size_t n;
    while (ss >> c >> n) { r << string(n, c); }
    return r.str();
}
```

5. In our main function, we construct a simple string with a lot of repetition, on which the algorithm works very well. Let's print the compressed version, and then the compressed and again decompressed version. In the end, we should get the same string as we initially constructed:

```
int main()
{
    string s {"aaaaaaaaabbbbbbbbbccccccccccc"};
    cout << compress(s) << '\n';
    cout << decompress(compress(s)) << '\n';
}
```

6. Compiling and running the program yields the following output:

```
$ ./compress
a9b9c11
aaaaaaaaabbbbbbbbbccccccccccc
```

How it works...

This program basically revolves around two functions: compress and decompress.

The decompress function is really simple because it only consists of variable declarations, a line of code, which actually does something, and the following return statement. The code line which does something is the following one:

```
while (ss >> c >> n) { r << string(n, c); }
```

It continuously reads the character, c, and the counter variable, n, out of the string stream, ss. The stringstream class hides a lot of string parsing magic from us at this point. While that succeeds, it constructs a decompressed string chunk into the string stream, from which the final result string can be returned back to the caller of decompress. If c = 'a' and n = 5, the expression string(n, c) will result in a string with the content, "aaaaa".

The compress function is more complex. We also wrote a little helper function for it. We called that helper function `occurences`. So, let's first have a glance at `occurrences`. The following diagram shows how it works:

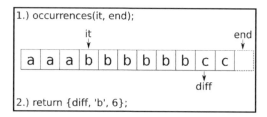

The `occurences` function accepts two parameters: an iterator pointing to the beginning of a character sequence within a range and the end iterator of that range. Using `find_if`, it finds the first character that is different from the character initially being pointed at. In the diagram, this is the iterator, `diff`. The difference between that new position and the old iterator position is the number of equal items (`diff - it` equals **6** in the diagram). After calculating this information, the `diff` iterator can be reused in order to execute the next search. Therefore, we pack `diff`, the character of the subrange, and the length of the subrange into a tuple and return it.

With the information lined up like this, we can jump from subrange to subrange and push the intermediate results into the compressed target string:

```
for (auto it (begin(s)); it != end_it;) {
    const auto [next_diff, c, n] (occurrences(it, end_it));
    r << c << n;
    it = next_diff;
}
```

There's more...

In step 4, we mentioned that the `decompress` function is not safe. Indeed, it can easily be *exploited*.

Imagine the following input string: `"a00000"`. Compressing it will result in the substring `"a1"` because there is only one character, `'a'`. That is followed by five times `'0'`, which will result in `"05"`. Together, this results in the compressed string `"a105"`. Unfortunately, this compressed string says *"105 times the character* `'a'`*"*. This has nothing to do with our initial input string. Even worse, if we decompress it, we get from a six-character string to a 105-character string. Imagine the same with larger numbers--the user can easily *blow up* our heap usage because our algorithm is not prepared for such inputs.

In order to prevent this, the compress function could, for example, reject input with numbers, or it could mask them in a special way. And the decompress algorithm could take another conditional, which puts an upper bound on the resulting string size. I am leaving this as an exercise for you.

7
Strings, Stream Classes, and Regular Expressions

We will cover the following recipes in this chapter:

- Creating, concatenating, and transforming strings
- Trimming whitespace from the beginning and end of strings
- Getting the comfort of `std::string` without the cost of constructing `std::string` objects
- Reading values from user input
- Counting all words in a file
- Formatting your output with I/O stream manipulators
- Initializing complex objects from file input
- Filling containers from `std::istream` iterators
- Generic printing with `std::ostream` iterators
- Redirect output to files for specific code sections
- Creating custom string classes by inheriting from `std::char_traits`
- Tokenizing input with the regular expression library
- Comfortably pretty printing numbers differently per context on the fly
- Catching readable exceptions from `std::iostream` errors

Introduction

This chapter is devoted to string handling, parsing, and printing of arbitrary data. For such jobs, STL provides its *I/O stream library*. The library basically consists of the following classes, which are each depicted in gray boxes:

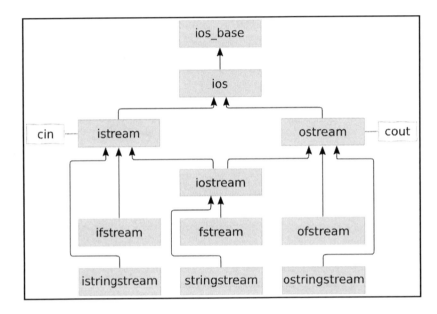

The arrows show the inheritance scheme of the classes. This might look very overwhelming at first, but we will get to use most of these classes in this chapter and get familiar with them class by class. When looking at those classes in the C++ STL documentation, we will not find them directly with these *exact* names. That is because the names in the diagram are what we see as application programmers, but they are really mostly just typedefs of classes with a `basic_` class name prefix (for example, we will have an easier job searching the STL documentation for `basic_istream` rather than `istream`). The `basic_*` I/O stream classes are templates that can be specialized for different character types. The classes in the diagram are specialized on `char` values. We will use these specializations throughout the book. If we prefix those class names with the w character, we get `wistream`, `wostream`, and so on--these are the specialization typedefs for `wchar_t` instead of `char`, for example.

At the top of the diagram, we see `std::ios_base`. We will basically never use it directly, but it is listed for completeness because all other classes inherit from it. The next specialization is `std::ios` which embodies the idea of an object which maintains a stream of data, that can be in *good* state, run *empty* of data state (EOF), or some kind of *fail* state.

The first specializations we are going to actually use are `std::istream` and `std::ostream`. The "i" and the "o" prefix stand for input and output. We have seen them in our earliest days of C++ programming in the simplest examples in form of the objects `std::cout` and `std::cin` (but also `std::cerr`). These are instances of those classes, which are always globally available. We do data output via `ostream` and input via `istream`.

A class which inherits from both `istream` and `ostream` is `iostream`. It combines both input and output capabilities. When we understand how all classes from the trio consisting of `istream`, `ostream` and `iostream` can be used, we basically are ready to immediately put all following ones to use, too:

`ifstream`, `ofstream` and `fstream` inherit from `istream`, `ostream` and `iostream` respectively, but lift their capabilities to redirect the I/O from and to files from the computer's *filesystem*.

The `istringstream`, `ostringstream` and `iostringstream` work pretty analogously. They help build strings in memory, and/or consuming data from them.

Creating, concatenating, and transforming strings

Even C++ programmers from the very old days will know about `std::string`. While string handling is tedious and painful in C, especially when parsing, concatenating, copying them, and so on, `std::string` is a real step forward regarding simplicity and safety.

Thanks to C++11, we don't even need to copy strings when we want to transfer ownership to some other function or data structure anymore because we can *move* them. This way, there's not much overhead involved in most cases.

The `std::string` got a few new features here and there over the last few standard increments. What is completely new in C++17 is `std::string_view`. We will play with both a bit (but there is another recipe, which concentrates more on `std::string_view`-only features) to get a feeling of them and how they work in the C++17 era.

How to do it...

We will create strings and string views and do basic concatenation and transformation with them in this section:

1. As always, we first include header files and declare that we use the `std` namespace:

```
#include <iostream>
#include <string>
#include <string_view>
#include <sstream>
#include <algorithm>

using namespace std;
```

2. Let's first create string objects. The most obvious way is instantiating an object a of class `string`. We control its content by giving the constructor a C-style string (which will be embedded in the binary as a static array containing characters after compiling). The constructor will copy it and make it the content of string object a. Alternatively, instead of initializing it from a C-style string, we can use the string literal operator `""`s. It creates a string object on the fly. Using that to construct object b, we can even use automatic type deduction:

```
int main()
{
    string a { "a"  };
    auto   b ( "b"s );
```

3. The strings we just created are *copying* their input from the constructor argument into their own buffer. In order to not copy, but *reference* the underlying string, we can use `string_view` instances. This class does also have a literal operator, and it is called `""sv`:

```
string_view c { "c"   };
auto        d ( "d"sv );
```

4. Okay, now let's play with our strings and string views. For both types, there are `operator<<` overloads for the `std::ostream` class, so they can be printed comfortably:

```
cout << a << ", " << b << '\n';
cout << c << ", " << d << '\n';
```

5. The string class overloads `operator+`, so we can *add* two strings and get their concatenation as a result. This way, `"a" + "b"` results in `"ab"`. Concatenating `a` and `b` this way is easy. With `a` and `c`, it is not that easy, because `c` is not a `string`, but a `string_view`. We have to get the string out of `c` first, and this can be done by constructing a new string from `c`, and then adding it to `a`. At this point one could ask, "Wait, why are you copying `c` into an intermediate string object just in order to add it to `a`? Can't you avoid that copy by using `c.data()`?" That is a nice idea, but it has a flaw--`string_view` instances do not have to carry zero-terminated strings. And this is a problem that can lead to buffer overflows:

```
cout << a + b << '\n';
cout << a + string{c} << '\n';
```

6. Let's create a new string, which contains all of the strings and string views we just created. By using `std::ostringstream`, we can *print* any variable into a stream object that behaves exactly like `std::cout`, but it doesn't print to the shell. Instead, it prints into a *string buffer*. After we streamed all the variables with some separating space between them using `operator<<`, we can construct and print a new string object from that with `o.str()`:

```
ostringstream o;
o << a << " " << b << " " << c << " " << d;
auto concatenated (o.str());
cout << concatenated << '\n';
```

7. We can now also transform that new string by converting all its letters to upper case, for example. The C library function `toupper`, which maps lower-case characters to upper-case characters and leaves other characters unchanged, is already available and can be combined with `std::transform` because a string is basically also an iterable container object with `char` items:

```
transform(begin(concatenated), end(concatenated),
          begin(concatenated), ::toupper);
cout << concatenated << '\n';
}
```

8. Compiling and running the program leads to the following output, which is just what we expected:

```
$ ./creating_strings
a, b
c, d
ab
ac
a b c d
A B C D
```

How it works...

Obviously, strings can be added with the + operator like numbers, but that has nothing to do with math but results in *concatenated* strings. In order to mix this with `string_view`, we need to convert to `std::string` first.

However, it is really important to note that when mixing strings and string views in code, we must never assume that the underlying string behind a `string_view` is *zero terminated*! This is why we would rather write `"abc"s + string{some_string_view}` than `"abc"s + some_string_view.data()`. Aside from that, `std::string` provides a member function, `append`, which can handle `string_view` instances, but it alters the string instead of returning a new one with the string view content appended.

 `std::string_view` is useful, but be cautious when mixing it with strings and string functions. We cannot assume that they are zero-terminated, which breaks things quickly in a standard string environment. Fortunately, there are often proper function overloads, which can deal with them the right way.

If we want to do complex string concatenation with formatting and so on, we should however not do that piece by piece on string instances. The `std::stringstream`, `std::ostringstream`, and `std::istringstream` classes are much better suited for this, as they enhance the memory management while appending, and provide all the formatting features we know from streams in general. The `std::ostringstream` class is what we chose in this section because we were going to create a string instead of parsing it. An `std::istringstream` instance could have been instantiated from an existing string, which we could have then comfortably parsed into variables of other types. If we want to combine both, `std::stringstream` is the perfect all-rounder.

Trimming whitespace from the beginning and end of strings

Especially when obtaining strings from user input, they are often polluted with unneeded white space. In another recipe, we removed excess whitespace that occurred between words.

Let's now have a look at strings that are surrounded by whitespace and remove that. The `std::string` has some nice helper functions for getting this job done.

 After reading this recipe that shows how to do this with plain string objects, make sure to also read the following recipe. There we will see how to avoid unnecessary copies or data modifications with the new `std::string_view` class.

How to do it...

In this section, we will write a helper function that identifies surrounding white space in a string and returns a copy without that, and then we are going to test it briefly.

1. As always, the header includes and using directive come first:

```
#include <iostream>
#include <string>
#include <algorithm>
#include <cctype>

using namespace std;
```

2. Our function to trim whitespace surrounding a string takes a const reference to an existing string. It will return a new string without any surrounding whitespace:

```
string trim_whitespace_surrounding(const string &s)
{
```

3. The `std::string` provides two handy functions, which help us a lot. The first is `string::find_first_not_of`, which accepts a string containing all the characters we want to skip over. This is, of course, whitespace, meaning the characters space `' '`, tab `'\t'`, and new line, `'\n'`. It returns us the first non-whitespace character position. If there is only whitespace in the string, it returns `string::npos`. This means that there is only an empty string left if we trim whitespace from it. So, in such a case, let's just return an empty string:

```
const char whitespace[] {" \t\n"};
const size_t first (s.find_first_not_of(whitespace));
if (string::npos == first) { return {}; }
```

4. We know now where the new string has to begin, but we don't yet know where it has to end. Therefore, we use the other handy string function `string::find_last_not_of`. It will return us the last character position in the string which is no whitespace:

```
const size_t last (s.find_last_not_of(whitespace));
```

5. Using `string::substr`, we can now return the part of the string, which is surrounded by whitespace but without the white space. This function takes two parameters--a *position* in the string to begin with and the *number of characters* after this position:

```
    return s.substr(first, (last - first + 1));
}
```

6. That's it. Let's write a main function in which we create a string that surrounds a text sentence with all kinds of whitespace, in order to trim it:

```
int main()
{
    string s {" \t\n string surrounded by ugly"
              " whitespace \t\n "};
```

7. We print the untrimmed and trimmed versions of the string. By surrounding the string with brackets, it's more obvious which whitespace belonged to it prior to trimming:

```
cout << "{" << s << "}\n";
cout << "{"
     << trim_whitespace_surrounding(s)
     << "}\n";
}
```

8. Compiling and running the program yields us the output we expected:

```
$ ./trim_whitespace
{
   string surrounded by ugly whitespace
   }
{string surrounded by ugly whitespace}
```

How it works...

In this section, we used `string::find_first_not_of` and `string::find_last_not_of`. Both functions accept a C-style string, which acts as a list of characters that should be skipped while searching a different character. If we have a string instance that carries the string, `"foo bar"`, and we call `find_first_not_of("bfo ")` on it, it will return us the value 5, because the `'a'` character is the first one that is not in the `"bfo "` string. The order of the characters in the argument string is not important.

The same functions exist with inverted logic, although we did not use them in this recipe: `string::find_first_of` and `string::find_last_of`.

Similar to iterator based functions, we need to check if these functions return an actual position in the string or a value that denotes that they did *not* find a character position fulfilling the constraints. If they did not find one, they return `string::npos`.

From the character positions we retrieved from these functions in our helper function, we built us a substring without surrounding whitespace, using `string::substring`. This function accepts a relative offset and a string length and then returns a new string instance with its own memory, which contains only that substring. For example, `string{"abcdef"}.substr(2, 2)` will return us a new string `"cd"`.

Getting the comfort of std::string without the cost of constructing std::string objects

The `std::string` class is a really useful class because it simplifies dealing with strings so much. A flaw is that if we want to pass around a substring of it, we need to pass a pointer and a length variable, two iterators, or a copy of the substring. We did that in the previous recipe, where we removed the surrounding whitespace from a string by taking a copy of the substring range that does not contain the surrounding whitespace.

If we want to pass a string or a substring to a library that does not even support `std::string`, we can only provide a raw string pointer, which is a bit disappointing, because it sets us back to the old C days. Just as with the substring problem, a raw pointer does not carry information about the string length with it. This way, one would have to implement a bundle of a pointer and a string length.

In a simplified way, this is exactly what `std::string_view` is. It is available since C++17 and provides a way to pair a pointer to some string together with that string's size. It embodies the idea of having a reference type for arrays of data.

If we design functions which formerly accepted `std::string` instances as parameters, but did not change them in a way that would require the string instances to reallocate the memory that holds the actual string payload, we could now use `std::string_view` and be more compatible with libraries that are STL-agnostic. We could let other libraries provide a `string_view` view on the payload strings behind their complex string implementations and then use that in our STL code. This way, the `string_view` class acts as a minimal and useful interface, which can be shared among different libraries.

Another cool thing is that `string_view` can be used as a non-copy reference to substrings of larger string objects. There are a lot of possibilities to use it profitably. In this section, we will play around with `string_view` in order to get a feeling for its ups and downs. We will also see how we can hide the surrounding whitespace from strings by adapting string views instead of modifying or copying the actual string. This method avoids unnecessary copying or data modification.

How to do it...

We are going to implement a function that relies on some `string_view` features, and then, we see how many different types we can feed into it:

1. The header includes and using directive come first:

```
#include <iostream>
#include <string_view>

using namespace std;
```

2. We implement a function that accepts a `string_view` as its only argument:

```
void print(string_view v)
{
```

3. Before doing anything with the input string, we remove any leading and trailing whitespace. We are not going to change the string, but the *view* on the string by narrowing it down to the actual non-whitespace part of the string. The `find_first_not_of` function will find the first character in the string, which is not space (' '), not a tab character ('\t'), and not a newline character ('\n'). With `remove_prefix`, we advance the internal `string_view` pointer to the first non-whitespace character. In case the string contains only whitespace, the `find_first_not_of` function returns the value npos, which is `size_type(-1)`. As `size_type` is an unsigned variable, this boils down to a very large number. So, we take the smaller one of both: `words_begin` or the string view's size:

```
const auto words_begin (v.find_first_not_of(" \t\n"));
v.remove_prefix(min(words_begin, v.size()));
```

4. We do the same with trailing whitespace. The `remove_suffix` shrinks down the view's size variable:

```
const auto words_end (v.find_last_not_of(" \t\n"));
if (words_end != string_view::npos) {
    v.remove_suffix(v.size() - words_end - 1);
}
```

5. Now we can print the string view and its length:

```
cout << "length: " << v.length()
     << " [" << v << "]\n";
}
```

6. In our main function, we play around with the new `print` function by feeding it with completely different argument types. First, we give it a runtime `char*` string from the `argv` pointer. At runtime, it contains the file name of our executable. Then, we give it an empty `string_view` instance. We then feed it with a C-style static character string, and with a `""sv` literal, which constructs us a `string_view` on the fly. And finally, we give it an `std::string`. The nice thing is that none of these arguments are modified or copied in order to call the `print` function. No heap allocations happen. For many and/or large strings, this is very efficient:

```
int main(int argc, char *argv[])
{
    print(argv[0]);
    print({});
    print("a const char * array");
    print("an std::string_view literal"sv);
    print("an std::string instance"s);
```

7. We did not test the whitespace removal feature. So, let's give it a string that has a lot of leading and trailing whitespace:

```
print(" \t\n foobar \n \t ");
```

8. Another cool feature is that the strings `string_view` gives us access to do not have to be *zero-terminated*. If we construct a string, such as `"abc"`, without a trailing zero, the `print` function can still safely handle it because `string_view` also carries the size of the string it points to:

```
char cstr[] {'a', 'b', 'c'};
print(string_view(cstr, sizeof(cstr)));
}
```

9. Compiling and running the program yields the following output. All the strings are correctly handled. The string we filled with lots of leading and trailing whitespace is correctly filtered, and the `abc` string without zero termination is also correctly printed without any buffer overflows:

```
$ ./string_view
length: 17 [./string_view]
length: 0 []
length: 20 [a const char * array]
length: 27 [an std::string_view literal]
length: 23 [an std::string instance]
length: 6 [foobar]
length: 3 [abc]
```

How it works...

We have just seen that we can call a function that accepts a `string_view` argument with basically anything that is string like in the sense that it stores characters in a contiguous way. *No copy* of the underlying string was made in any of our `print` calls.

It is interesting to note that in our `print(argv[0])` call, the string view automatically determined the string length because this is a zero-terminated string by convention. The other way around, one cannot assume that it is possible to determine a `string_view` instances's data length by counting the number of items until a zero terminator is reached. Because of this, we must always be careful about where we reach around a pointer to the string view data using `string_view::data()`. Usual string functions mostly assume zero termination and, thus, can buffer overflow very badly with raw pointers to the payload of a string view. It is always better to use interfaces that already expect a string view.

Apart from that, we get a lot of the luxury interface we know from `std::string` already.

 Use `std::string_view` for passing strings or substrings where you want to avoid copies or heap allocations, without losing the comfort of string classes. But be aware of the fact that `std::string_view` drops the assumption that strings are zero terminated.

Reading values from user input

A lot of recipes in this book read values from an input source, such as standard input or a file, and do something with it. This time we concentrate only on the reading and learn more about error handling, which becomes important if reading something from a stream did *not* go well and we need to handle it other than terminating the whole program.

We will only read from user input in this recipe, but as soon as we know how to do that, we also know how to read from any other stream. User input is read via `std::cin`, and that is essentially an input stream object, such as instances of `ifstream` and `istringstream` are.

How to do it...

In this section, we are going to read user input into different variables, and see how to handle errors, as well as how to do a little bit more complex tokenizing of input into useful chunks:

1. We only need `iostream` this time. So, let's include this single header and declare that we use the `std` namespace by default:

```
#include <iostream>

using namespace std;
```

2. Let's first prompt the user to enter two numbers. We will parse them into an `int` and a `double` variable. The user can separate them with white space. `1 2.3`, for example, is a valid input:

```
int main()
{
    cout << "Please Enter two numbers:\n> ";
    int x;
    double y;
```

3. Parsing and error checking is done at the same time in the condition part of our `if` branch. Only if both the numbers could be parsed are they meaningful to us and we print them:

```
if (cin >> x >> y) {
    cout << "You entered: " << x
         << " and " << y << '\n';
```

4. If the parsing did not succeed for any reason, we tell the user that the parsing did not go well. The `cin` stream object is now in a *fail state* and will not give us other input until we clear the fail state again. In order to be able to parse a new input afterward, we call `cin.clear()` and drop all input we received until now. The dropping is done with `cin.ignore`, where we specify that we are dropping the maximum number of characters until we finally see a newline character, which is also dropped. Everything after that is interesting input again:

```
    } else {
        cout << "Oh no, that did not go well!\n";
        cin.clear();
        cin.ignore(
            std::numeric_limits<std::streamsize>::max(),
            '\n');
    }
```

5. Let's now ask for some other input. We let the user enter names. As names can consist multiple words separated by spaces, the space character is not a good separator any longer. Therefore, we use `std::getline`, which accepts a stream object, such as `cin`, a string reference where it will copy the input into, and a separating character. Let's choose comma (,) as the separating character. By not just using `cin` alone and by using `cin >> ws` as a stream parameter for `getline` instead, we can make `cin` drop any leading whitespace before any name. In every loop step, we print the current name, but if a name is empty, we drop out of the loop:

```
    cout << "now please enter some "
            "comma-separated names:\n> ";
    for (string s; getline(cin >> ws, s, ',');) {
        if (s.empty()) { break; }
        cout << "name: \"" << s << "\"\n";
    }
}
```

6. Compiling and running the program leads to the following output, in which we assumingly entered only valid inputs. The numbers are "1 2", which are parsed correctly, and then we enter some names which are then also listed correctly. An empty name input in the form of two consecutive commas quits the loop:

```
$ ./strings_from_user_input
Please Enter two numbers:
> 1 2
You entered: 1 and 2
now please enter some comma-separated names:
```

```
> john doe,  ellen ripley,        alice,     chuck norris,,
name: "john doe"
name: "ellen ripley"
name: "alice"
name: "chuck norris"
```

7. When running the program again, while entering bad numbers in the beginning, we see that the program correctly takes the other branch, drops the bad input and correctly continues with the name listening. Play around with the `cin.clear()` and `cin.ignore(...)` lines to see how that tampers with the name reading code:

```
$ ./strings_from_user_input
Please Enter two numbers:
> a b
Oh no, that did not go well!
now please enter some comma-separated names:
> bud spencer, terence hill,,
name: "bud spencer"
name: "terence hill"
```

How it works...

We did some complex input retrieval in this section. The first noticeable thing is that we always did the retrieval and error checking at the same time.

The result of the expression `cin >> x` is again a reference to `cin`. This way, we can write `cin >> x >> y >> z >> ....` At the same time, it is possible to convert it into a Boolean value by using it in a Boolean context such as `if` conditions. The Boolean value tells us if the last read was successful. That is why we were able to write `if (cin >> x >> y) {...}`.

If we, for example, try to read an integer, but the input contains `"foobar"` as the next token, then parsing this into the integer is not possible and the stream object enters a *fail state*. This is only critical for the parsing attempt but not for the whole program. It is okay to reset it and then to try anything else. In our recipe program, we tried to read a list of names after a potentially failing attempt to read two numbers. In the case of a failing attempt to read those numbers in, we used `cin.clear()` to put `cin` back into a working state. But then, its internal cursor was still on what we typed instead of numbers. In order to drop this old input and clear the pipe for the names input, we used the very long expression, `cin.ignore(std::numeric_limits<std::streamsize>::max(),` `'\n');`. This is necessary to clear whatever is in the buffer at this point, because we want to start with a really fresh buffer when we ask the user for a list of names.

The following loop might look strange at first, too:

```
for (string s; getline(cin >> ws, s, ',');) { ... }
```

In the conditional part of the `for` loop, we use `getline`. The `getline` function accepts an input stream object, a string reference as an output parameter, and a delimiter character. By default, the delimiter character is the newline symbol. Here, we defined it to be the comma (`,`) character, so all the names in a list, such as `"john, carl, frank"`, are read individually.

So far, so good. But what does it mean to provide the `cin >> ws` function as a stream object? This makes `cin` first flush all the whitespace, which lead before the next non-whitespace character and after the last comma. Looking back at the `"john, carl, frank"` example, we would get the substrings `"john"`, `" carl"`, and `" frank"` without using `ws`. Notice the unnecessary leading space characters for `carl` and `frank`? These effectively vanish because of our `ws` pretreatment of the input stream.

Counting all words in a file

Let's say we read a text file and we want to count the number of words in the text. We define that one word is a range of characters between whitespace characters. How do we do it?

We could count the number of spaces, for example, because there must be spaces between words. In the sentence, `"John has a funny little dog."`, we have five space characters, so we could say there are six words.

What if we have a sentence with whitespace noise, such as "   John   has   \t a\nfunny little dog .''? There are way too many unnecessary spaces in this string, and it's not even only spaces. From the other recipes in this book, we already learned how we can remove such excess whitespace. So, we could first preprocess the string into a normal sentence form and then apply the strategy of counting space characters. Yes, that is doable, but there is a *much* easier way. Why shouldn't we use what the STL already provides us?

In addition to finding an elegant solution for this problem, we will let the user choose if we shall count the words from the standard input or a text file.

How to do it...

In this section, we will write a one-liner function that counts the words from an input buffer, and let the user choose where the input buffer reads from:

1. Let's include all the necessary headers first and declare that we use the `std` namespace:

```
#include <iostream>
#include <fstream>
#include <string>
#include <algorithm>
#include <iterator>

using namespace std;
```

2. Our `wordcount` function accepts an input stream, for example, `cin`. It creates an `std::input_iterator` iterator, which tokenizes the strings out of the stream and then feeds them to `std::distance`. The `distance` parameter accepts two iterators as arguments and tries to determine how many incrementing steps are needed in order to get from one iterator position to the other. For *random access* iterators, this is simple because they implement the mathematical difference operation (`operator-`). Such iterators can be subtracted from each other like pointers. An `istream_iterator` however, is a *forward* iterator and must be advanced until it equals the end iterator. Eventually, the number of steps needed is the number of words:

```
template <typename T>
size_t wordcount(T &is)
{
    return distance(istream_iterator<string>{is}, {});
}
```

3. In our main function, we let the user choose if the input stream will be `std::cin` or an input file:

```
int main(int argc, char **argv)
{
    size_t wc;
```

4. If the user launches the program in the shell together with a file name (such as `$ ./count_all_words some_textfile.txt`), then we obtain that filename from the `argv` command-line parameter array and open it, in order to feed the new input file stream into `wordcount`:

```
if (argc == 2) {
    ifstream ifs {argv[1]};
    wc = wordcount(ifs);
```

5. If the user launched the program without any parameter, we assume that the input comes from standard input:

```
} else {
    wc = wordcount(cin);
}
```

6. That's already it, so we just print the number of words we saved in the variable `wc`:

```
    cout << "There are " << wc << " words\n";
};
```

7. Let's compile and run the program. First, we feed the program from standard input without any file parameter. We can either pipe an echo call with some words into it or launch the program and enter some words from the keyboard. In the latter case, we can stop the input by pressing *Ctrl+D*. This is how echoing some words into the program looks:

```
$ echo "foo bar baz" | ./count_all_words
There are 3 words
```

8. When launching the program with its source code file as input, it will count how many words it consists of:

```
$ ./count_all_words count_all_words.cpp
There are 61 words
```

How it works...

There is not much left to say; most of it has been explained while implementing it as this program is very short. One thing we could elaborate on a bit is the fact that we used `std::cin` and an `std::ifstream` instance in a completely interchangeable way. The `cin` is of the `std::istream` type, and `std::ifstream` inherits from `std::istream`. Have a look at the class inheritance diagram at the beginning of this chapter. This way, they are completely interchangeable, even at runtime.

Keep your code modular by using stream abstractions. This helps decouple source code parts and makes your code easy to test because you can just inject any other matching type of stream.

Formatting your output with I/O stream manipulators

In many cases, just printing out strings and numbers is not enough. Sometimes, numbers need to be printed as decimal numbers, sometimes as hexadecimal, and sometimes even as octal. Sometimes we want to see a `"0x"` prefix in front of hexadecimal numbers, sometimes not.

When printing floating-point numbers, there are also a lot of things we may want to have an influence on. Should the decimal values always be printed with the same precision? Should they be printed at all? Or perhaps, we want a scientific notation?

Apart from scientific presentation and hexadecimal, octal, and so on, we also want to present the user output in a tidy form. Some output can be arranged in tables, for example, in order to make it as readable as possible.

All these things are, of course, possible with output streams. Some of these settings are also important when *parsing* values from input streams. In this recipe, we will get a feeling of such so-called **I/O manipulators** by playing around with them. Sometimes, they appear tricky, so we will also get into some details.

How to do it...

In this section, we will print numbers with wildly varying format settings, in order to get familiar with I/O manipulators:

1. First, we include all the necessary headers and declare that we use the `std` namespace by default:

```
#include <iostream>
#include <iomanip>
#include <locale>

using namespace std;
```

2. Next, we define a helper function that prints a single integer value with different styles. It accepts a padding width and a filling character for padding, which is set to space ' ' by default:

```
void print_aligned_demo(int val,
                        size_t width,
                        char fill_char = ' ')
{
```

3. With `setw`, we can set the minimum number of characters output for printing a number. If we print 123 with a width of 6, for example, we get "   123", or "123   ". We can control on which side the padding occurs with `std::left`, `std::right`, and `std::internal`. When printing numbers in the decimal form, `internal` looks identical to `right`. But if we print the value 0x1, for example, with a width of 6 and with `internal`, we get "0x   6". The `setfill` manipulator defines the character that will be used for padding. We will try different styles:

```
cout << "================\n";
cout << setfill(fill_char);
cout << left     << setw(width) << val << '\n';
cout << right    << setw(width) << val << '\n';
cout << internal << setw(width) << val << '\n';
}
```

4. In the main function, we start using the function we just implemented. At first, we print the value 12345, with a width of 15. We do this twice, but the second time, we use the '_' character for padding:

```
int main()
{
    print_aligned_demo(123456, 15);
    print_aligned_demo(123456, 15, '_');
```

5. Afterward, we print the value 0x123abc with the same width as before. However, before doing this, we apply std::hex and std::showbase to tell the output stream object cout that it should print numbers in the hexadecimal format and that it should prepend "0x" to them so that it is obvious that they are to be interpreted as hex:

```
cout << hex << showbase;
print_aligned_demo(0x123abc, 15);
```

6. We can do the same with oct, which tells cout to use the octal system for printing numbers. The showbase is still active, so 0 will be prepended to every printed number:

```
cout << oct;
print_aligned_demo(0123456, 15);
```

7. With hex and uppercase, we get the 'x' in "0x" printed upper case. The 'abc' in '0x123abc' is also upper cased:

```
cout << "A hex number with upper case letters: "
    << hex << uppercase << 0x123abc << '\n';
```

8. If we want to print 100 in the decimal format again, we have to remember that we switched the stream to hex before. By using dec, we can put it back to normal:

```
cout << "A number: " << 100 << '\n';
cout << dec;
cout << "Oops. now in decimal again: " << 100 << '\n';
```

9. We can also configure how Boolean values are printed. By default, `true` is printed as `1` and `false` as `0`. With `boolalpha`, we can set it to a text representation:

```
cout << "true/false values: "
     << true << ", " << false << '\n';
cout << boolalpha
     << "true/false values: "
     << true << ", " << false << '\n';
```

10. Let's have a look at floating-point variables of the `float` and `double` types. If we print a number such as `12.3`, it is printed as `12.3`, of course. If we have a number such as `12.0`, the output stream will just drop the decimal point, which we can change with `showpoint`. Using this, the decimal point is always displayed:

```
cout << "doubles: "
     << 12.3 << ", "
     << 12.0 << ", "
     << showpoint << 12.0 << '\n';
```

11. The representation of a floating-point number can be scientific or fixed. `scientific` means that the number is *normalized* to such a form that the first digit is the only digit before the decimal point, and then the exponent is printed, which is needed to multiply the number back to its actual size. For example, the value `300.0` would be printed as `"3.0E2"`, because 300 equals `3.0 * 10^2`. `fixed` reverts back to the normal decimal point notation:

```
cout << "scientific double: " << scientific
     << 123000000000.123 << '\n';
cout << "fixed      double: " << fixed
     << 123000000000.123 << '\n';
```

12. Apart from the notation, we can also decide with what precision a floating-point number is printed. Let's create a very small value and print it with 10 digits after the decimal point, and once with just one digit after the decimal point:

```
cout << "Very precise double: "
     << setprecision(10) << 0.0000000001 << '\n';
cout << "Less precise double: "
     << setprecision(1)  << 0.0000000001 << '\n';
}
```

13. Compiling and running the program yields us the following lengthy output. Those four first blocks of output are from the print helper function that tampered around with the `setw` and `left`/`right`/`internal` modifiers. Afterward, we played with the casing of base representations, Boolean representation, and floating-point formatting. It is a good idea to play with each of these to get familiar with them:

```
$ ./formatting
================
123456
          123456
          123456
================
123456_____
_____123456
_____123456
================
0x123abc
        0x123abc
0x        123abc
================
0123456
        0123456
        0123456
A hex number with upper case letters: 0X123ABC
A number: 0X64
Oops. now in decimal again: 100
true/false values: 1, 0
true/false values: true, false
doubles: 12.3, 12, 12.0000
scientific double: 1.230000E+11
fixed       double: 123000000000.123001
Very precise double: 0.0000000001
Less precise double: 0.0
```

How it works...

All these, sometimes pretty long, `<< foo << bar` stream expressions are really confusing if it is not clear to the reader what each of them does. Therefore, let's have a look at a table of existing formatting modifiers. They are all to be placed in a `input_stream >> modifier` or `output_stream << modifier` expression and then affect the following input or output:

Symbol	Meaning
`setprecision(int n)`	Sets the precision parameter when printing or parsing floating-point values.
`showpoint` / `noshowpoint`	Enables or disables the printing of the decimal point of floating-point numbers even if they do not have any decimal places.
`fixed` / `scientific` / `hexfloat` / `defaultfloat`	Numbers can be printed in a fixed style (which is the most intuitive one) or scientific style. `fixed` and `scientific` stand for these modes. `hexfloat` activates both modes, which formats floating-point numbers in hexadecimal floating-point notation. `defaultfloat` deactivates both modes.
`showpos` / `noshowpos`	Enable or disable printing a `'+'` prefix for positive floating-point values.
`setw(int n)`	Read or write exactly n characters. When reading, this truncates the input. When printing, padding is applied if the output would be shorter than n characters.
`setfill(char c)`	When applying padding (see `setw`), fill the output with character values, c. The default is space (`' '`).
`internal` / `left` / `right`	`left` and `right` control where the padding for fixed-width prints (see `setw`) occurs. `internal` puts padding characters in the middle between integers and their negative sign, the hex prefix and a hexadecimally printed value, or monetary units and values.
`dec` / `hex` / `oct`	Integral values can be printed and parsed in the decimal, hexadecimal, and octal base systems.

`setbase(int n)`	This is the numeric synonymous function to `dec`/`hex`/`oct`, which are equivalent if used with the values 10/16/8. Other values reset the base choice to 0, which leads to decimal printing again, or parsing based on the prefix of the input.
`quoted(string)`	Prints string in quotes or parse from quoted input, and then drops the quotes. `string` can be a String class instance or a C-style character array.
`boolalpha` / `noboolalpha`	Prints or parses Boolean values as/from alphabetical representation rather than 1/0 strings.
`showbase` / `noshowbase`	Enables or disables base-prefixes when printing or parsing numbers. For `hex`, this is `0x`; for `octal` it is 0.
`uppercase` / `nouppercase`	Enables or disables upper casing or alphabetical characters when printing floating-point and hexadecimal values.

The best way to get familiar with those is studying their variety a bit and playing with them.

When playing with them, however, we might have noticed already that most of these modifiers appear to be *sticky* and a few of them, not so. Sticky means that once applied, they appear to influence the input/output *forever* until they are reset again. The only non-sticky ones from this table are `setw` and `quoted`. They only affect the next item in the input/output. This is important to know because if we print some output with certain formatting, we should tidy up our stream object formatting settings afterward, because the next output from unrelated code may otherwise look crazy. Same applies to input parsing, where things can break with the wrong I/O manipulator options.

We did not really use any of those because they do not have to do anything with formatting, but for the reason of completeness, we should also have a look at some other stream state manipulators:

Symbol	Meaning
`skipws` / `noskipws`	Enables or disables the feature of input streams skipping whitespace
`unitbuf` / `nounitbuf`	Enables or disables immediate output buffer flushing after any output operation
`ws`	Can be used on input streams to skip any whitespace at the head of the stream
`ends`	Writes a string-terminating `'\0'` character into a stream

flush	Immediately flushes out whatever is in the output buffer
endl	Inserts a '\n' character into an output stream and flushes the output

From these, only `skipws/noskipws` and `unitbuf/nounitbuf` appear sticky.

Initializing complex objects from file input

Reading in individual integers, floats, and word strings is really easy, because the `>>` operator of input stream objects is overloaded for all these types, and input streams conveniently drop all in-between whitespace for us.

But what if we have a more complex structure that we want to read from an input stream, and if we need to read strings that contain more than one word (as they would normally be chunked into single words because of the whitespace skipping)?

For any type, it is possible to provide another input stream `operator>>` overload, and we are going to see how to do it.

How to do it...

In this section, we'll define a custom data structure and provide facilities to read such items from input streams as standard input:

1. We need to include some headers first and for comfort, we declare that we use the `std` namespace by default:

```
#include <iostream>
#include <iomanip>
#include <string>
#include <algorithm>
#include <iterator>
#include <vector>

using namespace std;
```

2. As a complex object example, we define a `city` structure. A city shall have a name, a population count, and geographic coordinates:

```
struct city {
    string name;
    size_t population;
    double latitude;
    double longitude;
};
```

3. In order to be able to read such a city from a serial input stream, we need to overload the stream function `operator>>`. In this operator, we first skip all the leading whitespace with `ws`, because we do not want whitespace to pollute the city name. Then, we read a whole line of text input. This implies that in the input file, there is a whole text line only carrying the name of a city object. Then, after a newline character, a whitespace-separated list of numbers follows, indicating the population, the geographic latitude, and the longitude:

```
istream& operator>>(istream &is, city &c)
{
    is >> ws;
    getline(is, c.name);
    is >> c.population
       >> c.latitude
       >> c.longitude;
    return is;
}
```

4. In our main function, we create a vector that can hold a range of city items. We fill it using `std::copy`. The input of the copy call is an `istream_iterator` range. By giving it the `city` struct type as a template parameter, it will use the `operator>>` function overload, which we just implemented:

```
int main()
{
    vector<city> l;
    copy(istream_iterator<city>{cin}, {},
        back_inserter(l));
```

5. In order to see whether our city parsing went right, we print what we got in the list. The I/O formatting, `left << setw(15) <<`, leads to the city name being filled with whitespace, so we get our output in a nicely readable form:

```
for (const auto &[name, pop, lat, lon] : l) {
    cout << left << setw(15) << name
         << " population=" << pop
         << " lat=" << lat
         << " lon=" << lon << '\n';
}
}
```

6. The text file from which we will feed our program looks like this. There are four example cities with their population count and geographical coordinates:

```
Braunschweig
250000 52.268874 10.526770
Berlin
4000000 52.520007 13.404954
New York City
8406000 40.712784 -74.005941
Mexico City
8851000 19.432608 -99.133208
```

7. Compiling and running the program yields the following output, which is what we expected. Try to tamper around with the input file by adding some unnecessary whitespace before the city names in order to see how it gets filtered out:

```
$ cat cities.txt  | ./initialize_complex_objects
Braunschweig    population=250000 lat=52.2689 lon=10.5268
Berlin          population=4000000 lat=52.52 lon=13.405
New York City   population=8406000 lat=40.7128 lon=-74.0059
Mexico City     population=8851000 lat=19.4326 lon=-99.1332
```

How it works...

This was another short recipe again. The only thing we did was creating a new struct `city`, then we overloaded `std::istream` iterator's `operator>>` for this type and that's it. This already enabled us to deserialize city items from standard input using `istream_iterator<city>`.

There might be an open question left regarding error checking. For that, let's have a look at the `operator>>` implementation again:

```
istream& operator>>(istream &is, city &c)
{
    is >> ws;
    getline(is, c.name);
    is >> c.population >> c.latitude >> c.longitude;
    return is;
}
```

We are reading a lot of different things. What happens if one of them fails and the next one doesn't? Does that mean that we are potentially reading all following items with a bad "offset" in the token stream? No, this cannot happen. As soon as one of these items cannot be parsed from the input stream, the input stream object enters an error state and refuses to parse anything further. This means that if for example `c.population` or `c.latitude` cannot be parsed, the remaining `>>` operands just "drop through", and we leave this operator function scope with a half-deserialized city object.

On the caller side, we are notified by this when we write `if (input_stream >> city_object)`. Such a streaming expression is implicitly converted to a bool value when used as a conditional expression. It returns `false` if the input stream object is in an error state. Knowing that we can reset the stream and do whatever is appropriate.

In this recipe, we did not write such `if` conditionals ourselves because we let `std::istream_iterator<city>` do the deserialization. The `operator++` implementation of this iterator class also checks for errors while parsing. If any errors occur, it will refuse iterating further. In this state, it returns `true` when it is compared to the end iterator, which makes the `copy` algorithm terminate. This way, we are safe.

Filling containers from std::istream iterators

In the last recipe, we learned how we can assemble compound data structures from an input stream and then fill lists or vectors with those.

This time, we make it a little bit harder by filling an `std::map` from standard input. The problem here is that we cannot just fill a single structure with values and push it back into a linear container like a list or a vector is because `map` divides its payload into key and value parts. It is, however, not completely different, as we will see.

After studying this recipe, we will feel comfortable with serializing and deserializing complex data structures from and to character streams.

How to do it...

We are going to define another structure like in the last recipe, but this time we are going to fill it into a map, which makes it more complicated because this container maps from keys to values instead of just holding all values in a list:

1. First, we include all the needed headers and declare that we use the `std` namespace by default:

```
#include <iostream>
#include <iomanip>
#include <map>
#include <iterator>
#include <algorithm>
#include <numeric>

using namespace std;
```

2. We want to maintain a little Internet meme database. Let's say a meme has a name, a description, and the year when it was born or invented. We will save them in an `std::map`, where the name is the key, and the other information is bunched up in a struct as the value associated with the key:

```
struct meme {
    string description;
    size_t year;
};
```

3. Let's first ignore the key and just implement a stream `operator>>` function overload for `struct meme`. We assume that the description is surrounded by quotation marks, followed by the year. This would look like `"some description" 2017` in a text file. As the description is surrounded by quotation marks, it can contain whitespace because we know that everything between the quotation marks belongs to it. By reading with `is >> quoted(m.description)`, the quotation marks are automatically used as delimiters and dropped afterward. This is very convenient. Just after that, we read the year number:

```
istream& operator>>(istream &is, meme &m) {
    return is >> quoted(m.description) >> m.year;
}
```

4. OK, now we take the meme's name as the key for the map into account. In order to insert a meme into the map, we need an `std::pair<key_type, value_type>` instance. `key_type` is `string`, of course, and `value_type` is `meme`. The name is allowed to contain spaces too, so we use the same `quoted` wrapper as for the description. `p.first` is the name and `p.second` is the whole `meme` structure associated with it. It will be fed into the other `operator>>` implementation that we just implemented:

```
istream& operator >>(istream &is,
                     pair<string, meme> &p) {
    return is >> quoted(p.first) >> p.second;
}
```

5. Okay, that's it. Let's write a main function, which instantiates a map, and fill that map. Because we overloaded the stream function `operator>>`, `istream_iterator` can deal with this type directly. We let it deserialize our meme items from standard input and use an `inserter` iterator in order to pump them into the map:

```
int main()
{
    map<string, meme> m;
    copy(istream_iterator<pair<string, meme>>{cin},
        {},
        inserter(m, end(m)));
```

6. Before we print what we have, let's first find out what's the *longest* meme name in the map. We use `std::accumulate` for this. It gets an initial value `0u` (u for unsigned) and will visit the map element-wise in order to *merge* them together. In terms of `accumulate`, merging usually means *adding*. In our case, we want no numeric *sum* of anything, but the largest string length. In order to get that, we provide `accumulate` a helper function, `max_func`, which takes the current maximum size variable (which must be `unsigned` because string lengths are unsigned) and compares it to the length of the current item's meme name string, in order to take the maximum of both values. This will happen for each element. The `accumulate` function's final return value is the maximum meme name length:

```
auto max_func ([](size_t old_max,
                  const auto &b) {
    return max(old_max, b.first.length());
});
size_t width {accumulate(begin(m), end(m),
                         0u, max_func)};
```

7. Now, let's quickly loop through the map and print each item. We use `<< left << setw(width)` to get a nice table-like printing:

```
for (const auto &[meme_name, meme_desc] : m) {
    const auto &[desc, year] = meme_desc;
    cout << left << setw(width) << meme_name
         << " : " << desc
         << ", " << year << '\n';
}
}
```

8. That's it. We need a small Internet meme database file, so let's fill a text file with some examples:

```
"Doge" "Very Shiba Inu. so dog. much funny. wow." 2013
"Pepe" "Anthropomorphic frog" 2016
"Gabe" "Musical dog on maximum borkdrive" 2016
"Honey Badger" "Crazy nastyass honey badger" 2011
"Dramatic Chipmunk" "Chipmunk with a very dramatic look" 2007
```

9. Compiling and running the program with the example meme database yields the following output:

```
$ cat memes.txt | ./filling_containers
Doge                : Very Shiba Inu. so dog. much funny. wow., 2013
Dramatic Chipmunk : Chipmunk with a very dramatic look, 2007
Gabe                : Musical dog on maximum borkdrive, 2016
Honey Badger        : Crazy nastyass honey badger, 2011
Pepe                : Anthropomorphic frog, 2016
```

How it works...

There were three specialties in this recipe. One was that we did not fill a normal vector or a list from a serial character stream, but a more complex container like `std::map`. The other was that we used those magic `quoted` stream manipulators. And the last was the `accumulate` call, which finds out the largest key string size.

Let's start with the `map` part. Our `struct meme` only contains a `description` field and `year`. The name of the Internet meme is not part of this structure because it is used as the key for the map. When we insert something into a map, we can provide an `std::pair` with a key type and a value type. This is what we did. We first implemented stream `operator>>` for `struct meme`, and then we did the same for `pair<string, meme>`. Then we used `istream_iterator<`**`pair<string, meme>`**`>{cin}` to get such items out of the standard input, and fed them into the map using `inserter(m, end(m))`.

When we deserialized meme items from the stream, we allowed the names and descriptions to contain whitespace. This was easily possible, although we only used one line per meme because we *quoted* those fields. An example of the line format is as follows: `"Name with spaces" "Description with spaces" 123`

When dealing with quoted strings both in input and output, `std::quoted` is a great help. If we have a string, `s`, printing it using `cout << quoted(s)` will put it in quotes. If we deserialize a string from a stream, for example, via `cin >> quoted(s)`, it will read the next quotation mark, fill the string with what is following, and continue until it sees the next quotation mark, no matter how many whitespace are involved.

The last strange looking thing was `max_func` in our accumulate call:

```
auto max_func ([](size_t old_max, const auto &b) {
    return max(old_max, b.first.length());
});

size_t width {accumulate(begin(m), end(m), 0u, max_func)};
```

Apparently, `max_func` accepts a `size_t` argument and another `auto`-typed argument which turns out to be a `pair` item from the map. This looks really weird at first as most binary reduction functions accept arguments of identical types and then merge them together with some operation, just as `std::plus` does. In this case, it is really different because we are not merging actual `pair` items. We only pick the key string length from every pair, *drop* the rest, and then reduce the resulting `size_t` values with the `max` function.

In the accumulate call, the first call of `max_func` gets the `0u` value we initially provided as the left argument and a reference to the first pair item on the right side. This results in a `max(0u, string_length)` return value, which is the left argument in the *next* call with the next pair item as the right parameter, and so on.

Generic printing with std::ostream iterators

It is pretty easy to print anything with output streams, as the STL is already shipped with many useful `operator<<` overloads for the most basic types. This way, data structures containing items of such types can easily be printed using the `std::ostream_iterator` class, which we've already done quite often in this book.

In this recipe, we will concentrate on how to do this with a custom type, and what else we can do to manipulate printing via template type choices without much code at the caller side.

How to do it...

We will play with `std::ostream_iterator` by enabling for combination with a new custom class and have a look into its implicit conversion capabilities, which can help us with printing:

1. The include files come first and then we declare that we use the `std` namespace by default:

```
#include <iostream>
#include <vector>
#include <iterator>
#include <unordered_map>
#include <algorithm>

using namespace std;
```

2. Let's implement a transformation function, which maps numbers to strings. It shall return `"one"` for the value 1, `"two"` for the value 2, and so on:

```
string word_num(int i) {
```

3. We fill a hash map with the mappings we need in order to access them later:

```
    unordered_map<int, string> m {
        {1, "one"}, {2, "two"}, {3, "three"},
        {4, "four"}, {5, "five"}, //...
    };
```

4. Now, we can feed the hash map's `find` function with the argument, `i`, and return what it finds. If it doesn't find anything, because there is no translation for a given number, we return the string, `"unknown"`:

```
    const auto match (m.find(i));
    if (match == end(m)) { return "unknown"; }
    return match->second;
};
```

5. Another thing with which we will play later with is `struct bork`. It only contains an integer and is also implicitly constructible from an integer. It has a `print` function, which accepts an output stream reference and prints the `"bork"` string repeatedly, depending on the value of its member integer `borks`:

```
struct bork {
    int borks;
```

```
    bork(int i) : borks{i} {}

    void print(ostream& os) const {
        fill_n(ostream_iterator<string>{os, " "},
            borks, "bork!"s);
    }
};
```

6. In order to gain convenience with `bork::print` we overload `operator<<` for stream objects, so they automatically call `bork::print` whenever `bork` objects are streamed into an output stream:

```
ostream& operator<<(ostream &os, const bork &b) {
    b.print(os);
    return os;
}
```

7. Now we can finally begin implementing the actual main function. We initially just create a vector with some example values:

```
int main()
{
    const vector<int> v {1, 2, 3, 4, 5};
```

8. Objects of type `ostream_iterator` need a template parameter, which denotes which type of variables they can print. If we write `ostream_iterator<T>`, it will later use `ostream& operator(ostream&, const T&)` for printing. This is exactly what we implemented before for the `bork` type, for example. This time, we are just printing integers, so it is `ostream_iterator<int>`. It shall use `cout` for printing, so we provide it as the constructor parameter. We go through our vector in a loop and assign each item `i` to the dereferenced output iterator. This is how stream iterators are used by STL algorithms too:

```
    ostream_iterator<int> oit {cout};
    for (int i : v) { *oit = i; }
    cout << '\n';
```

9. The output of the iterator we just produced is fine, but it prints the number without any separator. If we want a bit of separating whitespace between all printed items, we can provide a custom spacing string as a second parameter of the output stream iterator's constructor. This way, it prints "1, 2, 3, 4, 5, " instead of "12345". Unfortunately, we cannot easily tell it to drop the comma-space string after the last number, because the iterator does not know of its end before it reaches it:

```
ostream_iterator<int> oit_comma {cout, ", "};
for (int i : v) { *oit_comma = i; }
cout << '\n';
```

10. Assigning items to an output stream iterator in order to print them is not a wrong way to use it, but this is not what they were invented for. The idea is to use them in combination with algorithms. The simplest one is std::copy. We can provide the begin and end iterators of the vector as an input range and the output stream iterator as the output iterator. It will print all the numbers of the vector. Let's do that with both the output iterators and later compare the output with the loops we wrote before:

```
copy(begin(v), end(v), oit);
cout << '\n';
copy(begin(v), end(v), oit_comma);
cout << '\n';
```

11. Remember the function, word_num, which maps numbers to strings, as 1 to "one", 2 to "two", and so on? Yes, we can use those for printing too. We just need to use an output stream operator, which is template specialized on string because we are not printing integers any longer. And instead of std::copy, we use std::transform because it allows us to apply a transformation function to each item in the input range before copying it to the output range:

```
transform(begin(v), end(v),
          ostream_iterator<string>{cout, " "},
          word_num);
cout << '\n';
```

12. The last output line in this program finally puts `struct bork` to use. We could, but do not provide a transformation function to `std::transform`. Instead, we can just create an output stream iterator, which is specialized on the `bork` type in an `std::copy` call. This leads to the `bork` instances being *implicitly* created from the input range integers. That will give us some interesting output:

```
copy(begin(v), end(v),
    ostream_iterator<bork>{cout, "\n"});
}
```

13. Compiling and running the program yields us the following output. The first two lines are completely identical to the next two lines, which is what we suspected. Then, we get nice, written-out number strings in a line, followed by a lot of `bork!` strings. These occur in multiple lines because we used a `"\n"` separator string instead of spaces for those:

```
$ ./ostream_printing
12345
1, 2, 3, 4, 5,
12345
1, 2, 3, 4, 5,
one two three four five
bork!
bork! bork!
bork! bork! bork!
bork! bork! bork! bork!
bork! bork! bork! bork! bork!
```

How it works...

We have seen that `std::ostream_iterator` is really just a *syntax hack*, which kind of squeezes the act of printing into the form and syntax of an iterator. Incrementing such an iterator does *nothing*. Dereferencing it only returns us a proxy object whose assignment operator forwards its argument to an output stream.

Output stream iterators that are specialized on a type T (as in `ostream_iterator<T>`) work with all types for which an `ostream& operator<<(ostream&, const T&)` implementation is provided.

`ostream_iterator` always tries to call `operator<<` for the type it was specialized for, via its template parameter. It will try to implicitly convert types if the same is allowed. When we iterate over a range of A-typed items but we copy those items over to `output_iterator<B>` instances, this will work if A is implicitly convertible to B. We did exactly the same thing with `struct bork`: a `bork` instance is implicitly convertible from an integer value. That is why it was so easy to throw a lot of `"bork!"` strings onto the user shell.

If implicit conversion is not possible, we can do that ourselves, using `std::transform`, which is what we did in combination with the `word_num` function.

Note that it is, in general, *bad style* to allow implicit conversions for custom types because this is a common *source of bugs* that are really hard to find later. In our example use case, the implicit constructor is more useful than dangerous because the class is used for nothing else but printing.

Redirecting output to files for specific code sections

The `std::cout` provides a really nice way to print whatever we want, whenever we want because it is simple to use, easily extensible, and globally accessible. Even if we want to print special messages, such as error messages, which we want to isolate from normal messages, we can just use `std::cerr`, which is the same as `cout` but prints to the standard error channel instead of the standard output channel.

We might have some more complicated desires for logging sometimes. Let's say, for example, we want to *redirect* the output of a function to a file, or we want to *mute* the output of a function, without changing the function at all. Perhaps, it is a library function we cannot access the source code of. Maybe, it was never designed to write to a file but we want its output in a file.

It is indeed possible to redirect the output of stream objects. In this recipe, we are going to see how to do that in a very simple and elegant way.

How to do it...

We are going to implement a helper class that solves the problem of redirecting a stream and reverting that redirection again with constructor/destructor magic. And then we see how we can put it to use:

1. We only need the headers for input, output, and file streams this time. And we declare the `std` namespace as a default namespace for lookup:

```
#include <iostream>
#include <fstream>

using namespace std;
```

2. We implement a class, which holds a file stream object and a pointer to a stream buffer. The `cout` as a stream object has an internal stream buffer, which we can simply exchange. And while we exchange it, we can save what it was before, so we can *undo* any change later. We could look its type up in the C++ reference, but we can also use `decltype` to find out what type `cout.rdbuf()` returns. This is not generally good practice in all situations, but in this case, it's just a pointer type:

```
class redirect_cout_region
{
    using buftype = decltype(cout.rdbuf());
    ofstream ofs;
    buftype  buf_backup;
```

3. The constructor of our class accepts a filename string as its only parameter. The filename is used to initialize the file stream member, `ofs`. After initializing it, we can feed it into `cout` as a new stream buffer. The same function that accepts the new buffer also returns a pointer to the old one, so we can save it in order to restore it later:

```
public:
    explicit
    redirect_cout_region (const string &filename)
        : ofs{filename},
          buf_backup{cout.rdbuf(ofs.rdbuf())}
    {}
```

4. The default constructor does the same as the other constructor. The difference is, that it does not open any file. Feeding a default-constructed file stream buffer into the `cout` stream buffer leads to `cout` being kind of *deactivated*. It will just *drop* its input we give it for printing. This can also be useful in some situations:

```
redirect_cout_region()
    : ofs{},
      buf_backup{cout.rdbuf(ofs.rdbuf())}
{}
```

5. The destructor just restores our change. When an object of this class runs out of scope, the stream buffer of `cout` is the old one again:

```
~redirect_cout_region() {
    cout.rdbuf(buf_backup);
}
};
```

6. Let's mock an *output-heavy* function, so we can play with it later:

```
void my_output_heavy_function()
{
    cout << "some output\n";
    cout << "this function does really heavy work\n";
    cout << "... and lots of it...\n";
    // ...
}
```

7. In the main function, we first produce some completely normal output:

```
int main()
{
    cout << "Readable from normal stdout\n";
```

8. Now we're opening another scope, and the first thing we do in this scope is instantiating our new class with a text file parameter. File streams open files in read and write mode by default, so it creates this file for us. Any following output will now be redirected to this file, although we use cout for printing:

```
{
    redirect_cout_region _ {"output.txt"};
    cout << "Only visible in output.txt\n";
    my_output_heavy_function();
}
```

9. After leaving the scope, the file is closed and the output is redirected to the normal standard output again. Let's now open another scope in which we instantiate the same class, but via its default constructor. This way the following printed line of text will not be visible anywhere. It will just be dropped:

```
{
    redirect_cout_region _;
    cout << "This output will "
            "completely vanish\n";
}
```

10. After leaving that scope also, our standard output is resurrected and the last line of text output will be readable in the shell again:

```
    cout << "Readable from normal stdout again\n";
}
```

11. Compiling and running the program yields the output as we expected it. Only the very first and the very last lines of output are visible in the shell:

```
$ ./log_regions
Readable from normal stdout
Readable from normal stdout again
```

12. We can see that a new file, `output.txt`, has been created and contains the output of the first scope. The output of the second scope vanishes completely:

```
$ cat output.txt
Only visible in output.txt
some output
this function does really heavy work
... and lots of it...
```

How it works...

Every stream object has an internal buffer for which it acts as a front end. Such buffers are exchangeable. If we have a stream object, `s`, and want to save its buffer into a variable, `a`, and install a new buffer, `b`, this looks like the following: `a = s.rdbuf(b)`. Restoring it can be simply done with `s.rdbuf(a)`.

This is exactly what we did in this recipe. Another cool thing is that we can *stack* those `redirect_cout_region` helpers:

```
{
    cout << "print to standard output\n";

    redirect_cout_region la {"a.txt"};
    cout << "print to a.txt\n";
    redirect_cout_region lb {"b.txt"};
    cout << "print to b.txt\n";
}
cout << "print to standard output again\n";
```

This works because objects are destructed in the opposite order of their construction. The concept behind this pattern that uses the tight coupling between construction and destruction of objects is called **Resource Acquisition Is Initialization (RAII)**.

There is one really important thing that should be mentioned--the *initialization order* of the member variables of the `redirect_cout_region` class:

```
class redirect_cout_region {
    using buftype = decltype(cout.rdbuf());

    ofstream ofs;
    buftype  buf_backup;

public:
    explicit
    redirect_cout_region(const string &filename)
        : ofs{filename},
          buf_backup{cout.rdbuf(ofs.rdbuf())}
    {}

    ...
```

As we can see, the member, `buf_backup`, is constructed from an expression that depends on `ofs`. This obviously means that `ofs` needs to be initialized before `buf_backup`. Interestingly, the order in which these members are initialized does *not* depend on the order of the initializer list items. The initialization order only depends on the order of the *member declarations*!

> If one class member variable needs to be initialized after another member variable, they *must* also appear in that order in the class member declaration. The order of their appearance in the initializer list of the constructor is not critical.

Creating custom string classes by inheriting from std::char_traits

The `std::string` is extremely useful. However, as soon as people need a string class with slightly different semantics for string handling, some tend to write their *own* string class.

Writing your own string class is rarely a good idea because safe string handling is hard. Fortunately, `std::string` is only a specializing typedef of the template class, `std::basic_string`. This class contains all the complicated memory handling stuff, but it does not impose any policy on how strings are copied, compared, and so on. This is something that is imported into `basic_string` by accepting a template parameter that contains a traits class.

In this recipe, we will see how to build our own trait classes and, this way, how to create custom strings without reimplementing anything.

How to do it...

We are going to implement two different custom string classes: `lc_string` and `ci_string`. The first class constructs lower case strings from any string input. The other class does not transform any string, but it can do case-insensitive string comparison:

1. Let's include the few necessary headers first and then declare that we use the `std` namespace by default:

```cpp
#include <iostream>
#include <algorithm>
#include <string>

using namespace std;
```

2. Then we reimplement the `std::tolower` function, which is already defined in `<cctype>`. The already existing function is fine, but it is not `constexpr`. Some `string` functions are `constexpr` since C++17, however, and we want to be able to make use of that with our own custom string trait class. The function maps upper-case characters to lower case and leaves other characters unchanged:

```cpp
static constexpr char tolow(char c) {
    switch (c) {
    case 'A'...'Z': return c - 'A' + 'a';
    default:        return c;
    }
}
```

3. The `std::basic_string` class accepts three template parameters: the underlying character type, a character traits class, and an allocator type. We are only changing the character traits class in this section because it defines the behavior of strings. In order to reimplement only what should differ from the ordinary strings, we are publicly inheriting from the standard traits class:

```
class lc_traits : public char_traits<char> {
public:
```

4. Our class accepts input strings but transforms them to lower case. There is one function, which does this character-wise, so we can put our own `tolow` function here. This function is `constexpr`, which is why we reimplemented ourselves a `constexpr tolow` function:

```
static constexpr
void assign(char_type& r, const char_type& a ) {
    r = tolow(a);
}
```

5. The other function handles the copying of an entire string into its own memory. We use an `std::transform` call to copy all the characters from the source string to the internal destination string and, at the same time, map every character to its lower-case version:

```
static char_type* copy(char_type* dest,
                       const char_type* src,
                       size_t count) {
    transform(src, src + count, dest, tolow);
    return dest;
}
};
```

6. The other trait helps build a string class that effectively transforms strings to lower case. We are going to write another trait that leaves the actual string payload untouched but which is case insensitive when it comes to comparing strings. We inherit from the existing standard character traits class again, and this time, we redefine some other member functions:

```
class ci_traits : public char_traits<char> {
public:
```

7. The `eq` function tells whether two characters are equal. We do this too, but we compare their lower-case versions. This way `'A'` equals `'a'`:

```
static constexpr bool eq(char_type a, char_type b) {
    return tolow(a) == tolow(b);
}
```

8. The `lt` function tells whether the value of `a` is less than the value of `b`. We apply the correct logical operator for that, just after lower-casing both the characters again:

```
static constexpr bool lt(char_type a, char_type b) {
    return tolow(a) < tolow(b);
}
```

9. The last two functions worked on character-wise input and the next two functions work on string-wise input. The `compare` function works similar to the old-school `strncmp` function. It returns 0 if both the strings are equal within the length that `count` defines. If they differ, it returns a negative or positive number, which tells which input string is lexicographically smaller. Calculating the difference between both the characters at every position must, of course, be done on their lower-case versions. The nice thing is that this whole loop code has been part of a `constexpr` function since C++14:

```
static constexpr int compare(const char_type* s1,
                             const char_type* s2,
                             size_t count) {
    for (; count; ++s1, ++s2, --count) {
        const char_type diff (tolow(*s1) - tolow(*s2));
        if      (diff < 0) { return -1; }
        else if (diff > 0) { return +1; }
    }
    return 0;
}
```

10. The last function we need to implement for our case-insensitive string class is `find`. For a given input string, `p`, and length, `count`, it finds the position of a character, `ch`. Then, it returns a pointer to the first occurrence of that character, or it returns `nullptr` if there is none. The comparison in this function has to be done using the `tolow` "glasses" in order to make the search case-insensitive. Unfortunately, we cannot use `std::find_if`, because it is not `constexpr`, and must write a loop ourselves:

```
    static constexpr
    const char_type* find(const char_type* p,
                          size_t count,
                          const char_type& ch) {
        const char_type find_c {tolow(ch)};
        for (; count != 0; --count, ++p) {
            if (find_c == tolow(*p)) { return p; }
        }
        return nullptr;
    }
};
```

11. Okay, that's it for the traits. Since we have them in place now, we can define two new string class types. `lc_string` means *lower-case string*. `ci_string` means *case-insensitive string*. Both the classes only differ from `std::string` by their character traits class:

```
using lc_string = basic_string<char, lc_traits>;
using ci_string = basic_string<char, ci_traits>;
```

12. In order to make the output streams accept these new classes for printing, we quickly need to overload the stream `operator<<`:

```
ostream& operator<<(ostream& os, const lc_string& str) {
    return os.write(str.data(), str.size());
}
ostream& operator<<(ostream& os, const ci_string& str) {
    return os.write(str.data(), str.size());
}
```

13. Now we can finally begin implementing the actual program. Let's instantiate a normal string, a lower-case string, and a case-insensitive string, and print them immediately. They should all look normal on the terminal, but the lower case strings should be all lower-cased:

```
int main()
{
    cout << "    string: "
         << string{"Foo Bar Baz"} << '\n'
         << "lc_string: "
         << lc_string{"Foo Bar Baz"} << '\n'
         << "ci_string: "
         << ci_string{"Foo Bar Baz"} << '\n';
```

14. In order to test the case-insensitive string, we can instantiate two strings that are basically equal but differ in the casing of some characters. When doing a really case-insensitive comparison, they should appear equal nevertheless:

```
ci_string user_input {"MaGiC PaSsWoRd!"};
ci_string password   {"magic password!"};
```

15. So, let's compare them and print that they match if they do:

```
if (user_input == password) {
    cout << "Passwords match: \"" << user_input
         << "\" == \"" << password << "\"\n";
}
}
```

16. Compiling and running the program yields us the expected results. When we first printed the same string three times in different types, we got unchanged results, but the `lc_string` instance is all lower case. The comparison of the two strings that only differ in their character casing was indeed successful and yields us the right output:

```
$ ./custom_string
   string: Foo Bar Baz
lc_string: foo bar baz
ci_string: Foo Bar Baz
Passwords match: "MaGiC PaSsWoRd!" == "magic password!"
```

How it works...

All the subclassing, and function reimplementing we did will surely look a bit crazy for beginners. Where did all the function signatures come from, of which we *magically* knew that we need to reimplement?

Let's first have a look where `std::string` really comes from:

```
template <
    class CharT,
    class Traits    = std::char_traits<CharT>,
    class Allocator = std::allocator<CharT>
    >
class basic_string;
```

The `std::string` is really an `std::basic_string<char>` and that expands to `std::basic_string<char, std::char_traits<char>, std::allocator<char>>`. Okay, that is a long type description, but what does it mean? The point of all of this is that it is possible to base a string not only on single-byte `char` items but also on other, larger, types. This enables for string types, which can handle more than the typical American ASCII character set. This is not something we will have a look into now.

The `char_traits<char>` class, however, contains algorithms that `basic_string` needs for its operation. The `char_traits<char>` knows how to compare, find, and copy characters and strings.

The `allocator<char>` class is also a traits class, but its special job is handling string allocation and deallocation. This is not important for us at this time as the default behavior satisfies our needs.

If we want a string class to behave differently, we can try to reuse as much as possible from what `basic_string` and `char_traits` already provide. And this is what we did. We implemented two `char_traits` subclasses called `case_insentitive` and `lower_caser` and configured two completely new string types with them by using them as substitutes for the standard `char_traits` type.

In order to explore what other possibilities there are to adapt `basic_string` to your own needs, look up the C++ STL documentation for `std::char_traits` and see what other functions it has that can be reimplemented.

Tokenizing input with the regular expression library

When parsing or transforming strings in complex ways or breaking them into chunks, *regular expressions* are a great help. In many programming languages, they are already built in because they are so useful and handy.

If you do not know regular expressions yet, have a look at the *Wikipedia* article about them, for example. They will surely extend your horizon, as it is easy to see how useful they are when parsing any kind of text. Regular expressions can, for example, test whether an e-mail address string or an IP address string is valid, find and extract substrings out of large strings, which follow a complex pattern, and so on.

In this recipe, we will extract all the links out of an HTML file and list them for the user. The code will be amazingly short because we have regular expression support built in the C++ STL since C++11.

How to do it...

We are going to define a regular expression that detects links, and we apply it to an HTML file in order to pretty print all the links that occur in that file:

1. Let's first include all the necessary headers, and declare that we use the std namespace by default:

```
#include <iostream>
#include <iterator>
#include <regex>
#include <algorithm>
#include <iomanip>

using namespace std;
```

2. We will later generate an iterable range, which consists of strings. These strings always occur in pairs of a link and a link description. Therefore, let's write a little helper function, which pretty prints these:

```
template <typename InputIt>
void print(InputIt it, InputIt end_it)
{
    while (it != end_it) {
```

3. In each loop step, we increment the iterator twice and take copies of the link and the link description they contain. Between the two iterator dereferences, we add another guarding if branch that checks whether we prematurely reached the end of the iterable range, just for safety:

```
        const string link {*it++};
        if (it == end_it) { break; }
        const string desc {*it++};
```

4. Now, let's print the link with its description in a nicely prettified form and that's it:

```
cout << left << setw(28) << desc
    << " : " << link << '\n';
    }
}
```

5. In the main function, we are reading in everything that comes from standard input. To do this, we are constructing a string from the whole standard input via an input stream iterator. In order to prevent tokenizing, because we want the whole user input as-is, we use `noskipws`. This modifier deactivates whitespace skipping and tokenizing:

```
int main()
{
    cin >> noskipws;
    const std::string in {istream_iterator<char>{cin}, {}};
```

6. Now we need to define a regular expression that describes how we assume an HTML link to look. The parentheses, `()`, within the regular expression define groups. These are the parts of the link we want to access--the URL it links to, and its description:

```
const regex link_re {
    "<a href=\"([^\"]*)\"[^<]*>([^<]*)</a>"};
```

7. The `sregex_token_iterator` class has the same look and feel as of `istream_iterator`. We give it the whole string as iterable input range and the regular expression we just defined. There is also a third parameter, `{1, 2}`, which is an initializer list of integer values. It defines that we want to iterate over the groups 1 and 2 from the expressions it captures:

```
sregex_token_iterator it {
    begin(in), end(in), link_re, {1, 2}};
```

8. Now we have an iterator that will emit the links and link descriptions if it finds any. We provide it together with a default constructed iterator of the same type to the `print` function we implemented before:

```
    print(it, {});
}
```

9. Compiling and running the program gives us the following output. I ran the `curl` program on the ISO C++ homepage, which simply downloads an HTML page from the Internet. Of course, it would also be possible to write `cat some_html_file.html | ./link_extraction`. The regular expression we used is pretty much hardcoded to a fixed assumption of how links look in the HTML document. It may be exercised by you to make it more general:

```
$ curl -s "https://isocpp.org/blog" | ./link_extraction
Sign In / Suggest an Article : https://isocpp.org/member/login
Register                     : https://isocpp.org/member/register
Get Started!                 : https://isocpp.org/get-started
Tour                         : https://isocpp.org/tour
C++ Super-FAQ                : https://isocpp.org/faq
Blog                         : https://isocpp.org/blog
Forums                       : https://isocpp.org/forums
Standardization              : https://isocpp.org/std
About                        : https://isocpp.org/about
Current ISO C++ status       : https://isocpp.org/std/status
(...and many more...)
```

How it works...

Regular expressions (or *regex* in short) are extremely useful. They can look really cryptic, but it is worth learning how they work. A short regex can spare us writing many lines of code if we did the matching manually.

In this recipe, we first instantiated an object of type regex. We fed its constructor with a string that describes a regular expression. A very simple regular expression is " . ", which matches *every* character because a dot is the regex wildcard. If we write "a", then this matches only on the 'a' characters. If we write "ab*", then this means "one a, and zero or arbitrarily many b characters". And so on. Regular expressions are another large topic, and there are great explanations on Wikipedia and other websites or literature.

Let's have another look at our regular expression that matches what we assume to be HTML links. A simple HTML link can look like `<a href="some_url.com/foo">A great link</a>`. We want the `some_url.com/foo` part, as well as `A great link`. So we came up with the following regular expression, which contains *groups* for matching substrings:

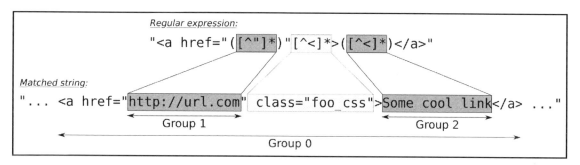

The whole match itself is always **Group 0**. In this case, this is the full `<a href .....</a>` string. The quoted `href`-part that contains the URL being linked to is **Group 1**. The `(` `)` parentheses in the regular expression define such a group of which we have 2. The other one is the part between the `<a ...>` and `</a>`, which contains the link description.

There are various STL functions that accept regex objects, but we directly used a regex token iterator adapter, which is a high-level abstraction that uses `std::regex_search` under the hood in order to automate recurring matching work. We instantiated it like this:

```
sregex_token_iterator it {begin(in), end(in), link_re, {1, 2}};
```

The begin and end part denote our input string over which the regex token iterator shall iterate and match all links. The `link_re` is, of course, the complex regular expression we implemented to match links. The `{1, 2}` part is the next complicated looking thing. It instructs the token iterator to stop on each full match and first yield Group 1, then after incrementing the iterator to yield Group 2, and after incrementing it again, it would finally search for the next match in the string. This somewhat intelligent behavior really spares us some code lines.

Let's have a look at another example to make sure we got the idea. Let's imagine the regular expression, `"a(b*)(c*)"`. It will match strings that contain an a character, then none or arbitrarily many b characters, and then none or arbitrarily many c characters:

```
const string s {" abc abbccc "};
const regex re {"a(b*)(c*)"};

sregex_token_iterator it {begin(s), end(s), re, {1, 2}};

print( *it ); // prints b
++it;
print( *it ); // prints c
++it;
print( *it ); // prints bb
++it;
print( *it ); // prints ccc
```

There is also the `std::regex_iterator` class, which emits the substrings that are *between* regex matches.

Comfortably pretty printing numbers differently per context on the fly

In the last recipe, we learned how to format the output with output streams. And while doing the same, we realized two facts:

- Most I/O manipulators are *sticky*, so we have to revert their effect after use in order to not tamper with other unrelated code, which also prints
- It can be very tedious and does not look very readable if we have to set up long chains of I/O manipulators in order to get only a few variables printed with specific formatting

A lot of people do not like I/O streams for such reasons, and even in C++, they still use `printf` for formatting their strings.

In this recipe, we will see how to format types on the fly without too much I/O manipulator noise in our code.

How to do it...

We are going to implement a class, `format_guard`, which can automatically revert any format setting. Additionally, we add a wrapper type, which can contain any value, but when it is printed, it gets special formatting without burdening us with I/O manipulator noise:

1. First, we include some headers and declare that we use the `std` namespace:

```
#include <iostream>
#include <iomanip>

using namespace std;
```

2. The helper class that tidies up our stream formatting states for us is called `format_guard`. Its constructor saves the formatting flags, which `std::cout` has set at the moment. Its destructor restores them to the state it had when the constructor was called. This effectively revokes any formatting settings that were applied in between:

```
class format_guard {
    decltype(cout.flags()) f {cout.flags()};
public:
    ~format_guard() { cout.flags(f); }
};
```

3. Another little helper class is `scientific_type`. Because it's a class template, it can wrap any payload type as a member variable. It basically does nothing:

```
template <typename T>
struct scientific_type {
    T value;
    explicit scientific_type(T val) : value{val} {}
};
```

4. We can define completely custom formatting settings for any type that was wrapped into `scientific_type` before because if we overload the stream `operator>>` for it, the stream library executes completely different code when printing such types. This way, we can print scientific values in scientific floating-point notation, with uppercase formatting and explicit + prefix if they have positive values. We do also use our `format_guard` class in order to tidy up all our settings when leaving this function again:

```
template <typename T>
ostream& operator<<(ostream &os, const scientific_type<T> &w) {
    format_guard _;
    os << scientific << uppercase << showpos;
    return os << w.value;
}
```

5. In the main function, we will first play around with the `format_guard` class. We open a new scope, first get an instance of the class, and then we apply some wild formatting flags to `std::cout`:

```
int main()
{
    {
        format_guard _;
        cout << hex << scientific << showbase << uppercase;
        cout << "Numbers with special formatting:\n";
        cout << 0x123abc << '\n';
        cout << 0.123456789 << '\n';
    }
```

6. After we printed some numbers with many formatting flags enabled, we left the scope again. While this happened, the destructor of `format_guard` tidied the formatting up. In order to test this, we are printing exactly the same numbers *again*. They should appear different:

```
    cout << "Same numbers, but normal formatting again:\n";
    cout << 0x123abc << '\n';
    cout << 0.123456789 << '\n';
```

7. Now we put `scientific_type` to use. Let's print three floating-point numbers in a row. We wrap the second number in `scientific_type`. This way, it is printed in our special scientific style, but the numbers before and after it get default formatting. At the same time, we avoid ugly formatting line *noise*:

```
cout << "Mixed formatting: "
     << 123.0 << " "
     << scientific_type{123.0} << " "
     << 123.456 << '\n';
}
```

8. Compiling and running the program yields us the following result. The first two numbers are printed with specific formatting. The next two numbers appear with default formatting, which shows us that our `format_guard` works just nicely. The three numbers in the last lines also look just as expected. Only the one in the middle has the formatting of `scientific_type`, the rest has default formatting:

```
$ ./pretty_print_on_the_fly
Numbers with special formatting:
0X123ABC
1.234568E-01
Same numbers, but normal formatting again:
1194684
0.123457
Mixed formatting: 123 +1.230000E+02 123.456
```

Catching readable exceptions from std::iostream errors

In *none* of the recipes in this chapter, we used *exceptions* to catch errors. While this is certainly possible, working on stream objects without exceptions is already very convenient. If we try to parse in 10 values, but this fails somewhere in the middle, the whole stream object sets itself into a fail state and stops further parsing. This way, we do not run into the danger of parsing variables from the wrong offset in the stream. We can just do the parsing in a conditional, such as `if (cin >> foo >> bar >> ...)`. If this fails, we handle it. It does not appear very advantageous to embrace parsing in a `try { ... } catch ...` block.

In fact, the C++ I/O stream library already existed before there were exceptions in C++. Exception support was added later, which might be an explanation why they are not a first-class supported feature in the stream library.

In order to use exceptions in the stream library, we must configure each stream object individually to throw an exception, whenever it sets itself into a fail state. Unfortunately, the error explanations in the exception objects, which we can then catch later, are not thoroughly standardized. This leads to not really helpful error messages, as we will see in this section. If we really want to use exceptions with stream objects, we can *additionally* poll the C library for filesystem error states to get some additional information.

In this section, we are going to write a program that can fail in different ways, handle those with exceptions, and see how to squeeze more information out of those afterward.

How to do it...

We will implement a program that opens a file (which might fail), and then we'll read an integer out of it (which might fail, too). We do this with activated exceptions and then we see how we can handle those:

1. First, we include some headers and declare that we use the std namespace:

```
#include <iostream>
#include <fstream>
#include <system_error>
#include <cstring>

using namespace std;
```

2. If we want to use stream objects with exceptions, we have to enable them first. In order to get a file stream object to throw an exception if the file we are letting it access does not exist, or if there are parsing errors, we need to set some fail bits in an exception mask. If we do something afterward that fails, it will trigger an exception. By activating failbit and badbit, we enable exceptions for filesystem errors and parsing errors:

```
int main()
{
    ifstream f;
    f.exceptions(f.failbit | f.badbit);
```

3. Now we can open a `try` block and access a file. If opening the file is successful, we try to read an integer from it. Only if both steps succeed, we print the integer:

```
try {
    f.open("non_existant.txt");

    int i;
    f >> i;

    cout << "integer has value: " << i << '\n';
}
```

4. In both the expected possibilities of an error, an instance of `std::ios_base::failure` is thrown. This object has a `what()` member function, which ought to explain what triggered the exception. Unfortunately, the standardization of this message was left out, and it does not give too much information. However, we can at least distinguish if there is a *filesystem* problem (because the file does not exist, for example) or a format *parsing* problem. The global variable, `errno`, has been there even before C++ was invented, and it is set to an error value, which we can check now. The `strerror` function translates from an error number to a human readable string. If `errno` is 0, there is, at least, no filesystem error:

```
catch (ios_base::failure& e) {
    cerr << "Caught error: ";
    if (errno) {
        cerr << strerror(errno) << '\n';
    } else {
        cerr << e.what() << '\n';
    }
}
}
```

5. Compiling the program and running it in two different scenarios yields the following output. If the file to be opened does exist but parsing an integer from it was not possible, we get an `iostream_category` error message:

```
$ ./readable_error_msg
Caught error: ios_base::clear: unspecified iostream_category error
```

6. If the file does *not* exist, we will be notified about this with a different message from `strerror(errno)`:

```
$ ./readable_error_msg
Caught error: No such file or directory
```

How it works...

We have seen that we can enable exceptions per stream object, `s`, with `s.exceptions(s.failbit | s.badbit)`. This means, that there is no way to use, for example, the `std::ifstream` instance's constructor for opening a file if we want to get an exception when opening that file is not possible:

```
ifstream f {"non_existant.txt"};
f.exceptions(...); // too late for an exception
```

This is a pity because exceptions actually promise that they make error handling less clumsy compared to old-school C-style code, which is riddled with loads of `if` branches, which handle errors after every step.

If we played around trying to provoke various reasons for streams to fail, we would realize that there are no different exceptions being thrown. This way, we can only find out *when* we get an error, but not *what* specific error (This is, of course, *not* true for exception handling in *general*, but for the STL stream library). That is why we additionally consulted the value of `errno`. This global variable is an ancient construct, which has already been used in the old days when there were no C++ or exceptions in general.

If any system-related function has seen an error condition, it is able to set the `errno` variable to something other than 0 (0 describes the absence of errors), and then the caller is able to read that error number and look up what its value means. The only problem with this is that when we have a multithreaded application, and all the threads use functions that can set this error variable, *whose* error value is it? If we read it even though there is no error, it could carry an error value because some *other* system function running in a *different thread* may have experienced an error. Luckily, this flaw has been gone since C++11, where every thread in a process sees its own `errno` variable.

Without elaborating the ups and downs of an ancient error indication method, it can give us useful extra information when an exception is triggered on system-based things such as file streams. Exceptions tell us *when* it happened, and `errno` can tell us *what* happened if it happened at the system level.

8
Utility Classes

In this chapter, we will cover the following recipes:

- Converting between different time units using `std::ratio`
- Converting between absolute and relative times with `std::chrono`
- Safely signalizing failure with `std::optional`
- Applying functions on tuples
- Quickly composing data structures with `std::tuple`
- Replacing `void*` with `std::any` for more type safety
- Storing different types with `std::variant`
- Automatically handling resources with `std::unique_ptr`
- Automatically handling shared heap memory with `std::shared_ptr`
- Dealing with weak pointers to shared objects
- Simplifying resource handling of legacy APIs with smart pointers
- Sharing different member values of the same object
- Generating random numbers and choosing the right random number engine
- Generating random numbers and letting the STL shape specific distributions

Introduction

This chapter is dedicated to utility classes that are very useful for solving very specific tasks. Some of them are indeed so useful that we will most probably see them extremely often in any C++ program snippet in the future or have at least already seen them sprinkled over all other chapters in this book.

The first two recipes are about measuring and taking the *time*. We will also see how to convert between different time units and how to jump between points in time.

Then, we will have a look at the `optional`, `variant`, and `any` types (which all came with C++14 and C++17) as well as some `tuple` tricks in another five recipes.

Since C++11, we also got sophisticated smart pointer types, namely `unique_ptr`, `shared_ptr`, and `weak_ptr`, which are an enormously effective help regarding *memory management*, which is why we will have a dedicated look at them in five recipes.

Finally, we will have a panoramic view of the library parts of the STL that are about generating *random numbers*. Apart from learning about the most important characteristics of the STL's random engines, we will also learn how to apply shaping to random numbers in order to get distributions that fit our actual needs.

Converting between different time units using std::ratio

Since C++11, the STL contains some new types and functions for taking, measuring, and displaying time. This part of the library exists in the `std::chrono` namespace and has some sophisticated details.

In this recipe, we will concentrate on measuring time spans and how to convert the result of the measurement between units, such as seconds, milliseconds, and microseconds. The STL provides facilities, which enable us to define our own time units and convert between them seamlessly.

How to do it...

In this section, we will write a little *game* that prompts the user to enter a specific word. The time that the user needs to type this word into the keyboard is measured and displayed in multiple time units:

1. At first, we need to include all the necessary headers. For reasons of comfort, we declare that we use the `std` namespace by default:

```
#include <iostream>
#include <chrono>
#include <ratio>
#include <cmath>
#include <iomanip>
#include <optional>

using namespace std;
```

2. The `chrono::duration` as a type for time durations usually refers to multiples or fractions of seconds. All the STL time duration units refer to integer typed duration specializations. In this recipe, we are going to specialize on `double`. In the recipe after this one, we will concentrate more on the existing time unit definitions that are already built into the STL:

```
using seconds = chrono::duration<double>;
```

3. One millisecond is a fraction of a second, so we define this unit by referring to seconds. The `ratio_multiply` template parameter applies the STL-predefined `milli` factor to `seconds::period`, which gives us the fraction we want. The `ratio_multiply` template is basically a meta programming function for multiplying ratios:

```
using milliseconds = chrono::duration<
    double, ratio_multiply<seconds::period, milli>>;
```

4. It's the same thing with microseconds. While a millisecond is a `milli`-fraction of a second, a microsecond is a `micro`-fraction of a second:

```
using microseconds = chrono::duration<
    double, ratio_multiply<seconds::period, micro>>;
```

5. Now we are going to implement a function, which reads a string from user input and measures how long it took the user to type the input. It takes no arguments and returns us the user input string as well as the elapsed time, bundled in a pair:

```
static pair<string, seconds> get_input()
{
    string s;
```

6. We need to take the time from the beginning of the period during which user input occurs and after it. Taking a time snapshot looks like this:

```
const auto tic (chrono::steady_clock::now());
```

7. The actual capturing of user input takes place now. If we are not successful, we just return a default-initialized tuple. The caller will see that he got an empty input string:

```
if (!(cin >> s)) {
    return {{}, {}};
}
```

8. In the case of success, we continue by taking another time snapshot. Then we return the input string and the difference between both time points. Note that both are absolute time points, but by calculating the difference, we get a duration:

```
    const auto toc (chrono::steady_clock::now());
    return {s, toc - tic};
}
```

9. Let's implement the actual program now. We loop until the user enters the input string correctly. In every loop step, we ask the user to please enter the string "C++17" and, then, call our get_input function:

```
int main()
{
    while (true) {
        cout << "Please type the word \"C++17\" as"
                " fast as you can.\n> ";
        const auto [user_input, diff] = get_input();
```

10. Then we check the input. If the input is empty, we interpret this as a request to exit the whole program:

```
if (user_input == "") { break; }
```

11. If the user correctly types `"C++17"`, we express our congratulations and then print the time the user needed to type the word correctly.
The `diff.count()` method returns the number of seconds as a floating point number. If we had used the original STL `seconds` duration type, then we would have got a *rounded* integer value, not a fraction. By feeding the milliseconds or microseconds `constructor` with our `diff` variable before calling `count()`, we get the same value transformed to a different unit:

```
if (user_input == "C++17") {
    cout << "Bravo. You did it in:\n"
        << fixed << setprecision(2)
        << setw(12) << diff.count()
        << " seconds.\n"
        << setw(12) << milliseconds(diff).count()
        << " milliseconds.\n"
        << setw(12) << microseconds(diff).count()
        << " microseconds.\n";
    break;
```

12. If the user has a typo in the input, we let him try again:

```
} else {
    cout << "Sorry, your input does not match."
            " You may try again.\n";
    }
  }
}
```

13. Compiling and running the program leads to the following output. At first, with a typo, the program repeatedly asks for the correct input word. After typing the word correctly, it displays how long it took us to type it in three different time units:

```
$ ./ratio_conversion
Please type the word "C++17" as fast as you can.
> c+17
Sorry, your input does not match. You may try again.
Please type the word "C++17" as fast as you can.
> C++17
```

```
Bravo. You did it in:
         1.48 seconds.
      1480.10 milliseconds.
   1480099.00 microseconds.
```

How it works...

While this section is all about converting between different time units, we first had to choose one of the three available clock objects. There is generally the choice between system_clock, steady_clock, and high_resolution_clock in the std::chrono namespace. What are the differences between them? Let's have a closer look:

Clock	Characteristics
system_clock	This represents the system-wide real-time "*wall*" clock. It is the right choice if we want to obtain the local time.
steady_clock	This clock is promised to be *monotonic*. This means that it will never be set back by any amount of time. This can happen to other clocks when their time is corrected by minimal amounts, or even when the time is switched between winter and summer time.
high_resolution_clock	This is the clock with the most fine-grained clock tick period the STL implementation can provide.

Since we measured the time distance, or duration from one absolute point in time and the other absolute point in time (which we captured in the variables tic and toc), we are not interested if those points in time were globally skewed. Even if the clock was 112 years, 5 hours, 10 minutes, and 1 second (or whatever) late or ahead of time, then this does not make a difference on the *difference between* them. The only important thing is that after we save the time point tic and before we save the time point toc, the clock must not be micro-adjusted (which happens on many systems from time to time) because that would distort our measurement. For these requirements, steady_clock is the optimal choice. Its implementation can be based on the processor's timestamp counter, which always counts up monotonously since the system was started.

Okay, now with the right time object choice, we are able to save points in time via `chrono::steady_clock::now()`. The now function returns us a `chrono::time_point<chrono::steady_clock>` typed value. The difference between two such values (as in `toc - tic`) is a *time span*, or *duration* of type `chrono::duration`. As this is the central type of this section, this gets a little complicated now. Let's have a closer look at the template type interface of `duration`:

```
template<
    class Rep,
    class Period = std::ratio<1>
> class duration;
```

The parameters we can change are called `Rep` and `Period`. Rep is easy to explain: this is just the numeric variable type that is used to save the time value. For the existing STL time units, this is usually `long long int`. In this recipe, we chose `double`. Because of our choice, we can save time values in seconds by default and then convert them to milli- or microseconds. If we save the time duration of `1.2345` seconds in the `chrono::seconds` type, then it would be rounded to one full second. This way, we would have to save the time difference between `tic` and `toc` in `chrono::microseconds` and could then convert to less-fine-grained units. With our `double` choice for `Rep`, we can convert up and down and lose only a minimal amount of precision, which does not hurt in this example.

We used `Rep = double` for all our time units, so they differed only in our choice of the `Period` parameter:

```
using seconds      = chrono::duration<double>;
using milliseconds = chrono::duration<double,
    ratio_multiply<seconds::period, milli>>;
using microseconds = chrono::duration<double,
    ratio_multiply<seconds::period, micro>>;
```

While `seconds` is the simplest unit to describe, as it works with `Period = ratio<1>`, the others have to be adjusted. As one millisecond is a thousandth of a second, we multiply the `seconds::period` (which is just a getter function to the `Period` parameter) with `milli`, which is a type alias for `std::ratio<1, 1000>` (`std::ratio<a, b>` represents the fractional value a/b). The `ratio_multiply` type is basically a *compile time function*, which represents the type that results from multiplying one ratio type with another.

Maybe this sounds too complicated, so let's have a look at an example:
`ratio_multiply<ratio<2, 3>, ratio<4, 5>>` results in `ratio<8, 15>` because `(2/3) * (4/5) = 8/15`.

Our resulting type definitions are equivalent to the following definitions:

```
using seconds      = chrono::duration<double, ratio<1, 1>>;
using milliseconds = chrono::duration<double, ratio<1, 1000>>;
using microseconds = chrono::duration<double, ratio<1, 1000000>>;
```

Having these types lined up, it is easy to convert between them. If we have a time duration d of type `seconds`, we can transform it to `milliseconds` just by feeding it through the constructor of the other type, that is, `milliseconds(d)`.

There's more...

In other tutorials or books, you might run across `duration_cast` whenever time durations are transformed. If we have a duration value of type `chrono::milliseconds` and want to transform it to `chrono::hours`, for example, we do indeed need to write `duration_cast<chrono::hours>(milliseconds_value)` because these units depend on *integer* types. Transforming from fine-grained units to less-fine-grained units leads to *precision loss* in that case, which is why we need a `duration_cast`. For `double`- or `float`-based duration units, this is not needed.

Converting between absolute and relative times with std::chrono

Until C++11, it was quite a hassle to take the wall clock time and *just print* it, because C++ did not have its own time library. It was always necessary to call functions of the C library, which looks very archaic, considering that such calls could be encapsulated nicely into their own classes.

Since C++11, the STL provides the `chrono` library, which makes time-related tasks much easier to implement.

In this recipe, we are going to take the local time, print it, and play around by adding different time offsets, which is a really comfortable thing to do with `std::chrono`.

How to do it...

We are going to save the current time and print it. Additionally, our program will add different offsets to the saved time point and print the resulting time points too:

1. The typical include lines come first; then, we declare that we use the `std` namespace by default:

```
#include <iostream>
#include <iomanip>
#include <chrono>

using namespace std;
```

2. We are going to print absolute time points. These will come along in the form of the `chrono::time_point` type template, so we will just overload the output stream operator for it. There are different ways to print the date and/or time part of a time point. We will just use the `%c` standard formatting. We could, of course, also print only the time, only the date, only the year, or whatever comes to our mind. All the conversions between the different types before we can finally apply `put_time` look a bit clunky, but we are only doing this once:

```
ostream& operator<<(ostream &os,
            const chrono::time_point<chrono::system_clock> &t)
{
    const auto tt   (chrono::system_clock::to_time_t(t));
    const auto loct (std::localtime(&tt));
    return os << put_time(loct, "%c");
}
```

3. There are already STL type definitions for `seconds`, `minutes`, `hours`, and so on. We will add the `days` type now. This is easy; we just have to specialize the `chrono::duration` template by referring to `hours` and multiply with `24`, because a full day has 24 hours:

```
using days = chrono::duration<
    chrono::hours::rep,
    ratio_multiply<chrono::hours::period, ratio<24>>>;
```

4. In order to be able to express a duration in multiples of days in the most elegant way, we can define our own `days` literal operator. Now, we can write `3_days` to construct a value that represents three days:

```
constexpr days operator ""_days(unsigned long long h)
{
    return days{h};
}
```

5. In the actual program, we will take a time snapshot, which we simply print afterward. This is very easy and comfortable because we already implemented the right operator overload for this:

```
int main()
{
    auto now (chrono::system_clock::now());
    cout << "The current date and time is " << now << '\n';
```

6. Having saved the current time in the `now` variable, we can add arbitrary durations to it and print those too. Let's add 12 hours to the current time and print what time we will have in 12 hours:

```
    chrono::hours chrono_12h {12};
    cout << "In 12 hours, it will be "
        << (now + chrono_12h) << '\n';
```

7. By declaring that we use the `chrono_literals` namespace by default, we unlock all the existing duration literals for hours, seconds, and so on. This way, we can elegantly print what time it was 12 hours and 15 minutes ago, or 7 days ago:

```
    using namespace chrono_literals;
    cout << "12 hours and 15 minutes ago, it was "
        << (now - 12h - 15min) << '\n'
        << "1 week ago, it was "
        << (now - 7_days) << '\n';
}
```

8. Compiling and running the program yields the following output. Because we used %c as the format string for time formatting, we get a pretty complete description in a specific format. By playing around with different format strings, we can get it in any format we like. Note that the time format is not 12 hours AM/PM but 24 hours because the app is run on a European system:

```
$ ./relative_absolute_times
The current date and time is Fri May  5 13:20:38 2017
In 12 hours, it will be Sat May  6 01:20:38 2017
12 hours and 15 minutes ago, it was Fri May  5 01:05:38 2017
1 week ago, it was Fri Apr 28 13:20:38 2017
```

How it works...

We obtained the current time point from std::chrono::system_clock. This STL clock class is the only one that can transform its time point values to a time structure that can be displayed as a human-readable time description string.

In order to print such time points, we implemented operator<< for output streams:

```
ostream& operator<<(ostream &os,
                    const chrono::time_point<chrono::system_clock> &t)
{
    const auto tt   (chrono::system_clock::to_time_t(t));
    const auto loct (std::localtime(&tt));
    return os << put_time(loct, "%c");
}
```

What happens here first, is that we transform from chrono::time_point<chrono::system_clock> to std::time_t. Values of this type can be transformed to a local wall clock relevant time value, which we do with std::localtime. This function returns us a pointer to a converted value (don't worry about the maintenance of the memory behind this pointer; it is a static object not allocated on the heap), which we can now finally print.

The std::put_time function accepts such an object together with a time format string. "%c" displays a standard date-time string, such as Sun Mar 12 11:33:40 2017. We could also have written "%m/%d/%y"; then the program would have printed the time in the format, 03/12/17. The whole list of existing format string modifiers for time is very long, but it is nicely documented to its full extent in the online C++ reference.

Aside from printing, we also added time offsets to our time point. This is very easy because we can express time durations, such as *12 hours and 15 minutes* as `12h + 15min`. The `chrono_literals` namespace already provides handy type literals for hours (`h`), minutes (`min`), seconds (`s`), milliseconds (`ms`), microseconds (`us`), and nanoseconds (`ns`).

Adding such a duration value to a time point value creates a new time point value because these types have the right `operator+` and `operator-` overloads, which is why it is so simple to add and display offsets in time.

Safely signalizing failure with std::optional

When a program communicates with the outside world and relies on values it gets from there, then all kinds of failures can happen.

This means that whenever we write a function that ought to return a value, but that can also possibly fail, then this must be reflected in some change of the function interface. We have several possibilities. Let's see how we can design the interface of a function that will return a string, but that could also fail:

- Use a success-indicating return value and output parameters: `bool get_string(string&);`
- Return a pointer (or a smart pointer) that can be set to `nullptr` if there is a failure: `string* get_string();`
- Throw an exception in the case of failure and leave the function signature very simple: `string get_string();`

All these approaches have different advantages and disadvantages. Since C++17, there is a new type that can be used to solve such a problem in a different way: `std::optional`. The notion of an optional value comes from purely functional programming languages (where they are sometimes called `Maybe` types) and can lead to very elegant code.

We can wrap `optional` around our own types in order to signal *empty* or *erroneous* values. In this recipe, we will learn how to do that.

How to do it...

In this section, we will implement a program that reads integers from the user and sums them up. Because the user can always input random things instead of numbers, we will see how `optional` can improve our error handling:

1. First, we include all the needed headers and declare that we use the `std` namespace:

```
#include <iostream>
#include <optional>

using namespace std;
```

2. Let's define an integer type, which, *maybe*, contains a value. The `std::optional` type does exactly that. By wrapping any type into `optional`, we give it an additional possible state, which reflects that it currently has *no* value:

```
using oint = optional<int>;
```

3. By having defined an optional integer type, we can express that a function that usually returns an integer can also possibly fail. If we take an integer from user input, this can possibly fail because the user might not always enter an integer even though we asked him to do so. Returning an optional integer is perfect in this case. If reading an integer succeeds, we feed it into the `optional<int>` constructor. Otherwise, we return a default constructed optional, which signals failure or emptiness:

```
oint read_int()
{
    int i;
    if (cin >> i) { return {i}; }
    return {};
}
```

4. We can do more than returning integers from functions that can possibly fail. What if we calculate the sum of two optional integers? This can only lead to a real numeric sum if both the operands contain an actual value. In any other case, we return an empty optional variable. This function needs a little more explanation: by implicitly transforming the `optional<int>` variables, a and b, to boolean expressions (by writing `!a` and `!b`), we get to know whether they contain actual values. If they do, we can access them like pointers or iterators by simply dereferencing them with `*a` and `*b`:

```
oint operator+(oint a, oint b)
{
    if (!a || !b) { return {}; }
    return {*a + *b};
}
```

5. Adding a normal integer to an optional integer follows the same logic:

```
oint operator+(oint a, int b)
{
    if (!a) { return {}; }
    return {*a + b};
}
```

6. Let's now write a program that does something with optional integers. We let the user enter two numbers:

```
int main()
{
    cout << "Please enter 2 integers.\n> ";
    auto a {read_int()};
    auto b {read_int()};
```

7. Then we add those input numbers and additionally add the value 10 to their sum. Since a and b are optional integers, sum will also be an optional integer type variable:

```
    auto sum (a + b + 10);
```

8. If a and/or b do not contain a value, then sum cannot possibly contain a value either. The nice thing about our optional integers now is that we do not need to explicitly check a and b. What happens when we sum up empty optionals is perfectly sane and defined behavior because we defined operator+ in a safe way for those types. This way, we can arbitrarily add many possibly empty optional integers, and we'll only need to check the resulting optional value. If it contains a value, then we can safely access and print it:

```
if (sum) {
    cout << *a << " + " << *b << " + 10 = "
         << *sum << '\n';
```

9. If the user enters something non-numeric, we error out:

```
} else {
    cout << "sorry, the input was "
            "something else than 2 numbers.\n";
}
}
```

10. That's it. When we compile and run the program, we get the following output:

```
$ ./optional
Please enter 2 integers.
> 1 2
1 + 2 + 10 = 13
```

11. Running the program again and entering something non-numeric yields the error message we prepared for this case:

```
$ ./optional
Please enter 2 integers.
> 2 z
sorry, the input was something else than 2 numbers.
```

How it works...

Working with optional is generally very simple and convenient. If we want to attach the notion of possible failure or optionality to any type T, we can just wrap it into std::optional<T> and that's it.

Whenever we get such a value from somewhere, we have to check whether it is in the empty state or whether it contains a real value. The `bool optional::has_value()` function does that for us. If it returns `true`, we may access the value. Accessing the value of an optional can be done with `T& optional::value()`.

Instead of always writing `if (x.has_value()) {...}` and `x.value()`, we can also write `if (x) {...}` and `*x`. The `std::optional` type defines explicit conversion to `bool` and `operator*` in such a way that dealing with an optional type is similar to dealing with a pointer.

Another handy operator helper that is good to know is the `operator->` overload of `optional`. If we have a `struct Foo { int a; string b; }` type and want to access one of its members through an `optional<Foo>` variable, `x`, then we can write `x->a` or `x->b`. Of course, we should first check whether `x` actually has a value.

If we try to access an optional value even though it does not have a value, then it will throw `std::logic_error`. This way, it is possible to mess around with a lot of optional values without always checking them. Using a `try-catch` clause, we could write code in the following form:

```
cout << "Please enter 3 numbers:\n";

try {
    cout << "Sum: "
        << (*read_int() + *read_int() + *read_int())
        << '\n';
} catch (const std::bad_optional_access &) {
    cout << "Unfortunately you did not enter 3 numbers\n";
}
```

Another gimmick of `std::optional` is `optional::value_or`. If we want to take an optional's value and fall back to a default value if it is in the empty state, then this is of help. `x = optional_var.value_or(123)` does this job in one concise line, where `123` is the fallback default value.

Applying functions on tuples

Since C++11, the STL provides `std::tuple`. This type allows us to sporadically *bundle* multiple values into a single variable and reach them around. The notion of tuples has been there for a long time in a lot of programming languages, and some recipes in this book are already devoted to this type because it is extremely versatile to use.

However, we sometimes end up with values bundled up in a tuple and then need to call functions with their individual members. Unpacking the members individually for every function argument is very tedious (and error-prone if we introduce a typo somewhere). The tedious form looks like this: `func(get<0>(tup), get<1>(tup), get<2>(tup), ...);`.

In this recipe, you will learn how to pack and unpack values to and from tuples in an elegant way, in order to call some functions that don't know about tuples.

How to do it...

We are going to implement a program that packs and unpacks values to and from tuples. Then, we will see how to call functions that know nothing about tuples with values from tuples:

1. First, we include a lot of headers and declare that we use the `std` namespace:

```cpp
#include <iostream>
#include <iomanip>
#include <tuple>
#include <functional>
#include <string>
#include <list>

using namespace std;
```

2. Let's first define a function that takes multiple parameters describing a student and prints them. A lot of legacy- or C-function interfaces look similar.:

```cpp
static void print_student(size_t id, const string &name, double gpa)
{
    cout << "Student " << quoted(name)
         << ", ID: "   << id
         << ", GPA: "  << gpa << '\n';
}
```

3. In the actual program, we define a tuple type on the fly and fill it with meaningful student data:

```
int main()
{
    using student = tuple<size_t, string, double>;
    student john {123, "John Doe"s, 3.7};
```

4. In order to print such an object, we can decompose it to its individual members and call `print_student` with those individual variables:

```
    {
        const auto &[id, name, gpa] = john;
        print_student(id, name, gpa);
    }
    cout << "-----\n";
```

5. Let's create a whole set of students in the form of an initializer list of student tuples:

```
auto arguments_for_later = {
    make_tuple(234, "John Doe"s,  3.7),
    make_tuple(345, "Billy Foo"s, 4.0),
    make_tuple(456, "Cathy Bar"s, 3.5),
};
```

6. We can still relatively comfortably print them all, but in order to decompose the tuple, we need to care how many elements such tuples have. If we have to write such code, then we will also have to restructure it in case the function call interface changes:

```
for (const auto &[id, name, gpa] : arguments_for_later) {
    print_student(id, name, gpa);
}
cout << "-----\n";
```

7. We can do better. Without even knowing the argument types of `print_student` or the number of members in a student tuple, we can directly forward the tuple's content to the function using `std::apply`. This function accepts a function pointer or a function object and a tuple and then *unpacks* the tuple in order to call the function with the tuple members as parameters:

```
apply(print_student, john);
cout << "-----\n";
```

8. This also works nicely in a loop, of course:

```
for (const auto &args : arguments_for_later) {
    apply(print_student, args);
}
cout << "-----\n";
}
```

9. Compiling and running the program shows that both ways work, as we assumed:

```
$ ./apply_functions_on_tuples
Student "John Doe", ID: 123, GPA: 3.7
-----
Student "John Doe", ID: 234, GPA: 3.7
Student "Billy Foo", ID: 345, GPA: 4
Student "Cathy Bar", ID: 456, GPA: 3.5
-----
Student "John Doe", ID: 123, GPA: 3.7
-----
Student "John Doe", ID: 234, GPA: 3.7
Student "Billy Foo", ID: 345, GPA: 4
Student "Cathy Bar", ID: 456, GPA: 3.5
-----
```

How it works...

The `std::apply` is a compile-time helper that helps us work more agnostic about the types we handle in our code.

Imagine we have a tuple `t` with the values (`123`, `"abc"s`, `456.0`). This tuple has the type, `tuple<int, string, double>`. Additionally, assume that we have a function `f` with the signature `int f(int, string, double)` (the types can also be references).

Then, we can write `x = apply(f, t)`, which will result in a function call, `x = f(123, "abc"s, 456.0)`. The `apply` method does even return to us what `f` returns.

Quickly composing data structures with std::tuple

Let's have a look at a basic use case for tuples that we most probably already know. We can define a structure as follows, in order to just bundle some variables:

```
struct Foo {
    int a;
    string b;
    float c;
};
```

Instead of defining a structure as in the preceding example, we can also define a tuple:

```
using Foo = tuple<int, string, float>;
```

We can access its items using the index number of the type from the type list. In order to access the first member of a tuple, t, we can use `std::get<0>(t)` to access the second member we write `std::get<1>`, and so on. If the index number is too large, then the compiler will even safely error out.

Throughout the book, we have already used the decomposition capabilities of C++17 for tuples. They allow us to decompose a tuple quickly by just writing `auto [a, b, c] = some_tuple` in order to access its individual items.

Composing and decomposing single data structures are not the only things we can do with tuples. We can also concatenate or split tuples, or do all kinds of magic. In this recipe, we will play around with such capabilities in order to learn how to do it.

How to do it...

In this section, we will write a program that can print any tuple on the fly. In addition to that, we will write a function that can *zip* tuples together:

1. We need to include a number of headers first and then we declare that we use the `std` namespace by default:

```
#include <iostream>
#include <tuple>
#include <list>
#include <utility>
#include <string>
#include <iterator>
```

```
#include <numeric>
#include <algorithm>

using namespace std;
```

2. As we will be dealing with tuples, it will be interesting to display their content. Therefore, we will now implement a very generic function that can print any tuple that consists of printable types. The function accepts an output stream reference `os`, which will be used to do the actual printing, and a variadic argument list, which carries all the tuple members. We decompose all the arguments into the first element and put it into the argument, `v`, and the rest, which is stored in the argument pack `vs...`:

```
template <typename T, typename ... Ts>
void print_args(ostream &os, const T &v, const Ts &...vs)
{
    os << v;
```

3. If there are arguments left in the parameter pack, `vs`, these are printed interleaved with `",  "` using the `initializer_list` expansion trick. You learned about this trick in the Chapter 4, *Lambda Expressions*:

```
    (void)initializer_list<int>{((os << ", " << vs), 0)...};
}
```

4. We can now print arbitrary sets of arguments by writing `print_args(cout, 1, 2, "foo", 3, "bar")`, for example. But this has nothing to do with tuples yet. In order to print tuples, we overload the stream output operator `<<` for any case of tuples by implementing a template function that matches on any tuple specialization:

```
template <typename ... Ts>
ostream& operator<<(ostream &os, const tuple<Ts...> &t)
{
```

5. Now it gets a little complicated. We first use a lambda expression that arbitrarily accepts many parameters. Whenever it is called, it prepends the `os` argument to those arguments and then calls `print_args` with the resulting new list of arguments. This means that a call to `capt_tup(...some parameters...)` leads to a `print_args(os, ...some parameters...)` call:

```
    auto print_to_os ([&os](const auto &...xs) {
        print_args(os, xs...);
    });
```

6. Now we can do the actual tuple unpacking magic. We use `std::apply` to unpack the tuple. All values will be taken out of the tuple then and lined up as function arguments for the function that we provide as the first argument. This just means that if we have a tuple, `t = (1, 2, 3)`, and call `apply(capt_tup, t)`, then this will lead to a function call, `capt_tup(1, 2, 3)`, which in turn leads to the function call, `print_args(os, 1, 2, 3)`. This is just what we need. As a nice extra, we surround the printing with parentheses:

```
    os << "(";
    apply(print_to_os, t);
    return os << ")";
}
```

7. Okay, now we wrote some complicated code that will make our life much easier when we want to print a tuple. But we can do a lot more with tuples. Let's, for example, write a function that accepts an iterable range, such as a vector or a list of numbers, as an argument. This function will then iterate over that range and then return us the *sum* of all the numbers in the range and bundle that with the *minimum* of all values, the *maximum* of all values, and the numeric *average* of them. By packing these four values into a tuple, we can return them as a single object without defining an additional structure type:

```
template <typename T>
tuple<double, double, double, double>
sum_min_max_avg(const T &range)
{
```

8. The `std::minmax_element` function returns us a pair of iterators that respectively point to the minimum and maximum values of the input range. The `std::accumulate` method sums up all the values in its input range. This is all we need to return the four values that fit in our tuple!

```
    auto min_max (minmax_element(begin(range), end(range)));
    auto sum     (accumulate(begin(range), end(range), 0.0));
    return {sum, *min_max.first, *min_max.second,
            sum / range.size()};
}
```

9. Before implementing the main program, we will implement one last magic helper function. I call it magic because it really looks complicated at first, but after understanding how it works, it will turn out as a really slick and nice helper. It will zip two tuples. This means that if we feed it a tuple, `(1, 2, 3)`, and another tuple, `('a', 'b', 'c')`, it will return a tuple `(1, 'a', 2, 'b', 3, 'c')`:

```
template <typename T1, typename T2>
static auto zip(const T1 &a, const T2 &b)
{
```

10. Now we arrived at the most complex lines of code of this recipe. We create a function object, `z`, which accepts an arbitrary number of arguments. It then returns another function object that captures all these arguments in a parameter pack, `xs`, but also accepts another arbitrary number of arguments. Let's sink this in for a moment. Within this inner function object, we can access both lists of arguments in the form of the parameter packs, `xs` and `ys`. And now let's have a look what we actually do with these parameter packs. The expression, `make_tuple(xs, ys)...`, groups the parameter packs item wise. This means that if we have `xs = 1, 2, 3` and `ys = 'a', 'b', 'c'`, this will result in a new parameter pack, `(1, 'a'), (2, 'b'), (3, 'c')`. This is a comma-separated list of three tuples. In order to get them all grouped in *one* tuple, we use `std::tuple_cat`, which accepts an arbitrary number of tuples and repacks them into one tuple. This way we get a nice `(1, 'a', 2, 'b', 3, 'c')` tuple:

```
auto z ([](auto ...xs) {
    return [xs...](auto ...ys) {
        return tuple_cat(make_tuple(xs, ys) ...);
    };
});
```

11. The last step is unwrapping all the values from the input tuples, `a` and `b`, and pushing them into `z`. The expression, `apply(z, a)`, puts all the values from `a` into the parameter pack `xs`, and `apply(..., b)` puts all the values of `b` into the parameter pack `ys`. The resulting tuple is the large zipped one, which we return to the caller:

```
    return apply(apply(z, a), b);
}
```

12. We invested a considerable amount of lines into helper/library code. Let's now finally put it to use. First, we construct some arbitrary tuples. The student contains ID, name, and GPA score of a student. The student_desc contains strings that describe what those fields mean in human-readable form. The std::make_tuple is a really nice helper because it automatically deduces the type of all the arguments and creates a suitable tuple type:

```
int main()
{
    auto student_desc (make_tuple("ID", "Name", "GPA"));
    auto student      (make_tuple(123456, "John Doe", 3.7));
```

13. Let's just print what we have. This is really simple because we just implemented the right operator<< overload for that:

```
cout << student_desc << '\n'
     << student      << '\n';
```

14. We can also group both the tuples on the fly with std::tuple_cat and print them like this:

```
cout << tuple_cat(student_desc, student) << '\n';
```

15. We can also create a new *zipped* tuple with our zip function and also print it:

```
auto zipped (zip(student_desc, student));
cout << zipped << '\n';
```

16. Let's not forget our sum_min_max_avg function. We create an initializer list that contains some numbers and feed it into this function. To make it a little bit more complicated, we create another tuple of the same size, which contains some describing strings. By zipping these tuples, we get a nice, interleaved output, as we will see when we run the program:

```
auto numbers = {0.0, 1.0, 2.0, 3.0, 4.0};
cout << zip(
        make_tuple("Sum", "Minimum", "Maximum", "Average"),
        sum_min_max_avg(numbers))
     << '\n';
}
```

17. Compiling and running the program yields the following output. The first two lines are just the individual `student` and `student_desc` tuples. Line 3 is the tuple composition we got by using `tuple_cat`. Line 4 contains the zipped student tuple. In the last line, we see the sum, minimum, maximum, and average value of the numeric list we last created. Because of the zipping, it is really easy to see what each value means:

```
$ ./tuple
(ID, Name, GPA)
(123456, John Doe, 3.7)
(ID, Name, GPA, 123456, John Doe, 3.7)
(ID, 123456, Name, John Doe, GPA, 3.7)
(Sum, 10, Minimum, 0, Maximum, 4, Average, 2)
```

How it works...

Some of the code in this section is admittedly complicated. We wrote an `operator<<` implementation for tuples, which looks very complex but supports all kinds of tuples that themselves consist of printable types. Then we implemented the `sum_min_max_avg` function, which just returns a tuple. Another very complicated thing to get our head around was the function `zip`.

The easiest part was `sum_min_max_avg`. The point about it is that when we define a function that returns an instance `tuple<Foo, Bar, Baz> f ()`, we can just write `return {foo_instance, bar_instance, baz_instance};` in that function to construct such a tuple. If you have trouble understanding the STL algorithms we used in the `sum_min_max_avg` function, then you might want to have a look at the Chapter 5, *STL Algorithm Basics* of this book, where we already had a closer look at them.

The other code was so complicated that we dedicate the specific helpers their own subsections:

operator<< for tuples

Before we even touched `operator<<` for output streams, we implemented the `print_args` function. Due to its variadic argument nature, it accepts any number and type of arguments, as long as the first one is an `ostream` instance:

```
template <typename T, typename ... Ts>
void print_args(ostream &os, const T &v, const Ts &...vs)
{
```

```
    os << v;

    (void)initializer_list<int>{((os << ", " << vs), 0)...};
}
```

This function prints the first item, v, and then prints all the other items from the parameter pack, vs. We print the first item individually because we want to have all items interleaved with ", " but we do not want this string leading or trailing the whole list (as in "1, 2, 3, " or ", 1, 2, 3"). We learned about the initializer_list expansion trick in Chapter 4, *Lambda Expressions*, in the recipe *Calling multiple functions with the same input*.

Having that function lined up, we have everything we need in order to print tuples. Our operator<< implementation looks as follows:

```
template <typename ... Ts>
ostream& operator<<(ostream &os, const tuple<Ts...> &t)
{
    auto capt_tup ([&os](const auto &...xs) {
        print_args(os, xs...);
    });

    os << "(";
    apply(capt_tup, t);
    return os << ")";
}
```

The first thing we do is defining the function object, capt_tup. When we call capt_tup(foo, bar, whatever), this results in the call, print_args(**os,** foo, bar, whatever). The only thing this function object does is prepend the output stream object os to its variadic list of arguments.

Afterward, we use std::apply in order to unpack all the items from tuple t. If this step looks too complicated, please have a look at the recipe before this one, which is dedicated to demonstrating how std::apply works.

The zip function for tuples

The zip function accepts two tuples, but looks horribly complicated, although it has a very crisp implementation:

```
template <typename T1, typename T2>
auto zip(const T1 &a, const T2 &b)
{
    auto z ([](auto ...xs) {
        return [xs...](auto ...ys) {
```

```
            return tuple_cat(make_tuple(xs, ys) ...);
        };
    });
    return apply(apply(z, a), b);
}
```

In order to understand this code better, imagine for a moment that the tuple `a` carries the values, `1, 2, 3`, and tuple `b` carries the values, `'a', 'b', 'c'`.

In such a case, calling `apply(z, a)` leads to a function call `z(1, 2, 3)`, which returns another function object that captures those values, `1, 2, 3`, in the parameter pack `xs`. When this function object is then called with `apply(z(1, 2, 3), b)`, it gets the values, `'a', 'b', 'c'`, stuffed into the parameter pack, `ys`. This is basically the same as if we called `z(1, 2, 3)('a', 'b', 'c')` directly.

Okay, now that we have `xs = (1, 2, 3)` and `ys = ('a', 'b', 'c')`, what happens then? The expression `tuple_cat(make_tuple(xs, ys) ...)` does the following magic; have a look at the diagram:

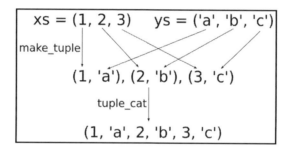

At first, the items from `xs` and `ys` are zipped together by interleaving them pairwise. This "pairwise interleaving" happens in the `make_tuple(xs, ys) ...` expression. This initially only leads to a variadic list of tuples with two items each. In order to get *one large* tuple, we apply `tuple_cat` on them and then we finally get a large concatenated tuple that contains all the members of the initial tuples in an interleaved manner.

Replacing void* with std::any for more type safety

It can happen that we want to store items of *any* type in a variable. For such a variable, we then need to be able to check whether it contains *anything*, and if it does, we need to be able to distinguish *what* it contains. All this needs to happen in a type-safe manner.

In the past, we were basically able to store pointers to various objects in a void* pointer. A void typed pointer alone cannot tell us what kind of object it points to, so we would need to handcraft some kind of additional mechanism that tells us what to expect. Such code quickly leads to quirky looking and unsafe code.

Another addition of C++17 to the STL is the std::any type. It is designed to hold variables of any kind and provides facilities that enable for type-safe inspection and access to it.

In this recipe, we will play around with this utility type in order to get a feeling of it.

How to do it...

We will implement a function that tries to be able to print everything. It uses std::any as its argument type:

1. First, we include some necessary headers and declare that we use the std namespace:

```
#include <iostream>
#include <iomanip>
#include <list>
#include <any>
#include <iterator>

using namespace std;
```

2. In order to reduce the number of angle bracket syntax in the following program, we define an alias for list<int>, which we will use later:

```
using int_list = list<int>;
```

3. Let's implement a function that claims to be able to print anything. The promise is that it prints anything provided as an argument in the form of an `std::any` variable:

```
void print_anything(const std::any &a)
{
```

4. The first thing we need to check is if the argument contains *anything* or if it is just an empty `any` instance. If it is empty, then there is no sense in trying to figure out how to print it:

```
if (!a.has_value()) {
    cout << "Nothing.\n";
```

5. If it is not empty, we can try to compare it with different types until we see a match. The first type to try is `string`. If it is a `string`, we can cast a to a `string` typed reference using `std::any_cast` and just print it. We put the string in quotes for cosmetic reasons:

```
} else if (a.type() == typeid(string)) {
    cout << "It's a string: "
         << quoted(any_cast<const string&>(a)) << '\n';
```

6. If it is not a `string`, it might be an `int`. In case this type matches, we can use `any_cast<int>` to obtain the actual `int` value:

```
} else if (a.type() == typeid(int)) {
    cout << "It's an integer: "
         << any_cast<int>(a) << '\n';
```

7. `std::any` does not only work with such simple types as `string` and `int`. We can also put a whole map or list or whatever composed complex data structure into an `any` variable. Let's see if the input is a list of integers, and if it is, we can just print it like we would print a list:

```
} else if (a.type() == typeid(int_list)) {
    const auto &l (any_cast<const int_list&>(a));
    cout << "It's a list: ";
    copy(begin(l), end(l),
        ostream_iterator<int>{cout, ", "});
    cout << '\n';
```

8. If none of these types match, we run out of type guesses. Let's give up in that case and tell the user that we have no idea how to print this:

```
    } else {
        cout << "Can't handle this item.\n";
    }
}
```

9. In the main function, we can now call this function with arbitrary types. We can call it with an empty `any` variable using `{}` or feed it with a string `"abc"` or an integer. Because `std::any` can be constructed from such types implicitly, there is no syntax overhead. We can even construct a whole list and throw it into this function:

```
int main()
{
    print_anything({});
    print_anything("abc"s);
    print_anything(123);
    print_anything(int_list{1, 2, 3});
```

10. If we are going to put objects that are really expensive to copy into an `any` variable, we can also perform an *in-place* construction. Let's try this with our list type. The `in_place_type_t<int_list>{}` expression is an empty object that gives the constructor of `any` enough information to know what we are going to construct. The second parameter, `{1, 2, 3}`, is just an initializer list that will be fed to the `int_list` embedded in the `any` variable for construction. This way, we avoid unnecessary copies or moves:

```
    print_anything(any(in_place_type_t<int_list>{}, {1, 2, 3}));
}
```

11. Compiling and running the program yields the following output, which is just what we expected:

```
$ ./any
Nothing.
It's a string: "abc"
It's an integer: 123
It's a list: 1, 2, 3,
It's a list: 1, 2, 3,
```

How it works...

The `std::any` type is similar in one regard to `std::optional`--it has a `has_value()` method that tells if an instance carries a value or not. But apart from that, it can contain literally *anything*, so it is more complex to handle compared with `optional`.

Before accessing the content of an `any` variable, we need to find out *what* type it carries and, then, *cast* it to that type.

Finding out if an `any` instance holds a type `T` value can be done with a comparison: `x.type() == typeid(T)`. If this comparison results in `true`, then we can use `any_cast` to get at the content.

Note that `any_cast<T>(x)` returns a *copy* of the internal `T` value in `x`. If we want a *reference* in order to avoid copying of complex objects, we need to use `any_cast<T&>(x)`. This is what we did when we accessed the internal `string` or `list<int>` objects in this section's code.

 If we cast an instance of `any` to the wrong type, it will throw an `std::bad_any_cast` exception.

Storing different types with std::variant

There are not only `struct` and `class` primitives in C++ that enable us to compose types. If we want to express that some variable can hold either some type `A` or a type `B` (or `C`, or whatever), we can use `union`. The problem with unions is that they cannot tell us they were actually initialized to which of the types that they can hold.

Consider the following code:

```
union U {
    int     a;
    char    *b;
    float   c;
};

void func(U u) { std::cout << u.b << '\n'; }
```

If we call the `func` function with a union that was initialized to hold an integer via member a, there is nothing that prevents us from accessing it, as if it was initialized to store a pointer to a string via member b. All kinds of bugs can be spread from such code. Before we start to pack our union with an auxiliary variable that tells us to what it was initialized in order to gain some safety, we can directly use `std::variant`, which came with C++17.

The `variant` is kind of the *new-school*, type-safe, and efficient union type. It does not use the heap, so it is as space-efficient and time-efficient as a union-based handcrafted solution could be, so we do not have to implement it ourselves. It can store anything apart from references, arrays, or the `void` type.

In this recipe, we will construct an example that profits from `variant` in order to get a feeling of how to use this cool new addition to the STL.

How to do it...

Let's implement a program that knows the types, `cat` and `dog`, and that stores a mixed list of cats and dogs without using any runtime polymorphy:

1. First, we include all the needed headers and define that we use the `std` namespace:

```
#include <iostream>
#include <variant>
#include <list>
#include <string>
#include <algorithm>

using namespace std;
```

2. Next, we implement two classes that have similar functionality but are not related to each other in any other way, in contrast to classes that, for example, inherit from the same interface or a similar interface. The first class is `cat`. A `cat` object has a name and can say *meow*:

```
class cat {
    string name;

public:
    cat(string n) : name{n} {}
```

```
    void meow() const {
        cout << name << " says Meow!\n";
    }
};
```

3. The other class is dog. A dog object does not say *meow* but *woof*, of course:

```
class dog {
    string name;
public:
    dog(string n) : name{n} {}
    void woof() const {
        cout << name << " says Woof!\n";
    }
};
```

4. Now we can define an animal type, which is just a type alias to std::variant<dog, cat>. This is basically the same as an old-school union but has all the extra features that variant provides:

```
using animal = variant<dog, cat>;
```

5. Before we write the main program, we implement two helpers first. One helper is an animal predicate. By calling is_type<cat>(...) or is_type<dog>(...), we can find out if an animal variant instance holds a cat or a dog. The implementation just calls holds_alternative, which is a generic predicate function for variant types:

```
template <typename T>
bool is_type(const animal &a) {
    return holds_alternative<T>(a);
}
```

6. The second helper is a structure that acts as a function object. It is a twofold function object because it implements operator() twice. One implementation is an overload that accepts dogs and the other accepts cats. For these types, it just calls the woof or the meow function:

```
struct animal_voice
{
    void operator()(const dog &d) const { d.woof(); }
    void operator()(const cat &c) const { c.meow(); }
};
```

7. Let's put these types and helpers to use. First, we define a list of `animal` variant instances and fill it with cats and dogs:

```
int main()
{
    list<animal> l {cat{"Tuba"}, dog{"Balou"}, cat{"Bobby"}};
```

8. Now, we print the contents of the list three times, and each time in a different way. One way is using `variant::index()`. Because `animal` is an alias of `variant<dog, cat>`, a return value of 0 means that the variant holds a `dog` instance. Index 1 means it is a `cat`. The order of the types in the variant specialization is the key here. In the switch case block, we access the variant with `get<T>` in order to get the actual `cat` or `dog` instance inside:

```
for (const animal &a : l) {
    switch (a.index()) {
    case 0:
        get<dog>(a).woof();
        break;
    case 1:
        get<cat>(a).meow();
        break;
    }
}
cout << "-----\n";
```

9. Instead of using the numeric index of the type, we can also explicitly ask for every type. The `get_if<dog>` returns a `dog`-typed pointer to the internal `dog` instance. If there is no `dog` instance inside, then the pointer is `null`. This way, we can try to get at different types until we finally succeed:

```
for (const animal &a : l) {
    if (const auto d (get_if<dog>(&a)); d) {
        d->woof();
    } else if (const auto c (get_if<cat>(&a)); c) {
        c->meow();
    }
}
cout << "-----\n";
```

10. The last and most elegant way is `variant::visit`. This function accepts a function object and a variant instance. The function object must implement different overloads for all the possible types the variant can hold. We implemented a structure with the right `operator()` overloads before, so we can use it here:

```
for (const animal &a : l) {
    visit(animal_voice{}, a);
}
cout << "-----\n";
```

11. At last, we will count the number of cats and dogs in the variant list. The `is_type<T>` predicate can be specialized on `cat` and `dog` and can then be used in combination with `std::count_if` to return us the number of instances of this type:

```
cout << "There are "
     << count_if(begin(l), end(l), is_type<cat>)
     << " cats and "
     << count_if(begin(l), end(l), is_type<dog>)
     << " dogs in the list.\n";
}
```

12. Compiling and running the program first yields the same list printed three times. After that, we see that the `is_type` predicates combined with `count_if` work just fine:

```
$ ./variant
Tuba says Meow!
Balou says Woof!
Bobby says Meow!
-----
Tuba says Meow!
Balou says Woof!
Bobby says Meow!
-----
Tuba says Meow!
Balou says Woof!
Bobby says Meow!
-----
There are 2 cats and 1 dogs in the list.
```

How it works...

The `std::variant` type is kind of similar to `std::any` because both can hold objects of different types, and we need to distinguish at runtime what exactly they hold before we try to access their content.

On the other hand, `std::variant` is different from `std::any` in the regard that we must declare what it shall be able to store in the form of a template type list. An instance of `std::variant<A, B, C>` *must* hold one instance of type A, B, or C. There is no possibility to hold *none* of them, which means that `std::variant` has no notion of *optionality*.

A variant of type, `variant<A, B, C>`, mimics a union type that could look like the following:

```
union U {
    A a;
    B b;
    C c;
};
```

The problem with unions is that we need to build our own mechanisms to distinguish if it was initialized with an A, B, or C variable. The `std::variant` type can do this for us without much hassle.

In the code in this section, we used three different ways to handle the content of a variant variable.

The first way was the `index()` function of `variant`. For a variant type `variant<A, B, C>` it can return index 0 if it was initialized to hold an A type, or 1 for B, or 2 for C, and so on for more complex variants.

The next way is the `get_if<T>` function. It accepts the address of a variant object and returns a T-typed pointer to its content. If the T type is wrong, then this pointer will be a `null` pointer. It is also possible to call `get<T>(x)` on a variant variable in order to get a reference to its content, but if that does not succeed, this function throws an exception (before doing such `get`-casts, checking for the right type can be done with the Boolean predicate `holds_alternative<T>(x)`).

The last way to access the variant is the `std::visit` function. It accepts a function object and a `variant` instance. The `visit` function then checks of which type the content of the variant is and then calls the right `operator()` overload of the function object.

For exactly this purpose, we implemented the `animal_voice` type because it can be used in combination with `visit` and `variant<dog, cat>`:

```
struct animal_voice
{
    void operator()(const dog &d) const { d.woof(); }
    void operator()(const cat &c) const { c.meow(); }
};
```

The `visit`-way of accessing variants can be considered the most elegant one because the code sections that actually access the variant do not need to be hardcoded to the types the variant can hold. This makes our code easier to extend.

 The claim that a `variant` type cannot hold *no* value was not completely true. By adding the `std::monostate` type to its type list, it can indeed be initialized to hold *no* value.

Automatically handling resources with std::unique_ptr

Since C++11, the STL provides smart pointers that really help keep track of dynamic memory and its disposal. Even before C++11, there was a class called `auto_ptr` that was already able to do automatic memory disposal, but it was easy to use the wrong way.

However, with the C++11-generation smart pointers, we seldom need to write `new` and `delete` ourselves, which is a really good thing. Smart pointers are a shiny example of automatic memory management. If we maintain dynamically allocated objects with `unique_ptr`, we are basically safe from memory leaks, because upon its destruction this class automatically calls `delete` on the object it maintains.

A unique pointer expresses ownership of the object it points to and follows its responsibility of freeing its memory again if it is no longer used. This class has the potential of relieving us forever from memory leaks (at least together with its companions `shared_ptr` and `weak_ptr`, but in this recipe, we solely concentrate on `unique_ptr`). And the best thing is that it imposes *no overhead* on space and runtime performance, compared with code with raw pointers and manual memory management. (Okay, it still sets its internal raw pointer to `nullptr` internally after destruction of the object it points to, which cannot always be optimized away. Most manually written code that manages dynamic memory does the same, though.)

In this recipe, we will a look at `unique_ptr` and how to use it.

How to do it...

We will write a program that shows us how `unique_ptr` handles memory by creating a custom type that adds some debug messages upon its construction and destruction. Then, we will play around with unique pointers, maintaining dynamically allocated instances of it:

1. First, we include the necessary headers and declare that we use the `std` namespace:

```
#include <iostream>
#include <memory>

using namespace std;
```

2. We are going to implement a little class for the object we are going to manage using `unique_ptr`. Its constructor and destructor print to the terminal, so we can see later when it is actually automatically deleted:

```
class Foo
{
public:
    string name;

    Foo(string n)
        : name{move(n)}
    { cout << "CTOR " << name << '\n'; }

    ~Foo() { cout << "DTOR " << name << '\n'; }
};
```

3. In order to see what limitations a function has that accepts unique pointers as arguments, we just implement one. It *processes* a Foo item by printing its name. Note that while unique pointers are smart, overhead-free, and comfortably safe, they can still be `null`. This means that we still have to check them before we dereference them:

```
void process_item(unique_ptr<Foo> p)
{
    if (!p) { return; }
    cout << "Processing " << p->name << '\n';
}
```

4. In the main function, we will open another scope, create two Foo objects on the heap, and manage both with unique pointers. We create the first one explicitly on the heap using the `new` operator and then put it into the constructor of the `unique_ptr<Foo>` variable, p1. We create the unique pointer, p2, by calling `make_unique<Foo>` with the arguments we would otherwise directly give the constructor of Foo. This is the more elegant way because we can use auto type deduction and the first time we can access the object, it is already managed by `unique_ptr`:

```
int main()
{
    {
        unique_ptr<Foo> p1 {new Foo{"foo"}};
        auto            p2 (make_unique<Foo>("bar"));
    }
```

5. After we left the scope, both objects are destructed immediately and their memory is released to the heap. Let's have a look at the `process_item` function and how to use it with `unique_ptr` now. If we construct a new Foo instance, managed by a `unique_ptr` in the function call, then its lifetime is reduced to the scope of the function. When `process_item` returns, the object is destroyed:

```
process_item(make_unique<Foo>("foo1"));
```

6. If we want to call `process_item` with an object that already existed before the call, then we need to *transfer ownership* because that function takes a `unique_ptr` by value, which means that calling it would lead to a copy. But `unique_ptr` cannot be copied, it can only be *moved*. Let's create two new `Foo` objects and move one into `process_item`. By looking at the terminal output later, we will see that `foo2` is destroyed when `process_item` returns because we transferred ownership to it. `foo3` will continue living until the main function returns:

```
        auto p1 (make_unique<Foo>("foo2"));
        auto p2 (make_unique<Foo>("foo3"));
        process_item(move(p1));
        cout << "End of main()\n";
    }
```

7. Let's compile and run the program. At first, we see the constructor and destructor calls of `foo` and `bar`. They are indeed destroyed just after the program leaves the additional scope. Note that the objects are destroyed in the opposite order of their creation. The next constructor line comes from `foo1`, which is the item we created during the `process_item` call. It is indeed destroyed immediately after the function call. Then we created `foo2` and `foo3`. `foo2` is destroyed immediately after the `process_item` call where we transferred the ownership. The other item, `foo3`, in comparison, is destroyed after the last code line in the main function:

```
$ ./unique_ptr
CTOR foo
CTOR bar
DTOR bar
DTOR foo
CTOR foo1
Processing foo1
DTOR foo1
CTOR foo2
CTOR foo3
Processing foo2
DTOR foo2
End of main()
DTOR foo3
```

How it works...

Handling heap objects with `std::unique_ptr` is really simple. After we initialized a unique pointer to hold a pointer to some object, there is *no way* we can accidentally *forget* about deleting it on some code path.

If we assign some new pointer to a unique pointer, then it will always first delete the old object it pointed to and then store the new pointer. On a unique pointer variable, x, we can also call `x.reset()` to just delete the object it points to immediately without assigning a new pointer. Another equivalent alternative to reassigning via `x = new_pointer` is `x.reset(new_pointer)`.

> There is indeed one single way to release an object from the management of `unique_ptr` without deleting it. The `release` function does that, but using this function is not advisable in most situations.

Since pointers need to be checked before they are actually dereferenced, they overload the right operators in a way that enables them to mimic raw pointers. Conditionals like `if (p) {...}` and `if (p != nullptr) {...}` perform the same way as we would check a raw pointer.

Dereferencing a unique pointer can be done via the `get()` function, which returns a raw pointer to the object that can be dereferenced, or directly via `operator*`, which again mimics raw pointers.

One important characteristic of `unique_ptr` is that its instances cannot be *copied* but can be *moved* from one `unique_ptr` variable to the other. This is why we had to move an existing unique pointer into the `process_item` function. If we were able to copy a unique pointer, then this would mean that the object being pointed to is owned by *two* unique pointers, although this contradicts the design of a *unique* pointer that is the *only owner* (and later the *"deleter"*) of the underlying object.

> Since there are data structures, such as `unique_ptr` and `shared_ptr`, there is rarely any reason to create heap objects directly with `new` and `delete` them manually. Use such classes wherever you can! Especially `unique_ptr` imposes *no* overhead at runtime.

Automatically handling shared heap memory with std::shared_ptr

In the last recipe, we learned how to use `unique_ptr`. This is an enormously useful and important class because it helps us manage dynamically allocated objects. However, it can only handle *single* ownership. It is not possible to let *multiple* objects own the same dynamically allocated object because, then, it would be unclear who has to delete it later.

The pointer type, `shared_ptr`, was designed for specifically this case. Shared pointers can be *copied* arbitrarily often. An internal reference counting mechanism tracks how many objects are still maintaining a pointer to the payload object. Only the last shared pointer that goes out of scope will call `delete` on the payload object. This way, we can be sure that we do not get memory leaks because objects are deleted automatically after use. At the same time, we can be sure that they are not deleted too early, or too often (every created object must only be deleted *once*).

In this recipe, you will learn how to use `shared_ptr` to automatically manage dynamic objects that are shared between multiple owners and see what's different when comparing it with `unique_ptr`:

How to do it...

We are going to write a program that is similar to the program we wrote in the `unique_ptr` recipe in order to get insights into the usage and principles of `shared_ptr`:

1. At first, we just include the necessary headers and declare that we use the `std` namespace by default:

```
#include <iostream>
#include <memory>

using namespace std;
```

2. Then we define a little helper class, which helps us see when instances of it are actually created and destroyed. We will manage instances of it with `shared_ptr`:

```
class Foo
{
public:
    string name;
    Foo(string n)
```

---
[368]

```
        : name{move(n)}
    { cout << "CTOR " << name << '\n'; }
    ~Foo() { cout << "DTOR " << name << '\n'; }
};
```

3. Next, we implement a function that takes a shared pointer to a `Foo` instance *by value*. Accepting shared pointers as arguments by value is more interesting than accepting them by reference because in this case, they need to be copied, which changes their internal reference counter, as we will see:

```
void f(shared_ptr<Foo> sp)
{
    cout << "f: use counter at "
         << sp.use_count() << '\n';
}
```

4. In the main function, we declare an empty shared pointer. By default constructing it, it is effectively a `null` pointer:

```
int main()
{
    shared_ptr<Foo> fa;
```

5. Next, we open another scope and instantiate two `Foo` objects. We create the first one using the `new` operator and then feed it into the constructor of a new `shared_ptr`. Then we create the second instance using `make_shared<Foo>`, which creates a `Foo` instance from the parameters we provide. This is the more elegant method because we can use auto type deduction and the object is already managed when we have the chance to access it for the first time. This is very similar to the `unique_ptr` recipe at this point:

```
    {
        cout << "Inner scope begin\n";
        shared_ptr<Foo> f1 {new Foo{"foo"}};
        auto            f2 (make_shared<Foo>("bar"));
```

6. Since shared pointers can be shared, they need to track how many parties share them. This is done with an internal reference counter or *use* counter. We can print its value using `use_count`. The value is exactly 1 at this point because we did not copy it yet. We can copy `f1` to `fa`, which increases the use counter to 2.

```
cout << "f1's use counter at " << f1.use_count() << '\n';
fa = f1;
cout << "f1's use counter at " << f1.use_count() << '\n';
```

7. While we're leaving the scope, the shared pointers `f1` and `f2` are destroyed. The `f1` variable's reference counter is decremented to 1 again, making `fa` the only owner of the `Foo` instance. While `f2` is destroyed, its reference counter is decremented to 0. In this case, the `shared_ptr` pointer's destructor will call `delete` on this object, which disposes of it:

```
    }
    cout << "Back to outer scope\n";

    cout << fa.use_count() << '\n';
```

8. Now, let's call the `f` function with our shared pointer in two different ways. At first, we call it naively by copying `fa`. The `f` function will then print that the reference counter has the value 2. In the second call to `f`, we move the pointer into the function. This makes `f` the only owner of the object:

```
    cout << "first f() call\n";
    f(fa);
    cout << "second f() call\n";
    f(move(fa));
```

9. After `f` is returned, the `Foo` instance is destroyed immediately because we do not have ownership of it any longer. Therefore, all the objects are already destroyed when the main function returns:

```
    cout << "end of main()\n";
}
```

10. Compiling and running the program yields the following output. In the beginning, we see "foo" and "bar" created. After we copied f1 (which points to "foo"), its reference counter was incremented to 2. While leaving the scope, "bar" is destroyed because the shared pointer to it being the subject of destruction is the only owner. The single 1 in the output is the reference count of fa, which is now the only owner of "foo". Afterward, we called function f twice. On the first call, we copied fa into it, which gave it a reference counter of 2 again. On the second call, we moved it into f, which did not alter its reference counter. Moreover, because f is the only owner of "foo" at this point, the object is destroyed immediately after f leaves the scope. This way, no other heap objects are destroyed after the last print line in main:

```
$ ./shared_ptr
Inner scope begin
CTOR foo
CTOR bar
f1's use counter at 1
f1's use counter at 2
DTOR bar
Back to outer scope
1
first f() call
f: use counter at 2
second f() call
f: use counter at 1
DTOR foo
end of main()
```

How it works...

When constructing and deleting objects, shared_ptr works basically like unique_ptr. Constructing shared pointers works similarly as creating unique pointers (although there is a function make_shared that creates shared objects as a pendant to unique_ptr pointer's make_unique function).

The major difference from `unique_ptr` is that we can copy the `shared_ptr` instances because shared pointers maintain a so-called *control block* together with the object they manage. The control block contains a pointer to the payload object and a reference counter or *use* counter. If there are N number of `shared_ptr` instances pointing to the object, then the use counter also has the value N. Whenever a `shared_ptr` instance is destructed, then its destructor decrements this internal use counter. The last shared pointer to such an object will hit the condition that it decrements the use counter to 0 during its destruction. This is, then, the shared pointer instance, which calls the `delete` operator on the payload object! This way, we can't possibly suffer from memory leaks because the object's use count is automatically tracked.

To illustrate this a bit more, let's have a look at the following diagram:

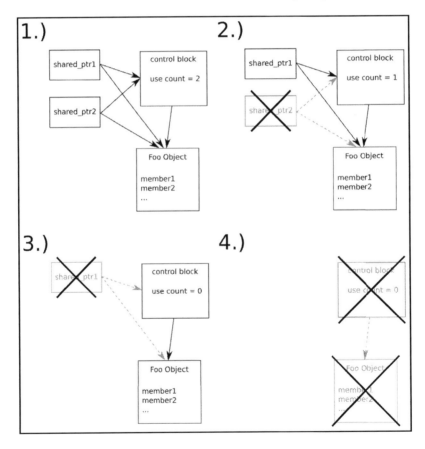

In step 1, we have two `shared_ptr` instances managing an object of type `Foo`. The use counter is at value 2. Then, `shared_ptr2` is destroyed, which decrements the use counter to 1. The `Foo` instance is not destroyed yet because there is still the other shared pointer. In step 3, the last shared pointer is destroyed too. This leads to the use counter being decremented to 0. Step 4 happens immediately after step 3. Both the control block and the instance of `Foo` are destroyed and their memory is released to the heap.

Equipped with `shared_ptr` and `unique_ptr`, we can automatically deal with most dynamically allocated objects without having to worry about memory leaks any longer. There is, however, one important caveat to consider--imagine we have two objects on the heap that contain shared pointers to each other, and some other shared pointer points to one of them from somewhere else. If that external shared pointer goes out of scope, then both objects still have the use counters with *nonzero* values because they reference *each other*. This leads to a *memory leak*. Shared pointers should not be used in this case because such cyclic reference chains prevent the use counter of such objects to ever reach 0.

There's more...

Look at the following code. What if you are told that it contains a potential *memory leak*?

```
void function(shared_ptr<A>, shared_ptr<B>, int);
// "function" is defined somewhere else

// ...somewhere later in the code:
function(new A{}, new B{}, other_function());
```

"Where is the memory leak?", one might ask, since the newly allocated objects A and B are immediately fed into `shared_ptr` types, and *then* we are safe from memory leaks.

Yes, it is true that we are safe from memory leaks as soon as the pointers are captured in the `shared_ptr` instances. The problem is a bit fiddly to grasp.

When we call a function, `f(x(), y(), z())`, the compiler needs to assemble code that calls `x()`, `y()`, and `z()` first so that it can forward their return values to `f`. What gets us very bad in combination with the example from before is that the compiler can execute these function calls to x, y, and z in *any* order.

Looking back at the example, what happens if the compiler decides to structure the code in a way where at first `new A{}` is called, then `other_function()`, and then `new B{}` is called, before the results of these functions are finally fed into `function`? If `other_function()` throws an exception, we get a memory leak because we still have an unmanaged object, A, on the heap because we just allocated it but did not have a chance to hand it to the management of `shared_ptr`. No matter how we catch the exception, the handle to the object is *gone* and we *cannot delete* it!

There are two easy ways to circumvent this problem:

```
// 1.)
function(make_shared<A>(), make_shared<B>(), other_function());

// 2.)
shared_ptr<A> ap {new A{}};
shared_ptr<B> bp {new B{}};
function(ap, bp, other_function());
```

This way, the objects are already managed by `shared_ptr`, no matter who throws what exception afterward.

Dealing with weak pointers to shared objects

In the recipe about `shared_ptr`, we learned how useful and easy to use shared pointers are. Together with `unique_ptr`, they pose an invaluable improvement for code that needs to manage dynamically allocated objects.

Whenever we copy `shared_ptr`, we increment its internal reference counter. As long as we hold our shared pointer copy, the object being pointed to will not be deleted. But what if we want some kind of *weak* pointer, which enables us to get at the object as long as it exists but does not prevent its destruction? And how do we determine if the object still exists, then?

In such situations, `weak_ptr` is our companion. It is a little bit more complicated to use than `unique_ptr` and `shared_ptr`, but after following this recipe, we will be ready to use it.

How to do it...

We will implement a program that maintains objects with `shared_ptr` instances, and then, we mix in `weak_ptr` to see how this changes the behavior of smart pointer memory handling:

1. At first, we include the necessary headers and declare that we use the `std` namespace by default:

```
#include <iostream>
#include <iomanip>
#include <memory>

using namespace std;
```

2. Next, we implement a class that prints a message in its destructor implementation. This way, we can simply check when an item is actually destroyed later in the program output:

```
struct Foo {
    int value;
    Foo(int i) : value{i} {}
    ~Foo() { cout << "DTOR Foo " << value << '\n'; }
};
```

3. Let's also implement a function that prints information about a weak pointer, so we can print a weak pointer's state at different points of our program. The `expired` function of `weak_ptr` tells us if the object it points to still really exists, because holding a weak pointer to an object does not prolong its lifetime! The `use_count` counter tells us how many `shared_ptr` instances are currently pointing to the object in question:

```
void weak_ptr_info(const weak_ptr<Foo> &p)
{
    cout << "---------" << boolalpha
         << "\nexpired:   " << p.expired()
         << "\nuse_count: " << p.use_count()
         << "\ncontent:   ";
```

4. If we want to access the actual object, we need to call the `lock` function. It returns us a shared pointer to the object. In case the object does *not exist* any longer, the shared pointer we got from it is effectively a `null` pointer. We need to check that, and then we can access it:

```
if (const auto sp (p.lock()); sp) {
    cout << sp->value << '\n';
} else {
    cout << "<null>\n";
}
}
```

5. Let's instantiate an empty weak pointer in the main function and print its content which is, of course, empty at first:

```
int main()
{
    weak_ptr<Foo> weak_foo;
    weak_ptr_info(weak_foo);
```

6. In a new scope, we instantiate a new shared pointer with a fresh instance of the `Foo` class. Then we copy it to the weak pointer. Note that this will not increment the reference count of the shared pointer. The reference counter is 1 because only one *shared* pointer owns it:

```
    {
        auto shared_foo (make_shared<Foo>(1337));
        weak_foo = shared_foo;
```

7. Let's call the weak pointer function before we *leave* the scope and, again, *after* we leave the scope. The `Foo` instance should be destroyed immediately, *although* a weak pointer points to it:

```
        weak_ptr_info(weak_foo);
    }
    weak_ptr_info(weak_foo);
}
```

8. Compiling and running the program yields us three times the output of the `weak_ptr_info` function. In the first call, the weak pointer is empty. In the second call, it already points to the `Foo` instance we created and is able to dereference it after *locking* it. Before the third call, we leave the inner scope, which triggers the destructor of the `Foo` instance, as we expected. Afterward, it is not possible to get at the content of the deleted `Foo` item via the weak pointer any longer, and the weak pointer correctly recognizes that it has expired:

```
$ ./weak_ptr
---------
expired:    true
use_count: 0
content:    <null>
---------
expired:    false
use_count: 1
content:    1337
DTOR Foo 1337
---------
expired:    true
use_count: 0
content:    <null>
```

How it works...

Weak pointers provide us a way to point at an object maintained by shared pointers without incrementing its use counter. Okay, a raw pointer could do the same, but a raw pointer cannot tell us if it is dangling or not. A weak pointer can!

In order to understand how weak pointers as an addition to shared pointers work, let's directly jump to an illustrating diagram:

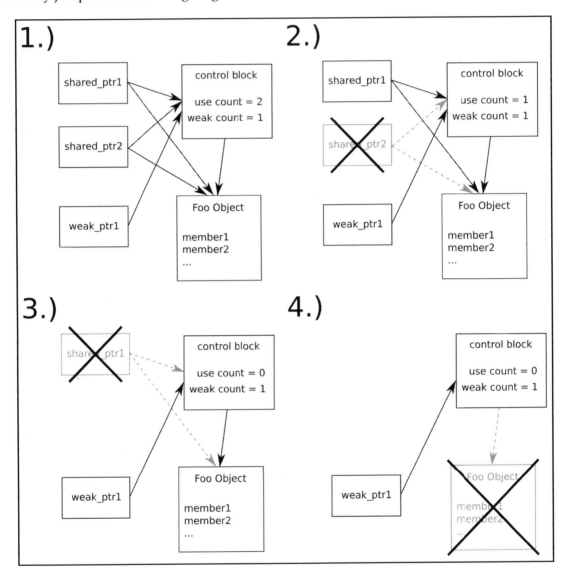

The flow is similar to the diagram in the recipe about shared pointers. In step 1, we have two shared pointers and a weak pointer pointing to the object of type `Foo`. Although there are three objects pointing to it, only the shared pointers manipulate its use counter, which is why it has the value 2. The weak pointer only manipulates a *weak counter* of the control block. In steps 2 and 3, the shared pointer instances are destroyed, which leads stepwise to a use counter of 0. In step 4, this results in the `Foo` object being deleted, but the control block *stays* there. The weak pointer still needs the control block in order to distinguish if it dangles or not. Only when the *last weak* pointer that still points to a control block *also* goes out of scope, the control block is deleted.

We can also say that a dangling weak pointer has *expired*. In order to check for this attribute, we can ask `weak_ptr` pointer's `expired` method, which returns a boolean value. If it is `true`, then we cannot dereference the weak pointer because there is no object to dereference any longer.

In order to dereference a weak pointer, we need to call `lock()`. This is safe and convenient because this function returns us a shared pointer. As long as we hold this shared pointer, the object behind it cannot vanish because we incremented the use counter by locking it. If the object is deleted, shortly before the `lock()` call, then the shared pointer it returns is effectively a `null` pointer.

Simplifying resource handling of legacy APIs with smart pointers

Smart pointers (`unique_ptr`, `shared_ptr`, and `weak_ptr`) are extremely useful, and it is, in general, safe to say that a programmer should *always* use these instead of allocating and freeing memory manually.

But what if objects cannot be allocated using the `new` operator and/or cannot be freed again using `delete`? Many legacy libraries come with their own allocation/destruction functions. It seems that this would be a problem because we learned that smart pointers rely on `new` and `delete`. If the creation and/or destruction of specific types of objects relies on specific factory functions' deleter interfaces, does this prevent us from getting the humongous benefits of smart pointers?

Not at all. In this recipe, we will see that we only need to perform very minimal customizations on smart pointers in order to let them follow specific procedures for allocation and destruction of specific objects.

How to do it...

In this section, we will define a type that cannot be allocated with `new` directly and, also, cannot be released again using `delete`. As this prevents it from being used with smart pointers directly, we perform the necessary little adaptions to instances of `unique_ptr` and `smart_ptr`:

1. As always, we first include the necessary headers and declare that we use the `std` namespace by default:

```
#include <iostream>
#include <memory>
#include <string>

using namespace std;
```

2. Next, we declare a class that has its constructor and destructor declared `private`. This way, we simulate the problem that we have to access specific functions that create and destroy instances of it:

```
class Foo
{
    string name;
    Foo(string n)
        : name{n}
    { cout << "CTOR " << name << '\n'; }
    ~Foo() { cout << "DTOR " << name << '\n'; }
```

3. The static methods, `create_foo` and `destroy_foo`, then create and destroy the `Foo` instances. They work with raw pointers. This simulates the situation of a legacy C API, which prevents us from using them with normal `shared_ptr` pointers directly:

```
public:
    static Foo* create_foo(string s) {
        return new Foo{move(s)};
    }

    static void destroy_foo(Foo *p) { delete p; }
};
```

4. Now, let's make such objects manageable by `shared_ptr`. We can, of course, put the pointer we get from `create_foo` into the constructor of a shared pointer. Only the destruction is tricky because the default deleter of `shared_ptr` would do it wrong. The trick is that we can give `shared_ptr` a *custom deleter*. The function signature that a deleter function or callable object needs to have is already the same as that of the `destroy_foo` function. If the function we need to call for destroying the object is more complicated, we can simply wrap it into a lambda expression:

```
static shared_ptr<Foo> make_shared_foo(string s)
{
    return {Foo::create_foo(move(s)), Foo::destroy_foo};
}
```

5. Note that `make_shared_foo` returns a usual `shared_ptr<Foo>` instance because giving it a custom deleter did not change its type. This is because `shared_ptr` uses virtual function calls to hide such details. Unique pointers do not impose any overhead, which makes the same trick unfeasible for them. Here, we need to change the type of the `unique_ptr`. As a second template parameter, we give it `void (*)(Foo*)`, which is exactly the type of pointer to the function, `destroy_foo`:

```
static unique_ptr<Foo, void (*)(Foo*)> make_unique_foo(string s)
{
    return {Foo::create_foo(move(s)), Foo::destroy_foo};
}
```

6. In the main function, we just instantiate both a shared pointer and a unique pointer instance. In the program output, we will see if they are really, correctly, and automatically destroyed:

```
int main()
{
    auto ps (make_shared_foo("shared Foo instance"));
    auto pu (make_unique_foo("unique Foo instance"));
}
```

7. Compiling and running the program yields the following output, which is luckily just what we expected:

```
$ ./legacy_shared_ptr
CTOR shared Foo instance
CTOR unique Foo instance
DTOR unique Foo instance
DTOR shared Foo instance
```

How it works...

Usually, `unique_ptr` and `shared_ptr` just call `delete` on their internal pointers, whenever they ought to destroy the object they maintain. In this section, we constructed a class which can neither be allocated the C++ way using `x = new Foo{123}` nor can it be destructed with `delete x` directly.

The `Foo::create_foo` function just returns a plain raw pointer to a newly constructed `Foo` instance, so this causes no further problems because smart pointers work with raw pointers anyway.

The problem we had to deal with is that we need to teach `unique_ptr` and `shared_ptr` how to *destruct* an object if the default way is *not* the right one.

In that regard, both the smart pointer types differ a little bit. In order to define a custom deleter for `unique_ptr`, we have to alter its type. Because the type signature of the `Foo` deleter is `void Foo::destroy_foo(Foo*);`, the type of the `unique_ptr` maintaining a `Foo` instance must be `unique_ptr<Foo, void (*)(Foo*)>`. Now, it can hold a function pointer to `destroy_foo`, which we provide it as a second constructor parameter in our `make_unique_foo` function.

If giving `unique_ptr` a custom deleter function forces us to change its type, why were we able to do the same with `shared_ptr` *without* changing its type? The only thing we had to do there was giving `shared_ptr` a second constructor parameter, and that's it. Why can't it be as easy for `unique_ptr` as it is for `shared_ptr`?

The reason why it is so simple to just provide `shared_ptr` some kind of callable deleter object without altering the shared pointer's type lies in the nature of shared pointers, which maintain a control block. The control block of shared pointers is an object with virtual functions. This means that the control block of a standard shared pointer compared with the type of a control block of a shared pointer with a custom deleter is *different*! When we want a unique pointer to use a custom deleter, then this changes the type of the unique pointer. When we want a shared pointer to use a custom deleter, then this changes the type of the internal *control block*, which is invisible to us because this difference is hidden behind a virtual function interface.

It would be *possible* to do the same trick with unique pointers, but then, this would imply a certain runtime overhead on them. This is not what we want because unique pointers promise to be completely *overhead free* at runtime.

Sharing different member values of the same object

Let's imagine we are maintaining a shared pointer to some complex, composed, and dynamically allocated object. Then, we want to start a new thread that does some time-consuming work on a member of this complex object. If we want to release this shared pointer now, the object will be deleted while the other thread is still accessing it. If we don't want to give the thread object the pointer to the whole complex object because that would mess with our nice interface, or for other reasons, does this mean that we have to do manual memory management now?

No. It is possible to use shared pointers that on one hand, point to a member of a large shared object, while on the other hand, perform automatic memory management for the entire initial object.

In this example, we will create such a scenario (without threads to keep it simple) in order to get a feeling for this handy feature of `shared_ptr`.

How to do it...

We are going to define a structure that is composed of multiple members. Then, we allocate an instance of this structure on the heap that is maintained by a shared pointer. From this shared pointer, we obtain more shared pointers that do not point to the actual object but to its members:

1. We include the necessary headers first and then declare that we use the `std` namespace by default:

```
#include <iostream>
#include <memory>
#include <string>

using namespace std;
```

2. Then we define a class that has different members. We will let shared pointers point to the individual members. In order to be able to see when the class is created and destroyed, we let its constructor and destructor print messages:

```
struct person {
    string name;
    size_t age;
    person(string n, size_t a)
        : name{move(n)}, age{a}
    { cout << "CTOR " << name << '\n'; }
    ~person() { cout << "DTOR " << name << '\n'; }
};
```

3. Let's define shared pointers that have the right types to point to the name and age member variables of a `person` class instance:

```
int main()
{
    shared_ptr<string> shared_name;
    shared_ptr<size_t> shared_age;
```

4. Next, we enter a new scope, create such a person object, and let a shared pointer manage it:

```
    {
        auto sperson (make_shared<person>("John Doe", 30));
```

5. Then, we let the first two shared pointers point to its name and age members. The trick is that we use a specific constructor of `shared_ptr`, which accepts a shared pointer and a pointer to a member of the shared object. This way, we can manage the object while not pointing at the object itself!

```
    shared_name = shared_ptr<string>(sperson, &sperson->name);
    shared_age  = shared_ptr<size_t>(sperson, &sperson->age);
}
```

6. After leaving the scope, we print the person's name and age values. This is only legal if the object is still allocated:

```
    cout << "name: "  << *shared_name
         << "\nage: " << *shared_age << '\n';
}
```

7. Compiling and running the program yields the following output. From the destructor message, we see that the object is indeed still alive and allocated when we access the person's name and age values via the member pointers!

```
$ ./shared_members
CTOR John Doe
name: John Doe
age:  30
DTOR John Doe
```

How it works...

In this section, we first created a shared pointer that manages a dynamically allocated `person` object. Then we made two other smart pointers point to the person object, but they both did not *directly* point to the person object itself but instead to its members, `name` and `age`.

To summarize what kind of scenario we just created, let's have a look at the following diagram:

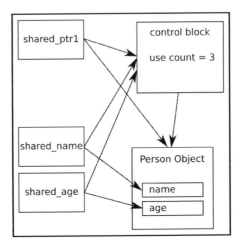

Note that `shared_ptr1` points to the `person` object directly, while `shared_name` and `shared_age` point to the `name` and the `age` members of the same object. Apparently, they still manage the object's entire lifetime. This is possible because the internal control block pointers still point to the same control block, no matter what sub-object the individual shared pointers point to.

In this scenario, the use count of the control block is 3. This way, the `person` object is not destroyed when `shared_ptr1` is destroyed because the other shared pointers still own the object.

When creating such shared pointer instances that point to members of the shared object, the syntax looks a bit strange. In order to obtain a `shared_ptr<string>` that points to the `name` member of a shared person, we need to write the following:

```
auto sperson (make_shared<person>("John Doe", 30));
auto sname   (shared_ptr<string>(sperson, &sperson->name));
```

In order to get a specific pointer to a member of a shared object, we instantiate a shared pointer with a type specialization of the member we want to access. This is why we write `shared_ptr<`**`string`**`>`. Then, in the constructor, we first provide the original shared pointer that maintains the `person` object and, as a second argument, the address of the object the new shared pointer will use when we dereference it.

Generating random numbers and choosing the right random number engine

In order to get random numbers for whatever purpose, C++ programmers usually basically used the `rand()` function of the C library before C++11. Since C++11, there has been a whole *suite* of random number generators that serve different purposes and have different characteristics.

These generators are not completely self-explanatory, so we will have a look at all of them in this recipe. In the end, we will see in what ways they differ, how to choose the right one, and that we will most probably never use all of them.

How to do it...

We will implement a procedure that prints a nice illustrating histogram of the numbers a random generator produces. Then, we will run all STL random number generator engines through this procedure and learn from the results. This program contains many repetitive lines, so it might be advantageous to just copy the source code from the code repository accompanying this book on the Internet instead of typing all the repetitive code manually.

1. At first, we include all the necessary headers and then declare that we use the `std` namespace by default:

```
#include <iostream>
#include <string>
#include <vector>
#include <random>
#include <iomanip>
#include <limits>
#include <cstdlib>
#include <algorithm>

using namespace std;
```

2. Then we implement a helper function, which helps us maintain and print some statistics for each type of random number engine. It accepts two parameters: the number of *partitions* and the number of *samples*. We will see immediately what these are for. The type of random generator is defined via the template parameter RD. The first thing we do in this function is define an alias type for the resulting numeric type of the numbers the generator returns. We also make sure that we have at least 10 partitions:

```
template <typename RD>
void histogram(size_t partitions, size_t samples)
{
    using rand_t = typename RD::result_type;
    partitions = max<size_t>(partitions, 10);
```

3. Next, we instantiate an actual generator instance of type RD. Then, we define a divisor variable called `div`. All random number engines emit random numbers within the range from 0 to RD::max(). The function argument, partitions, allows the caller to choose by how many partitions we divide every random number range. By dividing the largest possible value by the number of partitions, we know how large every partition is:

```
RD rd;
rand_t div ((double(RD::max()) + 1) / partitions);
```

4. Next, we instantiate a vector of counter variables. It is exactly as large as the number of partitions we have. Then, we get as many random values out of the random engine as the variable `samples` says. The expression, `rd()`, gets a random number from the generator and shifts its internal state to prepare it for returning the next random number. By dividing every random number by `div`, we get the partition number it falls into and can increment the right counter in the vector of counters:

```
vector<size_t> v (partitions);
for (size_t i {0}; i < samples; ++i) {
    ++v[rd() / div];
}
```

5. Now we have a nice coarse-grained histogram of sample values. In order to print it, we need to know a little bit more about its actual counter values. Let's extract its largest value using the `max_element` algorithm. We then divide this largest counter value by `100`. This way, we can divide all the counter values by `max_div` and print a lot of stars on the terminal without exceeding the width of `100`. If the largest counter contains a number less than `100`, because we did not use so many samples, we use `max` in order to get a minimal divisor of `1`:

```
rand_t max_elm (*max_element(begin(v), end(v)));
rand_t max_div (max(max_elm / 100, rand_t(1)));
```

6. Let's now print the histogram to the terminal. Every partition gets its own line on the terminal. By dividing its counter value by `max_div` and print so many asterisk symbols `'*'`, we get histogram lines that fit into the terminal:

```
for (size_t i {0}; i < partitions; ++i) {
    cout << setw(2) << i << ": "
         << string(v[i] / max_div, '*') << '\n';
}
}
```

7. Okay, that's it. Now to the main program. We let the user define how many partitions and samples should be used:

```
int main(int argc, char **argv)
{
    if (argc != 3) {
        cout << "Usage: " << argv[0]
             << " <partitions> <samples>\n";
        return 1;
    }
```

8. We then read those variables from the command line. Of course, the command line consists of strings, which we can convert to numbers using `std::stoull` (`stoull` is an abbreviation for **string** **to** **u**nsigned **long long**):

```
size_t partitions {stoull(argv[1])};
size_t samples    {stoull(argv[2])};
```

9. Now we call our histogram helper function on *every* random number engine the STL provides. This makes this recipe very long and repetitive. Better copy the example from the Internet. The output of this program is really interesting to look at. We start with `random_device`. This device tries to distribute the randomness equally over all the possible values:

```
cout << "random_device" << '\n';
histogram<random_device>(partitions, samples);
```

10. The next random engine we try is `default_random_engine`. What kind of engine this type refers to is implementation-specific. It can be *any* of the following random engines:

```
cout << "ndefault_random_engine" << '\n';
histogram<default_random_engine>(partitions, samples);
```

11. Then we try it on all the other engines:

```
cout << "nminstd_rand0" << '\n';
histogram<minstd_rand0>(partitions, samples);
cout << "nminstd_rand" << '\n';
histogram<minstd_rand>(partitions, samples);
cout << "nmt19937" << '\n';
histogram<mt19937>(partitions, samples);
cout << "nmt19937_64" << '\n';
histogram<mt19937_64>(partitions, samples);
cout << "nranlux24_base" << '\n';
histogram<ranlux24_base>(partitions, samples);
cout << "nranlux48_base" << '\n';
histogram<ranlux48_base>(partitions, samples);
cout << "nranlux24" << '\n';
histogram<ranlux24>(partitions, samples);
cout << "nranlux48" << '\n';
histogram<ranlux48>(partitions, samples);
cout << "nknuth_b" << '\n';
histogram<knuth_b>(partitions, samples);
}
```

12. Compiling and running the program yields interesting results. We will see a long list of output, and we'll see that all the random engines have different characteristics. Let's first run the program with `10` partitions and only `1000` samples:

```
$ ./random_generator 10 1000
random_device
0: ******************************************************************************
1: *************************************************************************
2: ***************************************************************************
3: ***********************************************************************
4: ***************************************************************************
5: *********************************************************************************
6: **************************************************************************
7: ***********************************************************************
8: **************************************************************************
9: ************************************************************************

default_random_engine
0: ****************************************************************************
1: ***************************************************************************
2: ***************************************************************************
3: ***********************************************************************
4: *****************************************************************************
5: ****************************************************************************
6: ****************************************************************************
7: ***********************************************************************
8: **************************************************************************
9: **************************************************************************

minstd_rand0
0: ****************************************************************************
1: *****************************************************************************
2: *************************************************************************
3: ***********************************************************************
4: *****************************************************************************
5: **************************************************************************
6: ****************************************************************************
7: **********************************************************************
8: ***********************************************************************
9: ***********************************************************************

minstd_rand
```

13. Then, we run the same program again. This time it is still `10` partitions but `1,000,000` samples. It becomes very obvious that the histograms look much *cleaner*, when we take more samples from them. This is an important observation:

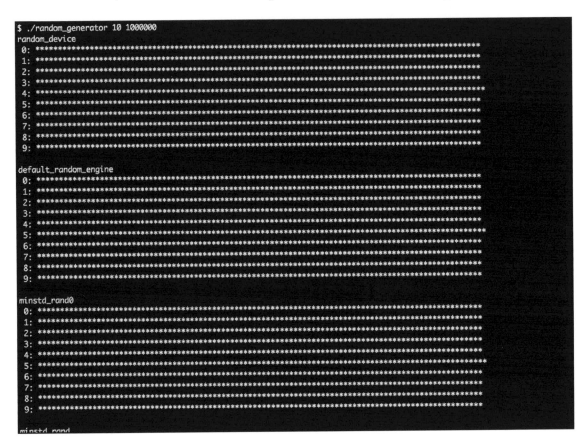

How it works...

In general, any random number generator needs to be instantiated as an object before use. The resulting object can be called like a function without parameters because it overloads `operator()`. Every call will then lead to a new random number. It is that simple.

In this section, we wrote a program that is much more complex than that in order to get a bit more information about random number generators. Please play around with the resulting program by launching it with different command-line arguments and realize the following facts:

- The more samples we take, the more equal our partition counters appear.
- The inequality of the partition counters wildly differs between individual engines.
- For a large number of samples, it becomes apparent that the *performance* of the individual random engines differs.
- Run the program with a low amount of samples multiple times. The distribution patterns look *the same* all the time--the random engines produce the *same* random number sequences repeatedly, which means they are *not random at all*. Such engines are called *deterministic* because their random numbers can be predicted. The only exception is `std::random_device`.

As we can see, there are a few characteristics to consider. For most standard applications, `std::default_random_engine` will be completely sufficient. Experts of cryptography or similarly security-sensitive topics will choose wisely between the engines they use, but for us average programmers, this is not too important when we write apps with some randomness.

We should carry home the following three facts from this recipe:

1. Usually, `std::default_random_engine` is a good default choice for the average application.
2. If we really need non-deterministic random numbers, `std::random_device` provides us such.
3. We can feed the constructor of any random engine with a *real* random number from `std::random_device` (or maybe a timestamp from the system clock), in order to make it produce different random numbers each time. This is called *seeding*.

 Note that `std::random_device` *can* possibly fall back to one of the deterministic engines if the library has no support for nondeterministic random engines.

Generating random numbers and letting the STL shape specific distributions

In the last recipe, we learned some bits about the STL random number engines. Generating random numbers this or the other way is often only half of the work.

Another question is, what do we need those numbers for? Are we programmatically "flipping a coin"? People used to do this using `rand()` % 2, which results in values of 0 and 1 that can then be mapped to *head* or *tail*. Fair enough; we do not need a library for that (although randomness experts know that just using the lowest few bits of a random number does not always lead to high-quality random numbers).

What if we want to model a die? Then, we could surely write `(rand() % 6) + 1`, in order to represent the result after rolling the die. There is still no pressing library needed for such simple tasks.

What if we want to model something that happens with an exact probability of 66%? Okay, then we can come up with a formula like `bool yesno = (rand() % 100 > 66)`. (Oh wait, should it be >=, or is > correct?)

Apart from that, how do we model an *unfair* die whose sides do not all have the same probability? Or how do we model more complex distributions? Such problems can quickly evolve to scientific tasks. In order to concentrate on our primary problems, let's have a look at what the STL already provides in order to help us.

The STL contains more than a dozen distribution algorithms that can shape random numbers for specific needs. In this recipe, we are going to have a very brief look at all of them, and a closer look at the most generally useful ones.

How to do it...

We are going to generate random numbers, shape them, and print their distribution patterns to the terminal. This way, we can get to know all of them and understand the most important ones, which is useful if we ever need to model something specific with randomness in mind:

1. At first, we include all the needed headers and declare that we use the `std` namespace:

```
#include <iostream>
#include <iomanip>
```

```
#include <random>
#include <map>
#include <string>
#include <algorithm>

using namespace std;
```

2. For every distribution the STL provides, we will print a histogram in order to see its characteristics because every distribution looks very special. It accepts a distribution as an argument and the number of samples that shall be taken from it. Then, we instantiate the default random engine and a map. The map maps from the values we obtained from the distribution to counters that count how often which value occurred. The reason for why we always instantiate a random engine is that all distributions are just used as a *shaping function* for random numbers that still need to be generated by a random engine:

```
template <typename T>
void print_distro(T distro, size_t samples)
{
    default_random_engine e;
    map<int, size_t> m;
```

3. We take as many samples as the `samples` variable says and feed the map counters with them. This way, we get a nice histogram. While calling `e()` alone would get us a raw random number from the random engine, `distro(e)` shapes the random numbers through the distribution object.

```
    for (size_t i {0}; i < samples; ++i) {
        m[distro(e)] += 1;
    }
```

4. In order to get a terminal output that fits into the terminal window, we need to know the *largest* counter value. The `max_element` function helps us in finding the largest value by comparing all the associated counters in the map and returning us an iterator to the largest counter node. Knowing this value, we can determine by what value we need to divide all the counter values in order to fit the output into the terminal window:

```
    size_t max_elm (max_element(begin(m), end(m),
        [](const auto &a, const auto &b) {
            return a.second < b.second;
        })->second);
    size_t max_div (max(max_elm / 100, size_t(1)));
```

5. Now, we loop through the map and print a bar of asterisk symbols `'*'` for all counters which have a significant size. We drop the others because some distribution engines spread the numbers over such large domains that it would completely flood our terminal windows:

```
for (const auto [randval, count] : m) {
    if (count < max_elm / 200) { continue; }
    cout << setw(3) << randval << " : "
        << string(count / max_div, '*') << '\n';
}
}
```

6. In the main function, we check if the user provided us exactly one parameter, which tells us how many samples to take from each distribution. If the user provided none or multiple parameters, we error out.

```
int main(int argc, char **argv)
{
    if (argc != 2) {
        cout << "Usage: " << argv[0]
            << " <samples>\n";
        return 1;
    }
```

7. We convert the command-line argument string to a number using `std::stoull`:

```
size_t samples {stoull(argv[1])};
```

8. At first, we try the `uniform_int_distribution` and `normal_distribution`. These are the most typical distributions used where random numbers are needed. Everyone who ever had stochastic as a topic in maths at school will most probably have heard about these already. The uniform distribution accepts two values, denoting the lower and the upper bound of the range they shall distribute random values over. By choosing 0 and 9, we will get equally often occurring values between (including) 0 and 9. The normal distribution accepts a *mean value* and a *standard derivation* as arguments:

```
cout << "uniform_int_distribution\n";
print_distro(uniform_int_distribution<int>{0, 9}, samples);
cout << "normal_distribution\n";
print_distro(normal_distribution<double>{0.0, 2.0}, samples);
```

9. Another really interesting distribution is `piecewise_constant_distribution`. It accepts two input ranges as arguments. The first range contains numbers that denote the limits of intervals. By defining it as `0, 5, 10, 30`, we get one interval that spans from `0` to `4`, then, an interval that spans from `5` to `9`, and the last interval spanning from `10` to `29`. The other input range defines the weights of the input ranges. By setting those weights to `0.2, 0.3, 0.5`, the intervals are hit by random numbers with the chances of 20%, 30%, and 50%. Within every interval, all the values are hit with equal probability:

```
initializer_list<double> intervals {0, 5, 10, 30};
initializer_list<double> weights {0.2, 0.3, 0.5};
cout << "piecewise_constant_distribution\n";
print_distro(
    piecewise_constant_distribution<double>{
        begin(intervals), end(intervals),
        begin(weights)},
    samples);
```

10. The `piecewise_linear_distribution` is constructed similarly, but its weight characteristics work completely differently. For every interval boundary point, there is one weight value. In the transition from one boundary to the other, the probability is linearly interpolated. We use the same interval list but a different list of weight values.

```
cout << "piecewise_linear_distribution\n";
initializer_list<double> weights2 {0, 1, 1, 0};
print_distro(
    piecewise_linear_distribution<double>{
        begin(intervals), end(intervals), begin(weights2)},
    samples);
```

11. The Bernoulli distribution is another important distribution because it distributes only *yes/no*, *hit/miss*, or *head/tail* values with a specific probability. Its output values are only `0` or `1`. Another interesting distribution, which is useful in many cases, is `discrete_distribution`. In our case, we initialize it to the discrete values `1, 2, 4, 8`. These values are interpreted as weights for the possible output values `0` to `3`:

```
cout << "bernoulli_distribution\n";
print_distro(std::bernoulli_distribution{0.75}, samples);
cout << "discrete_distribution\n";
print_distro(discrete_distribution<int>{{1, 2, 4, 8}}, samples);
```

12. There are a lot of different other distribution engines. They are very special and useful in very specific situations. If you have never heard about them, they *may* not be for you. However, since our program will produce nice distribution histograms, we will print them all, for curiosity reasons:

```
cout << "binomial_distribution\n";
print_distro(binomial_distribution<int>{10, 0.3}, samples);
cout << "negative_binomial_distribution\n";
print_distro(
    negative_binomial_distribution<int>{10, 0.8},
    samples);
cout << "geometric_distribution\n";
print_distro(geometric_distribution<int>{0.4}, samples);
cout << "exponential_distribution\n";
print_distro(exponential_distribution<double>{0.4}, samples);
cout << "gamma_distribution\n";
print_distro(gamma_distribution<double>{1.5, 1.0}, samples);
cout << "weibull_distribution\n";
print_distro(weibull_distribution<double>{1.5, 1.0}, samples);
cout << "extreme_value_distribution\n";
print_distro(
    extreme_value_distribution<double>{0.0, 1.0},
    samples);
cout << "lognormal_distribution\n";
print_distro(lognormal_distribution<double>{0.5, 0.5}, samples);
cout << "chi_squared_distribution\n";
print_distro(chi_squared_distribution<double>{1.0}, samples);
cout << "cauchy_distribution\n";
print_distro(cauchy_distribution<double>{0.0, 0.1}, samples);
cout << "fisher_f_distribution\n";
print_distro(fisher_f_distribution<double>{1.0, 1.0}, samples);
cout << "student_t_distribution\n";
print_distro(student_t_distribution<double>{1.0}, samples);
}
```

13. Compiling and running the program yields the following output. Let's first run the program with `1000` samples per distribution:

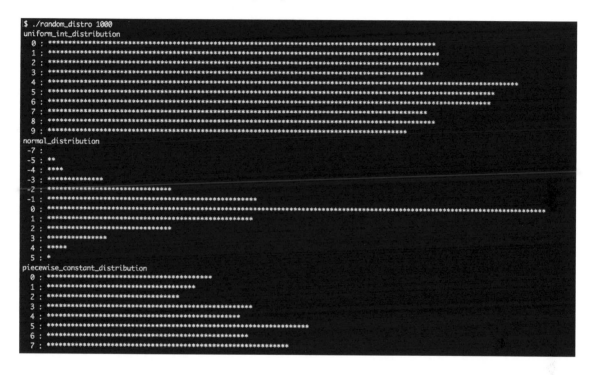

14. Another run with $1,000,000$ samples per distribution shows that the histograms appear much cleaner and more typical for each distribution. But we also see which ones are slow, and which ones are fast, while they are being generated:

```
$ ./random_distro 1000000
uniform_int_distribution
  0 : *********************************************************************
  1 : *********************************************************************
  2 : *********************************************************************
  3 : *********************************************************************
  4 : *********************************************************************
  5 : *********************************************************************
  6 : *********************************************************************
  7 : *********************************************************************
  8 : *********************************************************************
  9 : *********************************************************************
normal_distribution
 -5 : *
 -4 : ****
 -3 : **********
 -2 : *********************
 -1 : **********************************************
  0 : ***********************************************************************
  1 : **********************************************
  2 : *********************
  3 : **********
  4 : ****
  5 : *
piecewise_constant_distribution
  0 : ***************************************************
  1 : ***************************************************
  2 : ***************************************************
  3 : ***************************************************
  4 : ***************************************************
  5 : *********************************************************************
  6 : *********************************************************************
  7 : *********************************************************************
  8 : *********************************************************************
  9 : *********************************************************************
 10 : **********************************
 11 : **********************************
 12 : **********************************
 13 : **********************************
 14 : **********************************
 15 : **********************************
 16 : **********************************
 17 : **********************************
 18 : **********************************
 19 : **********************************
 20 : **********************************
```

How it works...

While we usually do not care too much about the random number engine, as long it is fast and produces numbers that are as random as possible, the distribution is something we *should* choose wisely, depending on the problem we like to solve (or create).

In order to use any distribution, we first need to instantiate a distribution object from it. We have seen that different distributions take different constructor arguments. In the recipe description, we went a bit too briefly over some distribution engines because most of them are too special and/or too complex to cover here. But don't worry, they are all documented in detail in the C++ STL documentation.

However, as soon as we have a distribution instantiated, we can call it like a function that accepts a random engine object as its only parameter. What happens then is that the distribution engine takes a random value from the random engine, applies some magic shaping (which completely depends on the choice of the distribution engine, of course), and then returns us a *shaped* random value. This leads to completely different histograms, as we saw after executing the program.

The most comprehensive way to get to know the different distributions is *playing* around with the program we just wrote. In addition to that, let's summarize the most important distributions. For all the distributions that occur in our program but not in the following table, please consult the C++ STL documentation if you are interested:

Distribution	Description
uniform_int_distribution	This distribution accepts a lower and an upper bound value as constructor arguments. It does, then, give us random numbers that always fall into the interval between (including) those bounds. The probability for each of the values in this interval is the same, which gives us a histogram with a *flat* shape. This distribution is representative of rolling a *die*, for example, because each side of the die has the same probability to occur.
normal_distribution	The normal distribution, or Gauss distribution, occurs practically everywhere in nature. Its STL version accepts a mean value and a standard derivation value as constructor parameters and forms a *roof*-like shape in the histogram. If we compare the body size or IQ of humans or other animals, or the grades of students, we will realize that these numbers are also normal-distributed.

`bernoulli_distribution`	The Bernoulli distribution is perfect if we want to flip a coin or get a yes/no answer. It emits only the values 0 or 1 and its only constructor parameter is the probability for the value of 1.
`discrete_distribution`	The discrete distribution is interesting if we only want a very limited, discrete set of values for which we want to define the probability for every individual value. Its constructor takes a list of weights and will emit random numbers with probabilities depending on their weight. If we want to model randomly distributed blood groups, of which there are only four different ones that have specific probabilities, then this engine is a perfect match.

9

Parallelism and Concurrency

In this chapter, we will cover the following recipes:

- Automatically parallelizing code that uses standard algorithms
- Putting a program to sleep for specific amounts of time
- Starting and stopping threads
- Performing exception-safe shared locking with `std::unique_lock` and `std::shared_lock`
- Avoiding deadlocks with `std::scoped_lock`
- Synchronizing concurrent `std::cout` use
- Safely postponing initialization with `std::call_once`
- Pushing the execution of tasks into the background using `std::async`
- Implementing the producer/consumer idiom with `std::condition_variable`
- Implementing the multiple producers/consumers idiom with `std::condition_variable`
- Parallelizing the ASCII Mandelbrot renderer using `std::async`
- Implementing a tiny automatic parallelization library with `std::future`

Introduction

Before C++11, C++ didn't have much support for parallelization. This does not mean that starting, controlling, stopping, and synchronizing threads was not possible, but it was necessary to use operating system-specific libraries because threads are inherently operating system-related.

With C++11, we got `std::thread`, which enables basic portable thread control across all operating systems. For synchronizing threads, C++11 also introduced mutex classes and comfortable RAII-style lock wrappers. In addition to that, `std::condition_variable` allows for flexible event notification between threads.

Some other really interesting additions are `std::async` and `std::future`--we can now wrap arbitrary normal functions into `std::async` calls in order to execute them asynchronously in the background. Such wrapped functions return `std::future` objects that promise to contain the result of the function later, so we can do something else before we wait for its arrival.

Another actually enormous improvement to the STL are *execution policies*, which can be added to 69 of the already *existing* algorithms. This addition means that we can just add a single execution policy argument to the existing standard algorithm calls in our old programs and get parallelization without complex rewrites.

In this chapter, we will go through all these additions in order to learn the most important things about them. Afterward, we'll have enough oversight of the parallelization support in the C++17 STL. We do not cover all the details, but the most important ones. The overview gained from this book helps in quickly understanding the rest of the parallel programming mechanisms, which you can always look up in the C++ 17 STL documentation online.

Finally, this chapter contains two bonus recipes. In one recipe, we will parallelize the Mandelbrot ASCII renderer from Chapter 6, *Advance Use of STL Algorithms*, with only minimal changes. In the last recipe, we will implement a tiny library that helps parallelizing complex tasks implicitly and automatically.

Automatically parallelizing code that uses standard algorithms

C++17 came with one really *major* extension for parallelism: *execution policies* for standard algorithms. Sixty nine algorithms were extended to accept execution policies in order to run parallel on multiple cores, and even with enabled vectorization.

For the user, this means that if we already use STL algorithms everywhere, we get a nice parallelization bonus for free. We can *easily* give our applications subsequent parallelization by simply adding a single execution policy argument to our existing STL algorithm calls.

In this recipe, we will implement a simple program (with a not too serious use case scenario) that lines up multiple STL algorithm calls. While using these, we will see how easy it is to use C++17 execution policies in order to let them run multithreaded. In the last subsections of this section, we will have a closer look at the different execution policies.

How to do it...

In this section, we will write a program that uses some standard algorithms. The program itself is more of an example of how real-life scenarios can look than doing actual real-life work situation. While using these standard algorithms, we are embedding execution policies in order to speed the code up:

1. First, we need to include some headers and declare that we use the std namespace. The execution header is a new one; it came with C++17:

```
#include <iostream>
#include <vector>
#include <random>
#include <algorithm>
#include <execution>

using namespace std;
```

2. Just for the sake of the example, we'll declare a predicate function that tells whether a number is odd. We will use it later:

```
static bool odd(int n) { return n % 2; }
```

3. Let's first define a large vector in our main function. We will fill it with a lot of data so that it takes some time to do calculations on it. The execution speed of this code will vary *a lot*, depending on the computer this code is executed on. Smaller/larger vector sizes might be better on different computers:

```
int main()
{
    vector<int> d (50000000);
```

4. In order to get a lot of random data for the vector, let's instantiate a random number generator along with a distribution and pack them up in a callable object. If this looks strange to you, please first have a look at the recipes that deal with random number generators and distributions in Chapter 8, *Utility Classes*:

```
mt19937 gen;
uniform_int_distribution<int> dis(0, 100000);
auto rand_num ([=] () mutable { return dis(gen); });
```

5. Now, let's use the `std::generate` algorithm to fill the vector with random data. There is a new C++17 version of this algorithm, which can take a new kind of argument: an execution policy. We put in `std::par` here, which allows for automatic parallelization of this code. By doing this, we allow for multiple threads to start filling the vector together, which reduces the execution time if the computer has more than one CPU, which is usually the case with modern computers:

```
generate(execution::par, begin(d), end(d), rand_num);
```

6. The `std::sort` method should also already be familiar. The C++17 version does also support an additional argument defining the execution policy:

```
sort(execution::par, begin(d), end(d));
```

7. The same applies to `std::reverse`:

```
reverse(execution::par, begin(d), end(d));
```

8. Then we use `std::count_if` to count all the odd numbers in the vector. And we can even parallelize that by just adding an execution policy again!

```
auto odds (count_if(execution::par, begin(d), end(d), odd));
```

9. This whole program did not do any *real* scientific work, as we were just going to have a look on how to parallelize standard algorithms, but let's print something in the end:

```
cout << (100.0 * odds / d.size())
     << "% of the numbers are odd.\n";
}
```

10. Compiling and running the program gives us the following output. At this point, it is interesting to see how the execution speed differs when using the algorithms without an execution policy compared with all the other execution policies. Doing this is left as an exercise for the reader. Try it; the available execution policies are seq, par, and par_vec. We should get different execution times for each of them:

```
$ ./auto_parallel
50.4% of the numbers are odd.
```

How it works...

Especially since this recipe did not distract us with any complicated real-life problem solution, we were able to fully concentrate on the standard library function calls. It is pretty obvious that the their parallelized versions are hardly different from the classic sequential ones. They only differ by *one additional* argument, which is the *execution policy*.

Let's have a look at the invocations and answer three central questions:

```
generate(execution::par, begin(d), end(d), rand_num);
sort(    execution::par, begin(d), end(d));
reverse( execution::par, begin(d), end(d));

auto odds (count_if(execution::par, begin(d), end(d), odd));
```

Which STL algorithms can we parallelize this way?

Sixty nine of the existing STL algorithms were upgraded to support parallelism in the C++17 standard, and there are seven new ones that also support parallelism. While such an upgrade might be pretty invasive for the implementation, not much has changed in terms of their interface--they all got an additional ExecutionPolicy&& policy argument, and that's it. This does *not* mean that we *always* have to provide an execution policy argument. It is just that they *additionally* support accepting an execution policy as their first argument.

These are the 69 upgraded standard algorithms. There are also the seven new ones that support execution policies from the beginning (highlighted in *bold*):

`std::adjacent_difference`	`std::inplace_merge`	`std::replace_if`
`std::adjacent_find`	`std::is_heap`	`std::reverse`
`std::all_of`	`std::is_heap_until`	`std::reverse_copy`
`std::any_of`	`std::is_partitioned`	`std::rotate`
`std::copy`	`std::is_sorted`	`std::rotate_copy`
`std::copy_if`	`std::is_sorted_until`	`std::search`
`std::copy_n`	`std::lexicographical_compare`	`std::search_n`
`std::count`	`std::max_element`	`std::set_difference`
`std::count_if`	`std::merge`	`std::set_intersection`
`std::equal`	`std::min_element`	`std::set_symmetric_difference`
`std::exclusive_scan`	`std::minmax_element`	`std::set_union`
`std::fill`	`std::mismatch`	`std::sort`
`std::fill_n`	`std::move`	`std::stable_partition`
`std::find`	`std::none_of`	`std::stable_sort`
`std::find_end`	`std::nth_element`	`std::swap_ranges`
`std::find_first_of`	`std::partial_sort`	`std::transform`
`std::find_if`	`std::partial_sort_copy`	**`std::transform_exclusive_scan`**
`std::find_if_not`	`std::partition`	**`std::transform_inclusive_scan`**
`std::for_each`	`std::partition_copy`	**`std::transform_reduce`**
`std::for_each_n`	`std::remove`	`std::uninitialized_copy`
`std::generate`	`std::remove_copy`	`std::uninitialized_copy_n`
`std::generate_n`	`std::remove_copy_if`	`std::uninitialized_fill`
`std::includes`	`std::remove_if`	`std::uninitialized_fill_n`
`std::inclusive_scan`	`std::replace`	`std::unique`
`std::inner_product`	`std::replace_copy`	`std::unique_copy`
	`std::replace_copy_if`	

Having these algorithms upgraded is great news! The more our old programs utilize STL algorithms, the easier we can add parallelism to them retroactively. Note that this does *not* mean that such changes make every program automatically *N* times faster because multiprogramming is quite a bit more complex than that.

However, instead of designing our own complicated parallel algorithms using `std::thread`, `std::async`, or by including external libraries, we can now parallelize standard tasks in a very elegant, operating system-independent way.

How do those execution policies work?

The execution policy tells which strategy we allow for the automatic parallelization of our standard algorithm calls.

The following three policy types exist in the `std::execution` namespace:

Policy	Meaning
`sequenced_policy`	The algorithm has to be executed in a sequential form similar to the original algorithm without an execution policy. The globally available instance has the name `std::execution::seq`.
`parallel_policy`	The algorithm may be executed with multiple threads that share the work in a parallel fashion. The globally available instance has the name `std::execution::par`.
`parallel_unsequenced_policy`	The algorithm may be executed with multiple threads sharing the work. In addition to that, it is permissible to vectorize the code. In this case, container access can be interleaved between threads and also within the same thread due to vectorization. The globally available instance has the name `std::execution::par_unseq`.

The execution policies imply specific constraints for us. The stricter the specific constraints, the more parallelization strategy measures we can allow:

- All element access functions used by the parallelized algorithm *must not* cause *deadlocks* or *data races*
- In the case of parallelism and vectorization, all the access functions *must not* use any kind of blocking synchronization

As long as we comply with these rules, we should be free from bugs introduced by using the parallel versions of the STL algorithms.

 Note that just using parallel STL algorithms correctly does not always lead to guaranteed speedup. Depending on the problem we try to solve, the problem size, and the efficiency of our data structures and other access methods, measurable speedup will vary very much or not occur at all. *Multiprogramming is still hard.*

What does vectorization mean?

Vectorization is a feature that both the CPU and the compiler need to support. Let's have a quick glance at a simple example to briefly understand what vectorization is and how it works. Imagine we want to sum up numbers from a very large vector. A plain implementation of this task can look like this:

```
std::vector<int> v {1, 2, 3, 4, 5, 6, 7 /*...*/};

int sum {std::accumulate(v.begin(), v.end(), 0)};
```

The compiler will eventually generate a loop from the `accumulate` call, which could look like this:

```
int sum {0};
for (size_t i {0}; i < v.size(); ++i) {
    sum += v[i];
}
```

Proceeding from this point, with vectorization allowed and enabled, the compiler could then produce the following code. The loop does four accumulation steps in one loop step and also does four times fewer iterations. For the sake of simplicity, the example does not deal with the remainder if the vector does not contain N * 4 elements:

```
int sum {0};
for (size_t i {0}; i < v.size() / 4; i += 4) {
    sum += v[i] + v[i+1] + v[i + 2] + v[i + 3];
}
// if v.size() / 4 has a remainder,
// real code has to deal with that also.
```

Why should it do this? Many CPUs provide instructions that can perform mathematical operations such as `sum += v[i] + v[i+1] + v[i + 2] + v[i + 3];` in just *one step*. Pressing as *many* mathematical operations into as *few* instructions as possible is the target because this speeds up the program.

Automatic vectorization is hard because the compiler needs to understand our program to some degree in order to make our program faster but without tampering with its *correctness*. At least, we can help the compiler by using standard algorithms as often as possible because those are easier to grasp for the compiler than complicated handcrafted loops with complex data flow dependencies.

Putting a program to sleep for specific amounts of time

A nice and simple possibility to control threads came with C++11. It introduced the `this_thread` namespace, which includes functions that affect only the caller thread. It contains two different functions that allow putting a thread to sleep for a certain amount of time, so we do not need to use any external or operating system-dependent libraries for such tasks any longer.

In this recipe, we concentrate on how to suspend threads for a certain amount of time, or how to put them to *sleep*.

How to do it...

We will write a short program that just puts the main thread to sleep for certain amounts of time:

1. Let's first include all the needed headers and declare that we'll use the `std` and `chrono_literals` namespaces. The `chrono_literals` namespace contains handy abbreviations for creating time-span values:

```
#include <iostream>
#include <chrono>
#include <thread>

using namespace std;
using namespace chrono_literals;
```

2. Let's immediately put the main thread to sleep for 5 seconds and 300 milliseconds. Thanks to `chrono_literals`, we can express this in a very readable format:

```
int main()
{
    cout << "Going to sleep for 5 seconds"
            " and 300 milli seconds.\n";
    this_thread::sleep_for(5s + 300ms);
```

3. The last sleep statement was `relative`. We can also express `absolute` sleep requests. Let's sleep until the point in time, which is *now* plus 3 seconds:

```
cout << "Going to sleep for another 3 seconds.\n";
this_thread::sleep_until(
    chrono::high_resolution_clock::now() + 3s);
```

4. Before quitting the program, let's print something else to signal the end of the second sleep period:

```
    cout << "That's it.\n";
}
```

5. Compiling and running the program yields the following results. Linux, Mac, and other UNIX-like operating systems provide the `time` command, which accepts another command in order to execute it and stop the time it takes. Running our program with `time` shows that it ran `8.32` seconds, which is roughly the `5.3` and 3 seconds we let our program sleep. When running the program, it is possible to count the time between the arrival of the printed lines on the terminal:

```
$ time ./sleep
Going to sleep for 5 seconds and 300 milli seconds.
Going to sleep for another 3 seconds.
That's it.
real  0m8.320s
user  0m0.005s
sys   0m0.003s
```

How it works...

The `sleep_for` and `sleep_until` functions have been added to C++11 and reside in the `std::this_thread` namespace. They block the current thread (not the whole process or program) for a specific amount of time. A thread does not consume CPU time while it is blocked. It is just put into an inactive state by the operating system. The operating system does, of course, remind itself of waking the thread up again. The best thing about this is that we do not need to care which operating system our program runs on because the STL abstracts this detail away from us.

The `this_thread::sleep_for` function accepts a `chrono::duration` value. In the simplest case, this is just `1s` or `5s + 300ms`, just like in our example code. In order to get such nice literals for time spans, we need to declare `using namespace std::chrono_literals;`.

The `this_thread::sleep_until` function accepts a `chrono::time_point` instead of a time span. This is comfortable if we wish to put the thread to sleep until some specific wall clock time.

The timing for waking up is only as accurate as the operating system allows. This will be generally accurate *enough* with most operating systems, but it might become difficult if some application needs nanosecond-granularity.

Another possibility to put a thread to sleep for a short time is `this_thread::yield`. It accepts *no* arguments, which means that we cannot know for how long the execution of a thread is placed back. The reason is that this function does not really implement the notion of sleeping or parking a thread. It just tells the operating system in a cooperative way that it can reschedule any other thread of any other process. If there are none, then the thread will be executed again immediately. For this reason, `yield` is often less useful than just sleeping for a minimal, but specified, amount of time.

Starting and stopping threads

Another addition that came with C++11 is the `std::thread` class. It provides a clean and simple way to start and stop threads, without any need for external libraries or to know how the operating system implements this. It's all just included in the STL.

In this recipe, we will implement a program that starts and stops threads. There are some minor details to know what to do with threads once they are started, so we will go through these too.

How to do it...

We will start multiple threads and see how our program behaves when we unleash multiple processor cores to execute parts of its code at the same time:

1. At first, we need to include only two headers and then we declare that we use the `std` and `chrono_literals` namespaces:

    ```
    #include <iostream>
    #include <thread>

    using namespace std;
    using namespace chrono_literals;
    ```

2. In order to start a thread, we need to be able to tell what code should be executed by it. So, let's define a function that can be executed. Functions are natural potential entry points for threads. The example function accepts an argument, `i`, which acts as the thread ID. This way we can tell which print line came from which thread later. Additionally, we use the thread ID to let all threads wait for different amounts of time, so we can be sure that they do not try to use `cout` at exactly the same time. If they did, that would garble the output. Another recipe in this chapter deals specifically with this problem:

    ```
    static void thread_with_param(int i)
    {
        this_thread::sleep_for(1ms * i);
        cout << "Hello from thread " << i << '\n';
        this_thread::sleep_for(1s * i);
        cout << "Bye from thread " << i << '\n';
    }
    ```

3. In the main function, we can, just out of curiosity, print how many threads can be run at the same time, using `std::thread::hardware_concurrency`. This depends on how many cores the machine really has and how many cores are supported by the STL implementation. This means that this might be a different number on every other computer:

```
int main()
{
    cout << thread::hardware_concurrency()
        << " concurrent threads are supported.\n";
```

4. Let's now finally start threads. With different IDs for each one, we start three threads. When instantiating a thread with an expression such as `thread t {f, x}`, this leads to a call of `f(x)` by the new thread. This ,way we can give the `thread_with_param` functions different arguments for each thread:

```
    thread t1 {thread_with_param, 1};
    thread t2 {thread_with_param, 2};
    thread t3 {thread_with_param, 3};
```

5. Since these threads are freely running, we need to stop them again when they are done with their work. We do this using the `join` function. It will *block* the calling thread until the thread we try to join returns:

```
    t1.join();
    t2.join();
```

6. An alternative to joining is *detaching*. If we do not call `join` or detach, the whole application will be terminated with a lot of smoke and noise as soon as the destructor of the `thread` object is executed. By calling `detach`, we tell `thread` that we really want to let thread number 3 to continue running, even after its `thread` instance is destructed:

```
    t3.detach();
```

7. Before quitting the main function and the whole program, we print another message:

```
    cout << "Threads joined.\n";
}
```

8. Compiling and running the code shows the following output. We can see that my machine has eight CPU cores. Then, we see the *hello* messages from all the threads, but the *bye* messages only from the two threads we actually joined. Thread 3 is still in its waiting period of 3 seconds, but the whole program does already terminate after the second thread has finished waiting for 2 seconds. This way, we cannot see the bye message from thread 3 because it was simply killed without any chance for completion (and without noise):

```
$ ./threads
8 concurrent threads are supported.
Hello from thread 1
Hello from thread 2
Hello from thread 3
Bye from thread 1
Bye from thread 2
Threads joined.
```

How it works...

Starting and stopping threads is a very simple thing to do. Multiprogramming starts to be complicated where threads need to work together (sharing resources, waiting for each other, and so on).

In order to start a thread, we first need some function that will be executed by it. The function does not need to be special, as a thread could execute practically every function. Let's pin down a minimal example program that starts a thread and waits for its completion:

```
void f(int i) { cout << i << '\n'; }

int main()
{
    thread t {f, 123};
    t.join();
}
```

The constructor call of `std::thread` accepts a function pointer or a callable object, followed by arguments that should be used with the function call. It is, of course, also possible to start a thread on a function that doesn't accept any parameters.

If the system has multiple CPU cores, then the threads can run parallel *and* concurrently. What is the difference between parallel and concurrent? If the computer has only one CPU core, then there can be a lot of threads that run in parallel but never concurrently because one CPU core can only run one thread at a time. The threads are then run in an interleaved way where every thread is executed for some parts of a second, then paused, and then the next thread gets a time slice (for human users, this looks like they run at the same time). If they do not need to share a CPU core, then they can run concurrently, as in *really at the same time.*

At this point, we have absolutely *no control* over the following details:

- The *order* in which the threads are interleaved when sharing a CPU core.
- The *priority* of a thread, or which one is more important than the other.
- The fact that threads are really *distributed* among all the CPU cores or if the operating system just pins them to the same core. It is indeed *possible* that all our threads run on only a single core, although the machine has more than 100 cores.

Most operating systems provide possibilities to control also these facets of multiprogramming, but such features are, at this point, *not* included in the STL.

However, we can start and stop threads and tell them when to work on what and when to pause. That should be enough for a large class of applications. What we did in this section was we started three additional threads. Afterward, we *joined* most of them and *detached* the last one. Let's summarize in a simple diagram what happened:

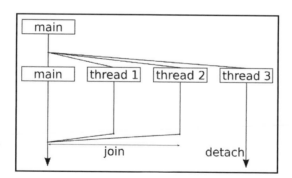

Reading the diagram from top to the bottom, it shows one point in time where we split the program workflow to four threads in total. We started three additional threads that did something (namely waiting and printing), but after starting the threads, the main thread executing the main function remained without work.

Whenever a thread has finished executing the function it was started with, it will return from this function. The standard library then does some tidy up work that results in the thread being removed from the operating system's schedule, and maybe in its destruction, but we do not need to worry about it.

The only thing we *need* to worry about is *joining*. When a thread calls function `x.join()` on another `thread` object, it is put to sleep until thread `x` returns. Note that we are out of luck if the thread is trapped in an endless loop! If we want a thread to continue living until it decides to terminate itself, we can call `x.detach()`. After doing so, we have no external control over the thread any longer. No matter what we decide--we *must* always *join* or *detach* threads. If we don't do one of the two, the destructor of the `thread` object will call `std::terminate()`, which leads to an abrupt application shutdown.

The moment when our main function returns, the whole application is, of course, terminated. However, at the same time, our detached thread, `t3`, was still sleeping before printing its *bye* message to the terminal. The operating system didn't care--it just terminated our whole program without waiting for that thread to finish. This is something we need to consider. If that additional thread had to complete something important, we would have to make the main function *wait* for it.

Performing exception safe shared locking with std::unique_lock and std::shared_lock

Since the operation of threads is a heavily operating system support-related thing and the STL provides good operating system-agnostic interfaces for that, it is also wise to provide STL support for *synchronization* between threads. This way, we can not only start and stop threads without external libraries but also synchronize them with abstractions from a single unified library: the STL.

In this recipe, we will have a look at STL mutex classes and RAII lock abstractions. While we play around with some of them in our concrete recipe implementation, we will also get an overview of more synchronization helpers that the STL provides.

How to do it...

We are going to write a program that uses an `std::shared_mutex` instance in its *exclusive* and *shared* modes and to see what that means. Additionally, we do not call the lock and unlock functions ourselves but do the locking with automatic unlocking using RAII helpers:

1. First, we need to include all necessary headers. Because we use STL functions and data structures all the time together with time literals, we declare that we use the `std` and `chrono_literal` namespaces:

```
#include <iostream>
#include <shared_mutex>
#include <thread>
#include <vector>

using namespace std;
using namespace chrono_literals;
```

2. The whole program revolves around one shared mutex, so let's define a global instance for the sake of simplicity:

```
shared_mutex shared_mut;
```

3. We are going to use the `std::shared_lock` and `std::unique_lock` RAII helpers. In order to make their names appear less clumsy, we define short type aliases for them:

```
using shrd_lck = shared_lock<shared_mutex>;
using uniq_lck = unique_lock<shared_mutex>;
```

4. Before beginning with the main function, we define two helper functions that both try to lock the mutex in *exclusive* mode. This function here will instantiate a `unique_lock` instance on the shared mutex. The second constructor argument `defer_lock` tells the object to keep the lock unlocked. Otherwise, its constructor would try to lock the mutex and then block until it succeeds. Then we call `try_lock` on the `exclusive_lock` object. This call will return immediately and its boolean return value tells us if it got the lock or if the mutex was locked already somewhere else:

```
static void print_exclusive()
{
    uniq_lck l {shared_mut, defer_lock};
    if (l.try_lock()) {
        cout << "Got exclusive lock.\n";
    } else {
```

```
            cout << "Unable to lock exclusively.\n";
        }
    }
```

5. The other helper function tries to lock the mutex in exclusive mode, too. It blocks until it gets the lock. Then we simulate some error case by throwing an exception (which carries just a plain integer number instead of a more complex exception object). Although this leads to an immediate exit of the context in which we hold a locked mutex, the mutex will cleanly be released again. That is because the destructor of `unique_lock` will release the lock in any case by design:

```
static void exclusive_throw()
{
    uniq_lck l {shared_mut};
    throw 123;
}
```

6. Now to the main function. First, we open up another scope and instantiate a `shared_lock` instance. Its constructor immediately locks the mutex in `shared` mode. We will see what this means in the next steps:

```
int main()
{
    {
        shrd_lck sl1 {shared_mut};
        cout << "shared lock once.\n";
```

7. Now we open yet another scope and instantiate a second `shared_lock` instance on the same mutex. We have two `shared_lock` instances now, and they both hold a shared lock on the mutex. In fact, we could instantiate arbitrarily many `shared_lock` instances on the same mutex. Then we call `print_exclusive`, which tries to lock the mutex in *exclusive* mode. This will not succeed because it is locked in *shared* mode already:

```
        {
            shrd_lck sl2 {shared_mut};
            cout << "shared lock twice.\n";
            print_exclusive();
        }
```

8. After leaving the latest scope, the destructor of the `shared_lock s12` releases its shared lock on the mutex. The `print_exclusive` function will again fail because the mutex is still in shared lock mode:

```
        cout << "shared lock once again.\n";
        print_exclusive();

    }
    cout << "lock is free.\n";
```

9. After leaving also the other scope, all `shared_lock` objects are destroyed, and the mutex is in unlocked state again. *Now* we can finally lock the mutex in exclusive mode. Let's do this by calling `exclusive_throw` and then `print_exclusive`. Remember that we throw an exception in `exclusive_throw`. But because `unique_lock` is an RAII object that gives us exception safety, the mutex will be unlocked again no matter how we return from `exclusive_throw`. This way `print_exclusive` will not block on an erroneously still locked mutex:

```
    try {
        exclusive_throw();
    } catch (int e) {
        cout << "Got exception " << e << '\n';
    }
    print_exclusive();
}
```

10. Compiling and running the code yields the following output. The first two lines show that we got the two shared lock instances. Then the `print_exclusive` function fails to lock the mutex in exclusive mode. After leaving the inner scope and unlocking the second shared lock, the `print_exclusive` function still fails. After leaving the other scope too, which finally released the mutex again, `exclusive_throw` and `print_exclusive` are finally able to lock the mutex:

```
$ ./shared_lock
shared lock once.
shared lock twice.
Unable to lock exclusively.
shared lock once again.
Unable to lock exclusively.
lock is free.
Got exception 123
Got exclusive lock.
```

How it works...

When looking at the C++ documentation, it is at first a little confusing that there are different mutex classes and RAII lock-helpers. Before looking at our concrete code sample, let us summarize what the STL has available for us.

Mutex classes

The term mutex stands for **mut**ual **ex**clusion. In order to prevent that concurrently running threads alter the same object in a non-orchestrated way that might lead to data corruption, we can use mutex objects. The STL provides different mutex classes with different specialties. They all have in common that they have a `lock` and an `unlock` method.

Whenever a thread is the first one to call `lock()` on a mutex that was not locked before, it owns the mutex. At this point, other threads will block on their `lock` calls, until the first thread calls `unlock` again. `std::mutex` can do exactly this.

There are many different mutex classes in the STL:

Type name	Description
mutex	Standard mutex with a `lock` and an `unlock` method. Provides an additional nonblocking `try_lock` method.
timed_mutex	Same as mutex, but provides additional `try_lock_for` and `try_lock_until` methods that allow for *timing out* instead of blocking forever.
recursive_mutex	Same as `mutex`, but if a thread locked an instance of it already, it can call `lock` multiple times on the same mutex object without blocking. It is released after the owning thread called `unlock` as often as it called `lock`.
recursive_timed_mutex	Provides the features of both `timed_mutex` and `recursive_mutex`.

Type name	Description
shared_mutex	This mutex is special in that regard, that it can be locked in *exclusive* mode and in *shared* mode. In exclusive mode, it shows the same behavior as the standard mutex class. If a thread locks it in shared mode, it is possible for other threads to lock it in shared mode, too. It will then be unlocked as soon as the last shared mode lock owner releases it. While a lock is locked in shared mode, it is not possible to obtain exclusive ownership. This is very similar to the behavior of shared_ptr, only that it does not manage memory, but lock ownership.
shared_timed_mutex	Combines the features of shared_mutex and timed_mutex for both exclusive and shared mode.

Lock classes

Everything is nice and easy as long as threads do just lock a mutex, access some concurrence protected object and unlock the mutex again. As soon as a forgetful programmer misses to unlock a mutex somewhere after locking it, or an exception is thrown while a mutex is still locked, things look ugly pretty quick. In the best case, the program just hangs immediately and the missing unlock call is identified quickly. Such bugs, however, are very similar to memory leaks, which also occur when there are missing explicit delete calls.

When regarding memory management, we have unique_ptr, shared_ptr and weak_ptr. Those helpers provide very convenient ways to avoid memory leaks. Such helpers exist for mutexes, too. The simplest one is std::lock_guard. It can be used as follows:

```
void critical_function()
{
    lock_guard<mutex> l {some_mutex};

    // critical section
}
```

`lock_guard` element's constructor accepts a mutex, on which it calls `lock` immediately. The whole constructor call will block until it obtains the lock on the mutex. Upon destruction, it unlocks the mutex again. This way it is hard to get the `lock`/`unlock` cycle wrong because it happens automatically.

The C++17 STL provides the following different RAII lock-helpers. They all accept a template argument that shall be of the same type as the mutex (although, since C++17, the compiler can deduce that type itself):

Name	Description
`lock_guard`	This class provides nothing else than a constructor and a destructor, which `lock` and `unlock` a mutex.
`scoped_lock`	Similar to `lock_guard`, but supports arbitrarily many mutexes in its constructor. Will release them in opposite order in its destructor.
`unique_lock`	Locks a mutex in exclusive mode. The constructor also accepts arguments that instruct it to timeout instead of blocking forever on the lock call. It is also possible to not lock the mutex at all, or to assume that it is locked already, or to only *try* locking the mutex. Additional methods allow to lock and unlock the mutex during the `unique_lock` lock's lifetime.
`shared_lock`	Same as `unique_lock`, but all operations are applied on the mutex in shared mode.

While `lock_guard` and `scoped_lock` have dead-simple interfaces that only consist of constructor and destructor, `unique_lock` and `shared_lock` are more complicated, but also more versatile. We will see in later recipes of this chapter, how else they can be used if not for plain simple lock regions.

Let's get back to the recipe code now. Although we only ran the code in single thread context, we have seen how it is meant to use the lock helpers. The `shrd_lck` type alias stands for `shared_lock<shared_mutex>` and allows us to lock an instance multiple times in shared mode. As long as `sl1` and `sl2` exist, no `print_exclusive` call is able to lock the mutex in exclusive mode. This is still simple.

Now let's get to the exclusively locking functions that came later in the main function:

```
int main()
{
    {
        shrd_lck sl1 {shared_mut};
        {
            shrd_lck sl2 {shared_mut};

            print_exclusive();
        }
        print_exclusive();
    }
    try {
        exclusive_throw();
    } catch (int e) {
        cout << "Got exception " << e << '\n';
    }
    print_exclusive();
}
```

One important detail is that after returning from `exclusive_throw`, the `print_exclusive` function is able to lock the mutex again, although `exclusive_throw` did not exit cleanly due to the exception it throws.

Let's have another look at `print_exclusive` because it used a strange constructor call:

```
void print_exclusive()
{
    uniq_lck l {shared_mut, defer_lock};

    if (l.try_lock()) {
        // ...
    }
}
```

We did not only provide `shared_mut` but also `defer_lock` as constructor arguments for `unique_lock` in this procedure. `defer_lock` is an empty global object that can be used to select a different constructor of `unique_lock` that simply does not lock the mutex. By doing so, we are able to call `l.try_lock()` later, which does not block. In case the mutex is locked already, we can do something else. If it was indeed possible to get the lock, we still have the destructor tidying up after us.

Avoiding deadlocks with std::scoped_lock

If deadlocks had occurred in road traffic, they would have looked like the following situation:

In order to get the traffic flow going again, we either need a large crane that randomly picks one car from the center of the street intersection and removes it. If that is not possible, then we need enough drivers to be cooperative. The deadlock can be solved by all drivers in one direction driving several meters backwards, making space for the other drivers to continue.

In multithreaded programs, such situations, of course, need to be avoided strictly by the programmer. It is however too easy to fail in that regard when the program is really complex.

In this recipe, we are going to write code which intentionally provokes a deadlock situation. Then we will see how to write code that acquires the same resources that led the other code into a deadlock, but use the new STL lock class std::scoped_lock that came with C++17, in order to avoid this mistake.

How to do it...

The code of this section contains two pairs of functions that ought to be executed by concurrent threads, and that acquire two resources in form of mutexes. One pair provokes a deadlock and the other avoids it. In the main function, we are going to try them out:

1. Let's first include all needed headers and declare that we use namespace `std` and `chrono_literals`:

```
#include <iostream>
#include <thread>
#include <mutex>

using namespace std;
using namespace chrono_literals;
```

2. Then we instantiate two mutex objects which we need in order to run into a deadlock:

```
mutex mut_a;
mutex mut_b;
```

3. In order to provoke a deadlock with two resources, we need two functions. One function tries to lock mutex A and then mutex B, while the other function will do that in the opposite order. By letting both functions sleep a bit between the locks, we can make sure that this code blocks forever on a deadlock. (This is for demonstration purposes. A program without some sleep lines might run successfully without a deadlock sometimes if we start it repeatedly.)
Note that we do not use the `'\n'` character in order to print a line break, but we use `endl`. `endl` does not only perform a line break but also flushes the stream buffer of `cout`, so we can be sure that prints are not bunched up and postponed:

```
static void deadlock_func_1()
{
    cout << "bad f1 acquiring mutex A..." << endl;
    lock_guard<mutex> la {mut_a};
    this_thread::sleep_for(100ms);
    cout << "bad f1 acquiring mutex B..." << endl;
    lock_guard<mutex> lb {mut_b};
    cout << "bad f1 got both mutexes." << endl;
}
```

4. As promised in the last step, `deadlock_func_2` looks exactly same as `deadlock_func_1`, but it locks mutex A and B in the opposite order:

```
static void deadlock_func_2()
{
    cout << "bad f2 acquiring mutex B..." << endl;
    lock_guard<mutex> lb {mut_b};
    this_thread::sleep_for(100ms);
    cout << "bad f2 acquiring mutex A..." << endl;
    lock_guard<mutex> la {mut_a};
    cout << "bad f2 got both mutexes." << endl;
}
```

5. Now we write a deadlock-free variant of those two functions we just implemented. They use the class `scoped_lock`, which locks all mutexes we provide as constructor arguments. Its destructor unlocks them again. While locking the mutexes, it internally applies a deadlock avoidance strategy for us. Note that both functions still use mutex A and B in opposite order:

```
static void sane_func_1()
{
    scoped_lock l {mut_a, mut_b};
    cout << "sane f1 got both mutexes." << endl;
}
static void sane_func_2()
{
    scoped_lock l {mut_b, mut_a};
    cout << "sane f2 got both mutexes." << endl;
}
```

6. In the main function, we will go through two scenarios. First, we use the *sane* functions in multithreaded context:

```
int main()
{
    {
        thread t1 {sane_func_1};
        thread t2 {sane_func_2};
        t1.join();
        t2.join();
    }
```

7. Then we use the deadlock-provoking functions that do not utilize any deadlock avoidance strategy:

```
    {
        thread t1 {deadlock_func_1};
        thread t2 {deadlock_func_2};
        t1.join();
        t2.join();
    }
}
```

8. Compiling and running the program yields the following output. The first two lines show that the *sane* locking function scenario works and both functions return without blocking forever. The other two functions run into a deadlock. We can tell that this is a deadlock because we see the print lines that tell that the individual threads try to lock mutexes A and B and then wait *forever*. Both do not reach the point where they successfully locked both mutexes. We can let this program run for hours, days, and years, and *nothing* will happen.

   This application needs to be killed from outside, for example by pressing the keys *Ctrl + C*:

```
$ ./avoid_deadlock
sane f1 got both mutexes
sane f2 got both mutexes
bad f2 acquiring mutex B...
bad f1 acquiring mutex A...
bad f1 acquiring mutex B...
bad f2 acquiring mutex A...
```

How it works...

By implementing code that willfully causes a deadlock, we've seen how quick such an unwanted scenario can happen. In a large project, where multiple programmers write code that needs to share a common set of mutex-protected resources, all programmers need to comply with the *same order* when locking and unlocking mutexes. While such strategies or rules are really easy to follow, they are also easy to forget. Another term for this problem is *lock order inversion*.

`scoped_lock` is a real help in such situations. It came with C++17 and works the same way as `lock_guard` and `unique_lock` work: its constructor performs the locking, and its destructor the unlocking of a mutex. `scoped_lock`'s specialty is that it can do this with *multiple* mutexes.

`scoped_lock` uses the `std::lock` function, which applies a special algorithm that performs a series of `try_lock` calls on all the mutexes provided, in order to prevent deadlocking. Therefore it is perfectly safe to use `scoped_lock` or call `std::lock` on the same set of locks, but in different orders.

Synchronizing concurrent std::cout use

One inconvenience in multithreaded programs is that we must practically secure *every* data structure they modify, with mutexes or other measures that protect from uncontrolled concurrent modification.

One data structure that is typically used very often for printing is `std::cout`. If multiple threads access `cout` concurrently, then the output will appear in interesting mixed patterns on the terminal. In order to prevent this, we would need to write our own function that prints in a concurrency-safe fashion.

We are going to learn how to provide a `cout` wrapper that consists of minimal code itself and that is as comfortable to use as `cout`.

How to do it...

In this section, we are going to implement a program that prints to the terminal concurrently from many threads. In order to prevent garbling of the messages due to concurrency, we implement a little helper class that synchronizes printing between threads:

1. As always, the includes come first:

```
#include <iostream>
#include <thread>
#include <mutex>
#include <sstream>
#include <vector>

using namespace std;
```

2. Then we implement our helper class, which we call pcout. The p stands for *parallel* because it works in a synchronized way for parallel contexts. The idea is that pcout publicly inherits from stringstream. This way we can use operator<< on instances of it. As soon as a pcout instance is destroyed, its destructor locks a mutex and then prints the content of the stringstream buffer. We will see how to use it in the next step:

```
struct pcout : public stringstream {
    static inline mutex cout_mutex;
    ~pcout() {
        lock_guard<mutex> l {cout_mutex};
        cout << rdbuf();
        cout.flush();
    }
};
```

3. Now let's write two functions that can be executed by additional threads. Both accept a thread ID as arguments. Then, their only difference is that the first one simply uses cout for printing. The other one looks nearly identical, but instead of using cout directly, it instantiates pcout. This instance is a temporary object that lives only exactly for this line of code. After all operator<< calls have been executed, the internal string stream is filled with what we want to print. Then pcout instance's destructor is called. We have seen what the destructor does: it locks a specific mutex all pcout instances share along and prints:

```
static void print_cout(int id)
{
    cout << "cout hello from " << id << '\n';
}
```

```
static void print_pcout(int id)
{
    pcout{} << "pcout hello from " << id << '\n';
}
```

4. Let's try it out. First, we are going to use `print_cout`, which just uses `cout` for printing. We start 10 threads which concurrently print their strings and wait until they finish:

```
int main()
{
    vector<thread> v;
    for (size_t i {0}; i < 10; ++i) {
        v.emplace_back(print_cout, i);
    }
    for (auto &t : v) { t.join(); }
```

5. Then we do the same thing with the `print_pcout` function:

```
    cout << "=====================\n";
    v.clear();
    for (size_t i {0}; i < 10; ++i) {
        v.emplace_back(print_pcout, i);
    }
    for (auto &t : v) { t.join(); }
}
```

6. Compiling and running the program yields the following result. As we see, the first 10 prints are completely garbled. This is how it can look like when `cout` is used concurrently without locking. The last 10 lines of the program are the `print_pcout` lines which do not show any signs of garbling. We can see that they are printed from different threads because their order appears randomized every time when we run the program again:

```
$ ./sync_cout
cout hello from cout hello from cout hello from cout hello from cout hello from
cout hello from cout hello from cout hello from cout hello from 0123cout hello f
rom 45678


9



pcout hello from 0
pcout hello from 2
pcout hello from 4
pcout hello from 1
pcout hello from 3
pcout hello from 5
pcout hello from 6
pcout hello from 7
pcout hello from 8
pcout hello from 9
```

How it works...

Ok, we've built this *"cout wrapper"* that automatically serializes concurrent printing attempts. How does it work?

Let's do the same steps our `pcout` helper does in a manual manner without any magic. First, it instantiates a string stream and accepts the input we feed into it:

```
stringstream ss;
ss << "This is some printed line " << 123 << '\n';
```

Then it locks a globally available mutex:

```
{
    lock_guard<mutex> l {cout_mutex};
```

In this locked scope, it accesses the content of string stream `ss`, prints it, and releases the mutex again by leaving the scope. The `cout.flush()` line tells the stream object to print to the terminal immediately. Without this line, a program might run faster because multiple printed lines can be bunched up and printed in a single run later. In our recipes, we will like to see all output lines immediately, so we use the `flush` method:

```
    cout << ss.rdbuf();
    cout.flush();
}
```

Ok, this is simple enough but tedious to write if we have to to the same thing again and again. We can shorten down the `stringstream` instantiation as follows:

```
stringstream{} << "This is some printed line " << 123 << '\n';
```

This instantiates a string stream object, feeds everything we want to print into it and then destructs it again. The lifetime of the string stream is reduced to just this line. Afterward, we cannot print it any longer, because we cannot access it. Which code is the last that is able to access the stream's content? It is the destructor of `stringstream`.

We cannot modify `stringstream` instance's member methods, but we can extend them by wrapping our own type around it via inheritance:

```
struct pcout : public stringstream {
    ~pcout() {
        lock_guard<mutex> l {cout_mutex};
        cout << rdbuf();
        cout.flush();
    }
};
```

This class *is still* a string stream and we can use it like any other string stream. The only difference is that it will lock a mutex and print its own buffer using `cout`.

We also moved the `cout_mutex` object into struct `pcout` as a static instance so we have both bundled in one place.

Safely postponing initialization with std::call_once

Sometimes we have specific code sections that can be run in parallel context by multiple threads with the obligation that some *setup code* must be executed exactly once before executing the actual functions. A simple solution is to just execute the existing setup function before the program enters a state from which parallel code can be executed from time to time.

The drawbacks of such an approach are the following ones:

- If the parallel function comes from a library, the user must not forget to call the setup function. That does not make the library easier to use.
- If the setup function is expensive in some way, and it might not even need to be executed in case the parallel functions that need this setup are not even always used, then we need code that decides when/if to run it.

In this recipe, we will have a look at `std::call_once`, which is a helper function that solves this problem for us in a simple to use and elegant implicit way.

How to do it...

We are going to write a program that starts multiple threads with exactly the same code. Although they are programmed to execute exactly the same code, our example setup function will only be called once:

1. First, we need to include all the necessary headers:

```
#include <iostream>
#include <thread>
#include <mutex>
#include <vector>

using namespace std;
```

2. We are going to use `std::call_once` later. In order to use it, we need an instance of `once_flag` somewhere. It is needed for the synchronization of all threads that use `call_once` on a specific function:

```
once_flag callflag;
```

3. The function which must be only executed once is the following one. It just prints a single exclamation mark:

```
static void once_print()
{
    cout << '!';
}
```

4. All threads will execute the print function. The first thing we do is calling the function once_print through the function std::call_once. call_once needs the variable callflag we defined before. It will use it to orchestrate the threads:

```
static void print(size_t x)
{
    std::call_once(callflag, once_print);
    cout << x;
}
```

5. Ok, let's now start 10 threads which all use the print function:

```
int main()
{
    vector<thread> v;
    for (size_t i {0}; i < 10; ++i) {
        v.emplace_back(print, i);
    }
    for (auto &t : v) { t.join(); }
    cout << '\n';
}
```

6. Compiling and running yields the following output. First, we see the exclamation mark from the once_print function. Then we see all thread IDs. call_once did not only make sure that once_print was only called once. Additionally, it synchronized all threads, so that no ID is printed *before* once_print was executed:

```
$ ./call_once
!1239406758
```

How it works...

std:call_once works like a barrier. It maintains access to a function (or a callable object). The first thread to reach it gets to execute the function. Until it has finished, any other thread that reaches the call_once line is blocked. After the first thread returns from the function, all other threads are released, too.

In order to organize this little choreography, a variable is needed from which the other threads can determine if they must wait and when they are released again. This is what our variable once_flag callflag; is for. Every call_once line also needs a once_flag instance as the argument prepending the function that shall be called only once.

Another nice detail is: If it happens, that the thread which is selected to execute the function in call_once *fails* because some *exception* is thrown, then the next thread is allowed to execute the function again. This happens in the hope that it will not throw an exception the next time.

Pushing the execution of tasks into the background using std::async

Whenever we want some code to be executed in the background, we can simply start a new thread that executes this code. While this happens, we can do something else and then wait for the result. It's simple:

```
std::thread t {my_function, arg1, arg2, ...};
// do something else
t.join(); // wait for thread to finish
```

But then the inconvenience starts: t.join() does not give us the return value of my_function. In order to get at that, we need to write a function that calls my_function and stores its return value in some variable that is also accessible for the first thread in which we started the new thread. If such situations occur repeatedly, then this represents quite a bunch of boilerplate code we have to write again and again.

Since C++11, we have std::async which can do exactly this job for us and not only that. In this recipe, we are going to write a simple program that does multiple things at the same time using asynchronous function calls. As std::async is a bit more powerful than that alone, we will have a closer look at its different facets.

How to do it...

We are going to implement a program that does multiple different things concurrently but instead of explicitly starting threads, we use `std::async` and `std::future`:

1. First, we include all necessary headers and declare that we use the `std` namespace:

```
#include <iostream>
#include <iomanip>
#include <map>
#include <string>
#include <algorithm>
#include <iterator>
#include <future>

using namespace std;
```

2. We implement three functions which have nothing to do with parallelism but do interesting tasks. The first function accepts a string and creates a histogram of all characters occurring within that string:

```
static map<char, size_t> histogram(const string &s)
{
    map<char, size_t> m;
    for (char c : s) { m[c] += 1; }
    return m;
}
```

3. The second function does also accept a string and returns a sorted copy of it:

```
static string sorted(string s)
{
    sort(begin(s), end(s));
    return s;
}
```

4. The third one counts how many vowels exist within the string it accepts:

```
static bool is_vowel(char c)
{
    char vowels[] {"aeiou"};
    return end(vowels) !=
            find(begin(vowels), end(vowels), c);
}
static size_t vowels(const string &s)
{
    return count_if(begin(s), end(s), is_vowel);
}
```

5. In the main function, we read the whole standard input into a string. In order to not segment the input into words, we deactivate `ios::skipws`. This way we get one large string, no matter how much white space the input contains. We use `pop_back` on the resulting string afterward because we got one string terminating `'\0'` character too much this way:

```
int main()
{
    cin.unsetf(ios::skipws);
    string input {istream_iterator<char>{cin}, {}};
    input.pop_back();
```

6. Now let's get the return values from all the functions we implemented before. In order to speed the execution up for very long input, we launch them *asynchronously*. The `std::async` function accepts a policy, a function, and arguments for that function. We call `histogram`, `sorted`, and `vowels` with `launch::async` as a policy (we will see later what that means). All functions get the same input string as arguments:

```
    auto hist        (async(launch::async,
                            histogram, input));
    auto sorted_str  (async(launch::async,
                            sorted,    input));
    auto vowel_count (async(launch::async,
                            vowels,    input));
```

7. The `async` calls return immediately because they do not actually execute our functions. Instead, they set up synchronization structures which will obtain the results of the function calls later. The results are now being calculated concurrently by additional threads. In the meantime, we are free to do whatever we want, as we can pick up those values later. The return values `hist`, `sorted_str` and `vowel_count` are of the types the functions `histogram`, `sorted`, and `vowels` return, but they were wrapped in a `future` type by `std::async`. Objects of this type express that they will contain their values at some point in time. By using `.get()` on all of them, we can make the main function block until the values arrive, and then use them for printing:

```
    for (const auto &[c, count] : hist.get()) {
        cout << c << ": " << count << '\n';
    }
    cout << "Sorted string: "
         << quoted(sorted_str.get()) << '\n'
         << "Total vowels: "
         << vowel_count.get()           << '\n';
}
```

8. Compiling and running the code looks like the following. We use a short example string that does not really make it worth being parallelized, but for the sake of this example, the code is nevertheless executed concurrently. Additionally, the overall structure of the program did not change much compared to a naive sequential version of it:

```
$ echo "foo bar baz foobazinga" | ./async
 : 3
a: 4
b: 3
f: 2
g: 1
i: 1
n: 1
o: 4
r: 1
z: 2
Sorted string: "   aaaabbbffginoooorzz"
Total vowels: 9
```

How it works...

If we would not have used `std::async` the serial unparallelized code could have looked as simple as that:

```
auto hist         (histogram(input));
auto sorted_str   (sorted(   input));
auto vowel_count  (vowels(    input));

for (const auto &[c, count] : hist) {
    cout << c << ": " << count << '\n';
}
cout << "Sorted string: " << quoted(sorted_str) << '\n';
cout << "Total vowels: "  << vowel_count        << '\n';
```

The only thing we did in order to parallelize the code was the following. We wrapped the three function calls into `async(launch::async, ...)` calls. This way these three functions are not executed by the main thread we are currently running in. Instead, `async` starts new threads and lets them execute the functions concurrently. This way we get to execute only the overhead of starting another thread and can continue with the next line of code, while all the work happens in the background:

```
auto hist         (async(launch::async, histogram, input));
auto sorted_str   (async(launch::async, sorted,    input));
auto vowel_count  (async(launch::async, vowels,    input));

for (const auto &[c, count] : hist.get()) {
    cout << c << ": " << count << '\n';
}
cout << "Sorted string: "
     << quoted(sorted_str.get()) << '\n'
     << "Total vowels: "
     << vowel_count.get()        << '\n';
```

While `histogram` for example, returns us a map instance, `async(..., histogram, ...)` does return us a map that was wrapped in a `future` object before. This `future` object is kind of an empty *placeholder* until the thread that executes the `histogram` function returns. The resulting map is then placed into the `future` object so we can finally access it. The `get` function then gives us access to the encapsulated result.

Let's have a look at another minimal example. Consider the following code snippet:

```
auto x (f(1, 2, 3));
cout << x;
```

Instead of writing the preceding code, we can also do the following:

```
auto x (async(launch::async, f, 1, 2, 3));
cout << x.get();
```

That's basically it. Executing tasks in the background might have never been easier in standard C++. There is still one thing left to resolve: What does `launch::async` mean? `launch::async` is a flag that defines the launch policy. There are two policy flags which allow for three constellations:

Policy choice	Meaning
`launch::async`	**The function is guaranteed to be executed by another thread.**
`launch::deferred`	The function is executed by the same thread, but later (*lazy evaluation*). Execution then happens when `get` or `wait` is called on the future. If *none* of both happens, the function is not called *at all*.
`launch::async | launch::deferred`	Having both flags set, the STL's `async` implementation is free to choose which policy shall be followed. This is the default choice if no policy is provided.

 By just calling `async(f, 1, 2, 3)` without a policy argument, we automatically select *both* policies. The implementation of `async` is then free to choose which policy to employ. This means that we cannot be *sure* that another thread is started at all, or if the execution is just deferred in the current thread.

There's more...

There is indeed one last thing we should know about. Suppose, we write code as follows:

```
async(launch::async, f);
async(launch::async, g);
```

This might have the motivation of executing functions f and g (we do not care about their return values in this example) in concurrent threads and then doing different things at the same time. While running such code, we will notice that the code *blocks* on this calls, which is most probably not what we want.

So why does it block? Isn't `async` all about nonblocking asynchronous calls? Yes it is, but there is one special peculiarity: if a future was obtained from an async call with the `launch::async` policy, then its destructor performs a *blocking wait*.

This means that *both* the async calls from this short example are blocking because the lifetime of the futures they return ends in the same line! We can fix this by capturing their return values in variables with a longer lifetime.

Implementing the producer/consumer idiom with std::condition_variable

In this recipe, we are going to implement a typical producer/consumer program with multiple threads. The general idea is that there is one thread that produces items and puts them into a queue. Then there is another thread that consumes such items. If there is nothing to produce, the producer thread sleeps. If there is no item in the queue to consume, the consumer sleeps.

Since the queue that both threads have access to is also modified by both whenever an item is produced or consumed, it needs to be protected by a mutex.

Another thing to consider is: What does the consumer do if there is no item in the queue? Does it poll the queue every second until it sees new items? That is not necessary because we can let the consumer wait for wakeup *events* that are triggered by the producer, whenever there are new items.

C++11 provides a nice data structure called `std::condition_variable` for this kind of events. In this recipe, we are going to implement a simple producer/consumer app that takes advantage of this.

How to do it...

We are going to implement a simple producer/consumer program which runs a single producer of values in its own thread, as well as a single consumer thread in another thread:

1. First, we need to perform all the needed includes:

```
#include <iostream>
#include <queue>
#include <tuple>
#include <condition_variable>
```

```
#include <thread>

using namespace std;
using namespace chrono_literals;
```

2. We instantiate a queue of simple numeric values and call it q. The producer will push values into it, and the consumer will take values out of it. In order to synchronize both, we need a mutex. In addition to that, we instantiate a condition_variable cv. The variable finished will be the producer's way to tell the consumer that no more values will follow:

```
queue<size_t>       q;
mutex               mut;
condition_variable cv;
bool                finished {false};
```

3. Let's first implement the producer function. It accepts an argument items which limits the maximum number of items for production. In a simple loop, it will sleep 100 milliseconds for every item, which simulates some computational *complexity*. Then we lock the mutex that synchronizes access to the queue. After successful production and insertion to the queue, we call cv.notify_all(). This function wakes the consumer up. We will see later at the consumer side how this works:

```
static void producer(size_t items) {
    for (size_t i {0}; i < items; ++i) {
        this_thread::sleep_for(100ms);
        {
            lock_guard<mutex> lk {mut};
            q.push(i);
        }
        cv.notify_all();
    }
```

4. After having produced all items, we lock the mutex again because we are going to change to set the finished bit. Then we call cv.notify_all() again:

```
    {
        lock_guard<mutex> lk {mut};
        finished = true;
    }
    cv.notify_all();
}
```

5. Now we can implement the consumer function. It takes no arguments because it will blindly consume until the queue runs empty. In a loop that is executed as long as `finished` is not set, it will first lock the mutex that protects both the queue and the `finished` flag. As soon as it has the lock, it calls `cv.wait` with the lock and a lambda expression as arguments. The lambda expression is a predicate that tells if the producer thread is still alive and if there is anything to consume in the queue:

```
static void consumer() {
    while (!finished) {
        unique_lock<mutex> l {mut};
        cv.wait(l, [] { return !q.empty() || finished; });
```

6. The `cv.wait` call unlocks the lock and waits until the condition described by the predicate function holds. Then, it locks the mutex again and consumes everything from the queue until it appears empty. If the producer is still alive, it will iterate through the loop again. Otherwise, it will terminate because `finished` is set, which is the producer's way to signal that there are no further items being produced:

```
        while (!q.empty()) {
            cout << "Got " << q.front()
                 << " from queue.\n";
            q.pop();
        }
    }
}
```

7. In the main function, we start a producer thread which produces 10 items, and a consumer thread. Then we wait until their completion and terminate the program:

```
int main() {
    thread t1 {producer, 10};
    thread t2 {consumer};
    t1.join();
    t2.join();
    cout << "finished!\n";
}
```

8. Compiling and running the program yields the following output. When the program is executed, we can see that there is some time (100 milliseconds) between each line, because the production of items takes some time:

```
$ ./producer_consumer
Got 0 from queue.
Got 1 from queue.
Got 2 from queue.
Got 3 from queue.
Got 4 from queue.
Got 5 from queue.
Got 6 from queue.
Got 7 from queue.
Got 8 from queue.
Got 9 from queue.
finished!
```

How it works...

In this recipe, we simply started two threads. The first thread produces items and puts them into a queue. The other takes items out of the queue. Whenever one of those threads touches the queue in any way, it locks the common mutex mut which is accessible for both. This way we made sure that it cannot happen that both threads manipulate the queue's state at the same time.

Apart from the queue and the mutex, we declared generally four variables that were involved in the producer-consumer thing:

```
queue<size_t>       q;
mutex               mut;
condition_variable  cv;
bool                finished {false};
```

The variable finished is easy to explain. It was set to true when the producer finished producing its fixed amount of items. When the consumer sees that this variable is true, it consumes the last items in the queue and stops consuming. But what is the condition_variable cv for? We used cv in two different contexts. One of the contexts was *waiting for a specific condition*, and the other was *signaling that condition*.

The consumer side that waits for a specific condition looks like this. The consumer thread loops over a block that first locks mutex mut in a unique_lock. Then it calls cv.wait:

```
while (!finished) {
    unique_lock<mutex> l {mut};

    cv.wait(l, [] { return !q.empty() || finished; });

    while (!q.empty()) {
        // consume
    }
}
```

This code is *somewhat* equivalent to the following alternative code. We will elaborate soon why it is not really the same:

```
while (!finished) {
    unique_lock<mutex> l {mut};

    while (q.empty() && !finished) {
        l.unlock();
        l.lock();
    }

    while (!q.empty()) {
        // consume
    }
}
```

This means that we generally first acquire the lock and then check what scenario we have:

1. Are there items to consume? Then keep the lock, consume, release the lock, and start over.
2. Else, if there are *no consumable items* but the producer is still *alive,* release the mutex to give the producer a chance of adding items to the queue. Then, try to lock it again in hope that the situation changes and we get to see situation 1.

The real reason why the cv.wait line is not equivalent to the while (q.empty() && ...) construct is, that we cannot simply loop over a l.unlock(); l.lock(); cycle. If the producer thread is inactive for some time, then this would lead to continuous locking and unlocking of the mutex, which makes no sense because it needlessly burns CPU cycles.

An expression like `cv.wait(lock, predicate)` will wait until `predicate()` returns `true`. But it does not do this by continuously unlocking and locking `lock`. In order to wake a thread up that blocks on the `wait` call of a `condition_variable` object, another thread has to call the `notify_one()` or `notify_all()` method on the same object. Only then the waiting thread(s) is/are kicked out of their sleep in order to check if `predicate()` holds.

The nice thing about the `wait` call checking the predicate is that if there is a *spurious* wakeup call, the thread will go to sleep immediately again. This means that it does not really harm the program flow (but maybe the performance) if we have too many notify calls.

On the producer side, we just called `cv.notify_all()` after the producer inserted an item to the queue and after it produced its last item and set the `finished` flag to `true`. This was enough to direct the consumer.

Implementing the multiple producers/consumers idiom with std::condition_variable

Let's pick up the producer/consumer problem from the last recipe and make it a bit more complicated: We make *multiple* producers produce items and *multiple* consumers consume them. In addition to that, we define that the queue shall not exceed a maximum size.

This way not only the consumers have to sleep from time to time if there are no items in the queue, but also the producers have to sleep from time to time when there are *enough* items in the queue.

We are going to see how to solve this problem with multiple `std::condition_variable` objects and will also use them in slightly different ways than in the last recipe.

How to do it...

In this section, we are going to implement a program just like in the recipe before, but this time with multiple producers and multiple consumers:

1. First, we need to include all needed headers and we declare that we use namespace `std` and `chrono_literals`:

```
#include <iostream>
#include <iomanip>
#include <sstream>
#include <vector>
#include <queue>
#include <thread>
#include <mutex>
#include <condition_variable>
#include <chrono>

using namespace std;
using namespace chrono_literals;
```

2. Then we implement the synchronized printing helper from the other recipe in this chapter because we are going to do a lot of concurrent printing:

```
struct pcout : public stringstream {
    static inline mutex cout_mutex;
    ~pcout() {
        lock_guard<mutex> l {cout_mutex};
        cout << rdbuf();
    }
};
```

3. All producers write values into the same queue and all consumers will also take values out of this queue. In addition to that queue, we need a mutex that protects both the queue and a flag that can tell if the production was stopped at some point:

```
queue<size_t> q;
mutex          q_mutex;
bool           production_stopped {false};
```

4. We are going to employ two different `condition_variables` in this program. In the single producer/consumer recipe, we had a `condition_variable` telling that there are new items in the queue. In this case, we make it a bit more complicated. We want the producers to produce until the queue contains a certain *stock amount* of items. If that stock amount is reached, they shall *sleep*. This way the `go_consume` variable can be used to wake up consumers which then, in turn, can wake up the producers with the `go_produce` variable again:

```
condition_variable go_produce;
condition_variable go_consume;
```

5. The producer function accepts a producer ID number, a total number of items to produce and a stock limit as arguments. It then enters its own production loop. There, it first locks the queue's mutex and unlocks it again in the `go_produce.wait` call. It waits for the condition that the queue size is below the `stock` threshold:

```
static void producer(size_t id, size_t items, size_t stock)
{
    for (size_t i = 0; i < items; ++i) {
        unique_lock<mutex> lock(q_mutex);
        go_produce.wait(lock,
            [&] { return q.size() < stock; });
```

6. After the producer was woken up, it produces an item and pushes it into the queue. The queue value is calculated from the expression `id * 100 + i`. This way we can later see which producer produced it because the hundreds in the number are the producer ID. We also print the production event to the terminal. The format of the printing may look strange, but it will align nicely with the consumer output in the terminal later:

```
q.push(id * 100 + i);
pcout{} << "   Producer " << id << " --> item "
        << setw(3) << q.back() << '\n';
```

7. After production, we can wake up sleeping consumers. A sleeping period of 90 milliseconds simulates that producing items takes some time:

```
        go_consume.notify_all();
        this_thread::sleep_for(90ms);
    }
    pcout{} << "EXIT: Producer " << id << '\n';
}
```

8. Now to the consumer function that only accepts a consumer ID as an argument. It shall continue waiting for items if the production has not stopped, or the queue is not empty. If the queue is empty, but the production has not stopped, then it is possible that there might be new items soon:

```
static void consumer(size_t id)
{
    while (!production_stopped || !q.empty()) {
        unique_lock<mutex> lock(q_mutex);
```

9. After locking the queue mutex, we unlock it again in order to wait on the `go_consume` event variable. The lambda expression argument describes that we want to return from the wait call when the queue contains items. The second argument `1s` tells that we do not want to wait forever. If it takes longer than 1 second, we want to drop out of the wait function. We can distinguish if the `wait_for` function returned because the predicate condition holds, or if we dropped out of it because of a timeout because it will return `false` in case of the timeout. If there are new items in the queue, we consume them and print this event to the terminal:

```
        if (go_consume.wait_for(lock, 1s,
                [] { return !q.empty(); })) {
            pcout{} << "                    item "
                    << setw(3) << q.front()
                    << " --> Consumer "
                    << id << '\n';
            q.pop();
```

10. After item consumption, we notify the producers and sleep for 130 milliseconds to simulate that consuming items is also time-consuming:

```
            go_produce.notify_all();
            this_thread::sleep_for(130ms);
        }
    }
    pcout{} << "EXIT: Producer " << id << '\n';
}
```

11. In the main function, we instantiate a vector for worker threads and another for consumer threads:

```
int main()
{
    vector<thread> workers;
    vector<thread> consumers;
```

12. Then we spawn three producer threads and five consumer threads:

```
    for (size_t i = 0; i < 3; ++i) {
        workers.emplace_back(producer, i, 15, 5);
    }
    for (size_t i = 0; i < 5; ++i) {
        consumers.emplace_back(consumer, i);
    }
```

13. We first let the producer threads finish. As soon as all of them have returned, we set the production_stopped flag, which will lead the consumers to finish, too. We need to collect those and then we can quit the program:

```
    for (auto &t : workers)   { t.join(); }
    production_stopped = true;
    for (auto &t : consumers) { t.join(); }
}
```

14. Compiling and running the program leads to the following output. The output is very long, which is why it is truncated here. We can see that the producers go to sleep from time to time, and let the consumers eat up some items until they finally produce again. It is interesting to alter the wait times for producers/consumers, as well as manipulating the number of producers/consumers and stock items because this completely changes the output patterns:

```
$ ./multi_producer_consumer
    Producer 0 --> item    0
    Producer 1 --> item 100
                   item    0 --> Consumer 0
    Producer 2 --> item 200
                   item 100 --> Consumer 1
                   item 200 --> Consumer 2
    Producer 0 --> item    1
    Producer 1 --> item 101
                   item    1 --> Consumer 0
...
    Producer 0 --> item   14
EXIT: Producer 0
    Producer 1 --> item 114
EXIT: Producer 1
                   item   14 --> Consumer 0
    Producer 2 --> item 214
EXIT: Producer 2
                   item 114 --> Consumer 1
                   item 214 --> Consumer 2
EXIT: Consumer 2
EXIT: Consumer 3
EXIT: Consumer 4
EXIT: Consumer 0
EXIT: Consumer 1
```

How it works...

This recipe is an extension of the preceding recipe. Instead of synchronizing only one producer with one consumer, we implemented a program that synchronizes M producers with N consumers. On top of that, not only the consumers go to sleep if there are no items for them left, but also the producers go to sleep as soon as the item queue becomes *too long*.

When multiple consumers wait for the same queue to fill up, then this would generally also work with the consumer code from the one producer/one consumer scenario. As long as only one thread locks the mutex that protects the queue and then takes items out of it, the code is safe. It does not matter how many threads are waiting for the lock at the same time. The same applies to the producers, as in both scenarios the only important thing is that the queue is never accessed by more than one thread at a time.

So what makes this program really more complex than just running the one producer/one consumer example with more threads is the fact that we make the producer threads stop as soon as the item queue length reached a certain threshold. In order to meet that requirement, we implemented two different signals with their own `condition_variable`:

1. The `go_produce` signals the event that the queue is not completely filled to the maximum and the producers may fill it up again.
2. The `go_consume` signals the event that the queue reached its maximum length and consumers are free to consume items again.

This way producers fill items into the queue and signal the `go_consume` event to the consuming threads, which wait on the following line:

```
if (go_consume.wait_for(lock, 1s, [] { return !q.empty(); })) {
    // got the event without timeout
}
```

The producers, on the other hand, wait on the following line until they are allowed to produce again:

```
go_produce.wait(lock, [&] { return q.size() < stock; });
```

One interesting detail is that we do not let consumers wait *forever*. In the `go_consume.wait_for` call, we additionally added a timeout argument of 1 second. This is the exit mechanism for consumers: if the queue is empty for longer than a second, maybe there are no active producers any longer.

For the sake of simplicity, the code tries to keep the queue length *always at the maximum*. A more sophisticated program could let the consumer threads push a wake-up notification, *only* if the queue has only *half* the size of its maximum length. This way producers would be woken up before the queue runs empty again, but not unnecessarily earlier when there are still enough items in the queue.

One situation that `condition_variable` solves elegantly for us is the following: If a consumer fires the `go_produce` notification, there might be a horde of producers racing to produce the next item. If only one item is missing, then there will only be one producer producing it. If all producers would always produce an item as soon as the `go_produce` event is fired, we would often see the case that the queue is filled above its allowed maximum.

Let's imagine the situation that we have $(max - 1)$ items in the queue and want one new item produced so that the queue is filled up again. No matter if a consumer thread calls `go_produce.notify_one()` (which would wake up only one waiting thread) or `go_produce.notify_all()` (which wakes up *all* waiting threads), we have the guarantee that only one producer thread will exit the `go_produce.wait` call, because, for all other producer threads, the `q.size() < stock` wait condition doesn't hold any longer as soon as they get the mutex after being woken up.

Parallelizing the ASCII Mandelbrot renderer using std::async

Remember the *ASCII Mandelbrot renderer* from `Chapter 6`, *Advanced Use of STL algorithms*? In this recipe, we will make it use threads in order to speed its calculation time a bit up.

First, we will modify the line in the original program that limits the number of iterations for every selected coordinate. This will make the program *slower* and its results *more accurate* than we can actually display on the terminal, but then we have a nice example target for parallelization.

Then, we will apply minor modifications to the program and see how the whole program runs faster. After those modifications, the program runs with `std::async` and `std::future`. In order to fully understand this recipe, it is crucial to understand the original program.

How to do it...

In this section, we take the ASCII Mandelbrot fractal renderer that we implemented in Chapter 6, *Advanced Use of STL Algorithms*. First, we are going to make the calculation take much more time by incrementing the calculation limit. Then we get some speedup by doing only four little changes to the program in order to parallelize it:

1. In order to follow the steps, it is best to just copy the whole program from the other recipe. Then follow the instructions in the following steps in order to do all needed adjustments. All differences from the original program are highlighted in *bold*.
    The first change is an additional header, `<future>`:

    ```
    #include <iostream>
    #include <algorithm>
    #include <iterator>
    #include <complex>
    #include <numeric>
    #include <vector>
    #include <future>

    using namespace std;
    ```

2. The `scaler` and `scaled_cmplx` functions don't need any change:

    ```
    using cmplx = complex<double>;
    static auto scaler(int min_from, int max_from,
                       double min_to, double max_to)
    {
        const int w_from {max_from - min_from};
        const double w_to {max_to - min_to};
        const int mid_from {(max_from - min_from) / 2 + min_from};
        const double mid_to {(max_to - min_to) / 2.0 + min_to};
        return [=] (int from) {
            return double(from - mid_from) / w_from * w_to + mid_to;
        };
    }
    template <typename A, typename B>
    ```

```
static auto scaled_cmplx(A scaler_x, B scaler_y)
{
    return [=](int x, int y) {
        return cmplx{scaler_x(x), scaler_y(y)};
    };
}
```

3. In the function `mandelbrot_iterations`, we are just going to increment the number of iterations in order to make the program a bit more computation-heavy:

```
static auto mandelbrot_iterations(cmplx c)
{
    cmplx z {};
    size_t iterations {0};
    const size_t max_iterations {100000};
    while (abs(z) < 2 && iterations < max_iterations) {
        ++iterations;
        z = pow(z, 2) + c;
    }
    return iterations;
}
```

4. Then we have a part of the main function that does not need any change again:

```
int main()
{
    const size_t w {100};
    const size_t h {40};
    auto scale (scaled_cmplx(
        scaler(0, w, -2.0, 1.0),
        scaler(0, h, -1.0, 1.0)
    ));
    auto i_to_xy ([=](int x) {
        return scale(x % w, x / w);
    });
```

5. In the `to_iteration_count` function, we do not call `mandelbrot_iterations(x_to_xy(x))` directly any longer, but make the call asynchronous using `std::async`:

```
    auto to_iteration_count ([=](int x) {
        return async(launch::async,
                     mandelbrot_iterations, i_to_xy(x));
    });
```

6. Before the last change, the function `to_iteration_count` returned us the number of iterations a specific coordinate needs for the Mandelbrot algorithm to converge. Now it returns a `future` variable that will contain the same value later because it is computed asynchronously. Because of this, we need a vector that holds all the future values, so let's just add one. The output iterator we provide `transform` as the third argument must be the begin iterator of the new output vector `r`:

```
vector<int> v (w * h);
vector<future<size_t>> r (w * h);
iota(begin(v), end(v), 0);
transform(begin(v), end(v), begin(r),
          to_iteration_count);
```

7. The `accumulate` call which did all the printing for us doesn't get `size_t` values as its second argument any longer, but `future<size_t>` values. We need to adapt it to this type (if we had used `auto&` as its type from the beginning then this would not even be necessary), and then we need to call `x.get()` where we just accessed `x` before, in order to wait for the value to arrive:

```
auto binfunc ([w, n{0}] (auto output_it, future<size_t> &x)
        mutable {
    *++output_it = (x.get() > 50 ? '*' : ' ');
    if (++n % w == 0) { ++output_it = '\n'; }
    return output_it;
}));
accumulate(begin(r), end(r),
           ostream_iterator<char>{cout}, binfunc);
}
```

8. Compiling and running gives us the same output as before. The only interesting difference is the execution speed. If we increase the number of iterations for the original version of the program, too, then the parallelized version should compute faster. On my computer with four CPU cores with hyperthreading (which results in 8 virtual cores), I get different results with GCC and clang. The best speedup is 5.3, and the worst is 3.8. The results will also vary across machines, of course.

How it works...

It is crucial to understand the whole program first because then it is clear that all the CPU-intense work happens in one line of code in the main function:

```
transform(begin(v), end(v), begin(r), to_iteration_count);
```

The vector v contains all the indices that are mapped to complex coordinates, which are then in turn iterated over with the Mandelbrot algorithm. The result of each iteration is saved in vector r.

In the original program, this is the single line which consumes all the processing time for calculating the fractal image. All code that precedes it is just set up work and all code that follows it is just for printing. This means that parallelizing this line is key to more performance.

One possible approach to parallelizing this is to break up the whole linear range from begin(v) to end(v) into chunks of the same size and distribute them evenly across all cores. This way all cores would share the amount of work. If we used the parallel version of std::transform with a parallel execution policy, this would exactly be the case. Unfortunately, this is not the right strategy for *this* problem, because every single point in the Mandelbrot set shows a very individual number of iterations.

Our approach here is to make every single vector item which represents an individually printed character cell on the terminal later an asynchronously calculated future value. As source and target vector are w * h items large, which means 100 * 40 in our case, we have a vector of 4000 future values that are calculated asynchronously. If our system had 4000 CPU cores, then this would mean that we start 4000 threads that do the Mandelbrot iteration really concurrently. On a normal system with fewer cores, the CPUs will just process one asynchronous item after the other per core.

While the transform call with the asynchronized version of to_iteration_count itself does *no calculation* but setting up of threads and future objects, it returns practically immediately. The original version of the program blocked at this point because the iterations took so long.

The parallelized version of the program does of course block *somewhere*, too. The function that prints all our values on the terminal must access the results from within the futures. In order to do that, it calls x.get() on all the values. And this is the trick: while it waits for the first value to be printed, a lot of other values are calculated at the same time. So if the get() call of the first future returns, the next future might be ready for printing already too!

In case w * h results in much larger numbers, there will be some measurable overhead in creating and synchronizing all these futures. In this case, the overhead is not too significant. On my laptop with an Intel i7 processor with 4 *hyperthreading* capable cores (which results in eight virtual cores), the parallel version of this program ran more than 3-5 times faster compared to the original program. The ideal parallelization would make it indeed 8 times faster. Of course, this speedup will vary between different computers, because it depends on a lot of factors.

Implementing a tiny automatic parallelization library with std::future

Most complex tasks can be broken down into subtasks. From all subtasks, we can draw an **directed acyclic graph (DAG)** that describes which subtask depends on what other subtasks in order to finish the higher level task. Let us, for example, imagine that we want to produce the string "foo bar foo bar this that ", and we can only do this by creating single words and concatenate those with other words, or with themselves. Let's say this functionality is provided by three primitive functions create, concat, and twice.

Taking this into account, we can draw the following DAG that visualizes the dependencies between them in order to get the final result:

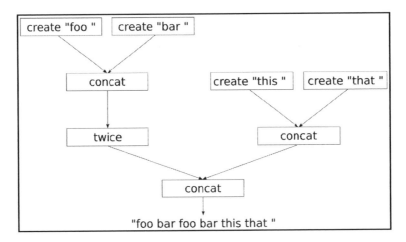

When implementing this in code, it is clear that everything can be implemented in a serial manner on one CPU core. Alternatively, all subtasks that depend on no other subtasks or other subtasks that already have been finished, can be executed *concurrently* on multiple CPU cores.

It might perhaps seem tedious to write such code, even with `std::async` because the dependencies between the subtasks need to be modeled. In this recipe, we will implement two little library helper functions that help to transform the normal functions `create`, `concat`, and `twice` to functions that work asynchronously. With those, we will find a really elegant way to set up the dependency graph. During execution, the graph will parallelize itself in a *seemingly intelligent* way in order to calculate the result as fast as possible.

How to do it...

In this section, we are going to implement some functions that simulate computation-intensive tasks that depend on each other, and let them run as parallel as possible:

1. Let's first include all the necessary headers:

```
#include <iostream>
#include <iomanip>
#include <thread>
#include <string>
#include <sstream>
#include <future>

using namespace std;
using namespace chrono_literals;
```

2. We need to synchronize concurrent access to `cout`, so let's use the synchronization helper from the other recipe in this chapter:

```
struct pcout : public stringstream {
    static inline mutex cout_mutex;
    ~pcout() {
        lock_guard<mutex> l {cout_mutex};
        cout << rdbuf();
        cout.flush();
    }
};
```

3. Now let's implement three functions which transform strings. The first function shall create an `std::string` object from a C-string. We let it sleep for 3 seconds to simulate that string creation is computation-heavy:

```
static string create(const char *s)
{
    pcout{} << "3s CREATE " << quoted(s) << '\n';
    this_thread::sleep_for(3s);
    return {s};
}
```

4. The next function accepts two string objects as arguments and returns their concatenation. We give it 5-second wait time to simulate that this is a time-consuming task:

```
static string concat(const string &a, const string &b)
{
    pcout{} << "5s CONCAT "
            << quoted(a) << " "
            << quoted(b) << '\n';
    this_thread::sleep_for(5s);
    return a + b;
}
```

5. The last computation-heavy function accepts a string and concatenates it with itself. It shall take 3 seconds to do this:

```
static string twice(const string &s)
{
    pcout{} << "3s TWICE " << quoted(s) << '\n';
    this_thread::sleep_for(3s);
    return s + s;
}
```

6. We could now already use those functions in a serial program, but we want to get some elegant automatic parallelization. So let's implement some helpers for this. *Attention please*, the following three functions look really complicated. `asynchronize` accepts a function `f` and returns a callable object that captures it. We can call this callable object with any number of arguments, and then it will capture those together with `f` in another callable object which it returns to us. This last callable object can be called without arguments. It does then call `f` asynchronously with all the arguments it captures:

```
template <typename F>
static auto asynchronize(F f)
```

```
{
    return [f](auto ... xs) {
        return [=] () {
            return async(launch::async, f, xs...);
        };
    };
}
```

7. The next function will be used by the function we declare in the next step afterward. It accepts a function `f`, and captures it in a callable object that it returns. That object can be called with a number of future objects. It will then call `.get()` on all the futures, apply `f` to them and return its result:

```
template <typename F>
static auto fut_unwrap(F f)
{
    return [f](auto ... xs) {
        return f(xs.get()...);
    };
}
```

8. The last helper function does also accept a function `f`. It returns a callable object that captures `f`. That callable object can be called with any number of callable objects as arguments, which it returns captured together with `f` in another callable object. That final callable object can then be called without arguments. It does then call all the callable objects that are captured in the `xs...` pack. These return futures which need to be unwrapped with `fut_unwrap`. The future-unwrapping and actual application of the real function `f` on the real values from the futures does again happen asynchronously using `std::async`:

```
template <typename F>
static auto async_adapter(F f)
{
    return [f](auto ... xs) {
        return [=] () {
            return async(launch::async,
                         fut_unwrap(f), xs()...);
        };
    };
}
```

9. Ok, that was maybe kind of a crazy ride that was slightly reminiscent of the movie *"Inception"* because of the lambda expressions that return lambda expressions. We will have a very detailed look at this voodoo-code later. Now let's take the functions `create`, `concat`, and `twice` and make them asynchronous. The function `async_adapter` makes a completely normal function wait for future arguments and return a future result. It is kind of a translating wrapper from the synchronous to the asynchronous world. We apply it to `concat` and `twice`. We must use `asynchronize` on `create` because it shall return a future, but we will feed it with real values instead of futures. The task dependency chain must begin with `create` calls:

```
int main()
{
    auto pcreate (asynchronize(create));
    auto pconcat (async_adapter(concat));
    auto ptwice  (async_adapter(twice));
```

10. Now we have automatically parallelizing functions that have the same names as the original synchronous ones, but with a p-prefix. Let us now set up a complex example dependency tree. First, we create the strings `"foo "` and `"bar "`, which we immediately concatenate to `"foo bar "`. This string is then concatenated with itself using `twice`. Then we create the strings `"this "` and `"that "`, which we concatenate to `"this that "`. Finally, we concatenate the results to `"foo bar foo bar this that "`. The result shall be saved in the variable `callable`. Then finally call `callable().get()` in order to start the computation and wait for its return value, in order to also print that. No computation is done before we call `callable()`, and after this call, all the magic starts:

```
    auto result (
        pconcat(
            ptwice(
                pconcat(
                    pcreate("foo "),
                    pcreate("bar "))),
            pconcat(
                pcreate("this "),
                pcreate("that "))));
    cout << "Setup done. Nothing executed yet.\n";
    cout << result().get() << '\n';
}
```

11. Compiling and running the program shows that all the `create` calls are performed at the same time, and then the other calls are performed. It looks as if they were scheduled intelligently. The whole program runs for 16 seconds. If the steps were not performed in parallel, it would take 30 seconds to complete. Note that we need a system with at least four CPU cores to be able to perform all `create` calls at the same time. If the system had fewer CPU cores, then some calls would have to share CPUs which would of course then consume more time:

```
$ ./chains
Setup done. Nothing executed yet.
3s CREATE "foo "
3s CREATE "bar "
3s CREATE "this "
3s CREATE "that "
5s CONCAT "this " "that "
5s CONCAT "foo " "bar "
3s TWICE  "foo bar "
5s CONCAT "foo bar foo bar " "this that "
foo bar foo bar this that
```

How it works...

A plain serial version of this program without any `async` and `future` magic would look like the following:

```
int main()
{
    string result {
        concat(
            twice(
                concat(
                    create("foo "),
                    create("bar "))),
            concat(
                create("this "),
                create("that "))) };

    cout << result << '\n';
}
```

In this recipe, we wrote the helper functions `async_adapter` and `asynchronize` that helped us create new functions from `create`, `concat`, and `twice`. We called those new asynchronous functions `pcreate`, `pconcat`, and `ptwice`.

Let us first ignore the complexity of the implementation of `async_adapter` and `asynchronize`, in order to first have a look what this got us.

The serial version looks similar to this code:

```
string result {concat( ... )};
cout << result << '\n';
```

The parallelized version looks similar to the following:

```
auto result (pconcat( ... ));
cout << result().get() << '\n';
```

Okay, now we get at the complicated part. The type of the parallelized result is not `string`, but a callable object that returns a `future<string>` on which we can call `get()`. This might indeed look crazy at first.

So, how and *why* did we exactly end up with callable objects that return futures? The problem with our `create`, `concat`, and `twice` methods is, that they are *slow*. (okay, we made them artificially slow, because we tried to model real life tasks that consume a lot of CPU time). But we identified that the dependency tree which describes the data flow has independent parts that could be executed in parallel. Let's have a look at two example schedules:

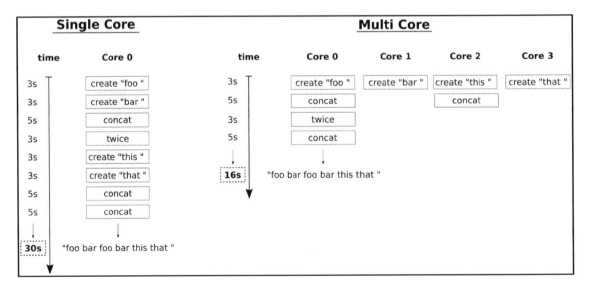

On the left side, we see a *single core* schedule. All the function calls have to be done one after each other because we have only a single CPU. That means, that when `create` costs 3 seconds, `concat` costs 5 seconds and `twice` costs 3 seconds, it will take 30 seconds to get the end result.

On the right side, we see a *parallel schedule* where as much is done in parallel as the dependencies between the function calls allow. In an ideal world with four cores, we can create all substrings at the same time, then concatenate them and so on. The minimal time to get the result with an optimal parallel schedule is 16 seconds. We cannot go faster if we cannot make the function calls themselves faster. With just four CPU cores we can achieve this execution time. We measurably achieved the optimal schedule. How did it work?

We could naively write the following code:

```
auto a (async(launch::async, create, "foo "));
auto b (async(launch::async, create, "bar "));
auto c (async(launch::async, create, "this "));
auto d (async(launch::async, create, "that "));
auto e (async(launch::async, concat, a.get(), b.get()));
auto f (async(launch::async, concat, c.get(), d.get()));
auto g (async(launch::async, twice, e.get()));
auto h (async(launch::async, concat, g.get(), f.get()));
```

This is a good start for a, b, c, and d, which represent the four substrings to begin with. These are created asynchronously in the background. Unfortunately, this code blocks on the line where we initialize e. In order to concatenate a and b, we need to call `get()` on both of them, which *blocks* until these values are *ready*. Obviously, this is not a good idea, because the parallelization stops being parallel on the first `get()` call. We need a better strategy.

Okay, so let us roll out the complicated helper functions we wrote. The first one is `asynchronize`:

```
template <typename F>
static auto asynchronize(F f)
{
    return [f](auto ... xs) {
        return [=] () {
            return async(launch::async, f, xs...);
        };
    };
}
```

When we have a function `int f(int, int)` then we can do the following:

```
auto f2 ( asynchronize(f) );
auto f3 ( f2(1, 2) );
auto f4 ( f3() );
int result { f4.get() };
```

`f2` is our asynchronous version of `f`. It can be called with the same arguments like `f`, because it *mimics* `f`. Then it returns a callable object, which we save in `f3`. `f3` now captures `f` and the arguments `1, 2`, but it did not call anything yet. This is just about the capturing.

When we call `f3()` now, then we finally get a future, because `f3()` does the `async(launch::async, f, 1, 2);` call! In that sense, the semantic meaning of `f3` is *"Take the captured function and the arguments, and throw them together into* `std::async`.".

The inner lambda expression that does not accept any arguments gives us an indirection. With it, we can set up work for parallel dispatch but do not have to call anything that blocks, *yet*. We follow the same principle in the much more complicated function `async_adapter`:

```
template <typename F>
static auto async_adapter(F f)
{
    return [f](auto ... xs) {
        return [=] () {
            return async(launch::async, fut_unwrap(f), xs()...);
        };
    };
}
```

This function does also first return a function that mimics `f` because it accepts the same arguments. Then that function returns a callable object that again accepts no arguments. And then that callable object finally differs from the other helper function.

What does the `async(launch::async, fut_unwrap(f), xs()...);` line mean? The
`xs()...` part means, that all arguments that are saved in pack `xs` are assumed to be
callable objects (like the ones we are creating all the time!), and so they are all called without
arguments. Those callable objects that we are producing all the time themselves produce
future values, on which we can call `get()`. This is where `fut_unwrap` comes into play:

```
template <typename F>
static auto fut_unwrap(F f)
{
    return [f](auto ... xs) {
        return f(xs.get()...);
    };
}
```

`fut_unwrap` just transforms a function `f` into a function object that accepts a range of
arguments. This function object does then call `.get()` on *all* of them and then finally
forwards them to `f`.

Take your time to digest all of this. When we used this in our main function, then the `auto
result (pconcat(...));` call chain did just construct a large callable object that contains
all functions and all arguments. No `async` call was done at this point yet. Then, when we
called `result()`, we *unleashed a little avalanche* of `async` and `.get()` calls that come just in
the right order to not block each other. In fact, no `get()` call happens before not all `async`
calls have been dispatched.

In the end, we can finally call `.get()` on the future value that `result()` returned, and
there we have our final string.

10
Filesystem

In this chapter, we will cover the following recipes:

- Implementing a path normalizer
- Getting canonical file paths from relative paths
- Listing all files in directories
- Implementing a grep-like text search tool
- Implementing an automatic file renamer
- Implementing a disk usage counter
- Calculating statistics about file types
- Implementing a tool that reduces folder size by substituting duplicates with symlinks

Introduction

Working with filesystem paths is always tedious if we don't have a library that helps us because there are many conditions that we need to handle.

Some paths are *absolute*, some are *relative*, and maybe they are not even straightforward because they also contain . (current directory) and . . (parent directory) indirections. Then, at the same time, different operating systems use the slash / to separate directories (Linux, MacOS, and different UNIX derivatives), or the backslash \ (Windows). And of course there are different types of files.

Since every other program that handles filesystem-related things needs such functionality, it is great to have the new filesystem library in the C++17 STL. The best thing about it is that it works the same way for different operating systems, so we don't have to write different code for versions of our programs that support different operating systems.

In this chapter, we will first see how the `path` class works, because it is most central to anything else in this library. Then, we will see how powerful but yet simple to use `directory_iterator` and `recursive_directory_iterator` classes are, while we do useful things with files. In the end, we will use some small and simple example tools that do some real-life tasks related to the filesystem. From this point, it will be easy to build more complex tools.

Implementing a path normalizer

We start this chapter with a very simple example around the `std::filesystem::path` class and a helper function that intelligently normalizes filesystem paths.

The result of this recipe is a little application that takes any filesystem path and returns us the same path in normalized form. Normalized means that we get an absolute path that contains no `.` or `..` path indirections.

While implementing that, we will also see what details we need to pay attention to when working with this basic part of the filesystem library.

How to do it...

In this section, we will implement a program that just accepts a filesystem path as a command-line argument and then prints it in normalized form.

1. Includes come first, and then we declare that we use namespace `std` and `filesystem`.

```
#include <iostream>
#include <filesystem>

using namespace std;
using namespace filesystem;
```

2. In the main function, we check whether the user provided a command-line argument. If that is not the case, we error out and print how to use the program. If a path was provided, we instantiate a `filesystem::path` object from it.

```
int main(int argc, char *argv[])
{
    if (argc != 2) {
        cout << "Usage: " << argv[0] << " <path>\n";
        return 1;
    }
    const path dir {argv[1]};
```

3. Since we can instantiate `path` objects from any string, we cannot be sure if the path really exists on the filesystem of the computer. In order to do that, we can use the `filesystem::exists` function. If it doesn't, we simply error out again.

```
    if (!exists(dir)) {
        cout << "Path " << dir << " does not exist.\n";
        return 1;
    }
```

4. Okay, at this point, we are pretty sure that the user provided some *existing* path knowing that we can ask for a normalized version of it, which we then print. `filesystem::canonical` returns us another `path` object. We could print it directly, but the `path` type overload of the `<<` operator surrounds paths with quotation marks. In order to avoid that, we can print a path through its `.c_str()` or `.string()` method.

```
    cout << canonical(dir).c_str() << '\n';
}
```

5. Let's compile the program and play with it. When we execute it in my home directory on the relative path `"src"`, it will print the full absolute path.

```
$ ./normalizer src
/Users/tfc/src
```

6. When we run the program in my home directory again, but give it a quirky relative path description that first enters my `Desktop` folder, then steps out of it again using `..`, then enters the `Documents` folder and steps out again in order to finally enter the `src` directory, the program prints the *same* path as before!

```
$ ./normalizer Desktop/../Documents/../src
/Users/tfc/src
```

How it works...

As a starter on `std::filesystem`, this recipe is still fairly short and straightforward. We initialized a `path` object from a string that contains a filesystem path description. The `std::filesystem::path` class plays a very central role whenever we use the filesystem library because most of the functions and classes relate to it.

Using the `filesystem::exists` function, we were able to check if the path really exists. Up to that point, we could not be sure about that, because it is indeed possible to create `path` objects that do not relate to an existing filesystem object. `exists` just accepts a `path` instance and returns `true` if it really exists. The function is already able to determine itself if we gave it an absolute or a relative path, which makes it very comfortable to use.

Finally, we used `filesystem::canonical` on the directory in order to print it in normalized form.

```
path canonical(const path& p, const path& base = current_path());
```

`canonical` accepts a path and as an optional second argument, it accepts another path. The second path `base` is prepended to path p if p is a relative path. After doing that, `canonical` tries to remove any `.` and `..` path indirections.

While printing, we used the `.c_str()` method on the canonicalized path. The reason for this is that the overload of `operator<<` for output streams surrounds paths with quotation marks, which we may not always want.

There's more...

`canonical` throws a `filesystem_error` type exception if the path we want to canonicalize does not exist. In order to prevent that, we checked our filesystem path with `exists`. But was that check really sufficient to avoid getting unhandled exceptions? No.

Both `exists` and `canonical` can throw `bad_alloc` exceptions. If those hit us, one could argue that the program is doomed anyway. A far more critical, and also much more probable problem would occur if, between us checking if the file exists and canonicalizing it, someone else renames or deletes the underlying file! In that case, `canonical` would throw a `filesystem_error`, although we checked for the file's existence before.

Most filesystem functions have an additional overload that takes the same arguments, but also an `std::error_code` reference.

```
path canonical(const path& p, const path& base = current_path());
path canonical(const path& p, error_code& ec);
path canonical(const std::filesystem::path& p,
               const std::filesystem::path& base,
               std::error_code& ec );
```

This way we can choose if we surround our filesystem function calls with `try-catch` constructs or check the errors manually. Note that this only changes the behavior of *filesystem-related* errors! With and without the `ec` parameter, more fundamental exceptions, for example, `bad_alloc`, can still be thrown if the system runs out of memory.

Getting canonical file paths from relative paths

In the last recipe, we already canonicalized/normalized paths. The `filesystem::path` class is, of course, capable of more things than just holding and checking paths. It also helps us in composing paths from strings easily, and also to decompose them again.

At this point, `path` does already abstract operating system details away from us, but there are also certain instances where we still need to keep such details in mind.

We will see how to deal with paths and their composition/decomposition by playing around with absolute and relative paths.

How to do it...

In this section, we will play around with absolute and relative paths in order to see the strengths of the `path` class and the helper functions around it.

1. First, we include all the necessary headers and declare that we use namespace `std` and `sfilesystem`.

```
#include <iostream>
#include <filesystem>

using namespace std;
using namespace filesystem;
```

2. Then, we declare an example path. At this point, it is not important that the text file it refers to really exists. There are some functions, however, that throw exceptions if the underlying file does not exist.

```
int main()
{
    path p {"testdir/foobar.txt"};
```

3. We will have a look at four different filesystem library functions now. `current_path` returns us the path the program is currently executed in, the *working directory*. `absolute` accepts a relative path like our path `p` and returns the absolute, nonambiguous path in the whole filesystem. `system_complete` does practically the same as `absolute` on Linux, MacOS, or UNIX-like operating systems. On Windows, we would get the absolute path additionally prepended by the disk volume letter (for example, `"C:"`). `canonical` does again the same as `absolute` does, but then additionally removes any `"."` (short for *"this directory"*) or `".."` (short for *"one directory up"*) indirections. We will play with such indirections in the following steps:

```
cout << "current_path      : " << current_path()
     << "\nabsolute_path    : " << absolute(p)
     << "\nsystem_complete  : " << system_complete(p)
     << "\ncanonical(p)     : " << canonical(p)
     << '\n';
```

4. Another nice thing about the `path` class is that it overloads the `/` operator. This way we can concatenate folder names and filenames using `/` and compose paths from that. Let's try it out and print a composed path.

```
cout << path{"testdir"} / "foobar.txt" << '\n';
```

5. Let's play with `canonical` and composed paths. By giving `canonical` a relative path such as `"foobar.txt"` and a composed absolute path `current_path() / "testdir"`, it should return us the existing absolute path. In another call, we give it our path p (which is `"testdir/foobar.txt"`) and provide it an absolute path that is `current_path()`, which directs us into `"testdir"` and up again. This should be the same as `current_path()`, because of the indirection. In both calls, `canonical` should return us the same absolute path.

```
cout << "canonical testdir    : "
     << canonical("foobar.txt",
                  current_path() / "testdir")
     << "\ncanonical testdir 2 : "
     << canonical(p, current_path() / "testdir/..")
     << '\n';
```

6. We can also test for the equivalence of two paths that are not canonical. `equivalence` canonicalizes the paths, which it accepts as arguments and returns `true` if they describe the same path after all. For this test, the path must really *exist*, otherwise, it throws an exception.

```
cout << "equivalence: "
     << equivalent("testdir/foobar.txt",
                   "testdir/../testdir/foobar.txt")
     << '\n';
}
```

7. Compiling and running the program yields the following output. `current_path()` returns the home folder on my laptop because I executed the application from there. Our relative path p has been prepended with this directory by `absolute_path`, `system_complete`, and `canonical`. We see that `absolute_path` and `system_complete` yield exactly the same path on my system because it is a Mac (it would be the same on Linux). On a Windows machine, `system_complete` would have prepended `"C:"`, or whatever drive the working directory is located in.

```
$ ./canonical_filepath
current_path    : "/Users/tfc"
absolute_path   : "/Users/tfc/testdir/foobar.txt"
system_complete : "/Users/tfc/testdir/foobar.txt"
canonical(p)    : "/Users/tfc/testdir/foobar.txt"
"testdir/foobar.txt"
canonical testdir   : "/Users/tfc/testdir/foobar.txt"
canonical testdir 2 : "/Users/tfc/testdir/foobar.txt"
equivalence: 1
```

8. We do not handle any exceptions in our short program. If we remove the `foobar.txt` file in the `testdir` directory, then the program aborts its execution due to an exception. The `canonical` function requires the path to exist. There is also a `weakly_canonical` function that does not come with this requirement.

```
$ ./canonial_filepath
current_path    : "/Users/tfc"
absolute_path   : "/Users/tfc/testdir/foobar.txt"
system_complete : "/Users/tfc/testdir/foobar.txt"
terminate called after throwing an instance of
'std::filesystem::v1::__cxx11::filesystem_error'
   what():  filesystem error: cannot canonicalize:
   No such file or directory [testdir/foobar.txt] [/Users/tfc]
```

How it works...

The goal of this recipe is to see how easy it is to compose new paths on the fly. This is mainly because the `path` class has a handy overload for the / operator. In addition to that, the filesystem functions get along well with relative and absolute paths, as well as with paths that contain . and .. indirections.

There is quite a jungle of functions that return parts of a `path` instance, with or without transformations. We are not going to list all functions there are here because a short glance into the C++ reference is the best way to get an oversight.

The member functions of the `path` class, however, might be worth a closer look. Let's see which part of a path is returned by what member function of `path`. The following diagram also shows how Windows paths are slightly different from UNIX/Linux paths.

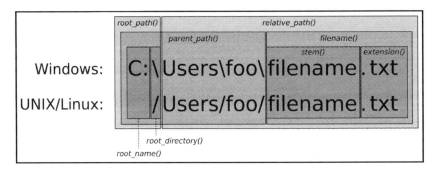

You can see that the diagram shows what the member functions of `path` return for an *absolute* path. For *relative* paths, `root_path`, `root_name`, and `root_directory` are empty. `relative_path` then just returns the path if it is relative already.

Listing all files in directories

Of course, every operating system that offers filesystem support also comes with some kind of utility that does just *list* all files within a directory in the filesystem. The simplest examples are the `ls` command on Linux, MacOS, and other UNIX-related operating systems. In DOS and Windows, there is the `dir` command. Both list all files in a directory and provide supplemental information such as file size, permissions, and so on.

Reimplementing such a tool is, however, also a nice standard task to get going with directory and file traversal. So, let's just do that!

Our own `ls`/`dir` utility will be able to list all items in a directory by name, indicate what kind of items there are, list their access permission flags, and display the number of bytes they occupy on the filesystem.

How to do it...

In this section, we will implement a little tool that lists all files in any user provided directory. It will not only list the filenames, but also their type, size, and access permissions.

1. First, we need to include some headers and declare that we use the namespaces `std` and `filesystem` by default.

```
#include <iostream>
#include <sstream>
#include <iomanip>
#include <numeric>
#include <algorithm>
#include <vector>
#include <filesystem>

using namespace std;
using namespace filesystem;
```

2. One helper function that we are going to need is `file_info`. It accepts a `directory_entry` object reference and extracts the path from it, as well as a `file_status` object (using the `status` function), which contains file type and permission information. Finally, it also extracts the size of the entry if it is a regular file. For directories or other special files, we plainly return a size of 0. All this information is bundled into a tuple.

```
static tuple<path, file_status, size_t>
file_info(const directory_entry &entry)
{
    const auto fs (status(entry));
    return {entry.path(),
            fs,
            is_regular_file(fs) ? file_size(entry.path()) : 0u};
}
```

3. Another helper function that we will need is `type_char`. A path cannot only represent directories and simple text/binary files. Operating systems provide a variety of other types that abstract something else, such as hardware device interfaces in the form of so-called character/block files. The STL filesystem library provides a lot of predicate functions for them. This way we can return the letter `'d'` for directories, the letter `'f'` for regular files, and so on.

```
static char type_char(file_status fs)
{
    if      (is_directory(fs))       { return 'd'; }
    else if (is_symlink(fs))         { return 'l'; }
    else if (is_character_file(fs))  { return 'c'; }
    else if (is_block_file(fs))      { return 'b'; }
    else if (is_fifo(fs))            { return 'p'; }
    else if (is_socket(fs))          { return 's'; }
    else if (is_other(fs))           { return 'o'; }
    else if (is_regular_file(fs))    { return 'f'; }
    return '?';
}
```

4. Yet another helper we will need is the `rwx` function. It accepts a `perms` variable (which is just an `enum` class type from the filesystem library) and returns a string such as `"rwxrwxrwx"` that describes the file's permission settings. The first group of `"rwx"` characters describes the *read, write, and execution* permissions for the owner of the file. The next group describes the same rights for all users that are part of the *user group* the file belongs to. The last character group describes which rights everyone else has for accessing the file. A string such as `"rwxrwxrwx"` means that everyone can access the object in any way. `"rw-r--r--"` means that only the owner can read and modify the file, while anyone else can only read it. We just compose a string from such read/write/execute character values, permission bit by permission bit. A lambda expression helps us with the repetitive work of checking if the `perms` variable p contains a specific owner bit and then returns `'-'` or the right character.

```
static string rwx(perms p)
{
    auto check ([p](perms bit, char c) {
        return (p & bit) == perms::none ? '-' : c;
    });
    return {check(perms::owner_read,    'r'),
            check(perms::owner_write,   'w'),
            check(perms::owner_exec,    'x'),
            check(perms::group_read,    'r'),
            check(perms::group_write,   'w'),
            check(perms::group_exec,    'x'),
            check(perms::others_read,   'r'),
            check(perms::others_write,  'w'),
            check(perms::others_exec,   'x')};
}
```

5. Finally, the last helper function accepts an integral file size and converts it to a better to read form. We just ignore the period while dividing numbers down and floor them to the nearest kilo, mega, or giga boundary.

```
static string size_string(size_t size)
{
    stringstream ss;
    if         (size >= 1000000000) {
        ss << (size / 1000000000) << 'G';
    } else if (size >= 1000000)     {
        ss << (size / 1000000) << 'M';
    } else if (size >= 1000)        {
        ss << (size / 1000) << 'K';
    } else { ss << size << 'B'; }
    return ss.str();
}
```

6. Now we can finally implement the main function. We begin with checking if the user provided a path in the command line. If he didn't, we just take the current directory ".". Then, we check if the directory exists. If it doesn't, we can't possibly list any files.

```
int main(int argc, char *argv[])
{
    path dir {argc > 1 ? argv[1] : "."};
    if (!exists(dir)) {
        cout << "Path " << dir << " does not exist.\n";
        return 1;
    }
}
```

7. Now, we will fill a `vector` with file information tuples just like our first helper function `file_info` returns from `directory_entry` objects. We instantiate a `directory_iterator` and give its constructor the `path` object, which we created in the last step. While iterating with the directory iterator, we transform the `directory_entry` objects to file information tuples and insert them into the vector.

```
vector<tuple<path, file_status, size_t>> items;
transform(directory_iterator{dir}, {},
    back_inserter(items), file_info);
```

8. Now we have all information saved in the vector items and can simply print it using all the helper functions we wrote.

```cpp
for (const auto &[path, status, size] : items) {
    cout << type_char(status)
        << rwx(status.permissions()) << " "
        << setw(4) << right << size_string(size)
        << " " << path.filename().c_str()
        << '\n';
}
}
```

9. Compiling and running the project with a file path in the offline version of the C++ documentation yields the following output. We see that the folder only contains directories and plain files because there are only 'd' and 'f' entries as first characters of all output lines. These files have different access permissions, and of course different sizes. Note that the files appear in alphabetical order of their names, but we cannot really rely on that because alphabetic ordering is not required by the C++17 standard.

```
$ ./list ~/Documents/cpp_reference/en/cpp
drwxrwxr-x     0B   algorithm
frw-r--r--    88K   algorithm.html
drwxrwxr-x     0B   atomic
frw-r--r--    35K   atomic.html
drwxrwxr-x     0B   chrono
frw-r--r--    34K   chrono.html
frw-r--r--    21K   comment.html
frw-r--r--    21K   comments.html
frw-r--r--   220K   compiler_support.html
drwxrwxr-x     0B   concept
frw-r--r--    67K   concept.html
drwxr-xr-x     0B   container
frw-r--r--   285K   container.html
drwxrwxr-x     0B   error
frw-r--r--    52K   error.html
```

How it works...

In this recipe, we iterated over files, and for every file, we checked its status and size. While all our per-file operations are fairly straightforward and simple, our actual directory traversal looked a bit magic.

In order to traverse our directory, we just instantiated a `directory_iterator` and then iterated over it. Traversing a directory is fantastically simple with the filesystem library.

```
for (const directory_entry &e : directory_iterator{dir}) {
    // do something
}
```

There is not much more to say about this class apart from the following things:

- It visits every element of the directory once
- The order in which the directory elements are iterated is unspecified
- Directory elements . and .. are already filtered out

However, it might be noticeable that `directory_iterator` seems to be an *iterator*, and an *iterable range* at the same time. Why? In the minimal `for` loop example we just had a look at, it was used as an iterable range. In the actual recipe code, we used it like an iterator:

```
transform(directory_iterator{dir}, {},
          back_inserter(items), file_info);
```

The truth is, it is just an iterator class type, but the `std::begin` and `std::end` functions provide overloads for this type. This way we can call the `begin` and `end` function on this kind of iterator and they return us iterators again. That might look strange at first sight, but it makes this class more useful.

Implementing a grep-like text search tool

Most operating systems come equipped with some kind of local search engine. Users can fire it up with some keyboard shortcut and then just enter what local file they are looking for.

Before such features came up, command-line users already searched through files with tools such as `grep` or `awk`. The user can simply type "`grep -r foobar .`" and the tool will crawl recursively through the current directory and find any file that contains the "`foobar`" string.

In this recipe, we will implement exactly such an application. Our little grep clone will just accept a pattern from the command line, and then recursively search through the directory we are in at the time of the application start. It will then print the name of every file that matches our pattern. The pattern matching will be applied linewise, so we can also print on which exact line numbers a file is matching the pattern.

How to do it...

We will implement a little tool that searches for user-provided text patterns in files. The tool works similar to the UNIX tool `grep`, but will not be as mature and powerful, for the sake of simplicity.

1. First, we need to include all the necessary headers and declare that we use namespace `std` and `filesystem`.

```
#include <iostream>
#include <fstream>
#include <regex>
#include <vector>
#include <string>
#include <filesystem>

using namespace std;
using namespace filesystem;
```

2. We implement a helper function first. It accepts a file path and a regular expression object that describes the pattern we are looking for. Then, we instantiate a `vector` that shall contain pairs of matching line numbers and their content. And we instantiate an input file stream object from which we will read and pattern-match the content, line by line.

```
static vector<pair<size_t, string>>
matches(const path &p, const regex &re)
{
    vector<pair<size_t, string>> d;
    ifstream is {p.c_str()};
```

3. We traverse the file line by line using the `getline` function. `regex_search` returns `true` if the string contains our pattern. If this is the case, then we put the line number and the string into the vector. Finally, we return all collected matches.

```
    string s;
    for (size_t line {1}; getline(is, s); ++line) {
        if (regex_search(begin(s), end(s), re)) {
            d.emplace_back(line, move(s));
        }
    }
    return d;
}
```

4. In the main function, we first check whether the user provided a command-line argument that we can use as the pattern. If not, we error out.

```
int main(int argc, char *argv[])
{
    if (argc != 2) {
        cout << "Usage: " << argv[0] << " <pattern>\n";
        return 1;
    }
```

5. Next, we construct a regular expression object from the input pattern. If the pattern is not a valid regular expression, this would lead to an exception. If such an exception occurs, we catch it and error out.

```
    regex pattern;
    try { pattern = regex{argv[1]}; }
    catch (const regex_error &e) {
        cout << "Invalid regular expression provided.n";
        return 1;
    }
```

6. Now, we can finally iterate over the filesystem and look for pattern matches. We use `recursive_directory_iterator` to iterate over all the files in the working directory. It works exactly like `directory_iterator` in the previous recipe, but it also descends down into subdirectories. This way we don't have to manage recursion. On every entry, we call our helper function `matches`.

```
    for (const auto &entry :
            recursive_directory_iterator{current_path()}) {
        auto ms (matches(entry.path(), pattern));
```

7. For every match (if any) we print the file path, its line number, and the matching line's complete content.

```
        for (const auto &[number, content] : ms) {
            cout << entry.path().c_str() << ":" << number
                 << " - " << content << '\n';
        }
    }
}
```

8. Let's prepare a file called `"foobar.txt"`, which contains some test lines we can search for.

```
foo
bar
baz
```

9. Compiling and running yields the following output. I launched the app in the `/Users/tfc/testdir` folder on my laptop, first with the pattern `"bar"`. Within that directory, it found the second line of our `foobar.txt` file and another file `"text1.txt"` that is located in `testdir/dir1`.

```
$ ./grepper bar
/Users/tfc/testdir/dir1/text1.txt:1 - foo bar bla blubb
/Users/tfc/testdir/foobar.txt:2 - bar
```

10. Launching the app again, but this time with the pattern `"baz"`, it finds the third line of our example text file.

```
$ ./grepper baz
/Users/tfc/testdir/foobar.txt:3 - baz
```

How it works...

Setting up and using a regular expression in order to filter the content of files is certainly the main task of this recipe. However, let's concentrate on `recursive_directory_iterator` because filtering recursively iterated files was just our motivation to use this special iterator class in this recipe.

Just like `directory_iterator`, `recursive_directory_iterator` iterates over elements of a directory. Its specialty is to do this recursively, as its name tells. Whenever it hits a filesystem element that is a *directory*, it will yield a `directory_entry` instance to this path, but then also descend down into it in order to iterate its children, too.

`recursive_directory_iterator` has some interesting member functions:

- `depth()`: This tells us how many levels the iterator has currently descended down into subdirectories.
- `recursion_pending()`: This tells us if the iterator is going to descend down after the element it currently points to.

- `disable_recursion_pending()`: This can be called to keep the iterator from descending into the next subdirectory if it is currently pointing to a directory into which it would descend. This means that calling this method has no effect if we call it *too early*.
- `pop()`: This aborts the current recursion level and goes one level up in the directory hierarchy to continue from there.

There's more...

Another thing to know about is the `directory_options` enum class. The constructor of `recursive_directory_iterator` does indeed accept a value of this type as a second argument. The default value which we have been implicitly using is `directory_options::none`. The other values are:

- `follow_directory_symlink`: This allows the recursive iterator to follow symbolic links to directories
- `skip_permission_denied`: This tells the iterator to skip directories that would otherwise result in errors because permission to access is denied by the filesystem

These options can be combined with the `|` operator.

Implementing an automatic file renamer

This recipe is motivated by a situation I find myself in pretty often. When collecting picture files from holidays, for example, from different friends and also different photo devices in one folder, the file endings often look different. Some JPEG files have a `.jpg` extension, some have `.jpeg`, and some others even have `.JPEG`.

Some people might prefer to homogenize all extensions. It would be useful to rename all files with a single command. At the same time, we could remove spaces `' '` and substitute them by underscores `'_'`, for example.

In this recipe, we will implement such a tool and call it `renamer`. It will accept a range of input patterns and their substitutes like this:

```
$ renamer jpeg jpg JPEG jpg
```

In that case, renamer will iterate recursively through the current directory and search for the patterns `jpeg` and `JPEG` in all filenames. It will substitute both with `jpg`.

How to do it...

We will implement a tool that recursively scans all files within a directory and matches their filenames with patterns. All matches are replaced with user provided tokens and the affected files are renamed accordingly.

1. First, we need to include a few headers and declare that we use namespaces `std` and `filesystem`.

```
#include <iostream>
#include <regex>
#include <vector>
#include <filesystem>

using namespace std;
using namespace filesystem;
```

2. We implement a short helper function that accepts an input file path in the form of a string and a range of replacement pairs. Each replacement pair consists of a pattern and its replacement. While looping through the replacement range, we use `regex_replace` to feed it with the input string and let it return the transformed string. Afterward, we return the resulting string.

```
template <typename T>
static string replace(string s, const T &replacements)
{
    for (const auto &[pattern, repl] : replacements) {
        s = regex_replace(s, pattern, repl);
    }
    return s;
}
```

3. In the main function, we first validate the command line. We accept command-line arguments in *pairs* because we want patterns together with their replacements. The first element of `argv` is always the executable name. This means that if the user provides at least one pair or more, then `argc` must be *odd* and not smaller than 3.

```
int main(int argc, char *argv[])
{
    if (argc < 3 || argc % 2 != 1) {
        cout << "Usage: " << argv[0]
            << " <pattern> <replacement> ...\n";
        return 1;
    }
```

4. Once we checked that there are pairs of input, we will fill a vector with these.

```
vector<pair<regex, string>> patterns;
for (int i {1}; i < argc; i += 2) {
    patterns.emplace_back(argv[i], argv[i + 1]);
}
```

5. Now we can iterate over the filesystem. For the sake of simplicity, we just define the application's current path as the directory to iterate over.
For every directory entry, we extract its original path to the `opath` variable. Then, we take only the filename without the rest of this path and transform it according to the list of patterns and replacements we collected before. We take a copy of `opath`, call it `rpath`, and replace its filename part with the new filename.

```
for (const auto &entry :
        recursive_directory_iterator{current_path()}) {
    path opath {entry.path()};
    string rname {replace(opath.filename().string(),
                          patterns)};
    path rpath {opath};
    rpath.replace_filename(rname);
```

6. For all files that are affected by our patterns, we print that we rename them. In case the resulting filename from replacing the patterns does already exist, we can't proceed. Let's just skip such files. We could of course alternatively just append some number to the path or something else to resolve the name clash.

```
if (opath != rpath) {
    cout << opath.c_str() << " --> "
         << rpath.filename().c_str() << '\n';
    if (exists(rpath)) {
        cout << "Error: Can't rename."
                " Destination file exists.\n";
    } else {
        rename(opath, rpath);
    }
}
}
}
```

7. Compiling and running the program in an example directory yields the following output. I have put some JPEG pictures into the directory but have given them different name endings jpg, jpeg, and JPEG. Then, I executed the program with the patterns jpeg and JPEG and chose jpg as the replacement for both. The result is a folder with homogenous filename extensions.

```
$ ls
birthday_party.jpeg    holiday_in_dubai.jpg  holiday_in_spain.jpg
trip_to_new_york.JPEG
$ ../renamer jpeg jpg JPEG jpg
/Users/tfc/pictures/birthday_party.jpeg --> birthday_party.jpg
/Users/tfc/pictures/trip_to_new_york.JPEG --> trip_to_new_york.jpg
$ ls
birthday_party.jpg    holiday_in_dubai.jpg holiday_in_spain.jpg
trip_to_new_york.jpg
```

Implementing a disk usage counter

We already implemented a tool that works like ls on Linux/MacOS, or dir on Windows, but just as these tools, it doesn't print the file size for *directories*.

In order to get the size equivalent of a directory, we would have to descend down into it and sum up the size of all files that it contains.

In this recipe, we will implement a tool that does just that. The tool can be run on any folder and will summarize the accumulated size of all directory entries.

How to do it...

In this section, we will implement an app that iterates over a directory and lists the file size of each entry. This is simple for regular files, but if we are looking at a directory entry that itself is a directory, then we have to look into it and summarize the size of all the files it holds.

1. First, we need to include all the necessary headers and declare that we use namespace `std` and `filesystem`.

```
#include <iostream>
#include <sstream>
#include <iomanip>
#include <numeric>
#include <filesystem>

using namespace std;
using namespace filesystem;
```

2. Then we implement a helper function that accepts a `directory_entry` as an argument and returns its size in the filesystem. If it is not a directory, we simply return the file size calculated by `file_size`.

```
static size_t entry_size(const directory_entry &entry)
{
    if (!is_directory(entry)) { return file_size(entry); }
```

3. If it is a directory, we need to iterate over all its entries and calculate their size. We end up calling our own `entry_size` helper function recursively if we stumble upon subdirectories again.

```
    return accumulate(directory_iterator{entry}, {}, 0u,
        [](size_t accum, const directory_entry &e) {
            return accum + entry_size(e);
        });
}
```

4. For better readability, we use the same `size_string` function as in other recipes in this chapter. It just divides large file sizes in to shorter and nicer ones to read strings with kilo, mega, or giga suffix.

```
static string size_string(size_t size)
{
    stringstream ss;
    if         (size >= 1000000000) {
        ss << (size / 1000000000) << 'G';
    } else if (size >= 1000000)    {
        ss << (size / 1000000) << 'M';
    } else if (size >= 1000)       {
        ss << (size / 1000) << 'K';
    } else { ss << size << 'B'; }
    return ss.str();
}
```

5. The first thing we need to do in the main function is to check whether the user provided a filesystem path on the command line. If that is not the case, we just take the current folder. Before proceeding, we check whether it exists.

```
int main(int argc, char *argv[])
{
    path dir {argc > 1 ? argv[1] : "."};
    if (!exists(dir)) {
        cout << "Path " << dir << " does not exist.\n";
        return 1;
    }
```

6. Now, we can iterate over all directory entries and print their sizes and names.

```
    for (const auto &entry : directory_iterator{dir}) {
        cout << setw(5) << right
             << size_string(entry_size(entry))
             << " " << entry.path().filename().c_str()
             << '\n';
    }
}
```

7. Compiling and running the program yields the following results. I launched it in a folder in the C++ offline reference. As it contains subfolders too, our recursive file size summary helper is immediately helpful.

```
$ ./file_size ~/Documents/cpp_reference/en/
  19M c
  12K c.html
 147M cpp
  17K cpp.html
  22K index.html
  22K Main_Page.html
```

How it works...

The whole program revolves around using `file_size` on regular files. If the program sees a directory, it recursively descends down into it and calls `file_size` on all its entries.

The only thing we did to distinguish if we call `file_size` directly or if we need the recursion strategy was asking the `is_directory` predicate. This works well for directories that only contain regular files and directories.

As simple as our example program is, it would crash under the following conditions, because of unhandled exceptions:

- `file_size` only works on regular files and symbolic links. It throws an exception in any other case.
- Although `file_size` works on symbolic links, it *still* throws an exception if we call it on a *broken* symbolic link.

In order to make this example recipe program more mature, we need more defensive programming against the wrong type of files and handling of exceptions.

Calculating statistics about file types

In the last recipe, we implemented a tool that lists the size of all members of any directory.

In this recipe, we will be counting sizes recursively, too, but this time we will accumulate the size of each file to their filename *extension*. This way we can print the user a table that lists how many files of each file type we have, and what the average size of such file types is.

How to do it...

In this section, we will implement a little tool that recursively iterates over a given directory. While doing that, it counts the number and size of all files, grouped by their extensions. Finally, it prints which filename extensions exist within that directory, how many there are per extension, and their average file size.

1. We need to include necessary headers and we declare that we use namespace `std` and `filesystem`.

```
#include <iostream>
#include <sstream>
#include <iomanip>
#include <map>
#include <filesystem>

using namespace std;
using namespace filesystem;
```

2. The `size_string` function was already helpful in other recipes. It transforms file sizes to human-readable strings.

```
static string size_string(size_t size)
{
    stringstream ss;
    if          (size >= 1000000000) {
        ss << (size / 1000000000) << 'G';
    } else if (size >= 1000000)     {
        ss << (size / 1000000) << 'M';
    } else if (size >= 1000)        {
        ss << (size / 1000) << 'K';
    } else { ss << size << 'B'; }
    return ss.str();
}
```

3. Then, we implement a helper function that accepts a `path` object as its argument and iterates over all files within that path. On its way, it collects all information in a map that maps from filename extensions to pairs that contain the total number and accumulated size of all files that have the same extension.

```
static map<string, pair<size_t, size_t>> ext_stats(const path &dir)
{
    map<string, pair<size_t, size_t>> m;
    for (const auto &entry :
            recursive_directory_iterator{dir}) {
```

4. If a directory entry is a directory itself, we skip it. Skipping it at this point does not mean that we are not recursively descending into it. `recursive_directory_iterator` still does that, but we do not want to look at the directory entries themselves.

```
        const path        p {entry.path()};
        const file_status fs {status(p)};
        if (is_directory(fs)) { continue; }
```

5. Next, we extract the extension part of the directory entry string. If it has no extension, we simply skip it.

```
        const string ext {p.extension().string()};
        if (ext.length() == 0) { continue; }
```

6. Next, we calculate the size of the file we are looking at. Then, we look up the aggregate object in the map for this extension. If there are yet none at this point, it is created implicitly. We simply increment the file count and add the file size to the size accumulator.

```
        const size_t size {file_size(p)};

        auto &[size_accum, count] = m[ext];
        size_accum += size;
        count       += 1;
    }
```

7. Afterward, we return the map.

```
        return m;
    }
```

8. In the main function, we take either a user-provided path from the command
line or the current directory. Of course, we need to check whether it
exists because it would not make sense to continue otherwise.

```
int main(int argc, char *argv[])
{
    path dir {argc > 1 ? argv[1] : "."};
    if (!exists(dir)) {
        cout << "Path " << dir << " does not exist.\n";
        return 1;
    }
```

9. We can immediately iterate over the map that ext_stats gives us. Because the
accum_size items in the map contain the sum of all files with the same
extension, we divide this sum by the total number of such files before printing it.

```
    for (const auto &[ext, stats] : ext_stats(dir)) {
        const auto &[accum_size, count] = stats;
        cout << setw(15) << left << ext << ": "
             << setw(4) << right << count
             << " items, avg size "
             << setw(4) << size_string(accum_size / count)
             << '\n';
    }
}
```

10. Compiling and running the program yields the following output. I gave it a
folder from the offline C++ reference as a command-line argument.

```
$ ./file_type ~/Documents/cpp_reference/
.css            :    2 items, avg size  41K
.gif            :    7 items, avg size 902B
.html           : 4355 items, avg size  38K
.js             :    3 items, avg size   4K
.php            :    1 items, avg size 739B
.png            :   34 items, avg size   2K
.svg            :   53 items, avg size   6K
.ttf            :    2 items, avg size 421K
```

Implementing a tool that reduces folder size by substituting duplicates with symlinks

There are a lot of tools that compress data in various ways. The most famous examples for file packing algorithms/formats are ZIP and RAR. Such tools try to reduce the size of files by reducing internal redundancy.

Before compressing files in archives, a very simple way to reduce disk usage is just *deleting duplicate* files. In this recipe, we will implement a little tool that crawls a directory recursively. While crawling, it will look for files that have the same content. If it finds such files, it will remove all duplicates but one. All removed files will be substituted with symbolic links that point to the now unique file. This saves spaces without any compression, while at the same time preserving all data.

How to do it...

In this section, we will implement a little tool that finds out which files in a directory are duplicates of each other. With that knowledge, it will remove all but one of all duplicated files, and substitute them with symbolic links, which reduces the folder size.

 Make sure to have a *backup* of your system's data. We will be playing with STL functions that remove files. A simply *misspelled* path in such a program can lead to a program that greedily removes too many files in unwanted ways.

1. First, we need to include the necessary headers and then we declare that we use namespace std and filesystem by default.

```
#include <iostream>
#include <fstream>
#include <unordered_map>
#include <filesystem>

using namespace std;
using namespace filesystem;
```

2. In order to find out which files are duplicates of each other, we will construct a hash map that maps from hashes of file content to the path of the first file from which that hash was generated. It would be a better idea to use a production hash algorithm for files such as MD5 or an SHA variant. In order to keep the recipe clean and simple, we just read the whole file into a string and then use the same hash function object that `unordered_map` already uses for strings to calculate hashes.

```
static size_t hash_from_path(const path &p)
{
    ifstream is {p.c_str(),
                    ios::in | ios::binary};
    if (!is) { throw errno; }
    string s;
    is.seekg(0, ios::end);
    s.reserve(is.tellg());
    is.seekg(0, ios::beg);
    s.assign(istreambuf_iterator<char>{is}, {});
    return hash<string>{}(s);
}
```

3. Then we implement the function that constructs such a hash map and deletes duplicates. It iterates recursively through a directory and its subdirectories.

```
static size_t reduce_dupes(const path &dir)
{
    unordered_map<size_t, path> m;
    size_t count {0};
    for (const auto &entry :
            recursive_directory_iterator{dir}) {
```

4. For every directory entry, it checks whether it is a directory itself. All directory items are skipped. For every file, we generate its hash value and try to insert it into the hash map. If the hash map already contains the same hash, then this means that we already inserted a file with the same hash. This means that we just found a duplicate! In case of a clash during insertion, the second value in the pair that `try_emplace` returns is `false`.

```
const path p {entry.path()};
if (is_directory(p)) { continue; }
const auto &[it, success] =
    m.try_emplace(hash_from_path(p), p);
```

5. Using the return values from `try_emplace`, we can tell the user that we just inserted a file because we have seen its hash for the first time. In case we found a duplicate, we tell the user what other file it is a duplicate of and delete it. After deletion, we create a symbolic link that replaces the duplicate.

```
if (!success) {
    cout << "Removed " << p.c_str()
         << " because it is a duplicate of "
         << it->second.c_str() << '\n';
    remove(p);
    create_symlink(absolute(it->second), p);
    ++count;
}
```

6. After the filesystem iteration, we return the number of files we deleted and replaced with symlinks.

```
    }
    return count;
}
```

7. In the main function, we make sure that the user provided a directory on the command line, and that this directory exists.

```
int main(int argc, char *argv[])
{
    if (argc != 2) {
        cout << "Usage: " << argv[0] << " <path>\n";
        return 1;
    }
    path dir {argv[1]};
```

```
    if (!exists(dir)) {
        cout << "Path " << dir << " does not exist.\n";
        return 1;
    }
```

8. The only thing we need to do now is to call `reduce_dupes` on this directory and print how many files it deleted.

```
    const size_t dupes {reduce_dupes(dir)};
    cout << "Removed " << dupes << " duplicates.\n";
}
```

9. Compiling and running the program on an example directory that contains some duplicate files looks like the following. I used the `du` tool to check the folder size before and after launching our program to demonstrate that the approach works.

```
$ du -sh dupe_dir
1.1M dupe_dir
$ ./dupe_compress dupe_dir
Removed dupe_dir/dir2/bar.jpg because it is a duplicate of
dupe_dir/dir1/bar.jpg
Removed dupe_dir/dir2/base10.png because it is a duplicate of
dupe_dir/dir1/base10.png
Removed dupe_dir/dir2/baz.jpeg because it is a duplicate of
dupe_dir/dir1/baz.jpeg
Removed dupe_dir/dir2/feed_fish.jpg because it is a duplicate of
dupe_dir/dir1/feed_fish.jpg
Removed dupe_dir/dir2/foo.jpg because it is a duplicate of
dupe_dir/dir1/foo.jpg
Removed dupe_dir/dir2/fox.jpg because it is a duplicate of
dupe_dir/dir1/fox.jpg
Removed 6 duplicates.
$ du -sh dupe_dir
584K dupe_dir
```

How it works...

We used the `create_symlink` function in order to make a filesystem entry point to another file in the filesystem. This way we can avoid having duplicate files. We could also have set a hard link using `create_hard_link`. Semantically, this is similar, but hard links have other technical implications than soft links. Different filesystem formats might not support hard links at all, or only a certain number of hard links that refer to the same file. Another problem is that hard links cannot link from one filesystem to the other.

However, apart from implementation details, there is one *blatant error* source when using `create_symlink` or `create_hard_link`. The following lines contain a bug. Can you spot it immediately?

```
path a {"some_dir/some_file.txt"};
path b {"other_dir/other_file.txt"};
remove(b);
create_symlink(a, b);
```

Nothing bad happens when executing this program, but the symlink will be *broken*. The symlink points to `"some_dir/some_file.txt"`, which is wrong. The problem is that it should really either point to `"/absolute/path/some_dir/some_file.txt"`, or `"../some_dir/some_file.txt"`. The `create_symlink` call uses a correct absolute path if we write it as follows:

```
create_symlink(absolute(a), b);
```

 `create_symlink` does not check whether the path we are linking to is *correct*.

There's more...

We already noticed that our hash function is a too simple one. For the sake of keeping this recipe simple and without external dependencies, we chose this way.

What is the problem with our hash function? There are actually two problems:

- We read the whole file into a string. This is disastrous for files that are larger than our system memory.
- The C++ hash function trait `hash<string>` is most probably not designed for such hashes.

If we are looking for a better hash function, we should take one that is fast, memory-friendly, and that makes sure that no two really large but different files get the same hash. The latter requirement is maybe the most important one. If we decide that one file is a duplicate of the other although they do not contain the same data, we surely have some *data loss* after deleting it.

Better hash algorithms are, for example, MD5 or one of the SHA variants. In order to get access to such functions in our program, we could use the OpenSSL cryptography API, for example.

Index

D

data structures
  composing, with std::tuple 346
deadlocks
  avoiding, with std::scoped_lock 426
dictionary merging tool
  implementing 211
different member values
  sharing, of same object 383
directories
  files, listing 479
disk usage counter
  implementing 491
distribution
  bernoulli_distribution 402
  discrete_distribution 402
  normal_distribution 401
  uniform_int_distribution 401

E

erase-remove idiom
  using, on std::vector 44
exception safe shared locking
  lock classes 423
  mutex classes 422
  std::shared_lock 418
  with std::unique_lock 418

F

failure
  signalizing, with std::optional 338
Fibonacci iterator 116
file input
  complex objects, initializing 291
file types
  statistics, calculating 494
files
  listing, in directories 479
  output, redirecting to 304
filtering
  algorithms, used 185
first in, first out (FIFO) 92
fold expressions
  about 33

handy helper functions, implementing 32
folder size
  reducing, with symlinks and tool implementing
    498
folding 33
format guard 321
format types
  implementing 320
formatting modifiers 289
forward iterator 100
Fourier transform formula
  about 228
  implementing, with STL numeric algorithms 228
fractal 241
functional objects
  reference link 152
functions
  applying, on tuples 343
  capture list 141
  composing, by concatenation 146
  constexpr 142
  defining, on run with lambda expressions 137
  exception attr 142
  mutable 142
  return type 142

G

generic data structures
  filling, iterator adapters used 109
grep-like text search tool
  implementing 484

H

handy helper functions
  implementing, with fold expressions 32
  multiple insertions, verifying 37
  multiple items, pushing into vector 39
  parameters, verifying within range 38
  ranges, matching against individual items 36
hash tables 44
header-only libraries
  enabling, with inline variables 29

Z

Printed in Great Britain
by Amazon